Hol.

W9-COG-860

𝕴𝖑𝖑𝖚𝖘𝖙𝖗𝖆𝖙𝖊𝖉 𝕰𝖉𝖎𝖙𝖎𝖔𝖓

THE DUTCH AND QUAKER COLONIES IN AMERICA

By JOHN FISKE

IN TWO VOLUMES

VOLUME II

THE DUTCH AND QUAKER COLONIES IN AMERICA
BY JOHN FISKE

ILLUSTRATED WITH
PORTRAITS, MAPS, FACSIMILES,
CONTEMPORARY VIEWS, PRINTS, AND
OTHER HISTORIC MATERIALS
IN TWO VOLUMES
VOLUME II.

Nieuw Nederlant is een seer schoon aengenaem gesont en lustigh lantschap daer het voor alderley slagh van menschen beter en ruymer aen de kost of gemackelycker door de werelt te geraken is als in Nederlant offte eenige andere quartieren des werelts mijn bekent.
ADRIAN van der DONCK, 1656

For I must needs tell you, if we miscarry it will be our own fault ; we have nobody else to blame ; for such is the happiness of our Constitution, that we cannot well be destroyed but by ourselves.
WILLIAM PENN, 1679

BOSTON AND NEW YORK
HOUGHTON, MIFFLIN AND COMPANY
The Riverside Press, Cambridge
M DCCCC III

CHAPTER XI

NEW YORK IN THE YEAR 1680

CONTENTS

CHAPTER XII

PENN'S HOLY EXPERIMENT

CONTENTS   ix

CHAPTER XV

KNICKERBOCKER SOCIETY

CHAPTER XVI

THE QUAKER COMMONWEALTH

CONTENTS

CHAPTER XVII

THE MIGRATIONS OF SECTS

NOTES ON THE ILLUSTRATIONS

All Masters of Ships Sloopes or any Vessells whatsoever as well English as Forreigners are hereby Required, that att their Arrivall into this Porte, or the places and Roades Adjacent, they shall Immediatly repaire before me and Acquaint me, from whence they Came, and whither they are Bound together with the Contents of their Lading; And in Case they intend to unload Any Goods, they are First to make A true Entry and Reporte of all Such Goods and Merchandize hee and they shall have on Board (as more plainly is Sett forth in An act of Parliament Entituled An Act for Incouraging of trade) And further that all Masters of ships Sloopes or any other Vessells that shall Lade any Goods in this Porte or the Places and Roades Adjacent within his Mats Commands, must first make Entry of his ship Sloope or Vessell Before hee take any Goods or Merchandize in and Declare what Parte or Place he is Bound for, And all the said Entryes are to be made both off ship & Goods as well Inwards as Outward Bound before Mr. Thomas Delavall who hath Commission from me to Receive them, Whereof they are not to faile Upon Penalty of the forfeitures and fines mentioned in the said Act GIVEN under my hand att James Fort &c. Sep. 13 1664

R. Nicolls

ONE OF GOVERNOR NICOLLS'S FIRST OFFICIAL ORDERS

THE DUTCH AND QUAKER COLONIES
IN AMERICA

CHAPTER X

THE ENGLISH AUTOCRATS

WHEN baffled Peter Stuyvesant with an aching heart turned over to Colonel Richard Nicolls the fair province of New Netherland, and the old local names — not yet old in years but destined to be forever venerable in memory — gave place to the name and titles of the new master ; when the little town on the tip end of Manhattan Island became New York, and Fort Amsterdam, its quaint citadel, became Fort James, and far up in the northern wilderness Dutch Orange received Scotch baptism as Albany ; the revolution was more quiet and peaceable than almost any A peaceful other that is recorded in history. Few political revolution changes have been greater in their consequences. By transferring from Dutch into English hands the strategic centre of antagonism to New France, it brought about an approach toward unity of political development in the English colonies and made it possible for them at length to come together in a great Federal Union. Such remote results were not within the ken of James, Duke of York. Thoughts of commerce rather than of empire filled his mind, and none could deny that the trade in peltries and the possession of a superb seaport were fit objects of princely care. A bigot and despot by natural temper, he had nothing to gain and everything to lose by exhibiting such qualities as Lord Proprietor of this Dutch domain. But for tact and moderation

VIEW OF NEW

this bloodless conquest could hardly have been made ; without continued moderation and tact it might prove hard to keep.   Conciliation was the watchword, and no better person
Richard   could have been found to carry out such a policy
Nicolls   than Richard Nicolls, one of the most genial and attractive figures in early American history.   He was honest and sensible, frank but courteous in speech, open-hearted and liberal-minded, a man of refined tastes and an excellent scholar withal, fond of his Greek and Latin books, and speaking Dutch and French like a native.   Wherever he went he won all hearts, and so it was in New Amsterdam. The citizens were undisturbed in person or property, and it was soon felt that their rights were better protected than ever before.   The old Dutch local government of burgomasters, schepens, and schout was retained for a year, and then those officers were replaced by mayor, aldermen, and sheriff.   A code of laws was promulgated, known as " The Duke's Laws," and none could complain of it as wanting in liberality.   The patroons were confirmed in their estates, henceforth called manors, jury trial was introduced and the criminal code amended, and it was provided that no Christian

AMSTERDAM, ABOUT 1650

should be in any wise molested for his religious opinions. The arrival of Englishmen upon the scene brought the Church of England and its services; but everything was amicably arranged, and for a time the Dutch Reformed service was held in the morning and the English in the afternoon at one and the same meeting-house.

While in these respects the duke's laws were so liberal, they provided nothing like constitutional government for the people of New York. There was no legal check upon Nicolls's arbitrary will; and if the four years of his governorship were long remembered as a kind of golden age in the history of the colony, it was purely because of his admirable character. As Samuel Maverick wrote to Lord Arlington, it was wonderful how this man A good autocrat could harmonize things in a world so full of strife; even the Indians felt the effects, and were "brought into such peaceful posture" as never before.

One of the most important series of transactions under the first English governor of New York was that which determined the boundaries of the province. Cartwright was sent up the North River, and met with no opposition at

Rensselaerwyck, Fort Orange, and Esopus. The submission was as peaceful as it had been at Manhattan. On the South River it was otherwise. Sir Robert Carr was sent

Sir Robert Carr at New Amstel with two of the frigates to demand the surrender of the Dutch fort at New Amstel. The garrison were ready to submit to the inevitable, but the commandant, Alexander Hinnoyossa, was determined to resist. A couple of broadsides from the frigates and a rush of English soldiers soon settled the business ; the fort was carried by storm, and of its defenders there were three killed and ten wounded. Carr now showed that he was made of very different stuff from Nicolls. He confiscated property for his private use and that of his son and friends ; he shipped the Dutch soldiers to Virginia, to be sold into servitude ; and he rifled people's houses, carrying away everything of value, even to the wearing apparel. It became necessary for Nicolls to follow him to the Delaware River and make him disgorge some of his plunder. The name New Amstel was changed to Newcastle, and Captain John Carr, son of Sir Robert, was put in command of the district. According to the charter which Lord Baltimore had obtained from Charles I., this whole western shore of Delaware Bay was part of Maryland ;[1] but the Duke of York showed small respect for his father's grants. He insisted upon keeping his own officers there, and thus Delaware remained an appendage to New York until 1682, when it was given to William Penn.

The eastern boundary was the next matter that required attention. It will be remembered that the charter obtained by Winthrop in 1662 made Connecticut extend to the Pacific Ocean, but the charter granted to the Duke of York in 1664 made the province of New York begin at the Connecticut River. If this latter provision had been sustained, it would have spoiled Connecticut, crippled Massachusetts, and prevented the existence of Vermont. The question had many complications. Both Connecticut and New Haven had ex-

[1] See my *Old Virginia and Her Neighbours*, Illustrated Edition, ii. 130.

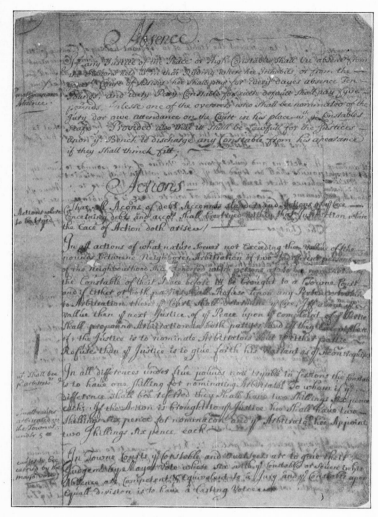

FIRST PAGE OF "THE DUKE'S LAWS"

ercised jurisdiction over portions of Long Island. The
Fall of the charter of 1662 extinguished the New Haven col-
republic of
New ony by annexing it to Connecticut, but the New
Haven Haven people had resisted this provision. Stam-
ford posed for the moment as an independent republic, but
Connecticut claimed jurisdiction over Stamford and over
Westchester County as well. The action of New Haven
tended to simplify matters. By the duke's charter New
York would have swallowed that colony. So between two
unpalatable cups New Haven chose the less bitter. The
"Christless rule" of democratic Connecticut was not so
bad as the equally Christless rule of despotically governed
New York. New Haven preferred to submit to the Winthrop charter. Everything now depended upon the justice
and wisdom of Nicolls ; his representations would have great
weight with the Duke of York and the king. Had he insisted upon the Connecticut River boundary he would probably have got it. But such a disregard for the Winthrop
charter seemed to him both dishonourable and contrary to
public policy, and he soon accepted a boundary line which
seemed fair to all parties. Connecticut was to have Stamford, but Westchester County was to belong to New York.
The dividing line was to start at Mamaroneck Creek and
The Con- run north-northwest until it should intersect the
necticut southern boundary of Massachusetts, keeping al-
boundary
ways as much as twenty miles distant from the
Hudson River. This sounded reasonable enough, but people's knowledge of American geography was still very slender. New York historians have accused the Connecticut
commissioners of playing a trick upon Governor Nicolls.[1]
Such charges are easy to make, but difficult to prove. It
does not seem likely that the Connecticut men, had they
correctly conceived the geography of the case, would have
proposed a line so ridiculous as to invite speedy exposure.
A line starting at Mamaroneck Creek and running north-
northwest would have crossed the Hudson River at Peeks-

[1] See, _e. g._, Brodhead's _History of the State of New York_, ii. 56.

kill and would have intersected the prolonged boundary of Massachusetts near the northwestern corner of Ulster County, five-and-thirty miles west of the river! The error was soon discovered, and was rectified in 1683, when the boundary was placed very nearly in its present position, though it was long before all questions connected with it were settled. This decision furnished a basis for determining afterwards the western boundary of Massachusetts and still later that of Vermont.

On the other hand, the whole of Long Island, having been expressly mentioned and given a central place in the grant to the Duke of York, was declared to be his. Nicolls named it Yorkshire and divided it into three ridings. Nantucket and Martha's Vineyard were likewise annexed to New York, and so remained until 1692, when they were handed over to Massachusetts. The name of Dukes County still commemorates the brief season when Martha's Vineyard was the property of James Stuart, Duke of York. The island of Pemaquid also, with a district of mainland between the Kennebec and St. Croix rivers, called the County of Cornwall, was included in James Stuart's proprietary domain; but this, with all the rest of Maine, was added to Massachusetts after the accession of William and Mary.

Yorkshire, Dukes County, and Cornwall

While Nicolls was busy settling boundaries and making the change from Dutch to English rule as pleasant as possible for all parties concerned, his colleagues Cartwright and Maverick were wasting breath and losing their tempers in the effort to outwit or browbeat the magistrates and parsons at Boston, — such men as Bellingham and Norton, Leverett and Simon Willard. In the summer of 1665 Cartwright sailed for England, carrying with him papers tending to convict the Massachusetts people of disloyalty. With this evidence he hoped to persuade the king to rescind their charter; but in mid-ocean he was captured by a Dutch cruiser, who seized all his papers and set him ashore in Spain, jocosely remarking that the climate

Cartwright sails for England, but lands in Spain

would cure the gout under which he was groaning.   By the time Cartwright arrived in London the king was too busy with the Dutch war to molest Massachusetts.   Thus the English capture of New Amsterdam, with the resulting complications, would seem to have given a fresh lease of life for twenty years to the charter of the stiff-necked Puritan republic.

After Cartwright's departure, Maverick stayed some time in Boston, ready to welcome the news of a *quo warranto ;* but none such came.   In January, 1667, Sir Robert Carr came to Boston from Delaware, intending to embark for England.   One cold Saturday evening Carr and Maverick, Pleasant with half-a-dozen boon companions, had grown Saturday evenings in somewhat noisy over a steaming bowl of grog at Boston the Ship Tavern, when a constable stepped in and told them to break up and go home.   They were dese-crating the Sabbath, which it was then the fashion to regard as beginning at sundown of Saturday.   But the company defied the constable and drove him away with blows.   On the next Saturday evening the party again assembled at the tavern, but prudently adjourned across the street to the house of a merchant named Kellond, where another con-stable, Arthur Mason, found them in a hilarious mood.   He told them it was well for them that they were in a private house, for had he found them across the way he would have haled them off to prison.   Angry words ensued, in the course of which Carr said that it was he who beat the con-stable, and he would do it again.   Mason retorted that it was lucky for the party that he was not the constable who found them at the tavern.   "Sir Robert asked if he dare meddle with the king's commissioners.   'Yes,' says Mason, 'and if the king himself had been there I would have carried him away'; upon which Maverick cried out, 'Treason!   Mason, thou shalt be hanged within a twelve-month.'   Sir Robert Carr spake to Sir Thomas Temple and some others of the company, to take notice of what passed, and the next day Maverick sent a note to Mr.

THE
CONDITIONS FOR NEW PLANTERS
In the Territories of His ROYAL HIGHNESS
THE
DUKE OF YORK

THE Purchases are to be made from the *Indian Sachims* and to be Recorded before the *Governour*.

The Purchasers are not to pay for their liberty of purchasing to the *Governour*.

The Purchasers are to set out a Town, and Inhabit together.

No purchaser shall at any time contract for himself with any *Sackim*, without consent of his Associates: or special Warrant from the *Governour*.

The Purchasers are free from all manner of Assessments or Rates for five years after their Town-plot is set out, and when the five years are expired, they shall only be liable to the publick Rates, and Payments according to the Customs of other Inhabitants both *English* and *Dutch*.

All Lands thus Purchased, and possest shall remain to the Purchasers, and their Heires, as free Lands to dispose of as they please.

In all Territories of his ROYAL HIGINES, Liberty of Conscience is allowed, Provided such Liberty is not converted to Licentiousness, or the disturbance of others, in the exercise of the Protestant Religion.

The several Townships have liberty to make their peculiar Laws, and Deciding all small Causes within themselves.

The Lands which I intend shall be first Planted, are those upon the West side of *Hudson-River*, &c, or adjoyning to the *Sopes*, but if any number of men sufficient for two or three, or more Towns, shall desire to plant upon any other Lands they shall have all due encouragement proportionable to their Quality, and undertakings.

Every Township is Obliged to pay their *Minister*, according to such agreement as they shall make with him, and no man to refuse his Proportion, the *Minister* being elected by the Major part of the Householders Inhabitants of the *Town*.

Every Township hath the free choice of all their officers both Civil, and Military, and all men who shall take the Oath of Allegiance to his *Majesty*, and are not Servants, or day-labourers but are admitted to enjoy *Town-lotts* are esteemed freemen of the Jurisdiction, and cannot forfeit the same without due process in Law.

R. Nicolls.

NICOLLS'S CONDITIONS FOR NEW PLANTERS

Bellingham the governor, charging Mason with high treason for the words spoken."[1] The governor behaved with tact and bound Mason over with sureties to answer at the next court. Presently Maverick, whose wrath had had time to cool, asked permission to withdraw his charge, inasmuch as he felt satisfied that Mason's words, though "rash and inconsiderate," were not malicious and indicated no " premeditated design" against his Majesty's government. Bellingham astutely replied that "the affair was of too high a nature for him to interpose in." The sagacious grand jury found simply "that the words charged were spoken," and the verdict of the court was that Mason should be "admonished in solemn manner" by the governor. Thus were the skirts of Massachusetts cleared of any insinuations of complicity with treason in which gossip-mongers might indulge. Hutchinson is right in saying that though the anecdote may seem trivial, it is full of instruction. As for the pot-valiant Sir Robert Carr, he sailed for England and died suddenly the day after landing. Maverick found the social atmosphere of Boston too austere, and was glad to remove to New York and accept from the duke the present of a house on Broadway, where he seems to have spent the remainder of his days.

The feeling of Nicolls toward Boston may be inferred from his remark, " Our time is lost upon men who are puffed up with the spirit of independency." He seems to have had no more sympathy than Stuyvesant with popular government ; and like his predecessor he found more or less trouble with the towns upon Long Island, which preferred the methods in vogue upon the Connecticut River to those of Manhattan. But his unfailing tact and good sense overcame all obstacles and made him a pattern for beneficent despots.

His attention was soon called in an unexpected way to the mainland west of the North River's mouth. Except for the settlements at Hoboken and Pavonia, and more recently at Bergen, in what is now Jersey City, little had been done in

[1] Hutchinson, *History of Massachusetts Bay*, Boston, 1764, i. 254.

that direction.   The Passaic and Raritan rivers flowed
Settle-
ments west
of the
Hudson through a wilderness as yet untrodden by white
men.   Nicolls named this fair country Albania
and felt a lively interest in its development.   In
1664 he granted the region west of the Achter Koll, or
Back Bay — which we now call Newark Bay — to several
families from Jamaica on Long Island.   From this place an
Indian trail furnished easy overland access to the hamlets on
the Delaware.   The patentees — John Ogden, Luke Watson, and their associates — numbered in all some eighty
persons.   They had scarcely begun to take possession when
Nicolls learned that the Duke of York had already given
away the whole territory between the North and South
The grant
to Berkeley
and
Carteret rivers.   It was so easy for a prince to show his
gratitude for favours received by making wholesale
gifts of unknown land in America!   The grantees
were Sir George Carteret and Lord Berkeley of Stratton.
The latter was the brother of Sir William Berkeley, the famous governor of Virginia, and figures occasionally in the
history of that commonwealth and of Carolina.   Carteret
belonged to a family which had for several generations been
prominent in the island of Jersey.   He defended his island
stoutly against the Roundhead soldiers, and he was the last
commander on British soil to lower the king's flag.   Both
Carteret and Berkeley seemed worthy of a reward for their
conspicuous and devoted loyalty, and one can easily fancy
James's comfortable sense of generosity tempered with thrift
as he looked over the map of New Netherland and marked
off this spacious unknown wilderness to bestow upon his
friends.   But when the affair came to Nicolls's ears, he
made such representations to the duke as to weaken his
belief in the thriftiness of the transaction and cause him to
repent of his haste.   He persuaded Berkeley and Carteret
to give back the land between the North and South rivers,
in exchange for an extensive tract to the west of the latter.
But this was encroaching upon Maryland, and gave rise to an
altercation between the Duke of York and Lord Baltimore.

FACSIMILE OF THE DUK

'S GRANT OF NEW JERSEY

The net result was that nothing further was done, and accordingly Carteret and Berkeley took possession of their proprietary domain.[1]

In August, 1665, Philip Carteret, a cousin of Sir George, arrived with several families and established himself just behind the Achter Koll, in the very region which Nicolls had granted to Ogden and his associates. The settlement was called Elizabethtown, after Elizabeth, wife of Sir George Carteret, a lady of somewhat Puritan proclivities, concerning whom Pepys testifies that "she cries out against the vices of the court, and how they are going to set up plays already. She do much cry out upon these things, and that which she believes will undo the whole nation." [2] Philip Carteret undertook to satisfy Nicolls's patentees by making compensation for the lands to which they laid claim, but Berkeley and Sir George refused to sanction this, on the ground that the Duke of York no longer owned the territory when his agent Nicolls made a grant of it ; so that the grant was simply void. Out of these circumstances grew various legal disputes which were not all disposed of until more than a century had elapsed.

Founding of Elizabethtown

The province thus carved out of New Netherland was named Nova Cæsarea, after the Latin name of the island of Jersey, the home of the Carterets. People, however, preferred the vernacular form of the name, and called it New Jersey. The form of government established by the proprietors, in their instrument known as the "Concessions," was a striking contrast to Nicolls's amiable

The name New Jersey

[1] Mellick, *The Story of an Old Farm, or Life in New Jersey in the Eighteenth Century*, Somerville, N. J., 1889, p. 105 ; a monograph of remarkable merit.
[2] Pepys' *Diary*, October 15, 1666.

despotism in New York. The sway of the governor, Philip Carteret, was limited not only by a council but also by an assembly elected by the people. Most liberal terms for purchasing lands were offered to settlers, and entire religious liberty was promised. The result of this was an immediate influx of settlers from New England. A party from the Piscataqua country founded Piscataway by the river Raritan ; others from Haverhill and Newbury made the beginnings of

ELIZABETH CASTLE, JERSEY, CARTERETS' STRONGHOLD

Woodbridge ; but the most important accession, in some respects, came from the lately extinguished republic of New Haven. There were many persons in that colony who could not endure the thought of annexation to Connecticut. The two communities stood for widely different ideas. Among all the New England colonies the Puritan theocracy was most dominant in New Haven, whereas in Connecticut it was weaker than anywhere else except Rhode Island. In New Haven none but church members qualified for communion could vote or hold office ; in Connecticut there was no such restriction. The tendencies of Connecticut, under the impress of the genius of Thomas Hooker, were democratic ; those

Unwillingness of New Haven leaders to be annexed to Connecticut

LETTER TO GOVERNOR WINTHROP

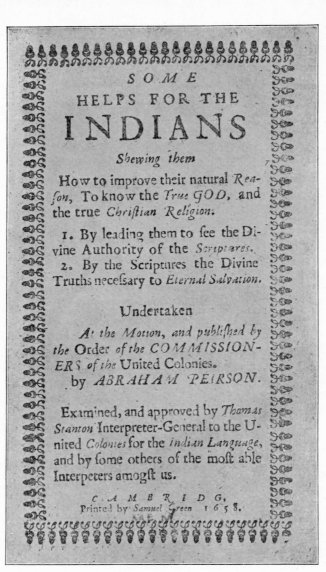

SOME
HELPS FOR THE
INDIANS
Shewing them

How to improve their natural *Reason*, To know the *True GOD*, and the true *Christian Religion.*

1. By leading them to see the Divine Authority of the *Scriptures.*
2. By the Scriptures the Divine Truths necessary to *Eternal Salvation.*

Undertaken

At the Motion, and published by the Order *of the* COMMISSIONERS *of the* United Colonies.
by *ABRAHAM PEIRSON.*

Examined, and approved by *Thomas Stanton* Interpreter-General to the United *Colonies* for the *Indian Language,* and by some others of the most able Interpeters amogst us.

C A M B R I D G,
Printed by *Samuel Green* 1 6 5 8.

TITLE OF ABRAHAM PIERSON'S "SOME HELPS"

of New Haven, under the guidance of John Davenport, were toward an aristocracy of "the saints." The civil magistrates there were "pillars of the church." Annexation to Connecticut meant giving votes and offices to men of unregenerate hearts ; it meant administering justice by codes of secular law instead of the inspired law of Moses ; it meant letting in a flood of democracy and ending forever the rule of the saints. Accordingly, when Davenport heard of the decision of the royal commissioners, he sadly exclaimed, "The cause of Christ in New Haven is miserably lost ! "

At this crisis the offer of complete civil and religious liberty in New Jersey produced a notable effect upon the New Haven towns. Those persons who were willing to be citizens of Connecticut (and these were a majority of the population, including probably most of the unenfranchised) might stay at home and be contented. The minority who could not abide the change might go to New Jersey and there live according to their theocratic notions. The removal of these irreconcilables tended to make the change easier for Connecticut. In 1665–67 several parties from Guilford, Branford, and Milford settled on the Passaic River and made the beginnings of a flourishing town there, which was at first called Milford, from the home of one of its founders, Robert Treat. But the name was soon changed to Newark, after the English home of its pastor, the venerable Abraham Pierson, a true spiritual brother of Davenport. As for Robert Treat, he returned in 1672 to Milford, played a distinguished part in King Philip's War, and afterward became governor of Connecticut. It is Pierson who must be regarded as the continuator of the New Haven colony's existence in that of its daughter, Newark. The larger part of his Branford congregation followed him thither, and their town constitution provided that none but communing church members should vote or be eligible to office. Sixty-four men signed this constitution, of whom twenty-three were from Branford, and forty-one from New Haven, Milford, and Guilford. Six out

Exodus from New Haven to New Jersey ; Robert Treat and Abraham Pierson

of this number made their marks, — a small proportion of
illiteracy for the seventeenth century.   It has been well said
that, "after 1666 the New Haven of Davenport and Eaton
must be looked for upon the banks, not of the Quinnipiac,
but of the Passaic.   The men, the methods, the laws, the
officers, that made New Haven town what it was in 1640,
disappeared from the Connecticut colony, but came to full
life again immediately in New Jersey." [1]   As for the aged
Davenport, he moved to Boston and became pastor of the
First Church there.

The government of New Jersey was similar in form to
the earlier governments founded in Virginia, Maryland, and
the New England colonies ; all alike were developments
from the ancient English county court.   The New Jersey
legislature consisted of governor, council, and representative assembly, and it was as well understood as in
New England or Virginia that there could be no
taxation save through the assembly.   But important constitutional questions came up at once for discussion,
as in the first years of Massachusetts.   The representatives
of the people were annoyed at the veto power exercised
over them by the governor and council, and accordingly
they insisted upon meeting in joint session where their own
numbers were sure to prevail.   This attempt was success-
fully resisted by the proprietors, but the immediate result
was that Governor Carteret's first assembly, which met in
1668, broke up in some disorder, and it was seven years
before there was another legal assembly.   There was also
the quarrel over quit-rents, which broke out in New Jersey
as in so many other colonies.   Quit-rents were always extremely unpopular.   Carteret's colonists refused to pay
them, and their opposition, organized as it was in town
meetings, was too strong to be overcome.   In 1671 the
towns chose an illegal assembly, with James Carteret,
a weak and debauched creature, a younger son of the lord-
proprietor, for its president.   For the moment constitutional

Constitu-
tional trou-
bles in New
Jersey

[1] Levermore, *The Republic of New Haven*, Baltimore, 1886, p. 120.

government, according to the "Concessions," seemed over-thrown, and Philip Carteret returned to England. The persistent energy of Sir George Carteret, backed by the Duke of York, presently restored order, but meanwhile Lord Berkeley lost his faith in the success of the enterprise and sold out for £1000 all his interest to a Quaker, John Fenwick, in trust for another Quaker, Edward Byllinge. This panic sale from Lord Berkeley to Quakers was one of the pivotal events in American history, for it soon resulted in bringing William Penn to the New World. But before we can enter upon this eventful story we must return for a while to the island of Manhattan and see what was going on there.

(marginal note: Lord Berkeley sells out his interest to a party of Quakers)

The peace of Breda, signed on St. Bartholomew's day, 1667, formally ceded New Netherland to the English, in exchange for Surinam in South America and the island of Poleron, one of the Banda group near the Moluccas. On New Year's, 1668, the peace was proclaimed in New York, and Governor Nicolls was able to add the welcome announce-ment that, for the next seven years at least, that province was to enjoy free trade with the Netherlands. Private affairs demanded Nicolls's presence in England, and the duke accepted his resignation. In New York there was universal sorrow at his departure; seldom has a public man been so beloved. At the house of the Dutch mayor, Cornelius Steenwyck, near the Whitehall, there was a farewell banquet. The *menu* has not come down to us, but an inventory of the things in the house has been preserved; and one feels that in those tapestried rooms, with their carved French cabinets, their velvet and Russia leather chairs, the muslin and "flowered tabby" curtains, the tall clock in the corner, and the paintings by Antwerp masters, there were the elements of refined com-fort. The Netherlanders at that time lived more luxuri-ously in their houses than any other people, and their habits had been carried with them to the New World. From

(marginal note: Departure of Govern-or Nicolls)

these last pleasant scenes the upright governor made his way back to England. He was soon to die a soldier's death. In the third naval war between the English and Dutch he served on the fleet and was killed at the battle of Solebay, May 28, 1672, at the early age of forty-seven.

Nicolls's successor, Francis Lovelace, a man of far less distinction for character and ability, was nevertheless a

Francis Lovelace worthy person, and New York was prosperous under his rule. The year of his arrival is memorable for the abolition of the two classes of "great burghers" and "small burghers," introduced by Stuyvesant in 1657. The distinction was imitated from the custom in Amsterdam and other Dutch cities. Members of the council, burgomasters and schepens, officers of the militia, and ministers of the gospel, with their descendants in the male line, were

Great and small burghers enrolled as great burghers; and other persons could be admitted to that class on payment of 50 guilders into the city treasury. These great burghers were eligible to public offices, and in case of conviction for a capital offence were exempt from confiscation or attainder. The class of small burghers comprised all other persons born in the city, or who had dwelt there for a year and six weeks; all men who were married to the daughters of burghers; all salaried servants of the West India Company; and all persons who kept a shop or permanently transacted business in the city. Strangers temporarily in the city could be enrolled in this class by paying a fee of 25 guilders. The privileges pertaining to it scarcely extended beyond sundry facilities for trading.[1] This division into classes proved very unpopular, and it was abolished in 1668 with general satisfaction.

Several families from Boston now bought estates in New York and came there to live, willing perhaps, like Maverick, to escape from the saintly rule of the "lords brethren." The most important and memorable act of Lovelace's administration was the establishment of a regular monthly

[1] O'Callaghan, *History of New Netherland*, ii. 341.

Deare S:

Fort James 27 of Decembr 1672

There presented you with 2 rarityes, & request of
the latest intelligence I could meete withall, and a Post-
by the first you will see what has beene acted on the Stage
of Europe, by the latter you will meete with a Monthly,
fresh Supply, so that if it receive but the same ardent incli
nations from you, as first it had from my selfe, by our
monthly advises, all publiqe occurrences, may bee transmitted
betwixt us togeather with severall other greate Conveniencys
of publiq importance, Consonant to the Commands layd upon
us by his Sacred Ma: who strictly injoints all his American
Subjects, to enter into a close correspondency with each other, this
I looke upon as the most Compendious meanes to begett a
mutuall understanding, and that it may receive all the
Countenance from you, for its future duration, I shall acquaint
you with the modell I have propos'd, and if you please but
to make an addition to it, or subtraction, or any other alteration, I shall bee ready to comply with you; this person

most facile way for a Post, which in processe
wise passages, and accommodation at Rivers, found
on this subject, shewing you understand the Scoope
if this can in came your Zeale to so publiq a

Lastly
to discover it further
(pro voluntate) this next Spring

... being both Actiue, Stoute and indefatigable, hee is sworne to his fidelity, I haue affixt an annuall Sallery on him, which togeather with the advantage of his letters, and other (shall hee portable Packes may afford him a handsom liuely hood, That form is the first Stage I haue designd him to Change his Horse, where Constantly I expect hee should haue a fresh and with a signification of Post hayes on the Superscription, and reciprocally wee expect ak to us free; each monday of the Month hee setts out from New Yorke, and is to returne within the Month from Boston to us againe, this Maile has diuers Baggs according to the Townes the letters are designd too, which are all sealb up, till theire arriuement, with the Seale of the Secretaries office, whos care it is on Satterday night to Seale them up; only Bye-letters are in an open Bagg to pro by the Stages. Thus you see the Scheme I haue drawne to pro mote so universall a good worke, that is to afford him directi- rance to so good Correspondence, I shall only beg of you your furthe where, and to whome to make his application too, uppon his arriued at Boston, as Likewise to afford him what letters you can to esta- blish him in that imployment there, shoulb see much aduenira goes to our designe, it in the intervalb you discoubt with somme of the most able woork-men, to marke out the best and

of tyme would see the Kings best high way, as like
or other necessary places, but I neede not inlardge my selfe
well as my selfe and therefore I intirely recommend it to you
conccrne, to haue the possibility of receauing a personall
I am with all respect   Your very affectionate friend Fra Lovelace.

mail service through southern New England between New York and Boston. This event may best be described by quoting the letter which Lovelace sent to Winthrop, at Hartford, in December, 1672 : "I here present you with two rarities, a pacquett of the latest intelligence I could meet withal, and a Post. By the first, you will see what has been acted on the stage of Europe ; by the latter you will meet with a monthly fresh supply ; so that if it receive but the same ardent inclinations from you as at first it hath from myself, by our monthly

The monthly mail between New York and Boston

VILLAGE OF HARLEM IN 1765

advisoes all publique occurrences may be transmitted between us, together with severall other great conveniencys of publique importance, consonant to the commands laid upon us by His sacred Majestie, who strictly injoins all his American subjects to enter into a close correspondency with each other. This I look upon as the most compendious means to beget a mutual understanding ; and that it may receive all the countenance from you for its future duration, I shall acquaint you with the model I have proposed ; and if you please but to make an addition to it, or substraction, or any other alteration, I shall be ready to comply with you. This person that has undertaken the imployment I conceaved most proper, being both active, stout, and indefatigable. He is sworne as to his fidelity. I have affixt an annuall sallery on him, which, together with the advantage of his letters and other small portable packes,

may afford him a handsome livelyhood. Hartford is the
first stage I have designed him to change his horse, where
constantly I expect he should have a fresh one lye. All
the letters outward shall be delivered gratis, with a signification of *Post Payd* on the superscription ; and reciprocally,
we expect all to us free. Each first Monday of the month
he sets out from New York, and is to return within the
month from Boston to us againe. The maile has divers
baggs, according to the townes the letters are designed to,
which are all sealed up till their arrivement, with the seale
of the Secretarie's Office, whose care it is on Saturday
night to seale them up. Only by-letters are in an open
bag, to dispense by the wayes. Thus you see the scheme
I have drawne to promote a happy correspondence. I shall
only beg of you your furtherance to so universall a good
work ; that is to afford him directions where and to whom
to make his application to upon his arrival at Boston ; as
likewise to afford him what letters you can to establish him
in that imployment there. It would be much advantagious
to our designe, if in the intervall you discoursed with some
of the most able woodmen, to make out the best and most
facile way for a Post, which in processe of tyme would be
the King's best highway ; as likewise passages and accommodation at Rivers, fords, or other necessary places." [1]

The first mail on the American continent started from
New York for Boston on New Year's day, 1673. The postman followed the Bowery Lane till it merged into the wagon-
road just finished to the new village of Harlem, where even
then the beer gave a foretaste of the preëminence in brewing
to which Manhattan has since attained. After a cooling
draught he was ready to go on his way past " Annie's
Hook," or Pelham Manor, to Greenwich and Stamford, and so on to New Haven, Hartford, and
Springfield, crossing all rivers and arms of the sea in boats,
as was necessary until the last years of the eighteenth

The post-
man's
route

[1] *General Entries*, iv. 243; *Mass. Hist. Soc. Trumbull Papers*,
MSS., xx. i 10.

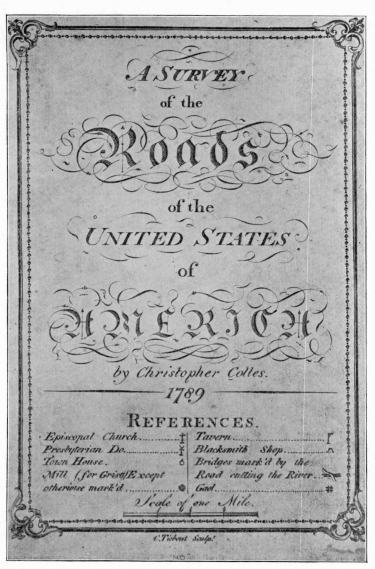

A SURVEY

of the

Roads

of the

UNITED STATES

of

AMERICA

by Christopher Colles.

—— 1789 ——

REFERENCES.

Episcopal Church............ ✝   Tavern............
Presbyterian Do.............. ✝   Blacksmith Shop............
Town House.............. ○   Bridges mark'd by the
Mill (for Grist) Except   Road cutting the River...
otherwise mark'd.............. ⊛   Gaol............ #

Scale of one Mile.

C. Tiebout sculp.t

TITLE OF COLLES'S "SURVEY OF THE ROADS"

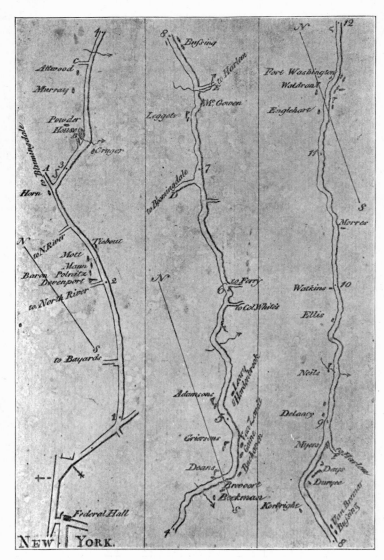

MAP OF HARLEM ROAD FROM NEW YORK

century. Now it was a stretch of newly built English wagon-road that our postman followed, but oftener a mere bridle-path, or an ancient Indian trail, and sometimes the way must needs be indicated by marking trees in the virgin forest. From Springfield eastward his path must have followed the same winding watercourses of which the Boston and Albany railroad now takes advantage, climbing near Quabaug (Brookfield) to a thousand feet above sea-level, then gently descending into the pleasant valley of the Charles. While our indefatigable carrier was thus earning his "handsome livelyhood," a locked box stood in the secretary's office in New York awaiting his return, and in it from day to day the little heap of eastward bound letters grew. When the postman returned with his prepaid mail

CORNER OF BROAD STREET AND EXCHANGE PLACE
Supposed View

he emptied his New York bag on a broad table in the coffee-house where citizens most did congregate. That locked box and that coffee-house table had in them the prophecy of the great post-office that now stands in the City Hall Park, and indirectly of all the post-offices, urban and rural, in English-speaking America. There was admirable foresight in Governor Lovelace's scheme. That indefatigable horseman of his was an indispensable instrument in " begetting a mutual understanding ; " he was one of the pioneers of our Federal Union.

Another prophetic incident of Lovelace's administration was the establishment of the first Merchants' Exchange, — a weekly meeting, on Friday mornings, at about the site where Exchange Place now crosses Broad Street. Some of the first American ships, moreover, were built at New York under this governor, and they were staunch craft.

Lovelace's rule, like that of Nicolls, was autocratic but in no wise oppressive. The change from Dutch to English rule had not yet bestowed English self-government upon the province of New York. The despotism of Kieft and Stuyvesant was continued, only now, instead of the iron clutch, it was a stroke of velvet. This was simply due to the different personal qualities of the rulers. The most restive part of the population, under this prolonged autocracy, was to be found in the English towns on Long Island. Their people persistently grumbled at this sort of government to which no Englishmen had from time immemorial been subjected. They wanted a representative assembly. In 1670 there was an approach toward an explosion. A tax was levied upon these Long Island towns to pay for repairs upon Fort James in New York. The case was quite similar to that of the tax levied by the governor and council of Massachusetts in 1631 upon the men of Watertown, to pay for a palisadoed wall in Cambridge. The men of Watertown refused to pay the tax, on the ground that they had no share in electing the authorities who levied it ; and this protest led at once to the introduction of representative government into the new-born commonwealth of Massachusetts. The first John Winthrop did not represent a would-be despotic authority in England, but Governor Lovelace did. Hence the protest of Long Island in 1670 was not so successful as that of Watertown in 1631. The towns drew up a remonstrance in which they declared that they would not yield to a demand for money to

The Long Island protest against arbitrary taxation

repair the fort; they might next be called upon to support the garrison, and there was no telling to what lengths the affair might go. They stoutly maintained that the principle of "no taxation without representation" — which England had asserted in 1265 and the Netherlands in 1477 — was their inalienable birthright. This remonstrance was pronounced seditious, and Lovelace ordered it to be publicly burned in the street before the City Hall. It is needless to add that Long Island remained disaffected and more or less turbulent.

Events in Europe were fast bringing about a fresh surprise for Manhattan. After the peace of Breda, Charles II. had entered into the famous Triple Alliance with Sweden and Holland, for the purpose of curbing the aggressive power of Louis XIV. As Bishop Burnet said, this was the best thing Charles II. ever did, and had he only adhered to this sound and manly policy it would have covered him with glory. But Louis well knew his cousin Charles's weaknesses. The blandishments of a new French mistress, and the promise of money enough to dispense with parliaments, were quite too much for the degenerate grandson of Henry of Navarre. He broke away from the Triple Alliance, scarcely two years old, and joined hands with Louis XIV. for the destruction of Holland. There followed, in rapid sequence, the fall and shameful murder of De Witt, the stride of the third William of Orange into the historic foreground, and one more wicked and terrible war between Englishmen and their Dutch cousins.

The Triple Alliance

War between England and Holland

And thus it happened that in the Christmas season of 1672, while the worthy Lovelace was setting afoot his postal scheme, a powerful Dutch fleet of fifteen ships, commanded by Cornelius Evertsen, was cruising in the West Indies to harass the English. By reinforcements this fleet was increased to three-and-twenty warships, carrying, besides their crews, 1600 troops. After finishing their business in the West Indies, these Dutchmen,

Admiral Evertsen's fleet

in July, 1673, visited Chesapeake Bay, destroying merchant vessels; and thence they kept on for New York, which had from the outset been their ultimate destination. Its recapture had been planned in Holland. On the morning of August 7 the ships dropped anchor off Staten Island; the next day they came up through the Narrows; the next they were ready to proceed to extremities.

The case was virtually a repetition of that of 1664. Governor Lovelace was absent on business, over on Long Island, but had he been on the spot it would have made no difference. The garrison of Fort James numbered scarcely eighty men. There was a brief exchange of volleys between the feeble fort and the majestic fleet, and a few lives were sacrificed, but resistance was hopeless. Before sunset of August 9 the ensign of the Dutch Republic floated over the fort, and the city on Manhattan passed once more under the sway of its founders. Once more there was a general change of nomenclature. The province resumed its old name of New Netherland, its eastern limit was pronounced to be that of the Hartford treaty of 1650,[1] and the whole of Long Island was declared to belong to it, but no claims were made upon Martha's Vineyard, Nantucket, or Pemaquid. Westward the claim took in whatever had been ruled by Stuyvesant, including New Sweden. Fort James was rechristened Fort Willem Hendrick, after the new stadholder, and the city was called New Orange. Esopus, which had exchanged its Indian name for Kingston, was now called Swanenburg. Albany received the name of Willemstadt, and its blockhouse that of Fort Nassau. As for Carteret's domain of New Jersey, it was baptized Achter Koll, or "Back Bay," from the broad sheet of water across which Elizabethtown was approached. A council of war was held by the officers of the fleet, and they appointed Anthony Colve, a captain of infantry, to be governor of New Netherland. All the places mentioned as within his jurisdiction sub-

Marginal notes: Capture of New York by the Dutch

Anthony Colve, governor of New Netherland

---

[1] See above, vol. i. p. 226.

mitted gracefully, and some of them very cheerfully, except on Long Island. There the Dutch towns, such as Brooklyn and Flatbush, rejoiced in the change of rulers ; even

CORNELIUS EVERTSEN

some of those towns where the English were a majority, such as Flushing and Jamaica, made no resistance. But the purely English towns in the East Riding — Southampton, Easthampton, Brookhaven, Southold, and Huntington — were extremely unwilling to yield ; and although they succumbed for a moment to the inexorable situation,[1] yet South-

---

[1] The "oath of fidelliti," which the inhabitants of these towns were required to take, is interesting as a quaint specimen of English written by a Dutch secretary : "Wee do sware in the presents of the Almightij God, that wee shall be true & faithfull to y⁰ high & mighty Lords y⁰

ampton published a protest and sent it all over New England, " in order to take off any aspersion cast upon us, as though we should freely submit to this foreign government." It became necessary for Governor Colve to "admonish" these froward eastern towns, but they did not cease to be thorns in the flesh. The appeal of Southampton was heard by sympathetic ears. Connecticut joined in the protest, angry letters passed between Colve and Winthrop, and presently Connecticut troops crossed the Sound. Scrimmages and reprisals on the high seas went on until Massachusetts also was aroused. Having seen some of her own ships captured and confiscated, Massachusetts decided that " God doth call them to do something in a hostile way for their own defence." Plymouth acquiesced in this policy, declaring that " just ground of a war" existed. Rhode Island, which was not a member of the Confederacy, took measures to defend her harbours against Dutch attacks ; while the three confederated colonies were planning an expedition which might have threatened not only Long Island, but Manhattan itself, for Evertsen's great fleet had sailed for Europe, leaving one frigate and one sloop-of-war to sustain Colve's government.

Danger of an attack by the New England Confederacy

It was indeed a precarious situation which depended upon the continued presence of a Dutch fleet in the midst of a European war that was straining Holland's resources. Fort Willem Hendrick, if good for anything, ought to be able to make it dangerous for hostile ships to enter either the East River or the North ; but as an instrument of war that fortress was now but little better than on the day when Dominie Megapolensis warned Stuyvesant of the folly of using it.

States Gennerall of yᵉ united Belgick Provinces, & his Serene hignesse the Prince of Orange, & to their Governᵣˢ here for the time being, and to yᵉ utmost of our power to prevent all what shall be attempted against the same, but uppon all occasions to behave ourselves as true & faitful subiects in conscience are bound to do, provided that wee shal not be forced in armes against our owne Nation if theij are sent bij a Lawful commission from his Majesty of England. Soo help us God." *New York Colonial Documents*, ii. 602.

Houses had been built and gardens planted so close to it as to interfere with firing. Colve felt bound to make How Governor Colve pulled down houses an effective weapon of it, and he decided that the offending houses must either be moved away or be pulled down. It was done as considerately as possible ; and here perhaps a few extracts from the contemporary records will help to bring the situation vividly before us.

It was announced that all persons injured in their property by the proposed work should be indemnified, either in

money or by a gift of real estate in some other locality. At a meeting held in the City Hall of New Orange, October 10, 1673, at which were present Governor Anthony The petitions Colve, Councillor Cornelius Steenwyck, and three burgomasters, Johannes van Brugh, Johannes de Peyster, and Ægidius Luyck, a number of petitions were heard, of which the following are samples : —

" Peter de Riemer is willing to remove his house, but requests Muyen's lot or one at the Water side instead.

" Lodewyck Pos requests the house next the City Hall ; otherwise 't will be impossible for him to move.

" Jacobus van de Water request's Pattison's house in Pearl Street, or a lot as near his former residence as possible, with satisfaction.

" George Cobbett says he is unable to move unless assisted.

" Jan Dircksen Meyer says he knows not whither to turn, but finally requests a lot behind The Five Houses, in Bridge Street.

" Andrew Meyer in like manner requests a lot there.

" Gerritt Hendricks, butcher, says he has been ruined by the English and is unable to move ; requests help and assistance.

" Peter Jansen Slott, by his father, requests a lot behind the City Hall.

" Simon Blanck requests accommodation for the winter, as his house cannot be moved ; asks a lot behind the Five Houses.

" Peter Stoutenburgh, absent.

" Martin Jansen Meyer says he is not able to move ; is offered a lot next to Kip in the valley, or recommended to look up another.

" Lysbeth Tyssen is told that her small houses will be examined, to see whether they cannot be spared.

" Peter Harmensen's little house is in like manner to be examined.

" Peter Jansen Mesier requests a place on the Water side ; otherwise cannot remove.

" Ephraim Herman requests satisfaction with others.

" Dr. Taylor's wife says that her husband is willing to risk his house, and to abide the result."

Steenwyck and the three burgomasters were then authorized to make an appraisal of the houses and lots which were to be destroyed or surrendered, and likewise of the houses and lots which they should think proper to bestow as indemnity.   By permission, two carpenters were added to this committee of appraisal.   After their work had been done a proclamation was issued, October 16 : —

" Whereas Fort Willem Hendrick and the city of New Orange situate on Manhatans Island is seriously encumbered and weakened by the houses, gardens, and orchards which The procla- lie so close under its walls and bulwarks that it is mation   impossible to defend it properly when occasion requires against its enemies, unless at least some of those houses, lots, and orchards be demolished and removed.   It is therefore considered necessary by the Governor-General, by and with the previous advice of his Council, to demolish, pull down, and remove the undernamed houses, gardens, and orchards, and the owners thereof are hereby most strictly ordered and commanded instantly to commence demolishing and pulling down their houses, gardens, and orchards, and to remove them to such lots as are laid out within this city by the Governor's order to that end and shall be shown to each of them by the Burgomasters."

A list of the doomed estates follows. The penalty for non-compliance with the order was forfeiture of the indemnity. In order to meet this extraordinary public outlay, a temporary tax was imposed. " It is resolved and ordered to collect from now henceforth until said indemnity and damage shall be prompt paid to said persons and no longer, to wit : —

" From all Beavers and peltries which will be exported from this government to Patria [the Netherlands] or elsewhere after the publication hereof, two and one half per cent.

" From Duffels and Blankets imported from Patria or elsewhere into this government, two per cent.

" And from powder, lead, muskets, wines, brandies, distilled waters, and rum, five per cent."

To this general proclamation was added the following specific notice : —

" Willem van Vredenburgh :

" You are hereby required and ordered, pursuant to the Proclamation, to demolish from garret to cellar your house and lot lying and being in Broadway, and to remove to the Company's garden, No. 1, for which removal you are allowed by arbitrators the sum of 330 florins, Wampum value, which shall be handed and paid you out of the extra duty which is ordered to be paid for that purpose."

A note in the records informs us that "a similar order is sent to the house of all the others mentioned in the Proclamation, except Dr. Taylor, Lysbet Tyssen, and Peter Harmsen, whose houses shall be still further examined, in order if possible to spare them." [1]

Colve was certainly a man of energy, for by the spring of 1674 his fortress was not only far advanced toward completion, but mounted 190 guns, collected from far and near, so that it might have made warm work for ships attempting

[1] *New York Colonial Documents*, ii. 630–635.

to enter either of the rivers. To meet such expenses the treasury had recourse not only to extraordinary duties, but also to wholesale confiscations. As no articles of capitulation had been agreed upon when New York surrendered to Admiral Evertsen, and no fettering promises had been made, it was considered quite right and legitimate tô confiscate all English and French property found in the city. Property belonging to persons actually living in Virginia, Maryland, or New England was exempted from this seizure. Those who suffered most were the friends and agents of the Duke of York, among them Lovelace, the ex-governor. This gentleman was of a speculating turn of mind, and had bought sundry snug bits of real estate and parcels of chattels, but without always paying for them on delivery; so that quite naturally he became involved in a Cretan labyrinth of debt. One of his purchases has achieved fame as the initial step in one of the most pertinacious cases of litigation known to modern history. In 1671 he bought the greater part of the "Dominie's Bowery," a farm of sixty-two acres on the North River between the present Fulton and Christopher streets, and mostly west of West Broadway. Lovelace bought it of the heirs of Anneke Jans, the widow of the stout Dominie Bogardus, who has already played his part in our narrative. The hitch in the transaction, which afterward opened the sluices of litigation, was the fact that one of the heirs did not join in the sale to Lovelace. But for that worthy himself there was a more fatal hitch, when the Dutch governor confiscated this purchase with all the rest of his property in New Netherland. No sooner had Lovelace returned from Long Island to Manhattan after its capture by the Dutch, than his creditors arrested him for debt. Concerning the great catastrophe the unfortunate man thus wrote to Governor Winthrop: "To be brief — it was *digitus Dei*, who exalts and depresses as he pleases, and to whom we must all submit. Would you be curious tô know what my losses amount to — I can in short resolve you. It was my all which ever I had been

Lovelace's purchases and debts

collecting ; too greate to misse in this wildernesse . . . I am now intending for England, with all the conveniency I may, unlesse prevented."[1] He was told that he might go within six weeks if he could first pay his debts, but as this was impossible, and there seemed to be nothing to be gained by holding him in durance, he was allowed to sail in the fleet for Holland.

The burgomasters and schepens of New Orange had requested the States General to undertake the government of the province of New Netherland, so auspiciously won back. Their High Mightinesses assented to this, and appointed, for governor of the province, Joris Andringa, who had been secretary to Admiral de Ruyter. For the moment it looked as if New Netherland, set free from the narrow and selfish tyranny of the West India Company, was about to enter upon a period of enhanced prosperity under the more liberal and far-sighted policy of the States General. But it had been otherwise decreed. The prosperity was indeed to come, but under other rulers. Diplomacy quickly undid the work of Admiral Evertsen.

This war, in which France and England were united against Holland, very closely concerned the interests of the House of Hapsburg, in Spain and Austria. The purpose of Louis XIV. was to conquer and annex to France as much as possible of the ancient Middle Kingdom, or Lotharingia, and more especially Franche Comté and the Spanish Netherlands. It therefore became Spain's interest to defend her old adversary, the Dutch Netherlands ; and the interest of the Empire was similar, since if France should succeed in swallowing Franche Comté she would next attempt to swallow Alsace. As for the Dutch, they were hard pressed by the united strength of France and England, and willing to pay something for relief. Under these circumstances Spanish diplomacy prevailed upon the States General to make peace with England upon the basis of a mutual restoration of conquests and the payment of

The situation in Europe

[1] Brodhead, ii. 215.

a liberal war indemnity from the Dutch into the English treasury.   Upon such terms Charles II. was willing to make peace, the more so since the recent events had brought about the rise of his nephew, the Prince of Orange, to the head of affairs and the downfall of De Witt.   Moreover, since Spain and the Empire were coming into the lists against France, it became possible for Charles to gain his personal ends without the trouble of fighting.   His abiding need was of money, to preserve as far as possible his in- dependence of Parliament, and to support his innu- merable mistresses.   "There are two paymasters to whom we may apply.   The one is Parliament, the other is Louis XIV.   In these years he sets himself up to auction.   As the feeling against France is constantly growing in Parliament, it becomes a principle with Charles that by opposing Louis he can obtain money from Parliament, and on the other hand that on condition of restraining, thwarting, or pro- roguing Parliament, he can obtain money from Louis.   Dur- ing this period Louis is contending against a great coalition. It lies with Charles to decide the issue of the European war, which is particularly dependent on him.   He has ceased to aid France ; what if he should strike in on the other side ? If Louis does not wish to see this happen, Louis must pay !" [1]

New policy of Charles II.

In accordance with this Machiavellian policy, Charles pro- rogued his Parliament in 1675, and got £100,000 from his French cousin ; in 1677 he made his demand greater and got £180,000 for a similar service ; in 1678 he wanted £600,000 for turning Parliament out of doors, and upon Louis's refusal our merry monarch turned around and got £600,000 from Parliament, in the expectation that it would be used in a war against Louis !

Such was the course upon which Charles was feeling inclined to enter at the beginning of the year 1674, and accordingly it became easy to detach him from the alliance with France.   At the eleventh hour Louis came forward

[1] Seeley, *The Growth of British Policy*, ii. 213.

with a handsome offer of money, but it was too late. A treaty was signed at Westminster, February 19, between the British king and their High Mighti- nesses at the Hague, and among its provisions was one which finally shaped the destiny of New Netherland, and made it an English province. On the 11th of July following, the treaty was proclaimed at the City Hall of New Orange. It marked the beginnings of greater changes than anybody could foresee. The end of the unnatural estrangement between English and Dutch was approaching; children born that year in London and Amsterdam were still in the schoolroom when the Prince of Orange was hailed as King of England.

The treaty of Westminster did not put New Netherland back into the hands of the Duke of York. The crown lawyers decided that his title was extinguished by the Dutch conquest, and that the treaty handed it over from the States General to Charles II. Accordingly that monarch granted it afresh to his brother. The new grant was not a confirmation of the old grant of 1664; it made no allusion to it and took no heed of several important things that had been done under it. It gave to the Duke of York the whole territory between the Connecticut and Delaware rivers, in utter disregard alike of Nicolls's arrangements with Winthrop and of the claims of Berkeley and Carteret. Thus were the seeds of further vexation and bickering plentifully sown. As for the sturdy Carteret, he entered his protest immediately and with so much vigour that he quite won over Charles, and then James thought it best to yield. But like a true Stuart he could not do anything without creating fresh entanglements. He had once granted New Jersey to Berkeley and Carteret jointly; he now made a fresh grant of the eastern part to Carteret in severalty, while he took no notice of the western part, which Berkeley had sold to a couple of Quakers, and for which he had pocketed the purchase-money, £1000. Lord Berkeley had gone as ambassador to France; and as for such little

The treaty of Westminster, Feb. 19, 1674

Conflicting claims

folk as Friends Byllinge and Fenwick, the duke had apparently forgotten their existence. The boundary between East Jersey and West Jersey was declared in Carteret's patent to be a straight line running from Barnegat Creek on the seacoast to a small tributary of the Delaware River next below the mouth of Rankokus Kill. The patent conveyed the territory of East Jersey to Carteret, but without any powers of sovereignty. As for Staten Island, concerning which some question had arisen, it was "adjudged to belong to New York."

The next thing to be done was to send a governor to take possession of New York. Poor Lovelace had fallen from favour. The Dutch had once confiscated his property; the

Edmund Andros, the new governor

Duke of York now confiscated it again, to satisfy debts due to himself, amounting — as he said — to £7000. The unfortunate ex-governor died before his accounts were settled. For his successor the duke's

THE ANDROS SEAL

choice fell upon an energetic young man whose name has left behind it in America some harsh and jarring memories, — Edmund Andros, major in Prince Rupert's regiment of dragoons.

Massachusetts writers have been apt to deal too severely with Andros, for it was in Boston that his hand was felt most heavily. To class him with vulgar tyrants would be grossly unjust. As to his personal integrity and his general rectitude of purpose

His character

there can be no doubt. His administrative ability also was unquestionable; but while broad-minded in some ways, there were streaks of narrowness in his mind and he was deficient in tact and sympathy. He was not the sort of man who would find it easy to wield arbitrary power according to James Stuart's notions without making it oppressive. But he was immeasurably better in all ways than the princes whom he served; and if his career in the New World had ended with his governorship of New York, his name would have escaped the odium which has been visited upon it.

Andros belonged to a family eminent in the history of the little island of Guernsey, where his father was lord of the manor of Sausmarez and bailiff of the island. The father was also an officer of the royal household. Edmund was born in London in 1637, was brought up at court with the children of Charles I., and shared their exile. At that time he served for a while in the Dutch army, and became familiar with the Dutch language, while he could His early also speak French fluently. These were useful ac- life complishments in a governor of New York. Of the dozen or more languages in vogue there, next after Dutch and English came French, because of the large numbers of Huguenots and Walloons who had found homes in Manhattan.

We shall have occasion hereafter to comment upon the peculiar comradeship between Quakers and Roman Catholics which signalized the courts of the last two Stuart kings. We may see an illustration of it in some of James's appointments for New York. Governor Andros was a member of the Church of England. With him was joined, as lieutenant-governor, Anthony Brockholls, who was a Quakers Roman Catholic, disqualified from holding office and Catholics in England; while the collector of the port was William Dyer, formerly secretary of Rhode Island, whose Quaker wife had been cruelly hanged on Boston Common in 1660.

On an October day of 1674 the English frigates Diamond

Anthos Brockholls

and Castle sailed into the bay of New York, bringing Major Andros and his companions, among whom was Philip Carteret returning to the governorship of New Jersey. The

surrender of the city by Colve was an affair of bows and
Arrival of
Andros in
New York smiles and pretty speeches. Andros regaled the
city officials in his cabin with "ye beste of vitayles
and drink," and Colve, not to be outdone in hospi-
tality, presented to his successor his own handsome carriage
with three finely caparisoned horses. The liberal terms
formerly granted by Colonel Nicolls were renewed; the
"Duke's Laws" were proclaimed once more in force; city
officers were appointed, of whom some were English, some
Dutch, and some French; and the Andros government
seemed to be going into peaceful operation. At Albany
and Kingston there was no opposition, but on the eastern
end of Long Island there was grumbling. On November 14
Andros issued a proclamation reinstating the magistrates
of the several towns who had been in office under Lovelace
at the moment of the Dutch conquest. When this document was received on Long Island the towns of Southold,
The Long
Island
towns Easthampton, and Southampton held town meetings and instructed their magistrates to inform the
governor that they were not under his jurisdiction,
but under that of Governor Winthrop of Connecticut. With
the help of that colony they had cast off the rule of the
Dutch, and they did not feel authorized to separate themselves from her without her express consent. Andros replied that if the three towns did not at once comply with
his proclamation they would be dealt with as if in rebellion;
at the same time he thanked Connecticut for her services in
restoring these towns to the Duke of York's allegiance;
and thus Winthrop and the three towns, on the whole,
deemed acquiescence the best policy.

　More serious trouble broke out at Manhattan in the following March, when Andros issued a proclamation requiring all
citizens of the province of New York to take the same oath
of allegiance which Nicolls had exacted in 1664. The articles
The oath of
allegiance of capitulation between Nicolls and Stuyvesant had
contained provisions that the Dutch might "enjoy
the liberty of their consciences in divine worship and church

discipline," that they might retain "their own customs concerning their inheritances," that all public records should be respected, and various other safeguards against oppression. When Nicolls demanded the oath of allegiance, Cornelius Steenwyck and several other burghers were unwilling to take it unless Nicolls should expressly declare that the articles of capitulation were " not in the least broken or intended to be broken by any words or expressions in the said oath ; " and to this Nicolls readily assented. Now the same objection was urged before Andros by eight leading burghers. Four of these — Cornelius Steenwyck, Johannes van Brugh, Johannes de Peyster, and Jacob Kip — had urged it before Nicolls ; the others were Nicholas Bayard, William Beekman, Ægidius Luyck, and Anthony de Milt. It was evident that the action of these gentlemen would determine that of many other citizens, and Andros saw fit to charge them with a wish to stir up rebellion. He insisted that they should take the oath without any qualification or proviso. Then the eight recusant burghers replied that if they could not be allowed to take the oath now as they had taken it for Nicolls, they hoped they might be permitted to sell their estates and move away from New York. The governor answered by sending them to jail, from which they were released only on giving bonds to appear before the next court of assizes, to be tried for mutinous and inflammatory behaviour. The case came up in the following October, when the accusation was adroitly modified, and the defendants were charged with having violated an act of Parliament by engaging in trade without having taken the oath of allegiance. On this charge conviction was inevitable, and the penalty was forfeiture of goods. Thus driven to the wall, the recusant burghers were fain to secure a remission of the penalty by taking the oath unconditionally ; and such other citizens as had been waiting to follow their example presently came forward and took the oath likewise.[1]

[1] *Minutes of Common Council,* i. 9–11 ; *Colonial Documents,* iii. 233–239.

The affair thus ended in a complete victory for Andros, but it was not to his credit for wisdom and tact that there should have been any such affair at all.   His refusal to grant the very reasonable request of the burghers was indeed not a heinous act of tyranny ; his inability to see anything but sedition in it was a kind of weakness. not uncommon with arbitrary rulers ; and his willingness to remit all penalties on carrying his point was surely not the mark of a truculent temper.   The incident shows Andros in no worse light than that in which Stuyvesant often appeared, but at the same time it plainly shows his inferiority to Nicolls.   His want of tact was the more blameworthy in that Nicolls had once granted the same request that was now made, and no harm whatever had come of it.   Andros showed himself in this instance incapable of profiting by his predecessor's experience.

Andros showed a want of tact

The popular discontent, which in the city and throughout the province had so readily acquiesced in the first change from Dutch to English rule, was still far from abated.   Many of the best citizens had hoped that the change would result in self-government with a regular legislative assembly.   The question had been more or less talked about under Nicolls and Lovelace ; now it was brought up afresh, and the demand for an assembly was so emphatic that Andros felt it necessary to consult his master about it. At first Andros was opposed to the demand, as we learn from the following letter written to him by the Duke of York, in April, 1675 : —

Demand for a representative assembly

" Touching Generall Assemblyes wch ye people there seem desirous of in imitacōn of their neighbour Colonies, I thinke you have done well to discourage any mocōn of y^{t} kind, both as being not at all comprehended in yor Instructions nor indeed consistent wth ye forme of governm^{t} already established, nor necessary for ye ease or redresse of any grievance y^{t} may happen, since y^{t} may be as easily obtained by any peticōn or other addresse to you at their Generall Assizes (wch is once a yeare) where the same per-

The duke's letters

sons (as Justices) are usually present, who in all probability would be theire Representatives if another constitucōn were allowed." [1]

But apparently in the course of that year the views of Governor Andros underwent some change, for in January, 1676, the duke thus advises him : —

"I have formerly writt to you touching Assemblyes in those countreys and have since observed what severall of your lattest letters hint about that matter. But unless you had offered what qualificacōns are usuall and proper to such Assemblyes, I cannot but suspect they would be of dangerous consequence, nothing being more knowne then [*i. e.* than] the aptnesse of such bodyes to assume to themselves many priviledges wch prove destructive to, or very oft disturbe, the peace of ye governm^t wherein they are allowed. Neither doe I see any use of them, wch is not as well provided for, whilest you and your Councell governe according to ye laws established (thereby preserving evary man's property inviolate) and whilest all things that need redresse may be sure of finding it, either at ye Quarter Sessions or by other legall and ordinary wayes, or lastly by appeale to myselfe. *But howsoever if you continue of ye same opinion, I shall be ready to consider of any proposalls you shall send to y^t purpose.*" [2]

The last sentence, which I have italicized, indicates that the governor had suggested the feasibleness and prudence of yielding to the popular demand for a legislature. It seems, moreover, to show the duke in one of his gracious moods. Nothing, however, came of the discussion, and the rule of Andros continued without constitutional check. There can be no question as to his faithfulness to his master, or as to his unflagging zeal for the interests of the city and province which had been committed to his care. In municipal reforms he was most energetic, and he found an able ally in the wealthy and accomplished Stephanus van Cortlandt,[3] the

[1] *Colonial Documents*, iii. 230.　　　　[2] *Id.*, iii. 235.
[3] His name is commemorated in Cortlandt Street, leading from Broadway down to the Pennsylvania Railroad's ferry.

first mayor of New York who was born in the city.   Van
Cortlandt's beautiful wife, Gertrude Schuyler, was an espe-
Municipal   cial favourite with Mrs. Andros, and there was warm
improve-   friendship between the husbands, so that mayor
ments   supported governor with more than ordinary alac-
rity.   Van Cortlandt laid out and graded Broadway for
some distance beyond the city wall; and seven wells were
sunk, which proved useful in cases of fire, though the water
was too brackish for drinking.   Andros was a stickler for
cleanliness and obliged every householder on certain stated
days to set out by the wayside his litter and garbage in barrels or tubs, for the city's carts to take away.   Andros also
built a market-house on Broad Street, and a wharf on the
East River, he had decrepit houses thoroughly repaired, or if
not worth repairing and liable to become dangerous, he had
them pulled down.   Tidy housekeeping was a hobby to which
he was always ready to give personal supervision.   When
building was going on he would stand by and give orders to
the workmen, or would even in his zeal pick up a foot-rule
and measure a board to see if it would fit.   It goes without
saying that trade and currency would engage the attention
of such a man.   He fostered trades and tradesmen with rules
and regulations until it was a wonder that New York had any
Currency   trade left.   Even the quantity of brine in which the
             farmer might immerse his blocks of fat pork was
minutely prescribed.   As for prices, they were of course fixed
by ordinance.   The currency of the province was in that un-
fathomable chaos which has always had so many admirers
in the New World, — specie, beaver skins, white and black
wampum, with relative values perpetually shifting, — and in
the attempt to introduce something like order and stability
Andros struggled manfully but in vain.   Another crying
evil was intemperance.   It was said, perhaps with some
Dram-   exaggeration, that one quarter of all the houses in
shops   the city were places for retailing beer and spirits,
and it could not be denied that the streets were too noisy
with tipplers.   The vehement mood in which Andros ap-

proached such matters is shown by his ordinance that if any man were to be seen drunk on the street, and the magistrates should be unable to discover where he had got his liquor, they were empowered forthwith to clap a fine upon every house in that street! How far this superlative edict was enforced we do not know.

In spite of his zeal and diligence the prosperity of New York did not come up to its governor's wishes and expectations, and although inducements were held out to immigrants, yet the population did not increase so rapidly as was desired. It seemed to Andros necessary for the general welfare that the thriving towns and teeming fields of Connecti- *Andros* cut should be added to his province ; or, as he him- *covets* self would have honestly said, to assert the duke's *cut* rightful authority over this eastern portion of his province. At the same time both Andros and the duke knew that some discretion was needful in proceeding against a colony chartered by the king, to say nothing of the facts that Connecticut single-handed was stronger than New York, and that she was loosely confederated with Massachusetts and Plymouth, upon whose aid in certain emergencies she could count.

In the spring of 1675 Andros sent a message to Hartford, requesting the General Court to make arrangements for turning over that town and all the country west of the Connecticut River to the Duke of York. The court replied by alleging the award of the royal commissioners of 1664, which gave to Connecticut a boundary twenty miles east *and lays* of the Hudson River. Andros rejoined that the *claim to it* alleged award had never been confirmed by the king, and was now quite superseded by the new royal grant to the duke. The men of Connecticut refused to admit this claim, and their contumacy was declared by Andros and his council to be tantamount to rebellion. In June "hee sent home Captⁿ Salisbury for England to let his Royal Highness know how impossible it was for this Government to subsist without the addition of Connecticut." [1]

[1] Governor Dongan's report of 1687 to the Lords of Trade, in O'Cal-

In the answer to Salisbury's message, which did not come for nearly a year, the duke's secretary wrote to Andros: "Upon the whole you will see that His Roy[ll] H[ss] is willing things should rest as they are at present, but he is not sorry you have revived this clayme because possibly some good use may be hereafter made of it."[1]

But the ship that carried Captain Salisbury had scarcely sailed (July 2, 1675) when a courier from Hartford came spurring down the Bowery Lane (July 4) with the shocking news of the Indian massacre at Swanzey. The long-drawn chapter of horrors known as King Philip's War had begun. Andros at once wrote to Winthrop: "I am very much troubled at the Christians' misfortunes and hard disasters in those parts, being so overpowered by such heathen. Hereupon I have hastened my coming to your parts, and added a force to be ready to take such resolutions as may be fit for me upon this extraordinary occasion, with which I intend, God willing, to set out this evening, and to make the best of my way to Connecticut River, His Royal Highness' bounds there."[2]

Breaking out of King Philip's War

If the good people at Hartford had been at all slow to dread the coming of Andros with his Danaan gift of reinforcements, this last ominous allusion would have quickened them. They promptly recalled the force which they had despatched in aid of Plymouth, and they sent Captain Thomas Bull, with 100 men, to hold the fort at Saybrook. The General Court was at once assembled, and unanimously adopted a protest against "Major Andros and all his aiders and abettors, as disturbers of the public peace of his Majesty's good subjects." It was resolved that they should "use their utmost power and endeavour (expecting

Connecticut prepares to resist Andros

laghan's *Documentary History of New York*, i. 187. Dongan goes on to say, "Much less can it subsist now without it, being at more expense than in the time of Sir Edmond, having lost Delaware, etc. . . . I hope his Ma[ty] will bee graciously pleased to add that Colony to this which is the Centre of all His Dominions in America."

[1] *Colonial Documents*, iii. 236.

[2] *Connecticut Colonial Records*, ii. 579.

therein the assistance of Almighty God) to defend the good people of the Colony from the said Major Andros's attempts."

On the 8th of July Andros arrived at Saybrook with three sloops-of-war, and found the fort already occupied by Captain Bull, and the royal standard floating over it, upon which it was neither prudent nor proper to fire. Andros sent a message up to Hartford, renewing his demand for territory, and asking for a "direct and effectual answer," for which he said he should wait. As for his aid against Indians, he hinted that the Connecticut people did not seem over eager for it. Captain Bull told him that if he wished to be helpful against Philip's Indians he had better lose no time in sailing to Mount Hope Bay. After two days Andros came ashore and had an interview on the river's bank with Bull and his officers. Andros insisted upon having the duke's patent read aloud, but Bull's party refused to listen and walked away, saying it was no business of theirs. When the reading was finished, Andros said he should now depart unless they wished him to stay. The officers replied that they were not instructed to ask him to stay, but they had something to read aloud for his benefit, and they went on to read the protest of the General Court in which Andros was set down as a disturber of the public peace. He exclaimed that this was a poor requital for his kindness in offering aid against the savages; and so the colloquy ended. As his vessels got under weigh he was courteously saluted by the guns of the fort, and the salute was returned. Then with swelling canvas the governor's ships sailed out of the beautiful river and sped away over the majestic waters of the Sound with prows turned southward for Long Island. When the affair was reported to the Hartford magistrates, they commended Bull and his officers for what they had done, but wished that it might have been done less mildly. It would have been well, they said, if the reading of the patent had been drowned in a boom and clatter of drums.[1] Eighteen years later, as we shall see, a very

> *Andros baffled at Saybrook*

[1] *Connecticut Colonial Records*, ii. 262, 334, 339-343, 579-584. Dr.

doubtful tradition credits Captain Wadsworth with remembering this hint and acting upon it.[1]

From Southold, where Andros landed, he sent a few soldiers to protect his master's islands of Nantucket and Martha's Vineyard. He returned through Long Island to Manhattan, and exacted fresh assurances of good behaviour from all the Algonquin sachems in the neighbourhood. After a few weeks the rumour of Jesuit intrigues in the Mohawk valley led him to visit the Long House in person, to counteract this dangerous influence.

The Iroquois league was now at the height of its power. These barbarians had never forgotten Champlain's attack

Courcelle

upon them at Ticonderoga,[2] and seldom let slip any opportunity for harassing the French. They became so vexatious that early in 1666 Courcelle, the governor of Canada, set out with a party on snow-shoes to invade the Mohawk country. Courcelle with much difficulty reached Schenectady, the most advanced outpost of New Netherland, where he first learned of the capture of the province by Colonel Nicolls. He was obliged to retrace his steps without chastising the barbarians, for, hard as the advance had been through a frozen wilderness, he feared that sudden thaws and vernal mud might make retreat impossible. In the autumn of the same year Courcelle returned with the Marquis de Tracy, lieutenant-general of New France, and a powerful force of 1300 men, and they succeeded in burning five of the Mohawk " castles," or palisaded villages, and destroying an immense

French invasion of the Mohawk country

Trumbull's account, in his *History of Connecticut*, i. 330, perhaps needs a little pruning.

[1] See below, p. 204.   [2] See above, vol. i. p. 83.

quantity of food that had been stored for the winter. The French beheld with astonishment how much these keen-witted barbarians had learned from the Dutch.[1] Not only had they grown expert in the use of firearms and many carpenters' tools, but their forts were stout quadrangles twenty feet high, with formidable bastions at the corners. The destruction of these elaborate strongholds made a deep impression upon the dusky brethren of the Long House, for it showed them that their eastern door, at least, might be beaten in by Onontio[2] and his pale-faced children.

Governor Nicolls held that this French invasion of the Mohawk country was a trespass on the territory of New York, since he recognized a kind of Dutch overlordship over the Long House, and held that their rights of suzerainty had now passed over to the English. For a moment Nicolls dreamed of a general attack upon Canada, in which the New England colonies should take part, but such a scheme found little favour. A war against New France meant a war against Algonquins and in aid of Iroquois, and was likely to infuriate the Algonquins of New England, whose love for their brethren of Canada may not have been strong, but whose hate for the Iroquois surpassed the hatreds of hell. Nicolls encouraged the Mohawks to resist the French, but neither under his administration nor that of Lovelace were adequate measures taken for securing a permanent Anglo-Iroquois alliance.

Meanwhile the sagacious and indefatigable rulers of New France were as ready to try persuasion as violence, and they found consummate instruments in the Jesuits. These de-

[1] Parkman, *Old Régime*, i. 257.

[2] *Onontio* (occasionally written *Yonnondio*) means Big Mountain, and is the Iroquois translation of the name of Charles de Montmagny, who was governor of Canada from 1636 to 1648. All the French governors of Canada were thereafter called Onontio by the Iroquois, among whom it was customary for the hereditary chief to inherit the name as well as the office of his predecessor. In like manner all the governors of Pennsylvania were called *Onas*, which means Quill, and is a translation of the name Penn. See Parkman's *Jesuits*, ii. 102.

voted missionaries addressed themselves to the task of con-
verting the Iroquois to Christianity and turning their hearts
to an alliance with Onontio.   With the Mohawks, who had

French
intrigues
with the
Long
House

suffered the chief damage from the French, the
case was hopeless ; but the other tribes — Oneidas,
Onondagas, Cayugas, and Senecas — were more
ready to listen.   Some headway was made, and a
few tawny warriors were baptized, while Courcelle began
building a fortress at Cataraqui, where the river St. Lawrence flows out of Lake Ontario.   This stronghold, which
was finished in 1673 by Frontenac, and bore his name for
more than eighty years, stood on the site of the present
city of Kingston.   Its immediate purpose was to serve as a
base for expeditions across Lake Ontario against the central
and western tribes of the Long House, and to cut off the
lucrative fur trade in which these barbarians were the pur-
veyors for the Dutch and English in New York.

The moment when Andros was governor of New York
was therefore a critical moment.   If the Jesuit missionaries

A critical
moment

had won over the Long House, it is not improbable that New York would have become, and might
perhaps have remained, a French province.   Possibly the formation of the American Union might have been prevented.
Certainly the history of the eighteenth and nineteenth centuries would have been modified in many important particulars.

There was imminent danger that the short-sighted policy
of the Duke of York would play directly into the hands of
the French.   For a while James did what he could to favour
the Jesuit missionaries, wishing to see the heathen of the

The duke's
mistaken
policy

New World brought into the fold of Rome, and
failing to realize that every point gained by those
good Jesuits was a nail in the coffin of his own
American interests.   At times, however, he seemed to wake
up to the gravity of the situation, which Andros, being on
the spot, understood much better than he.   In the terrible
summer of 1675, when the Wampanoags were working such

havoc in the Plymouth colony and the Nipmucks in the central highlands of Massachusetts, while on the other hand the frontier settlements in Virginia and Maryland were being goaded into a war set afoot by wandering Susquehannocks,[1] it was clearly a time for preserving friendly relations with the formidable Long House. Scarcely had Andros returned from his Connecticut expedition when he made up his mind to go in person to the Mohawks and secure their favour and that of their confederates.

His journey took him far into the Indian country. It was a pleasant voyage, of course, to Albany, making a brief stop at Esopus. After landing at Albany his party struck into the great Indian trail, the course of which has been closely followed in later days by the Erie Canal and the New York Central Railroad. After a march of about sixteen miles they came upon the Mohawk River, at a fording-place, where there was a tiny Dutch hamlet founded fourteen years before by Arendt van Corlear, a man of noble and generous nature. As a commissioner of Rensselaerwyck he had long been well known to the Indians, in whose minds his name stood as a synonym for truth and integrity. In 1667 this good Corlear came to a melancholy end. As he was sailing on Lake Champlain he passed a rock whereon the waves were wont to dash and fly up wildly, and Indian folklore told of an ancestral Indian who haunted the spot and controlled the weather, so that passing canoes always threw a pipe or other small gift to this genius of the lake and prayed for a favourable wind. But Corlear not only neglected this wise precaution, but in his contempt for such heathen fancies made an unseemly gesture as he passed the rock ; whereat the offended spirit blew a sudden gust which capsized his boat and drowned him.[2]

The Indian name of the village founded by Corlear was Onoaligone, but the village itself was known to Indians

Journey of Andros into the wilderness

Fate of Arendt van Corlear

---

[1] See *Old Virginia and Her Neighbours*, ii. Illustrated Edition, 51–55.
[2] Colden's *History of the Five Nations*, London, 1755, i. 32.

and French simply as "Corlear's." The Dutch inhabitants, however, transferred to it the Iroquois name Schenectady, which was originally applied to the country about the site
Corlear's village, Schenectady of Albany.[1] At this Dutch village of Schenectady, the remotest western outpost of civilization, the governor and his retinue made a brief halt. At that fording-place the trail divided, one branch crossing the river, the other following its windings closely upon the southern bank. This southern trail would bring Andros through the three principal Mohawk castles; the first one being on the west bank of Schoharie Creek at its junction with the river, the second at Canajoharie, and the third on the site of the present town absurdly named "Danube," in Herkimer County. Soon after leaving
Andros arrives in the Oneida country this stronghold the trail passed from the territory of the Mohawks into that of the Oneidas, and there was no other stopping-place until the party arrived at a hill around the base of which the trail made a very noticeable curve. Here at the Oneida stronghold known as Nundadasis, or "around the hill," hard by the site of the city of Utica, this inland journey came to an end.

To this rendezvous in the depths of the primeval forest came chiefs from all the Five Nations, even from the fur-
Great conference with the Indians thest Seneca villages on the southern shore of Lake Erie. There was a grand powwow which lasted for several days. It was the season for green succotash and for mallards and teal, with the red man's inevi-

[1] The meaning of Schenectady is variously rendered. Morgan, whose familiarity was greatest with the Seneca dialect, makes it mean " Beyond-the-openings " (*i. e.* in the hills); see his *League of the Iroquois*, Rochester, 1851, p. 415. David Cusick, the Tuscarora (in his *History of the Six Nations*, Lockport, 1848) makes it mean " Beyond-the-pine-plains," and Beauchamp (*Indian Names in New York*, Fayetteville, 1893) got the same interpretation from some Onondagas.

table gala dish of boiled dog. Solemn speeches were made, wampum belts were exchanged, and many a ring of blue smoke curled from the pipe of peace, as it was made clear to all that the wicked Onontio sought to bring ruin upon the Long House, while the English were its steadfast friends, even as the Dutch had been before them. The Indians' vivid sense of the continuity between these two was shown when they bestowed upon Andros the name of their old friend Corlear. As in their minds the Dutch power whose friendship they valued was personified in Corlear, the particular Dutchman with whom they chiefly had dealings on matters of public interest, so now the English power was personified in Andros. Since he stood for exactly the same things as their former ally, he too was Corlear, and by that name the governors of New York were henceforth known in the Long House for more than a hundred years.

An immediate result of this auspicious conference with the Five Nations was the organization of a Board of Commissioners of Indian Affairs, with its headquarters at Albany. From that time forth the proximity of Albany to the Long House made it one of the most important towns in English America, as was shown in 1754, when it was selected as the place of meeting for the famous Congress at which Benjamin Franklin's plan for a Federal Union was propounded. For secretary of his Board of Commissioners Andros appointed a young Scotchman, the scion of a family long famous in Scotland and destined to further fame in America. Robert Livingston was the son of an eminent Presbyterian minister of Roxburghshire, who migrated to Rotterdam soon after Charles II. came to the throne. At about the age of twenty Robert came to America and settled in Albany, where he was almost immediately made town clerk. His appointment within another year to such a responsible post on the Indian Commission was an early testimony to the ability and force of character that were afterward shown in many ways. In 1679 he married Alida, sister of Peter

The Board of Indian Commissioners

Robert Livingston

Schuyler and widow of Dominie Nicholas van Rensselaer, — an alliance of three names potent in the history of the New World. Peter Schuyler, who was afterward mayor of Albany, exerted greater influence over the Iroquois than any other man before the arrival of William Johnson in the next century. On the whole, the founding of the Indian Commission was probably the most important act of Andros's administration, and the value of the work accomplished by a little group of able men at Albany is not likely to be overrated.

Andros continued, like his Dutch predecessors, to supply the Iroquois with muskets and ammunition, and this was probably the source of the rumour, which was believed in Boston, that Philip's Indians were supplied with powder at Albany. The governor was naturally indignant at this vile slander. He had left most stringent orders at Albany prohibiting the sale of firearms or powder to any Algonquin, under penalty of £10 fine for every quarter of a pound of powder, or in aggravated cases the offender might even be put to death. Therefore "hee sent two gentlemen to Boston

Andros's relations with New England

to complaine of such an aspersion, demanding itt might bee made appeare, or falce informer punished ; They by a letter cleare the Magistrates butt nott Generalty, still asperced wthout any known cause, complaint, or notice." The "Generalty" of people anywhere in the New England Confederacy were not willing to deprive themselves of any excuse for hating the representative of that "man of sin," James Stuart, and even when Andros sincerely wished to aid them his generosity must reach them through that colony of heretics with which the "lords brethren" refused to own fellowship. "Upon notice of want, though unasked, hee sent six barrels of powder and some match to Roade Island, which they thankfully accepted, and afterward lent part of it to New England fforces in want, att their fight in Narrogansett country."[1] Some of the powder burnt in destroying the swamp fortress on

[1] *New York Colonial Documents*, iii. 254.

Ro: Livingston Seir.

that terrible December Sunday came therefore from the much hated governor of New York.

The New England historians of this war lose sight of King Philip after the Brookfield fight in August, 1675, and he first reappears in Mrs. Rowlandson's narrative for February, 1676. The New York archives show that in November and December he was in the mountains of Berkshire accompanied by 1000 warriors, and on one occasion came within forty miles of Albany. His purpose may probably have been to bring the Mohegans of the Housatonic valley [1] into the general crusade against the English, and with this large force he may have hoped to destroy Albany.[2] The alarm was sent to New York,

King Philip in the Berkshire mountains

[1] The same who had afterward a romantic history under the name of Stockbridge Indians, and are forever associated with the names of John Sergeant, David Brainerd, and Jonathan Edwards. See Davidson, *Muh-he-ka-ne-ok: a History of the Stockbridge Nation*, Milwaukee, 1893.

[2] Increase Mather credits him with a more Machiavellian purpose : " We hear that Philip, being this winter entertained in the Mohawk country, made it his design to breed a quarrel between the English and them ; to effect which, divers of our returned captives do report that he resolved to kill some scattering Mohawks, and then to say that the English had done it. But one of those whom he thought to have killed was only wounded, and got away to his countrymen, giving them to understand that not the English, but Philip, had killed the men ; so that, instead of bringing the Mohawks upon the English, he brought them upon himself. Thus the heathen are sent down into the pit that they made ; in the net which they had laid is their own foot taken ; the Lord is known by the judgment which he executeth ; the wicked is snared in the work of his own hands." Mather's *Brief History of the War with the Indians*, Boston, 1676, p. 38. I agree with Dr. Palfrey in suspecting this to be a " wild story," and I doubt if anything could have induced the Wampanoag chief to risk his scalp in the Mohawk country ; nevertheless the diplomacy ascribed to him is characteristically Indian, and the tale may be based upon facts. No such explanation, however, is needed for the Mohawk attack upon Philip, since the Mohawks were in close alliance with the English. My statement (*Beginnings of New England*, Illustrated Edition, p. 257), " What [Philip] had been doing, or where he had been, since the Brookfield fight in August, was never known," needs some modification. When

and the governor at once wrote to Hartford and to Boston for permission to bring a force of English and Iroquois into New England to attack their Algonquin foes.   The request was refused, which indicates that it was suspected of being a ruse to cover a real design upon the west bank of the Connecticut River.   Then Andros went up to Albany with six sloops and there met a large force of exulting Mohawks, loaded with the scalps of Philip's warriors whom they had defeated and chased through Berkshire.[1]   It was immediately after this defeat that Philip, moving eastward, attacked Lancaster with a strong party of Nipmucks.

After the summer of 1676 the war came to an end in southern New England, with the almost complete extermination of Narragansetts, Wampanoags, and Nipmucks, but it was kept up two years longer by the Tarratines on the Maine coast.   Massachusetts and Connecticut wished to deal directly with the Mohawks, to obtain military aid from them, but Andros would not allow this.   He was willing, however, to have envoys from Boston and Hartford meet envoys from the Long House in his presence at Albany and negotiate to their hearts' content.   Sundry questions connected with the Indian troubles at the South, which had ensued after the overthrow of the Susquehannocks by the Senecas, brought envoys likewise from Virginia and Maryland to Albany.   In 1677 Andros dealt a blow at the Tarratines in the interest of the Duke of York.

War with the Tarratines

He sent a force which took possession of Pemaquid and built a fort there : but here he contrived to irritate Massachusetts by forbidding the curing of fish except upon the islands and one small spot near the fort.

In the autumn of 1677 Andros went to England on private business, leaving Brockholls in charge of his province. He was knighted in approval of his official conduct, and returned to New York in the autumn of 1678.   With him

I wrote it, I knew Mather's story, to which I attached no importance, but I had not seen the paper in the New York archives.

[1] *New York Colonial Documents*, iii. 255.

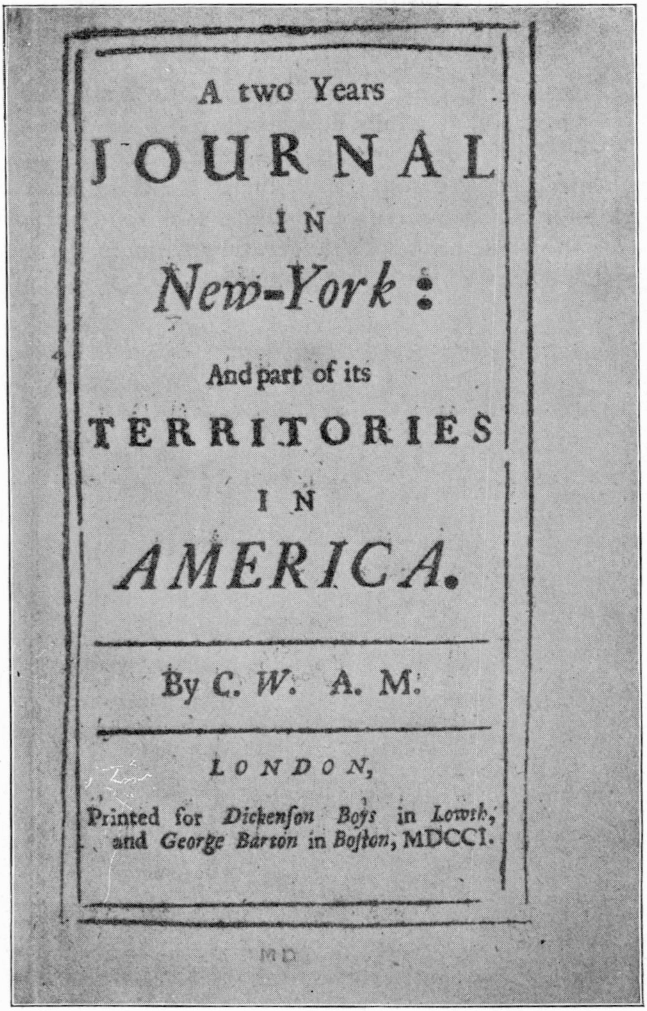

A two Years

JOURNAL

IN

New-York :

And part of its

TERRITORIES

IN

AMERICA.

By C. W. A. M.

LONDON,

Printed for *Dickenson Boys* in *Lowth*, and *George Barton* in *Boston*, MDCCI.

TITLE OF WOLLEY'S "TWO YEARS' JOURNAL"

came Rev. Charles Wolley, a young Cambridge graduate,

Andros
visits Eng-
land, is
knighted,
and returns
to New
York
who, after his return to England three years later, published a book which was widely read, entitled " A Two Years' Journal in New York." It was in the next year, moreover, that New York was visited and carefully described by two very keen and intelligent Dutch observers, the so-called Labadist emissaries, Jasper Dankers and Peter Sluyter. Let us seize this occasion for taking a survey of the city as it appeared in the days of the Duke of York's autocratic governors. For this purpose, we shall do best to take our start in a new chapter.

CHAPTER XI

NEW YORK IN THE YEAR 1680

LATE in the autumn of 1680 the good people of Manhattan were overcome with terror at a sight in the heavens such as has seldom greeted human eyes. An enormous comet, perhaps the most magnificent one on record, suddenly made its appearance. At first it was tailless and dim, like a nebulous cloud, but at the end of a week the tail began to show itself and in a second week had attained a length of 30 degrees; in the third week it extended to 70 degrees, while the whole mass was growing brighter. After five weeks it seemed to be absorbed into the intense glare of the sun, but in four days more it reappeared like a blazing sun itself in the throes of some giant convulsion and threw out a tail in the opposite direction as far as the whole distance between the sun and the earth. Sir Isaac Newton, who was then at work upon the mighty problems soon to be published to the world in his "Principia," welcomed this strange visitor as affording him a beautiful instance for testing the truth of his new theory of gravitation.[1] But most people throughout the civilized world, the learned as well as the multitude, feared that the end of all things was at hand. Every church in Europe, from the grandest cathedral to the humblest chapel, resounded with supplications, and in the province of New York a day of fasting and humiliation was appointed, in order that the wrath of God might be assuaged. Let us take a brief survey of the little city on Manhattan Island, upon which Newton's comet looked down, while Dominie Nieuwenhuysen and Dominie Frazius were busy with prayers to avert the direful omen.

The great comet

---

[1] Newton's *Principia*, book iii. prop. 41.

To a visitor sailing up the harbour the most conspicuous objects would have been Fort James, standing on the present Battery and mounting forty-seven guns, and a little to the west of it the principal town windmill.[1] Fort James On the other side, near the present South Ferry, scarcely less conspicuous, was the stone Government House, built by Stuyvesant, the name of which was afterward changed by Governor Dongan to Whitehall. Hard by was the governor's dwelling-house. Going up Whitehall Street, one would espy the warehouse and bakery that had once belonged to the West India Company, and the brewery, convenient for governor and dominie. Near it stood the Dutch parsonage with its quaint flower-beds gorgeous in colours and bordered with closely trimmed box. Coming to the Bowling Green, the belfry of Kieft's church of St. Nicholas would be seen peering over the walls of the fort at the graveyard on the west side of Broadway. Just north of the wall stood the town pump. Stepping back to Whitehall and turning eastward, we come upon the jail and the stocks. Pearl Street, the oldest in the city, was then the river bank, and was often called Waterside or the Strand, but the old name has prevailed, which is said to have been given it from the abundant heaps of oyster-shells, highly prized for the excellence of their lime. The quaint Dutch houses, with their gables and weathercocks and small-paned dormer windows, were built of bricks baked in Holland, cemented with mortar made from this lime. They retained the high stoop (*stoep*, *i. e.* steps), which in the Fatherland raised the best rooms above the risk of inundation, and thus bequeathed to modern New York one of its most distinctive architectural features.

From Pearl Street in a gentle curve ran northward to the city wall a street most suggestive of Holland, with a stream flowing through its centre diked on both sides like a Dutch

[1] This description partly follows the map of "The Towne of Mannados, or New Amsterdam, in 1661," of which the original is in the British Museum.

canal. This was rightly called Broad Street, for it was
seventy-two feet in width. Its canal was spanned Broad
by several wooden foot-bridges and one "for cat- Street
tell and waggons." At about the time which our narrative
has reached, Governor Andros had the canal effaced and
the road built solidly over it, and from that day to this the
stream has continued to flow under Broad Street, doing

SMIT'S V'LEI

duty as a sewer.[1] Two spacious docks were then built at the
foot of the street, between the jail and Whitehall, which
greatly increased the facilities for shipping. Walking up
Pearl Street as far as the present No. 73, opposite Coenties
Slip, one would come upon the old Stadt Huys, which served
as a city hall until 1699, when a new one was built on Wall
Street, facing the head of Broad. In that new City Hall
the eccentric Charles Lee spent the year 1777 as a prisoner, and on its balcony in 1789, the object of his jealous
hatred, George Washington, was inaugurated President of
the United States.

Where Pearl Street crossed Wall, there was the Water

[1] Hill and Waring, *Old Wells and Water-Courses of the Island
of Manhattan*, p. 310.

Gate through the tall palisadoed structure. A little below, the burgher's battery of ten guns frowned upon the river; The Water Gate just at the gate was a demi-lune called the Fly (V'lei) blockhouse; and a short distance above stood the slaughter-houses, which Andros had banished from the city. Proceeding northward, we enter a bright green marshy valley drained by a brook, where groups of laughing women might be seen washing clothes, as one often sees them to-day in France. The brook and the verdure have Maiden Lane long since departed, but the brookside path still keeps the name of Maiden Lane. On the East River, at the foot of this path, is a busy blacksmith's forge, from which the valley is known as Smit's Vallei, shortened in common parlance to V'lei. A few steps above the smithery bring us to the site of Peck Slip, where a boat is moored to a tree growing on the bank. A horn hangs upon this tree, and if we take it down and blow, a farmer will emerge from his house near by and ferry us over to Brooklyn for three stivers in wampum, or about six cents in our modern reckoning. But we will leave the horn un- sounded, for after a brief visit to Isaac Allerton's big tobacco warehouse, between the present Cliff Street and Shoe- makers' Land Fulton Ferry, we must walk through Shoemakers' Land. Until 1676 the tanneries were on Broad Street, but Andros then declared them a nuisance and ordered them out of the city; whereupon their owners bought the land now enclosed between Broadway, Ann, Gold, and John streets, and did there tan hides and make boots. After twenty years this odorous business was moved a little further north, to Beekman's Swamp, which has re- mained for two centuries the principal home of the city's leather trade.

From the western border of Shoemakers' Land a south- ward walk on Broadway outside the wall, a country road among woods and fields, brings us down to the Land Gate. Of peril from savage foes or from wild beasts in this open country, not much was to be apprehended in 1678, although the young parson Wolley tells with much unction of the part which he took in a bear hunt near Maiden Lane. But the military defences were kept up and increased The Land until the end of the century, chiefly in view of Gate possible danger from France. At the Land Gate (Broadway and Wall Street) a large stone salient was added, mounting several guns, and known by the name " Hollandia ; " while a similar structure, called " Zelandia," stood where Wall was crossed by King (now William) Street. The site of Greenwich Street was then a long steep bluff with its base washed by the North River, and presently the wall was continued and carried southward, crowning the bluff and reinforced by three stout bastions, until it reached Fort James. There were no buildings of note west of Broadway except the Lutheran church and parsonage, near the Land Gate.

Manhattan north of the city wall was an undulating woodland, with many rocky hills and considerable areas of salt marshes partially drained by sluggish streams. In several favoured localities were flourishing boweries (Dutch *bouw-eries, i. e.* farms) with smiling orchards and gardens. The main thoroughfare started at the Land Gate as the northward extension of Broadway ; at the site of Ann Street it was deflected eastward and followed the direction of Park Row and Chatham Street into the Bowery Lane, so called from Stuyvesant's country seat, which it passed. Walking northward from the point of deflection, one would have on the right hand Beekman's Swamp and on the left hand the grazing-ground long known as the Flats, then as the Common or the Fields, now as the City Hall Park. In time The it came to supersede the Bowling Green as a place Common for great open-air assemblies ; there it was, in 1774, that the youthful Alexander Hamilton, a student at King's College, began his public career, just a century after the first coming of Andros to govern New York. During those hundred years the changes of landscape in that neighborhood were not great. The most notable feature was the large pond which covered the area now bounded by Baxter, White,

THE COLLECT

Elm, Duane, and Park streets. Around the shores of this bright and sparkling sheet of water stood a village of Man-
The Collect, or Fresh Water
hattan Indians before the white intruders came to their island. For Indians, Dutch, and English it was a bountiful reservoir of dainty fish, and in the winter it was the gay scene of skating parties. It was sometimes called the Fresh Water, sometimes the Collect, of which more anon. To the south of it was a much smaller pond known as the Little Collect, and on the narrow isthmus between, about at the present junction of Duane and Centre streets, the City Magazine or Powder House was built in 1728. There it has been supposed that the French fort of Norumbega may have stood in 1542, when it was visited by Jean Allefonsce.[1]

This deep and limpid lake, the Collect, was at the divide between the two watersheds into the East and North rivers. Its surface was at the level of a ridge of high land, from which, in the southeast and northwest directions, there ran two deep depressions, separating the lower end of Manhattan
Wolfert's Marsh
from the broader region above. These depressions were salt marshes. The easterly one, called Wolfert's Marsh, extended to the East River, and through it

[1] See above, vol. i. p. 67.

flowed the Old Kill on about the line of Roosevelt Street. The wayfarer on his way up from the city, just before reaching the brink of Wolfert's Marsh, might quench his thirst at a copious spring, called the Tea Water Pump, which remained famous until the middle of the nineteenth century. After passing this natural fountain, he would come to the

KISSING BRIDGE

descent into the marshy ravine, a descent so steep that the high road was constrained to make a sharp curve from the line of Park Row eastward through a bit of William and Pearl, and back again. After the descent, he would cross the Old Kill upon the Kissing Bridge, where, if he happened to be walking or driving with a lady companion, it was his privilege to kiss her. On the further

The Kissing Bridge

side of the stream another sharp curve (the cause of the opening at Chatham Square) was made necessary by the abrupt ascent.[1] At the top of the hill stood Wolfert Webber's tavern, and a little beyond it a tall windmill built in 1662. In this neighbourhood were a few farms kept by free negroes. Some distance further out one would pass the ancient mile-stone, which still stands on the Bowery opposite Rivington Street, " on which, if it does not happen to be covered over with bills, one may still read the legend, 2 miles to City Hall." [2] Still further north, near the Ninth Street station of the Third Avenue elevated railroad, came the cluster of settlements known as the Bowery Village, founded by Stuyvesant on his own territory. There were the clanking smithery, the church where the town schoolmaster, Dominie Selyns, preached on Sundays, and the inn where good entertainment was furnished for man and beast.

The Bowery Village

About a mile above the Bowery Village, the road began to make its way over wild and rugged hills, with few traces of human occupation save at the well-kept farm of Jacobus Kip, at that deep bight of the East River between Thirty-third and Thirty-seventh streets which is still known as Kip's Bay. Kip's massive and stately house, which he built in 1655, being then secretary of New Netherland, was demolished in 1851, because it occupied the space where Thirty-fifth Street now crosses Second Avenue. After leaving this farm behind and proceeding for another half mile, one would come upon another indentation of the river, which the Dutch called Deutel (i. e. Wedge) Bay, a name which in English mouths soon became Turtle Bay. Into it, near the foot of Forty-seventh Street, emptied a brook which, from its sources near Ninth Avenue and Seventy-second Street, meandered across the island, leaving a modern vestige of itself in the lake near the Plaza in Cen-

Kip's Bay

Turtle Bay

[1] In this account I have been much assisted by Hill and Waring, *Old Wells and Water-Courses*, an admirable monograph.

[2] Hewitt's *The Bowery*, p. 372.

LISPENARD'S MEADOWS

tral Park. Some of this brook's water was utilized in turning the wheels of Mynheer de Voor's grist-mill, whereby it
was commonly known as Voor's Mill-stream. The bridge
on which our high road was carried over it afforded our wayfarer a second opportunity for kissing the damsel beside him
without fear of rebuke. Just above this bridge there stood
for more than a century Old Cato's Inn, renowned for its
suppers of fish and game. Nothing else do we en-
counter that calls for mention here until we arrive   Harlem
at the Flats, where the village of Harlem had reached a
flourishing condition by 1660.

We may now return to the place where Broadway was
deflected into Park Row, and thence take a fresh northward
start on the other side of the Common, along the present
line of Broadway. In the days of Andros this was merely
a walk across the fields, but afterwards the prolongation of
Broadway began as a ropewalk. By 1776 that thoroughfare,
with the streets west of it, had been laid out and partially
occupied with houses as far up as Reade Street. There
the land descended into the great hollow through which
flowed the Collect's western outlet down to the Hudson
River. Its breadth was rather more than half a mile, from

the line of Duane to that of Spring Street, which received its name from one of the rivulets which swelled the volume

The Great Kill and Lispenard's Meadows of the Groote (*i. e.* Great) Kill, as the main outlet was called.   Up this Groote Kill the red men used to paddle their canoes laden with oysters, and from the heaps of shells on the shores of the pond came the Dutch name Kolch Hoek (*i. e.* Shell Point), which the English corrupted into Collect.   The wide region which the stream imperfectly drained was afterward long known as Lispenard's Meadows.   Part of it was excellent grazing-land, but it was largely swamp, with treacherous quagmires here and there in which cattle were engulfed.   Its perils were illustrated by grewsome incidents, as when a puzzled pedestrian after nightfall, losing his way where Greene Street now crosses Grand, stepped into a deep pool and was drowned.   Through its insidious and spongy wastes, musical with bull-frogs, many a zealous angler made his way, while the fowler with his shot-gun was sure to find woodcock and snipe abounding.   After 1730 the region was regarded as a lurking-place of miasma, and from time to time portions were filled in by dumping stones and earth.   At length the whole space was filled up, while the Groote Kill was straightened and deepened and confined between plank walls, so as to become a canal in a street one hundred feet wide.   Such

Canal Street was the origin of Canal Street.   Early in the nineteenth century the city had come to envelop the beautiful Collect, which became a receptacle for rubbish and filth until it was voted a nuisance and obliterated.   On a rising ground to the west of the water had formerly stood the gallows.   In 1838, on a spot which had been in the central portion of the lake, was built the city prison, that noble but dismal specimen of Egyptian architecture commonly known as The Tombs.

On the bank of the North River, half a mile or so above the northern confines of Lispenard's Meadows, there was an interesting hamlet, at first accessible only by the river and afterward by foot-paths.   It was originally an Indian

village rejoicing in the name of Sappokanican, and occupied
a very defensible position between the steep river bank and
Minetta Brook, a stream which still flows in its old
course, though no longer visible. Two rivulets, Sappokani-can, or Greenwich.
arising the one near the site of Calvary Church
and the other at Sixth Avenue and Seventeenth Street,
came together between Fifth and Sixth avenues a little
below Twelfth Street. Their junction formed Minetta
Brook, which, after curving eastward enough to touch

CANAL STREET

Clinton Place, flowed across Washington Square and down
into the North River, through a small swamp between
Charlton and West Houston streets, known as Minetta
Water. It was a clear swift brook abounding in trout, and
its left bank was high and covered with dense forest. The
space enclosed between its right bank and the North River
(through the centre of which Christopher Street now runs)
was a vast and smiling field, salubrious and fertile. Indian

hamlets not unfrequently migrate with very little ado, and as to what became of Sappokanican we are not informed, but it is on record that Director Van Twiller procured it for his own behoof in 1633 and made it a tobacco plantation. It was known in his time as the Bossen Bouwerie (*i. e.* Forest Farm), and the quality of its tobacco was highly esteemed. By 1727 there was a flourishing village there and the English had begun to call it Greenwich. It was then connected with the city by a good road, nearly identical with Greenwich Street, crossing Lispenard's Meadows and the Minetta Water on causeways.

In the time of Andros, and long after, there was nothing on the west side of the island above Greenwich that calls for special mention in our narrative. Greenwich is mentioned, by its old Indian name, in the journal of the two Labadist emissaries, Jasper Dankers and Peter Sluyter, who visited New York in the autumn of 1679. They were representatives of a small sect of Mystics or Quietists lately founded by one Jean de Labadie. While their theology was mainly that of the Reformed Dutch Church, their aim was to restore sundry customs of primitive Christians, including community of goods. The result of this visit to New York was the grant of a large tract of land on Bohemia Manor, in Maryland, on which a company of Labadists settled in 1683.[1] The worthy brethren, Dankers and Sluyter, left an interesting journal of their visit, which was discovered a few years ago ; and they made some quite artistic pencil sketches of the city withal, which are extremely precious as historical documents.[2] A few extracts from their diary will be found instructive.

The ancient custom of robbing innocent travellers for the gratification of thick-witted and sordid hucksters, which still

Dankers and Sluyter

[1] See *Old Virginia and Her Neighbours*, Illustrated Edition, ii. 128.

[2] An English translation of their Journal, edited by H. C. Murphy, forms the first volume of the *Memoirs of the Long Island Historical Society*, Brooklyn, 1867. It contains excellent engravings of the pictures.

of linen. This being finished, we sent our goods in a cart to our lodgings, paying for the two heavy chests and straw beds and other goods from the public storehouse to the Smit's Valey, 16 stivers of zeawan (*i. e.* wampum), equal to 3½ stivers in the money of Holland. This finished the day, and we retired to rest. On Tuesday we remained at home for the purpose of writing, but in the afternoon, finding that many goods had been discharged from the ship, we went to look after our little package, which also came. I declared it, and it was examined. I had to pay 24 guilders in zeawan, or 5 guilders in the coin of Holland. I brought it to the house and looked the things all over, rejoicing that we were finally rid of that miserable set and the ship, the freight only remaining to be paid, which was fixed at 4 guilders in coin.

" As soon as we had dined we sent off our letters, and this being all accomplished we started at two o'clock for Long Island. . . . The water by which it is separated

East River

from the Manhattans is improperly called the East River, for it is nothing else than an arm of the sea, beginning in the Bay on the west and ending in the sea [*i. e.* the Sound] on the east. After forming in this passage several islands, this water is as broad before the city as the Y before Amsterdam,[1] but the ebb and flood tides are stronger. . . . We three crossed, my comrade and self, with Gerrit [a fellow-passenger returning from Holland] for our guide, in a rowboat, which in good weather and tide carries a sail. When we had crossed . . . we went on up the hill along open roads

Brooklyn

slightly wooded, through the first village, called Breuckelen, which has an ugly little church standing in the middle of the road. Having passed through here, we struck off to the right in order to go to Gowanes. We went upon several plantations where Gerrit was acquainted with almost all the people, who made us very welcome, sharing

---

[1] A slight exaggeration. The Y or Ij, an arm of the Zuyder Zee, is considerably more than a mile in breadth before Amsterdam, while the East River, at Peck Slip, in the seventeenth century, was about three fifths of a mile.

prevails at the port of New York, was attended with more
or less delay and personal inconvenience, as it is to-day. If
all the curses upon "protectionism" that have been wasted
during two and a half centuries on those inhospitable docks
could some day take effect and bury the foul iniquity deeper
than Malebolge, what a gain for civilization it would be!

> " S' io avessi le rime aspre e chiocce,
>   Come si converrebbe al tristo buco!" [1]

It would indeed take rhymes rough and hoarse to do justice
to such a theme. The unvarnished tale of Messrs. Dankers
and Sluyter has a familiar sound. Arriving in the harbour
on Saturday evening, they were allowed to go ashore for
Sunday and hear some New World preaching. On Monday
morning " we went on board ship in order to obtain our
travelling bag and clothes for the purpose of having them
washed, but when we came on board we could not get ashore
again before the afternoon, when the passengers' goods were
to be delivered. All our goods which were between decks
were taken ashore and carried to the public store- The cus-
house, where they had to be examined, but some tom-house
time elapsed before it was done, in consequence of the exam-
iners being elsewhere. At length, however, one Abraham
Lennoy, a good fellow apparently, befriended us. He examined our chest only, without touching our bedding or anything else. I showed him a list of the tin which we had in
the upper part of our chest, and he examined it and also the
tin, and turned up a little more what was in the chest and
with that left off, without looking at it closely. [A little
shamefast wert thou then, worthy Lennoy, at the dirty work
for which government hired thee? or, perchance, did a Labadist guilder or two, ever so gently slipped into thy palm,
soften the asperities?] He demanded four English shillings
for the tin, remarking at the same time that he had observed
some other small articles, but would not examine them
closely, though he had not seen either the box or the pieces

---

[1] Dante, *Inferno*, xxxii. 1.

up the chimney, of clear oak and hickory, of which they made not the least scruple of burning profusely.   We let it penetrate us thoroughly.   There had been already thrown upon it, to be roasted, a pailful of Gowanes oysters, which are the best in the country.   They are quite as good as those of England, and better than those we ate at Falmouth.   I had to try some of them raw.   They are large and full, some of them not less than a foot long. . . . Everybody keeps the shells for the purpose of burning them into lime.   They pickle

SIMON AESEN (DE HART)

the oysters in small casks, and send them to Barbadoes and the other islands.   We had for supper a roasted haunch of venison, which he had bought of the Indians for 3½ guilders of zeawan [*i. e.* 15 cents] and which weighed 30 lbs.   The meat was exceedingly tender and good, and also quite fat. It had a slight spicy flavour.   We were also served with wild turkey, which was also fat and of a good flavour ; and a wild goose, but that was rather dry. . . . We saw here, lying in a heap, a whole hill of watermelons as large as pumpkins, which Symon was going to take to the city to sell. . . . It was very late at night when we went to rest in a Kermis bed, as it is called,[1] in the corner of the hearth, alongside of a good fire."

Next morning, after their host and hostess had gone with their marketing to the city, our three friends made their way on foot to Najack (Fort Hamilton), where they came upon a great field of ripe maize, which their diary calls " Turkish wheat."   The epithet is interesting as a survival from the time when America was supposed to be Asia.   Just as the American bird which in French is called " Indian fowl " is called in English a "turkey," so this "Turkish wheat " is only another name for " Indian corn."

Fort Hamilton

---

[1] Kermis was a great fair or festival, in the Low Countries, with much dancing and frolic.   A Kermis bed would be an extra bed for such occasions when the house was full of company.

with us bountifully whatever they had, whether milk, cider,
fruit, or tobacco, and especially and most of all, miserable rum
or brandy brought from Barbadoes and the other islands, and
called by the Dutch *kill-devil*.   All these people are very
fond of it, most of them extravagantly so, although it is very
dear and has a bad taste.   It is impossible to tell how many
peach trees we passed, all laden with fruit to breaking down,
and many of them actually broken down.   We came to a
place surrounded with such trees from which so many had
fallen off that the ground could not be discerned, and you
could not put your foot down without trampling them, and
notwithstanding such large quantities had fallen off, the
trees were still as full as they could bear.   The hogs and
other animals mostly feed on them.   This place belongs to
the oldest European woman in the country.   We went into
her house where she lives with her children.   She was sitting
by the fire, smoking tobacco incessantly, one pipe after
another.   We inquired after her age, which the children told
us was about a hundred years. . . .   She had been about fifty
years now in the country, and had above seventy children and
grandchildren.   We tasted here for the first time smoked
twælft [*i. e.* twelfth, meaning striped bass], a fish so called
because it is caught in season next after the elft [*i. e.* eleventh, meaning shad].   It was salted a little and then smoked,
and although now a year old, it was still perfectly good and
in flavour not inferior to smoked salmon.   We drank here
also the first new cider, which was very fine.

   "We proceeded on to Gowanes, . . . where we arrived
in the evening at one of the best friends of Gerrit, named
Symon.[1]   He was very glad to see us, and so was   Gowanus
his wife.   He took us into the house and entertained us exceedingly well.   We found a good fire, half way

   [1] This was Simon de Hart.   Our Labadists follow the ancient usage
in which the forename was of more importance than the surname.   The
house where they were so well regaled " is still standing, having been in
the possession of the descendants of Simon de Hart ever since."   Mrs.
Lamb's *History of the City of New York*, i. 287.

The adjective occurs with the same meaning in the next sentence : "We soon heard a noise of pounding, like threshing, and went to the place whence it proceeded, and found there an old Indian woman busily employed beating Turkish beans out of the pods by means of a stick, which she did with astonishing force and dexterity.   Gerrit inquired of her, in the Indian language which he spoke perfectly well, how old she was, and she answered eighty years ; at which we were still more astonished that so old a woman should still have so much strength and courage to work as she did.   We

SIMON DE HART'S HOUSE

went thence to her habitation, where we found the whole troop together, consisting of seven or eight families, and twenty or twenty-two persons.   Their house was low and long, about sixty feet long and fourteen or fifteen wide.   The bottom was earth, the sides and roof were made of reed and the bark of chestnut trees ; the posts or columns were limbs of trees stuck in the ground

An Algonquin household

and all fastened together. The ridge of the roof was open about half a foot wide from end to end, in order to let the smoke escape, in place of a chimney. On the sides of the house the roof was so low that you could hardly stand under it. The entrances, which were at both ends, were so small that they had to stoop down and squeeze themselves to get through them. The doors were made of reed or flat bark. In the whole building there was no iron, stone, lime, or lead.

"They build their fire in the middle of the floor, according to the number of families, so that from one end to the other each boils its own pot and eats when it likes, not only the families by themselves, but each Indian alone when he is hungry, at all hours, morning, noon, and night. By each fire are the cooking utensils, consisting of a pot, a bowl or calabash, and a spoon also made of a calabash. These are all that relate to cooking. They lie upon mats, with their feet towards the fire on each side of it. They do not sit much upon anything raised up, but, for the most part, sit upon the ground, or squat on their ankles. Their other household articles consist of a calabash of water, out of which they drink, a small basket in which to carry their maize and beans, and a knife. The implements are, for tillage, merely a small sharp stone ; for hunting, a gun and pouch for powder and lead ; for fishing, a canoe without mast or sail, and not a nail in any part of it, though it is sometimes full forty feet in length, fish-hooks and lines, and scoop to paddle with in place of oars. . . .

"All who live in one house are generally of one stock, as father and mother, with their offspring. Their bread is maize pounded in a block by a stone, but not fine ; this is mixed with water and made into a cake, which they bake under the hot ashes. They gave us a small piece when we entered, and although the grains were not ripe, and it was half-baked and coarse grains, we nevertheless had to eat it, or at least not throw it away before them, which they would have regarded as a great sin, or a great affront. We chewed a little of it and managed to hide it.   We had also to drink out of their calabashes the water, which was very good.

"Here we saw the Indians who had come on board the ship when we arrived.   They were all joyful at the visit of our Gerrit, who had long dwelt thereabouts and was an old acquaintance of theirs.   We gave them two jews-harps, whereat they were much pleased and at once began to play them, and fairly well.   Some of their chiefs — who are their priests and medicine-men and could speak good Dutch — were busy making shoes of deer-leather, which they make soft by long working it between the hands.   They had dogs, besides fowls and hogs, which they are gradually learning from Europeans how to manage.   Toward the last we asked them for some peaches, and their reply was 'Go and pick some,' which shows their politeness!   However, not wishing to offend them, we went out and pulled some.   Although they are such a poor miserable people, they are licentious and proud, and much given to knavery and scoffing.   As we noticed an extremely old woman (not less than a hundred, one would think), some saucy young fellows jeeringly answered, 'Twenty years.'   We observed the manner in which they travel with their children, a woman having one which she carried on her back.   The little thing clung tight around her neck like a cat, and was held secure by a piece of duffels, their usual garment."

A most admirable and lifelike description of an aboriginal dwelling!   Our Labadist friends were keen observers, and deft with pen as well as pencil.   We cannot recount all their experiences, but may follow them on their trip to the extreme north of Manhattan.   After leaving the Bowery Tavern they proceeded "through the woods to New Harlem, a rather large village directly opposite the place where the northeast creek [Harlem River] and the East River come together, situated about three hours' journey from New Amsterdam, like as the old Harlem in Europe is situated about three hours' distance from the old Amsterdam.   As our guide, Gerrit, had some business here,

A night at Harlem

and found many acquaintances, we remained over night at
the house of a man named Geresolveert,[1] the schout of the
village, who had formerly lived in Brazil, and whose heart
was still full of it.   His house was all the time filled with
people, mostly drinking that execrable rum.   He had also
James   the best cider we have tasted.   Among the crowd
Carteret   we found a person of quality, an Englishman,
namely, Captain Carteret,[2] whose father is in great favour
with the king, and he himself had assisted in sundry exploits
in the king's service.   He commanded the English forces
which went in 1660 to retake St. Kitts. . . .   The king has
given to his father, Sir George Carteret, the entire government of the lands west of the North River, in New Netherland, with power to appoint as governor whom he pleases ;
and at this present time there is a governor over it by his
appointment, another Carteret, his nephew, I believe,[3] who
resides at Elizabethtown, in New Jersey. . . . This son is
a very profligate person.   He married a merchant's daughter here, and has so treated his wife that her father has
been compelled to take her home again.   He runs about
among the farmers, and stays where he can find most to
drink, and sleeps in barns on the straw.   If he would conduct himself properly he might hold the highest positions,
for he has studied the moralities, and seems to have been
of a good understanding ; but that is all now drowned.
His father, who will no longer acknowledge him as his son,[4]
allows him yearly as much only as is necessary to live."

[1] O delicious ! a Dutch translation of Resolved, a Puritan forename
by no means uncommon in those days.   The person meant was Resolved
Waldron, constable of Harlem.

[2] See above, p. 18.   James Carteret was a legitimate younger son of
Sir George, not an illegitimate son, as has sometimes been said.   See
Burke's *Dormant and Extinct Peerages*, p. 108.

[3] W. L. Stone (*Hist. New York City*, p. 63) makes him a brother of
Sir George ; Broadhead (*Hist. New York*, ii. 84) makes him a cousin ;
and Burke does not elucidate the matter.   The names Philip and
George had for at least four centuries been so thickly iterated among
the Carterets that their use as distinctive appellations was lost.

[4] Hence probably the rumour of illegitimacy.

The morning after this hilarious night at the schout's, our friends set out from Harlem village to go up to the end of the island, and perhaps it may have been the thirst which sometimes ensues upon such nights that made them exclaim over the deliciousness of the juicy morning peaches. "When we were not far from the point of Spyten Duyvil we could see on our left hand the rocky cliffs of the main- Spyten land on the other side of the North River, these Duyvil cliffs standing straight up and down, with the grain, just as if they were antimony.   We crossed over the Spyten Duyvil in a canoe, and paid nine stivers fare [or about eighteen cents] for us three, which was very dear.   We followed the opposite side of the land, till we came to the house of one Valentyn, a great acquaintance of our Gerrit's. He had gone to the city, but his wife, though she did not know Gerrit or us, was so much rejoiced to see Hollanders that she hardly knew what to do for us.   She set before us what she had.   We left after breakfasting. Her son showed us the way, and we came to a road entirely covered with peaches. We asked the boy why they left them to lie there, and why the hogs did not eat them. He answered, we do not know what to do with them, there are so many ; the hogs are satiated with them and will not eat any more. . . . We pursued our way now a small distance through the woods and over the hills, and then back again along the shore to a point where lived an Englishman named Webblingh, who was standing ready to cross over.   He carried us over with him, and refused to take any pay for our passage, offering us at the same time some of his rum, a liquor which is everywhere.

"We were now again at New Harlem, and dined with Geresolveert, at whose house we had slept the night before, and who made us welcome.   It was now two o'clock ; and leaving there we crossed the island, which takes about three quarters of an hour to do, and came to the North River, which we followed a little within the woods, as far as Sappokanican, where Gerrit had a sister and some friends.

There we rested ourselves and drank some good beer, which
was very refreshing.   We then kept on our way
along the shore to the city, where we arrived in
the evening very tired, having walked this day
about forty miles.   I must add, in passing through this
island we sometimes encountered such a sweet smell in the
air that we stood still, because we did not know what it was
we were meeting."

The good
beer of
Greenwich

In the course of their adventures our worthy friends inform
us that they talked with "the first male born of Europeans
in New Netherland," a brewer named Jean Vigné.   His
parents were from Valenciennes, and he was now about
sixty-five years of age."   Their pictures of the
clergy are not flattering.   They heard a venerable
minister "from the up-river country at Fort Orange," who
was called Dominie Schaats, whose demeanour was so rough
and outlandish that they suspected him of indulgence in the
ubiquitous rum.   They tell us that Dominie Nieuwenhuysen
was " a thick, corpulent person, with a red and bloated face,
and of very slabbering speech."   On one Sunday they went
at noon " to hear the English minister, whose service took
place after the Dutch church was out.   There were not above
twenty-five or thirty people in the church.   The first thing
that occurred was the reading of their prayers and ceremonies out of the prayer-book, as is done in all Episcopal
churches.   A young man then went into the pulpit and
preached, who thought he was performing wonders ; but he
had a little book in his hand out of which he read his ser-
mon, which was from a quarter to half an hour long.   With
this the services were concluded, whereat we could not be
sufficiently astonished.

Three
dominies

This young parson was Mr. Charles Wolley, who came in
1678 with Andros.   We may now let him speak for himself,
and first as to the climate : " It is of a sweet and wholesome
breath, free from those annoyances which are commonly
ascribed by naturalists for the insalubriety of any Country,
viz. . . . stagnant Waters, lowness of Shoars, inconstancy

of Weather [!], and the excessive heat of the Summer [! !] ;
it is gently refreshed, fanned, and allayed by con- Mr. Wolley
stant breezes from the Sea. . . . Nature kindly on the
New York
drains and purgeth [the land] by Fontanels and climate
Issues of running waters in its irriguous Valleys, and shelters
it with the umbrellas of all sorts of Trees . . . ; which Trees
and Plants do undoubtedly, tho' insensibly, suck in and
digest into their own growth and composition those subter-
raneous Particles and Exhalations, which otherwise wou'd be
attracted by the heat of the Sun, and so become matter for
infectious Clouds and malign Atmospheres. . . . I myself,
a person of a weakly Stamen and a valetudinary Constitution,
was not in the least indisposed in that Climate during my
residence there, the space of three years."

Allowing for a somewhat too roseate tint in the references
to the freedom from fickle weather and torrid heat, this is
an excellent description of the breezy and salubrious air of
Manhattan. As for the people, they impressed Mr. Wolley
as extremely " high-flown religionists," but he had never
visited Boston or New Haven. Even in this comparatively
tolerant New Netherland, the ministers of different churches
sometimes would not take tea together, and our young
Cambridge friend did not relish such narrowness.

"There were two Ministers, or Dominies as they were
called there, the one a Lutheran or High-Dutch,[1] the other
a Calvinist or Low Dutchman,[2] who behaved themselves
one towards another so shily and uncharitably as if Luther
and Calvin had bequeathed and entailed their virulent and
bigoted Spirits upon them and their heirs forever. They
had not visited or spoken to each other with any respect
for six years together before my being there, with A Latin
whom I being much acquainted, I invited them supper
both with their Vrows to a Supper one night unknown to
each other, with an obligation that they should not speak
one word of Dutch, under the penalty of a bottle of Madeira,

[1] Dominie Bernhardus Frazius.
[2] Dominie Nieuwenhuysen.

alledging I was so imperfect in that Language that we could not manage a sociable discourse.   So accordingly they came, and at the first interview they stood so appalled as if the Ghosts of Luther and Calvin had suffered a transmigration, but the amaze soon went off with a *salve tu quoque* and a Bottle of Wine, of which the Calvinist Dominie was a true Carouzer, and so we continued our *Mensalia* the whole evening in Latine, which they both spoke so fluently and promptly that I blushed at myself with a passionate regret that I could not keep pace with them. . . . As to the Dutch language, in which I was but a smatterer, I think it lofty, majestic, and emphatical." [1]

The intemperate zeal of red-faced Dominie Nieuwenhuysen sometimes hurried him into a pace which he could not keep up. Dominie Nicholas van Rensselaer, having been ordained in England by a bishop, had come to be minister at Albany as colleague to the aged Dr. Schaats, whose oratory seemed to our Labadist visitors so uncouth.   Nieuwenhuysen denied that ordination by an English bishop could confer the right to administer sacraments in the Dutch Reformed Church, and he therefore insisted that Van Rensselaer should be forbidden to baptize children ; but when the point was argued before Andros and his council, the zealous Calvinist was obliged to recede from his position.   An attempt was soon afterward made to convict Van Rensselaer of doctrinal heresy.   Charges of "false preaching" were brought against him by Jacob Leisler, a wealthy German, one of Nieuwenhuysen's deacons, and a young English protégé of his, named Jacob Milborne.   The result of the trial was the acquittal of Van Rensselaer, while Leisler and Milborne were obliged to pay the costs.   We shall by and by meet the deacon and his friend under very different circumstances.   Already this incident shows the existence of two mutually repugnant trends of feeling in the Dutch church at New York ; the one aristocratic, liberal, mellow, and inclined to fraternize with Episcopacy ; the

Dominie Van Rensselaer

[1] Wolley's *Journal*, pp. 55, 56.

A

Brief Defcription

OF

NEW-YORK

Formerly Called

New-Netherlands.

With the Places thereunto Adjoyning.

Together with the
Manner of its Scituation, Fertility of the Soyle,
Healthfulnefs of the Climate, and the
Commodities thence produced.

ALSO

Some Directions and Advice to fuch as fhall go
thither: An Account of what Commodities they fhall
take with them; The Profit and Pleafure that
may accrew to them thereby.

LIKEWISE

A Brief RELATION of the Cuftoms of the
Indians there.

By *DANIEL DENTON.*

LONDON,
Printed for *John Hancock*, at the firft Shop in *Popes-Head-Alley* in
Cornhil at the three Bibles, and *William Bradley* at the three Bibles
in the Minories, 1670.

TITLE OF DENTON'S "NEW YORK"

other democratic, fanatical, bitter, and Puritanical. Such antagonisms were to bear fruit in deadly feuds.

According to Andros's own report, the province of New York consisted of twenty-four towns, villages, or parishes, divided into six precincts for courts of quarter sessions. The total value of the estates was about £150,000, equivalent to at least $3,000,000 of the present day. A merchant worth £1000 ($20,000) was deemed rich, and a planter with half that amount in chattels was accounted very well off. The population of the city since 1664 had increased from about 1600 to about 3500. Three ships, eight sloops, and seven boats were owned in the city, and of these craft four had been built there. The revenue of the province was £2000, not enough "by a greate deale," which was a source of worry to the Duke of York. The lack of servants was also quite generally felt; there were a few black slaves, chiefly from Barbadoes, worth about £30 a head. The principal exports were furs, lumber, tar, and bolted flour; which paid for £50,000 of manufactured goods imported from England. There were no beggars in the province, but of all poor and disabled persons due care was taken. There were twenty churches — Reformed Dutch, Lutheran, Independent, Presbyterian, Baptist, Quaker, and Jew — all self-supporting; but there was a scarcity of ministers, which was an inconvenience in respect of funerals, weddings, and christenings.[1]

Estates and revenues

The scarcity of clergymen led the way to an interesting development. We have already seen that the Reformed Dutch Church in New York accepted ordination at the hands of an English bishop as sufficient qualification for the ministry; but this was not enough. The methods of the Dutch Church must be expanded to fit the occasion. In 1678 Laurentius van Gaasbeeck was sent out to be minister at Esopus, under the authority of the Classis, or supreme ecclesiastical body, of Amsterdam. Before his arrival the spiritual interests of Esopus

Formation of an independent Classis

[1] *New York Colonial Documents*, iii. 245, 260–262.

were cared for temporarily by Petrus Tesschenmaeker, a young graduate of Utrecht, who had lately come over. Tesschenmaeker was a bachelor of divinity, but had not been ordained. Upon the arrival of the new dominie at Esopus, this young man received a call to the church at Newcastle on the Delaware, which furthermore requested that he might be ordained without the cumbrous formality of crossing the ocean to Holland. Hereupon Andros directed Nieuwenhuysen with any three or more clergymen to form themselves into a Classis, and after duly examining Tesschenmaeker to ordain him if they saw fit. This was done, the action of the New York dominies was approved by the Classis of Amsterdam, and thus in a most pleasant and sensible fashion was the Dutch Church in America made practically independent of the fatherland.[1]

The insufficiency of revenue was to a great extent reme- The flour died by the ordinances concerning the bolting of monopoly flour. First it was ordered that all flour for exportation should be bolted and duly inspected and the barrels properly marked before they could be shipped. Then it was further ordered that all inspection of flour must take place in the city of New York. These arrangements conferred upon the city for some years a lucrative monopoly.

One order, to which the duke attached great importance, required that all vessels with cargoes bound for any port within the original territory of New Netherland should enter at the New York custom-house. The duke insisted that Sir Edmund should rigorously enforce this order, and the immediate result was trouble with New Jersey.

It will be remembered that in 1664 the Duke of York had granted New Jersey jointly to Sir George Carteret and Lord Berkeley as lords proprietary, and under this grant had exercised powers of sovereignty in the eastern and northern parts of that fine province. Practically there had come about an ill-defined separation between Carteret's actual do-

<hr/>

[1] Dankers and Sluyter's *Journal*, iii. 222 ; *Book of General Entries*, xxxii. 61 ; Demarest, *History of the Reformed Dutch Church*, p. 183.

main and the southwestern region, which Berkeley soon sold

Affairs in
New Jersey to a couple of Quakers.   The Dutch conquest of 1673 was held to have extinguished all these rights, and apparently vested them in the States General, which by the treaty of Westminster next year handed them over to Charles II., who forthwith by a bran-new patent granted New Netherland over again to his brother James.   Then James granted East Jersey to Carteret in severalty, but without conferring upon him any power of sovereignty. The Quaker purchasers of West Jersey were ignored, but a boundary line between the two Jerseys was summarily indicated.   Now the affairs of West Jersey need not concern us at present ; we shall by and by come to them in connection with the career of William Penn.   But with regard to East Jersey an interesting question is suggested.   Did the new grant to Sir George Carteret make him a lord proprietor, responsible only to the crown ?   or was he simply a lord of the manor, answerable to his immediate overlord, the Duke of York ?   In other words, was East Jersey a part of the province of New York, or was it quite distinct and independent, as Maryland was independent of Virginia, and Connecticut of Massachusetts ?   The style of the grant, which conferred upon Sir George no power of sovereignty, would plainly imply the former alternative.   But Governor Philip Carteret, from the moment of his return in 1674, acted upon the latter.   He called an assembly, which enacted laws as formerly, and he declared Elizabethtown to be a free port.

The duke's order, that all ships bound to any port within the original New Netherland must enter and clear at New York, brought this question to a trial.   In the spring of Andros
asserts
sovereignty
over East
Jersey 1680, acting upon express instructions from the duke, Sir Edmund Andros began seizing ships which went on their way to Elizabethtown without entering and paying custom-house fees at New York.   He accompanied this action with a polite note to Governor Carteret, announcing his design to build a fortress at Sandy Hook.   But in thus taking New Jersey soil for a

A

FURTHER ACCOUNT

O F

New JERSEY,

In an Abstract of

L E T T E R S

Lately Writ from thence,

By several Inhabitants there Resident.

Printed in the Year 1676.

TITLE OF "A FURTHER ACCOUNT"

public purpose, he would gladly satisfy all claims of individual proprietors who might be dispossessed or damaged. Thus did Sir Edmund blandly assert the right of eminent domain over the territory that had been granted to Carteret. The reply of Philip Carteret denied Sir Edmund's right either to make Jersey-bound ships pay fees and duties at the port of New York, or to put up any public building on Jersey soil. This attitude of the governor of East Jersey was warmly supported by the assembly, which voted to indemnify the owners of any ship that might be seized by the governor of New York.

Carteret resists

In reading what follows it should be borne in mind that Andros and Carteret had for many years been warm friends ; their wives also were devotedly attached to each other ; and often did their boats ply to and fro past Bergen Point for suppers and other social merriment at each other's houses. Now when Carteret declared that any attempt of New York to build a fort at Sandy Hook would be resisted, Sir Edmund answered this defiance of his old friend by sending his secretary to Elizabethtown, to read aloud before the people a proclamation forbidding "Captain Philip Carteret, with all other pretended magistrates civil or military authorized by him," from exercising any kind of jurisdiction over his Majesty's subjects anywhere within the bounds of the king's patent to the Duke of York.   Not content with thus implicitly deposing Carteret from his governorship, the proclamation called upon the people to surrender him as a prisoner to Andros.[1] This fulmination met with no cordial reception.   Carteret sent an appeal to the king and began gathering troops.

Andros deposes Carteret

It was not an army, however, but only his ordinary retinue,

---

[1] Leaming and Spicer, *Grants, Concessions, and Original Constitutions of New Jersey*, London, 1758, pp. 112–137, 674–677 ; Whitehead's *East Jersey under the Proprietary Governments*, p. 71 ; *Newark Town Records*, p. 78 ; Dankers and Sluyter, *Journal*, pp. 277–347.

that Sir Edmund took with him a week later, when he crossed the Achter Koll.   He was politely received, and took dinner at Carteret's house, and over their nuts and Madeira the twain argued the question of jurisdiction and quoted parchments and letters at each other, but all to no purpose.   So Andros went back to his sloop, escorted by his affectionate friend, with compliments to Lady Andros and the usual military salute.   But after three weeks had passed without Carteret's giving any sign of sub- *Arrest of* mission, on the last day of April, Andros sent a *Carteret* party of soldiers to arrest him.   The order was carried out with shocking brutality.   These ruffians broke open Carteret's doors at midnight, dragged him from his bed, and carried him in his night-dress to New York, where some clothes were given him, and he was flung into jail to await his trial on a charge of riotously presuming to exercise unlawful jurisdiction over his Majesty's subjects.

Of this shameful affair Carteret wrote to a friend in England, " I was so disabled by the bruises and the hurts I then received, that I fear I shall never be the same man again." [1] He was an athletic and high-spirited gentleman, and evidently was not taken without a desperate struggle.   A few black eyes and a broken jaw or so, fairly dis- *His trial* tributed among his captors, would have been no *and acquittal* more than their desert.   After four weeks of jail, a special court of assizes was assembled, and Sir Edmund took his seat as presiding justice amid the rattle of drums and fanfare of trumpets.   Arraigned before this tribunal, Carteret first demurred to its jurisdiction, but was overruled.   Then he argued that his conduct as governor of East Jersey had been entirely legal "and by virtue of power derived from the king."   His arguments and proofs convinced the jury, and they acquitted him.   Andros could not conceal his chagrin ; he tried to browbeat the jurors, and sent them out twice to reconsider their verdict, but they were immovable, and Carteret scored a triumph.   Even now,

[1] *New Jersey Colonial Documents*, 1st series, i. 316, 317.

however, Andros would not allow him to return to New
Jersey until he had extorted from him a promise that he
would not "assume any authority or jurisdiction there, civil
or military." [1]

At length, early in June, the deposed governor was
escorted back to Elizabethtown, with much politeness and
ceremony, by his loving friends, Sir Edmund and Lady
Andros.   One would like to know how the dinner passed off
Carteret's
return to
Elizabeth-
town at Mrs. Carteret's, and what Sir Edmund had to
say about the conduct of his ruffians.   Attempts
have been made to excuse him for his part in the
transaction, on the ground that he was only carrying out
the duke's orders.   Nevertheless, while it would be hardly
just to charge upon Andros all the brutality of his myr-
midons, the whole affair helps us to understand the intense
hatred which he inspired in people at a later period.   In his
eagerness to serve his master, we see him carrying out
orders with needless violence and even behaving most rep-
rehensibly, as in his attempt to overawe the jurymen.   Our
old comparison recurs to us as we feel that such was not
the way in which Nicolls would have given effect to the
duke's orders.

The people of East Jersey submitted to the appointment
of sundry officers by Andros, but their assembly refused to
adopt the Duke's Laws.   News of all these proceedings was
sent by the deposed governor to Lady Carteret, widow of
of Sir George, who had lately died.   These were people of
great influence at court, and accordingly the duke deemed
it best not to take to himself too much responsibility for the
acts of his agent.   He told Lady Carteret that he
The duke
relin-
quishes
East Jer-
sey to the
Carterets "doth wholly disown and declare that Sir Edmund
Andros had never any such order or authority from
him for the doing thereof," — a characteristic specimen of Stuart veracity.   Presently James executed
a paper relinquishing his claim upon East Jersey, and con-

<hr />

[1] Leaming and Spicer, *Grant's Concessions, etc.*, pp. 678–684; Dankers
and Sluyter, *Journal*, pp. 347–351; Whitehead's *East Jersey*, pp. 73, 74.

firming it in the proprietorship of young Sir George Carteret, grandson and heir of the original grantee; and so the quarrel ended in the discomfiture of Andros.

Questions of ownership and jurisdiction had been coming up in West Jersey likewise, which ended in this same year 1680 in the duke's relinquishing all his claims in favour of Friend Byllinge and other Quakers. But I must reserve this story for a while until it can fall into its proper place in the line of causation which led to the founding of Pennsylvania. We must bid adieu for a season to the pleasant country between the North and South rivers of New Netherland. We have to view the career of a man of extraordinary and varied powers, uniting after a fashion all his own the wisdom of the serpent with the purity of the dove,[1] who was able at once to be a leader of one of the most iconoclastic and unpopular of Christian sects, and to retain the admiring friendship of one of the most bigoted kings that ever sat upon a throne. We must make the acquaintance of William Penn, who, take him for all in all, was by far the greatest among the founders of American commonwealths.

and West Jersey to Byllinge and his friends

[1] I leave this sentence as I first wrote it in 1882. I was not then aware that Benjamin Franklin had alluded to Penn as uniting " the subtlety of the serpent with the innocence of the dove." (See his *Works*, ed. Sparks, iii. 123.) Franklin's phrase, however, is intended for a sneer, as his context shows, while mine is meant to convey accurate but unstinted praise.

CHAPTER XII

At the time of our Declaration of Independence the only
states in which all Christian sects stood socially and politically on an equal footing were Pennsylvania and Delaware,
the two states which had originally constituted the
palatinate or proprietary domain of William Penn.
Rhode Island, indeed, had been founded upon
equally liberal principles, but during the strong
wave of anti-Catholic feeling that passed over the country
in the time of James II., a clause depriving Papists of the
franchise found its way into the statute book and it was not
repealed until 1783. If Roger Williams had lived a few
years longer, it is not likely that this one stain upon the
noble record of Rhode Island would have been permitted.
As for Pennsylvania, if there was anything which she stood
for in the eyes of the world, it was liberty of conscience.
Her fame had gone abroad over the continent of Europe.
In Voltaire's writings Pennsylvania more than once receives
admiring mention as the one favoured country in the world
where men can be devoutly religious and still refrain from
tearing one another to pieces.

There was something more than satire in the suggested
antithesis; as with most of Voltaire's keen-edged remarks,
there was deep and earnest meaning behind it. Until quite
modern times toleration was found only in union with indif-
ference. In religious matters the Gallio, who "cared for none
of those things," might refuse to play the part of a persecutor, but the most devout and disinterested zeal for religion
was apt to be combined with more or less fanatical intoler-

ance.   Various causes from time to time contributed to this,
but the deepest and most abiding cause was the
imperfect separation between religion and politics.   Identity of
                                                        civil and
If we carry our thoughts back to primeval ages, we   religious
                                                        life in
see that there was no such separation ; religious life   primitive
                                                        ages.
and civil life were identical.   The earliest glimpses
we can get of the human race show us nowhere anything like
a nation, but everywhere small tribes perpetually encroaching upon one another and perpetually fighting to escape
annihilation.   The state of things among the American
Indians of the seventeenth century may serve to illustrate
what had been going on over a large part of the earth's surface for at least 300,000 or 400,000 years.   From the Aus-
tralian stage of human existence up to the Iroquois stage
there was in many respects an enormous advance toward
civilization, but the omnipresence of exterminating warfare
continued, and enables us to understand that fea-   Need for
ture of primeval times.   In such a stage of society   conformity
almost every act of tribal life is invested with religious significance, and absolute conformity to tribal rules and observ-
ances is enforced with pitiless rigour.   The slightest neglect
of an omen, for example, might offend some tutelar deity
and thus bring on defeat ; it is therefore unhesitatingly punished with death.   It is an important part of the duties
of medicine-men to take cognizance of the slightest offences
and lapses.   In early society the enforced conformity relates
chiefly to matters of ritual and ceremony ; questions of
dogma arise at a later stage, after a considerable development in human thinking.   But to whatever matter the
enforcement of conformity relates, there can be no doubt as
to the absolute necessity of it in early society.   No liberty
of divergence can be allowed to the individual without
endangering the community.

As a kind of help toward the illustration of this point, let
me cite a familiar instance of persecution in modern times
and in a highly civilized community, where some of the conditions of primitive society had been temporarily reproduced.

In 1636 there were about 5000 Englishmen in New England, distributed in more than twenty villages, mostly on the shores of Massachusetts Bay, but some as remote as the Connecticut River. Such a concerted Indian assault upon them as was actually made forty years later, in King Philip's war, might have overwhelmed them. Such an assault was contemplated by the Pequots and dreaded throughout the settlements, and the train-bands were making ready for war, when a certain number of Boston men refused to serve. There were a few persons of influence in Boston, called Antinomians, of whom the one best remembered is Anne Hutchinson. According to them it made a great difference to one's salvation whether one were under a "covenant of grace" or only under a "covenant of works." The men who in a moment of peril to the commonwealth refused to march against the enemy alleged as a sufficient reason that they suspected their chaplain of being under a "covenant of works," and therefore would not serve with him. Under such circumstances Mrs. Hutchinson and

The Antinomians and the Pequot war

FACSIMILE OF ORDER EXPELLING MRS. HUTCHINSON FROM BOSTON

the other Antinomians were banished from Boston. A disagreement upon a transcendental question of theology was breeding sedition and endangering the very existence of the state. Those who defend the government of Massachusetts for banishing Mrs. Hutchinson rest their defence upon such grounds. Without feeling called upon to decide that question, we can see that the case is historically instructive in a high degree.

Now when we come to early society, the military urgency is incessant and imperative, and all other things must yield to it. It is sustained by the feeling of corporate responsibility which is universal among tribal communities. The tribe is regarded as responsible for the acts of each one of its individuals. Religious sanctions and penalties are visited upon everything. What we call conventionalities are in the tribal stage of society regarded as sacraments, and thus the slightest infringement is liable to call down upon the whole tribe the wrath of some offended tutelar deity, in the shape of defeat or famine or pestilence. In such a stern discipline there is no room for divergence or dissent. And such was undoubtedly the kind of training under which all our ancestors were reared, from far-off ages of which only a geologic record remains down to the mere yesterday that witnessed the building of the Pyramids. Under such rigid training were formed, through wave after wave of conquest, the great nations of prechristian times.

It is not strange that it has taken the foremost races of men three or four thousand years to free themselves from the tyranny of mental habits which had been engrained into them for three or four hundred thousand. A careful study of the history of religious persecution shows us that sometimes politics and sometimes religion have been most actively concerned in it. The persecution of Christians by the Roman emperors was chiefly political, because Christianity asserted a dominion over men paramount to that of the emperor. The persecution of the Albigenses by Pope Innocent III. was largely political, because that heresy threatened the very continuance of the Papacy as part of the complex government of mediæval Europe. Innocent, like the heathen emperors, was fighting in self-defence. So, too, a considerable part of the mutual persecutions of Catholics and Protestants in the sixteenth and seventeenth centuries was simply downright warfare in which A kills B to prevent B from killing A. But if we consider the nature of the religious motives that have entered into persecution, whether they have been dominating motives or have simply been enlisted in furtherance of political ends, we find that they have always been rooted in the ancient notion of corporate responsibility. Let us get rid of the unclean thing lest we be cursed for its sake; such has been the feeling which has more than anything else sustained persecution. The Spanish prelates, for example, who urged the banishment of the Moriscos, loudly asseverated that the failure to suppress the Dutch Netherlands was a mark of God's displeasure that such people were allowed to stay in Spain. Was God likely to aid the Spaniards in exterminating infidels abroad while they were so sinful as to harbour infidels in their own country? So when Queen Mary Tudor was led by domestic disappointments to fancy herself undergoing divine punishment, she quickly reached the conclusion that she had not been sufficiently zealous in purging the kingdom of heresy, and this particular act of logic kindled the flames for more than fifty Protestants. In the sixteenth century this way of looking at things (which I now take pains to explain to my readers) would not have needed a word of explanation for anybody; it was simply a piece of plain common sense, self-evident to all!

Now inasmuch as this notion of corporate responsibility Reasons for the prolonged vitality of the persecuting spirit is a survival from the very infancy of the human race, since the rigorous restriction of individuality persisted through countless generations of men to whom it proved indispensably useful, it is not strange that, since it has come to be recognized as harmful and stigmatized as persecution, it has been found so hard to kill. The conditions of tribal society long ago ceased to exist in Europe. Instead of tribes, the foremost races of men are organized in a complicated fashion as nations ; instead of tutelar deities they have reached sundry more or less imperfect forms of monotheism ; and with the advance of knowledge the conception of natural law has destroyed a host of primitive superstitions. Religion is no longer in the old materialistic way but in a much higher and more spiritual way implicated with each act of life. Part of this great change is due to the mighty influence exerted by the mediæval Church as a spiritual power distinct from and often opposed to the temporal power. In Christianity the separation of church from state took its rise ; and while religion was made an affair of mankind, not of localities or tribes, the importance of the individual was greatly increased.

Now if we look at religious persecution from the point of view of modern society, it is easy to see that it is an unmitigated evil. The evolution of a higher civil- *Importance* ization can best be attained by allowing to indi- *of preserv-* vidual tastes, impulses, and capacities the freest *ing varia-* *tions* possible play. Procrustes-beds are out of fashion ; we no longer think it desirable that all people should act alike. From a Darwinian standpoint we recognize that an abundance of spontaneous variation is favourable to progress. A wise horticulturist sees signs of promise in many an aberrant plant and carefully nurtures it. If you wish to produce a race of self-reliant, inventive, and enterprising Yankees, you must not begin by setting up a winnowing machine for picking out and slaughtering all the men and women who are bold enough and bright enough to do their own thinking, and earnest enough to talk about it to others. Such an infernal machine was the Inquisition ; it weeded out the sturdiest plants and saved the weaker ones, thus lowering the average capacity of the people wherever it was in vigorous operation. As a rule it has been persons of a progressive type who have become objects of persecution, and when they have fled from their native land they have added strength to the country that has received them. In the history of what has been done by men who speak English, it is a fact of cardinal importance that England has never had an Inquisition, but has habitually sheltered religious refugees from other countries.

Such is the scientific aspect of the case. But it has a purely religious aspect from which we are brought to the same conclusion. The moment we cease to regard religious truth as a rigid body of formulas, imparted to mankind once for all and incapable of further interpretation or expansion; the moment we come to look upon religion as part of the soul's development under the immediate influence of the Spirit of God; the moment we concede to individual judgment some weight in determining what the individual form of religious expression shall be, — that moment we have taken the first step toward the conclusion that a dead uniformity of opinion on religious questions is undesirable. In the presence of an Eternal Reality which confessedly transcends our human powers of comprehension in many ways, we are not entitled to frown or to sneer at our neighbour's view, but if we give it due attention we may find in it more or less that is helpful and uplifting which we had overlooked. Thus, instead of mere toleration we rise to a higher plane and greet the innovator with words of cordial welcome. Such a state of things, on any general scale, can hardly yet be said to have come into existence, but in the foremost communities many minds have come within sight of it, and some have attained to it. So in past times we find here and there some choice spirit reaching it. Especially in the seventeenth century, when Protestantism was assuming sundry extreme forms, and when one of the symptoms of the age was the demonstration, by Hobbes and Locke, of the relativity of all knowledge, there were active leaders of men who attained to this great breadth of view. For example, Sir Henry Vane, whom Milton, in that sonnet which is the most glorious tribute ever paid by a man of

From a religious point of view the innovator should be welcomed

Vane's heavenly speech

letters to a statesman, calls Religion's "eldest son," — Sir
Henry Vane once exclaimed in Parliament, "Why should
the labours of any be suppressed, if sober, though never so
different? We now profess to seek God, we desire to see
light!" Roger Williams called this a "heavenly speech."
It merited Milton's encomium : —

> " To know
> Both Spiritual and Civil, what each means,
> What serves each, thou hast learn'd, which few have done."

It was greatly to the credit of Oliver Cromwell as a statesman that he usually exhibited this large-minded and generous
tolerance.   It was Cromwell, for example, who en-   Cromwell's
couraged Jews to come to England, where they   tolerance
had not been allowed since 1290.[1] So a Rhode Island
statute of 1684, the year after Roger Williams's death, and
in accordance with his principles, expressly admits Jewish
immigrants to all the rights and privileges of citizens.   These
men — Vane and Williams, Milton and Cromwell — had
reached a very modern standpoint in such matters.

Just at the zenith of Cromwell's career that notable phase
of religious development known as Quakerism appeared upon
the scene.   Quakerism was the most extreme form which
Protestantism had assumed.   In so far as Protestantism
claimed to be working a reformation in Christianity by retaining the spiritual core and dropping off the non-essential
integuments, the Quakers carried this process about as far
as it could go.   There have always been two sides to
Quakerism, the rationalistic side, whereby it has   Quietists
sometimes drawn upon itself the imputation of   and
Socinianism or Deism, and the mystic side, where-   Quakers
by it shows traces of kinship with various sects of Quietists.
John Tauler, the mighty Dominican preacher in the days
of the Black Death, seems in many respects a forerunner
of the Quakers.   Thomas à Kempis, author of the most
widely read Christian book after the Bible, belonged to the
same class of minds.   Without much organization or ma-

[1] Masson's *Milton*, v. 71.

chinery as a sect, such men were known in the thirteenth and fourteenth centuries as " Friends of God." A group of them which attained to some organization in Holland about 1360 came to be known as " Brethren of the Common Life." It was among these people that Thomas à Kempis was trained at Deventer ; their influence upon Dutch culture was very great, and I dare say the mildness and tolerance of the Netherlands in matters of religion owes much to them.

The founder of Quakerism, George Fox, was born in Leicestershire, in 1624, the son of a prosperous weaver, known to his neighbours as " righteous Christopher Fox." An origin among Leicester weavers is suggestive of Dutch influences, but in the lack of detailed evidence it is George Fox easy to make too much of such suggestions. At an early age and with scanty education, George Fox became a lay preacher. His aim was not to gather disciples about him and found a new sect, but to purify the Church from sundry errors, doctrinal and practical. The basis of his teaching was the belief that each soul is in religious matters answerable not to its fellows, but to God alone, without priestly mediation, because the Holy Spirit is immediately present in every soul, and is thus a direct source of illumination. From this central belief flowed two important practical consequences, both essentially modern ; one was complete toleration, the other was complete equality of human beings before the law, and hence the condemnation of slavery, in which Quakers have generally been foremost. Fox's extreme democracy was shown in the refusal to take off his hat, and in the avoidance of the plural pronoun of dignity. His rejection of a priesthood extended to all ordained and salaried preachers. He cared little for communion with bread and wine in comparison with communion in spirit, and set more value upon the baptism of repentance than upon the baptism of water. He regarded the inner light as a more authoritative guide than Scripture, since it was the interpreter to which the sacred text must ultimately be

referred ; but he was far from neglecting the written word. On the contrary, his deference to it was often extremely scrupulous, as when he understood the injunction, " Swear not at all," as a prohibition of judicial oaths, and the commandment, " Thou shalt not kill," as a condemnation of all warfare.   Fox was a man of rare executive power ; " I never saw the occasion," said Penn, " to which he was not equal."   He was a man of lofty soul and deep spiritual insight ; and before his commanding presence and starlike eyes the persecutor often quailed.

It was customary at that moment of religious upheaval for independent preachers and laymen to invade the pulpits and exhort the congregations after the unceremonious manner described by Sir Walter Scott in " Woodstock."   Unseemly brawls were apt to result, in the course of which the preacher was dragged before the nearest magistrate.   Fox tells us how on one of these occasions, *Origin of the epithet "Quaker"* at Derby in 1650, he was taken before Justice Bennett, " who was the first that called us Quakers, because I bade him tremble at the word of the Lord."   Fox and his early followers were often put in jail, not so much for teaching heresy as for breaking the peace.   The absence of ecclesiastical organization made them seem like vagrant ranters, and their refusals to pay tithes, or to testify under oath, or to lift their hats before a magistrate, kept them perpetually liable to punishment for contempt of court.   Cromwell was indisposed to annoy them, and his relations with Fox were friendly, yet between 1650 and 1658 several hundred Quakers were put into jail, usually for such breaches of custom and etiquette.

It was, moreover, not always possible to distinguish offhand between the followers of George Fox and those of other enthusiasts who were swarming in England.   Such a preacher was James Naylor, who had been a cav- *Crazy enthusiasts* alry officer in Cromwell's army, but turned prophet and went stark mad, calling himself "the Prince of Peace, the Fairest among Ten Thousand, and the Altogether Lovely."

This Naylor marched through the streets of Wells and Glas-
tonbury, while the people threw down their cloaks to serve
as mats for his feet, and sang " Hosanna in the highest." On
one occasion he was believed to have raised a dead woman
to life. Other prophets, not easy to deal with, were those
who thought it needful to remove all their clothing in order
to "testify in the sight of the Lord." In a very few instances disciples of Fox seem to have taken part in such
performances, but so little care was taken to discriminate
that Quakers had to bear the odium of the whole. They
were regarded as a set of ignorant and lawless fanatics, like
John of Leyden and the Anabaptists of Münster ; and until
the truth about them came to be better understood, the
general feeling toward them was one of horror and dread.

Under these circumstances it was impossible for Quakers
to avoid persecution had they wished to avoid it. But, on
the contrary, they courted it. It was their business to
reform the whole of Christendom, not to gather themselves
into some quiet corner where they might worship unmolested.
They were inspired by an aggressive missionary zeal which
was apt to lead them where their company was not
wanted, and so it happened in the case of Massachusetts. The ideal of the Quakers was flatly
antagonistic to that of the settlers of Massachusetts. The
Christianity of the former was freed from Judaism as far as
was possible ; the Christianity of the latter was heavily
encumbered with Judaism. The Quaker aimed at complete
separation between church and state ; the government of
Massachusetts was patterned after the ancient Jewish theocracy, in which church and state were identified. The
Quaker was tolerant of differences in doctrine ; the Calvinist regarded such tolerance as a deadly sin. For these
reasons the arrival of a few Quakers in Boston in 1656 was
considered an act of invasion and treated as such. Under
various penalties Quakers were forbidden to enter any of the
New England colonies except Rhode Island. There they
were welcomed, but that did not content them. The pen-

Missionary zeal of the Quakers

Milk for Babes;
AND
Meat for strong Men.
A
FEAST
OF
FAT THINGS:
WINE *well refined on the* LEES.

O come yong Men and Maidens, old Men and
Babes, drink abundantly of the Streams that run from
the Fountain, that you may feel a Well-spring of living
Water in your selves, springing up to Eternal Life; that
as he lives (even CHRIST JESUS) from whence all the
Springs do come, so you may live also, and partake of
his Glory that is ascended at the right-hand of the Father, far above Principalities and Powers.

Being the breathings of the Spirit through his Servant *JAMES*
NAYLOR, written by him in the time of the confinement of
his outward man in Prison.

The Third Edition.

London, Printed in the Year, 1668.

TITLE OF NAYLOR'S "MILK FOR BABES"

alties against them were heaviest in Massachusetts, and thither they turned their chief attention. They came not to minister unto sound Rhode Island, but unto sick Massachusetts. The Puritan theocracy was their man of sin. They made up their minds to overthrow it, and they succeeded, because the party of the unenfranchised people in Boston were largely in sympathy with them. The furious scene in the council-room, when the venerable Endicott smote upon the table and threatened to go and end his days in England, marked the downfall of the theocratic ideal. Henceforth there was to be room for heretics in Massachusetts. The lesson has since been well improved, and all that now remains is to set up, on Boston Common, the scene of their martyrdom, a fitting monument to the heroes that won the victory.

The accession of Charles II. is commonly cited as the cause of this victory of the Quakers in Boston ; but there can be no doubt that the chief cause was the disagreement between the people of Boston and their theocratic government, and the moment when it proved impossible to execute the sentence upon Wenlock Christison, the battle was virtually decided. As for Charles II., we shall see how his policy led him more and more to extend his favour to Quakers. At first their refusal to take the oath of allegiance cost them dear ; for many people, unable to understand their scruples, could not see in such contumacy anything but an evidence of disloyalty. Many were sent to Barbadoes and Jamaica, where they were sold into temporary slavery, like that of the white servants in Virginia. In 1662 they were forbidden to hold meetings, and their meeting-houses were closed by the police.

Charles II. and the oath of allegiance

It is at about this time that William Penn may be said to have made his first appearance in history. He was born in London in 1644. His father, Sir William Penn, was a distinguished admiral in the navy of the Commonwealth, but afterward became a warm friend of Charles II. His mother was a Dutch lady, Margaret Jasper, daughter of a wealthy merchant of Rotterdam,—a fact which was probably of importance in view of Penn's future social relations and connections upon the continent of Europe.   As a child Penn was educated at Chigwell, where dwelt the eccentric John Saltmarsh, whose book entitled "Sparkles of Glory" is one of the most remarkable productions of English mysticism, and in some places reads

Early years of William Penn

WILLIAM PENN

like a foreshadowing or prophecy of Penn's own ideas.   It is not unlikely that Saltmarsh's book may have suggested to Penn the memorable experience which he had at the age of eleven.   One day when alone in his chamber "he was suddenly surprised with an inward comfort ; and, as he thought, an external glory in the room, which gave rise to religious emotions, during which he had the strongest conviction of the being of a God, and that the soul of man was capable of enjoying communication with Him.   He believed also that the seal of Divinity had been put upon him at this moment, and that he had been awakened or called upon to a holy life." [1]   From that time forth he felt that he had a mission in the world.   After the Chigwell school, he studied with a private tutor on Tower Hill until he was sixteen, when he saw the formal entry of Charles II. into the city across London Bridge.   Admiral Penn was that year elected to Parliament, and William was matriculated at Christ Church, Oxford, where he remained two years.   There he acquired a high reputation as a scholar and as an athlete, enthusiastic in field sports, a good oarsman, and a lover of Greek. Among the languages which he could speak fluently were Latin, Italian, French, German, and Dutch.   At Oxford, along with sundry other students, he became converted to

His conversion to Quakerism

Quakerism, refused to wear surplices, forsook chapel worship, and got into trouble.   There is a story that he was expelled from the college, but it is not well supported, and it seems more likely that his father took him away.   He was then sent with some fashionable friends to Paris, in the hope of curing him of his Quaker notions.   He was in his nineteenth year, tall, lithe, and strongly built, a picture of manly beauty, with great lustrous eyes under wide arching brows, a profusion of dark hair falling in curls upon his shoulders, a powerful chin, a refined and sensitive mouth.   He seems to have been a skilful swordsman, for when attacked one evening on the street by a desperado who threatened his life, Penn overcame and disarmed the wretch without wounding him.   He spent a year or more in hard study at the Huguenot college in Saumur, and then travelled for a year in Italy.   After that he studied law at Lincoln's Inn, and presently visited Ire-

[1] Stoughton's *Penn*, p. 8.

land, where he was thrown into prison for attending a Quaker meeting at Cork.

Sir William Penn, who was a good churchman, was shocked and disgusted at the sort of reputation his son was earning, and we get glimpses of contention in the household.

ADMIRAL PENN

"You may *thee* and *thou* other folk as much as you like," quoth the angry father, "but don't you dare to *thee* and *thou* the king, or the Duke of York, or me."[1]   Young **Trouble at** William did dare, however, even so far as to wear **home** his hat in the royal presence, which only amused the merry monarch.   One day when William met him, the king took off his hat.   "Why dost thou remove thy hat, friend

[1] For the use of these pronouns in the seventeenth century, see below, p. 116.

Charles ? " quoth the young man.   " Because," said the king,
" wherever I am, it is customary for only one to remain covered!"   But the admiral did not take it so pleasantly ; he
threatened to turn his obstinate son out of doors without
a shilling. Lady Penn implored, and one of the family
friends, a nobleman of the court, insisted that Sir William
ought to be proud of a son of such varied accomplishments
and lofty character, in spite of a few eccentricities of demeanour.   It is sad to relate that the father's threat was
carried out ; but it was only for a time.   Admiration for
dauntless courage and high principle at length prevailed with
the old naval hero, and he called his son home again and
ever after held him in reverence.

In 1670 the admiral died, commending William with his
last breath to the especial care of the Duke of York.
William was left in possession of an ample fortune, and
devoted himself to writing and preaching in defence and
explanation of Quakerism.   His learning and eloquence, with a certain sobriety of mind that qualified his mysticism, made many converts ; nor is it
unlikely that his high social position and gallant bearing
were helpful to the cause in some quarters.   It was largely
due to Penn that current opinion gradually ceased to con-
found the disciples of Fox with the rabble of Antinomian
fanatics with which England was then familiar, and to put
them upon a plane of respectability, by the side of Presbyterians and other Dissenters.   Again and again, while
engaged in this work, Penn was thrown into prison and kept
there for months, sometimes in the Tower, like a gentleman,
but once for six months in noisome Newgate, along with
common criminals.   These penalties were mostly for breaking the Conventicle Act.   The reports of the trials are often
very interesting, by reason of the visible admiration felt by
the honest judges for the brilliant prisoner.   " I vow, Mr.
Penn," quoth Sir John Robinson from the bench one day,
" I vow, Mr. Penn, I am sorry for you.   You are an ingenious
gentleman, all the world must allow you, and do allow you,

Penn's ser-
vices to
Quakerism

that ; and you have a plentiful estate ; why should you render yourself unhappy by associating with such a simple people ? " Sometimes the prisoner's ingenuity and resourcefulness would baffle the prosecutor, and in despair of other means of catching him the magistrate would tender the oath of allegiance. But Penn's subtlety was matched by his boldness : once when the judge insulted him by a remark derogatory to his character, the reply came quickly and sharply, " I trample thy slander as dirt under my feet ! " And this boldness was equalled by his steadfastness : once the Bishop of London sent word to him in the Tower, that he must either withdraw certain statements or die a prisoner. " Thou mayest tell him," said Penn to the messenger, "that my prison shall be my grave before I will budge a jot, for I owe obedience of my conscience to no mortal man." *His courage*

During these years Penn kept publishing books and pamphlets, controversial or expository, wherein he argues and persuades with logic and with eloquence, and is not always meek ; sometimes the keen blade leaps from the scabbard and deals a mortal thrust. Mrs. Samuel Pepys read one of these treatises aloud to her husband, who calls it extremely well written and " a serious sort of book, not fit for every one to read." The titles of these books give an inkling of their savour : " Truth Exalted," " The Guide Mistaken," " A Seasonable Caveat against Popery," etc. The one which Mr. Pepys would not recommend to all readers was entitled " The Sandy Foundation Shaken," which was clearly open to the charge of Socinianism. Grave accusations of heresies were brought against Penn, to which he made reply in his " Innocency with her Open Face," some quotations from which will give us an impression of his style : — *Some of his writings*

" It may not be unreasonable to observe, that however industrious some (and those dissenters too) have been to represent me as a person disturbing the civil peace, I have not violated any truly fundamental law which relates to external propriety and good behaviour, and not to religious appre-hensions ; it being the constant principle of myself and friends to maintain good works and keep our consciences void of offence, paying active or passive obedience, suitable to the meek example of our Lord Jesus Christ. Nor would I have any ignorant how forward I was by messages, letters, and visits, to have determined this debate in a sober and select assembly, notwithstanding the rude entertainment we had met with before ; but con-trary to their own appointments our adversaries failed us, which necessitated me to that defence ;[1] and finding the truth so prest with slander, I cannot but say I saw my just call to her relief ; but alas ! how have those two or three extemporary sheets been tost, tumbled, and torn on all hands, yea, aggravated to a monstrous design, even the subversion of the Christian religion, than which there could be nothing more repugnant to my principle and purpose ; wherefore how very intemperate have all my adversaries been in their revilings, slanders, and defamations ! using the most opprobrious terms of seducer, heretic, blasphemer, deceiver, Socinian, Pelagian, Simon Magus, im-piously robbing Christ of his divinity, for whom the vengeance of the great day is reserved, etc. Nor have these things been whispered, but in one book and pulpit after another have been thundered out against me, as if some bull had lately been arrived from Rome ; and all this acted under the foul pretence of zeal and love to Jesus Christ, whose meek and gentle example always taught it for a principal mark of true Christianity to suffer the most outrageous injuries, but never to return any. . . . Tell me,

If you will not talk with me, I must write

You call names at me instead of using argument

[1] A discussion in a Presbyterian meeting-house in London, between Penn with some friends and the Presbyterian minister, Thomas Vin-cent, had ended in an attempt to silence the Quakers by uproar. Penn persisted even after the lights were put out, but then yielded to Vin-cent's promise to meet him again in a fair and open discussion. It proved impossible, however, to make Vincent keep his promise, and so Penn had recourse to the press, and published his *The Sandy Foundation Shaken*. See Stoughton's *William Penn*, p. 57.

I pray, did Luther, that grand reformer whom you so much reverence, justly demand from the emperor at the Diet of Worms . . . that none should sit upon his doctrines but the scripture ; and in case they should be cast, that no other sentence should be passed upon him than what Gamaliel offered to the Jewish council ? If it were not of God it would not stand ; and if you will not censure him who first arraigned the Christian world (so called) at the bar of his private judgment (that had so many hundred years soundly slept, without so much as giving one considerable shrug or turn during that tedious winter-night of dark apostasy), but justify his proceedings, can you so furiously assault others ?

If you do not blame Luther for asserting the right of private judgment, why blame me ?

" But above all you, who refuse conformity to others, and that have been writing these eight years for liberty of conscience, . . . what pregnant testimonies do you give of your unwillingness to grant that to others you so earnestly beg for yourselves ? Doth it not discover your injustice, and plainly express that only want of power hinders you to act ? But of all Protestants in general I demand, do you believe that persecution to be Christian in yourselves that you condemned for antichristian in the Papists ? You judged it a weakness in their religion, and is it cogent argument in yours ? Nay, is it not the readiest way to enhance and propagate the reputation of what you would depress ? If you were displeased at their assuming an infallibility, will you believe it impossible in yourselves to err ? Have Whitaker, Reynolds, Laud, Owen, Baxter, Stillingfleet, Poole, etc., disarmed the Romanists of these inhuman weapons, that you might employ them against your inoffensive countrymen ? Let the example and holy precepts of Christ dissuade you, who came not to destroy but save ; and soberly reflect upon his equal law of doing as you would be done unto. . . . Have a care you are not upon one of Saul's errands to Damascus, and helping the mighty against God and his anointed ; and rather choose by

When you persecute others, you assume your own infallibility, as much as the Papists do

But you cannot hurt us, for if God is with us, who can be against us ?

fair and moderate debates, not penalties ratified by imperial decrees, to determine religious differences. . . . But if you are resolved severity shall take its course, in this our case can never change nor happiness abate ; for no human edict can possibly deprive us of His glorious presence, who is able to make the dismallest prisons so many receptacles of pleasure, and whose heavenly fellowship doth unspeakably replenish our solitary souls with divine consolation." [1]

It is interesting to see how Penn's argument partly anticipates that of John Stuart Mill, in his famous "Essay on Liberty." The extent to which the sense of an ever present God replenished his soul with divine consolation is No Cross, shown in one of his most important works, " No no Crown Cross, no Crown," written in the Tower of London in the year 1668. It is as beautiful as its title, albeit we must make allowance for the peculiar prolixity which English writers of the seventeenth century seldom succeeded in avoiding. In spite of this drawback the book abounds in the eloquence that wins the soul : —

" This made the prophet David say, ' The King's daughter is all glorious within, her clothing is of wrought gold.' What is the glory that is within the true church, and that gold that makes up that inward glory ? Tell me, O superstitious man ! is it thy stately temples, altars, carpets, tables, tapestries ; thy vestments, organs, voices, candles, lamps, censers, plate, and jewels, with the like furniture of thy worldly Religion temples ? No such matter; they bear no proporthrives not tion with the divine adornment of the King of upon out-ward show heaven's daughter, the blessed and redeemed church of Christ. Miserable apostasy that it is ! and a wretched supplement in the loss and absence of the apostolic life, the spiritual glory of the primitive church.

" But yet some of these admirers of external pomp and glory in worship would be thought lovers of the Cross, and to that end have made to themselves many. But alas ! what hopes can there be of reconciling that to Christianity, that

[1] Penn's *Select Works*, London, 1825, i. 163–165.

NO
Cross, no Crovvn:
Or several Sober
REASONS
Against

Hat-Honour, Titular-Respects, You to a single Person, with the *Apparel* and *Recreations* of the Times:

Being inconsistant with Scripture, Reason, and the Practice, as well of the best Heathens, as the holy Men and Women of all Generations; and consequently fantastick, impertinent and sinfull.

With Sixty Eight Testimonies of the most famous Persons, of both former and latter Ages for further confirmation.

In Defence of the poor despised *Quakers*, against the Practice and Objections of their Adversaries.

By W. Penn j.

An humble Disciple, and patient Bearer of the Cross of Jesus.

But Mordecai *bowed not,* Esth. 3. 2. Adam *where art thou!* Gen. 3. *In like manner the women adorn themselves in modest Apparal, with brodered hair,* &c. 1 Tim. 2. 9. *Thy Law is my Meditation all the day,* Psal. 119. 97.

Printed in the Year, 1669.

TITLE OF "NO CROSS, NO CROWN"

the nearer it comes to its resemblance, the farther off it is in reality ? . . . It is true, they have got a cross, but it seems to be in the room of the true one ; and so mannerly, that it will do as they will have it that wear it ; for instead of mortifying their wills by it, they made it and use it according to them ; so that the cross is become their ensign that do nothing but what they list.   Yet by that they would be thought his disciples, that never did his own will but the will of his heavenly Father.

It is but a false cross that comports with self-indul-gence

" This is such a cross as flesh and blood can carry, for flesh and blood invented it ; therefore not the cross of Christ that is to crucify flesh and blood.   Thousands of them have no more virtue than a chip ; poor empty shadows, not so much as images of the true one.   Some carry them for charms about them, but never repel one evil with them.   They sin with them upon their backs ; and though they put them in their bosoms, their beloved lusts lie there too without the least disquiet.   They are as dumb as Elijah's mock-gods ; no life nor power in them (1 Kings xviii. 27). . . . Is it possible that such crosses should mend their makers ?   Surely not. . . .

Religion is not a fetish, but a disci-pline

" Nor is a recluse life (the boasted righteousness of some) much more commendable, or one whit nearer to the nature of the true cross ; for if it be not unlawful as other things are, it is unnatural, which true religion teaches not.   The Christian convent and monastery are within, where the soul is encloistered from sin.   And this religious house the true followers of Christ carry about with them, who ex-empt not themselves from the conversation of the world, though they keep themselves from the evil of the world in their conversation.   That is a lazy, rusty, unprofitable self-denial, burdensome to others to feed their idleness ; religious bedlams, where people are kept up lest they should do mischief abroad. . . . No thanks if they commit not what they are not tempted to commit.   What the eye views not, the heart craves not, as well as rues not.

Better re-sist temp-tation than flee from it

The cross of Christ is of another nature ; it truly overcomes the world, and leads a life of purity in the face of its allurements. They that bear it are not thus chained up for fear they should bite, nor locked up lest they should be stole away ; no, they receive power from Christ their captain, to resist the evil and do that which is good in the sight of God. . . . What a world should we have if everybody, for fear of transgressing, should mew himself up within four walls ! . . .

"Not that I would be thought to slight a true retirement ; for I do not only acknowledge but admire solitude. Christ himself was an example of it ; he loved and chose to frequent mountains, gardens, seasides. They are requisite to the growth of piety ; and I reverence the virtue that seeks and uses it, wishing there were more of it in the world ; but then it should be free, not constrained. What benefit to the mind to have it for a punishment, not for a pleasure ? Nay, I have long thought it an error among all sorts that use not monastic lives, that they have no retreats for the afflicted, the tempted, the solitary, and the devout ;[1] where they might undisturbedly wait upon God, pass through their religious exercises, and being thereby strengthened may with more power over their own spirits enter into the business of the world again ; though the less the better, to be sure. For divine pleasures are to be found in a free solitude."[2]

The wholesomeness of solitude

From such sweet reflections we come now and then upon quaint arguments in justification of sundry peculiarities of the Friends, as for example their plainness of attire : "Were it possible that any one could bring us father Adam's girdle and mother Eve's apron, what laughing, what fleering, what mocking of their homely fashion would there be ! surely their tailor would find but little custom, although we read

[1] It was such a want that the noble and saintlike Nicholas Ferrar sought to satisfy in his Protestant monastery of Little Gidding. See my *Old Virginia and Her Neighbours*, Illustrated Edition, i. 196.
[2] Penn's *Select Works*, i. 368–371.

it was God himself that made them coats of skins. . . . How many pieces of ribband, and what feathers, lace-bands, and the like, did Adam and Eve wear in Paradise or out of it? What rich embroideries, silks, points, etc., had Abel, Enoch, Noah, and good old Abraham? Did Eve, Sarah, Susannah, Elizabeth, and the Virgin Mary use to curl, powder, patch, paint, wear false locks of strange colours, rich points, trimmings, laced gowns, embroidered petticoats, shoes with slipslaps laced with silk or silver lace and ruffled like pigeons' feet, with several yards of ribbands? How many plays did Jesus Christ and the apostles recreate themselves at? What poets, romances, comedies, and the like did the apostles and saints use to pass away their time withal? . . . But if I were asked, whence came them [these follies]; I would quickly answer, from the Gentiles that knew not God, . . . an effeminate Sardanapalus, . . . a comical Aristophanes, a prodigal Charaxus, a luxurious Aristippus . . . [from] such women as the infamous Clytemnestra, the painted Jezebel, the lascivious Campaspe, the most immodest Posthumia, the costly Corinthian Lais, the impudent Flora, the wanton Egyptian Cleopatra, and most insatiable Messalina; persons whose memories have stunk through all ages and carry with them a perpetual rot. These and not the holy self-denying men and women in ancient times were devoted to the like recreations and vain delights." [1]

The follies of fashion

Or, as concerns the use of "thou" and "thee" for "you," the modern reader needs to be reminded of the English usage in Penn's time, which made the Quaker innovation seem especially heinous. The usage in English was like that in French to-day, and analogous to the German, Italian, and Spanish usage. The singular pronoun was reserved for solemn invocations to the Deity, or for familiar intercourse with the members of one's family, including the servants; for addressing parents, however (especially the father), or social superiors or equals

"Thee" and "thou"

[1] Penn's *Select Works*, i. 482.

outside the circle of familiarity, the plural was necessary.
The rule was much like that which governs the use of the
Christian name to-day; you may call your wife, or sister,
or brother, or children, or the housemaid, by the forename;
but to address father or mother in that way is felt to be
disrespectful, and to address a lady so, unless she is an
intimate acquaintance, is an unwarrantable liberty. In the
seventeenth century, to "thou" (French *tutoyer*) a lady was
as rude as to call her Lizzie or Jane; to "thou" one's father
was much like addressing him as Tom or Jack. Probably
few things did so much to make the Quakers shock people's
sense of the proprieties as their use of the pronouns, which
was in later days imitated by the Jacobins of the French
Revolution. "There is another piece of our non-conformity
to the world, that renders us [*i. e.* makes us seem] very
clownish to the breeding of it, and that is, Thou for You,
and that without difference or respect to persons; a thing
that to some looks so rude, it cannot well go down without
derision or wrath." Nevertheless, says Penn, we Friends
have good reasons and high authorities on our side. "Luther,
the great reformer, was so far from condemning our plain
speech that in his 'Ludus' he sports himself with You to
a single person as an incongruous and ridiculous speech,
viz. *Magister, vos estis iratus?* 'Master, are You angry?'
as absurd with him in Latin as 'My masters, art Thou
angry?' is in English. Erasmus, a learned man and an
exact critic in speech, not only derides it, but bestows a
whole discourse upon rendering it absurd; plainly manifest-
ing . . . that the original of this corruption was the corruption of flattery. Lipsius affirms of the ancient Romans,
that the manner of greeting now in vogue was not in use
among them. . . . Is it not as proper to say, 'Thou lovest,'
to ten men, as to say, 'You love,' to one man? . . . Is it
reasonable that children should be whipt at school for putting
You for Thou, as having made false Latin; and yet that we
must be (though not whipt) reproached, and often abused,
when we use the contrary propriety of speech? . . . It can-

not be denied that the most famous poems, dedicated to love or majesty, are written in this style [*i. e.* with Thou]. Read of each in Chaucer, Spenser, Waller, Cowley, Dryden, etc. Why then should it be so homely, ill-bred, and insufferable in us? This, I conceive, can never be answered. . . . [The other style] was first ascribed in way of flattery to proud popes and emperors, imitating the heathen's vain homage to their gods ; . . . for which reason, You, only to be used to many, became first spoken to one. It seems the word Thou looked like too lean and thin a respect ; and therefore some, bigger than they should be, would have a style suitable to their own ambition. . . . It is a most extravagant piece of pride in a mortal man to require or expect from his fellow-creature a more civil speech . . . than he is wont to give the immortal God his Creator, in all his worship to him. . . . Say not, I am serious about slight things ; but beware you of levity and rashness in serious things. . . . But I would not have thee think it is a mere Thou or Title, simply or nakedly in themselves, we boggle at, or that we would beget or set up any form inconsistent with severity or true civility ; . . . but the esteem and value the vain minds of men do put upon them constrains us to testify so steadily against them."[1]

The use of "you" in place of "thou" is undemocratic

Other things in Penn's career beside the free circulation of his heretical books occur to remind us that in the England of Charles II., in spite of grave shortcomings, we are in a free country. Attacks upon liberty are made in courts of justice, but are apt to fail of success. Such a damnable iniquity as the Dreyfus case, which has made every true lover of France put on mourning, shows us that the Paris of Zola still has lessons of vital importance to learn from the London of Congreve and Aphra Behn. In 1670 Penn was arraigned before the Lord Mayor's court for infringing the Conventicle Act and provoking a riot by speaking in Gracechurch Street to an

Memorable scene in the Lord Mayor's court, 1670

[1] Penn's *Select Works*, i. 421–428.

12.

THE
Peoples {Ancient and Just} Liberties
ASSERTED,

IN THE

TRYAL

OF

William Penn, and *William Mead,*

At the Sessions held at the *Old-Baily* in *London,* the first, third, fourth and fifth of *Sept.* 70. against the most Arbitrary procedure of that Court.

Isa. 10. 1, 2. *Wo unto them that Decree Unrighteous Decrees, and write grievousness, which they have prescribed ; to turn away the Needy from Judgment, and to take away the right from the Poor, &c.*
Psal. 94. 20. *Shall the Throne of Iniquity have fellowship with thee, which frameth mischief by a Law.*

Sic volo, sic jubeo, stat pro ratione voluntas.

Old-Baily, 1st. 3d. 4th, 5th of *Sept.* 1670.

Printed in the Year, 1670.

TITLE OF " THE PEOPLE'S ANCIENT AND JUST LIBERTIES "

unlawful assembly.   He argued his own case, and proved much more than a match for the recorder.   The twelve jurors failed to agree, and were sent out again and again after a scolding from the Court.   At length they brought in the verdict, " Guilty of speaking in Gracechurch Street," but this was not enough.   So they were locked up for the night " without meat, drink, fire, or tobacco," and next morning the question was put to them, "Guilty, or not guilty ? "   The foreman replied, " Guilty of speaking in Gracechurch Street," and stopped, whereupon the Lord Mayor added, "to an unlawful assembly."   " No, my lord," said the foreman, " we give no other verdict than we gave last night."   So these brave men were scolded again, locked up again for several hours, and again brought into court, but their spirit was not quelled.   " Is William Penn, the prisoner, guilty or not guilty ? " asked the mayor.   " Not guilty, my lord." Then the mayor, quite beside himself with rage, proceeded to fine each of the jurors in a sum equivalent to about $30, with jail until it should be paid.   " What is all this for ? " exclaimed Penn.   " For contempt of court," quoth the Lord Mayor.   But his was not the last word on the subject. The case was taken to the Court of Common Pleas, which summarily quashed the mayor's order and set free the sturdy jurors.   Thus justice triumphed, and Penn straightway published his own account of the affair, in a pamphlet entitled, " The People's Ancient and Just Liberties Asserted." [1]

In 1672 Penn was married to Gulielma Maria, daughter
Penn's of Sir William Springett, a noted officer of the Par-
marriage, liamentary army who had lost his life in the Civil
and charm- ing home War.   This lady was celebrated for beauty, wit, and accomplishments, and had withal a handsome estate at Worm-

[1] Penn's *Select Works*, i. 179–223.   At one point in the trial, the recorder, John Howell, exclaimed : " Till now I never understood the reason of the policy and prudence of the Spaniards in suffering the Inquisition among them.   And certainly it will never be well with us, till something like the Spanish Inquisition be in England." *Id.* p. 194.

inghurst, in Sussex, overlooking the beautiful South Downs. There all the things that make life delightful seemed to be combined, — books and flowers, cultivated friends, the supreme restfulness of rural England with its tempered

Guli Penn

sunshine, its gentle showers, and the tonic fragrance of the salt sea. In this blest retreat Penn spent his happiest days, but he was often called upon to leave it. One of his first visitors was his friend George Fox, who had lately re-turned from a journey through the American colonies, and had much to tell. The time had arrived when matters of business were to turn Penn's attention deci-sively toward America, but while these matters of business were taking shape he visited Holland and travelled in the lower parts of Germany with a party of friends, holding meetings at all times and places, here and there meeting with rebuffs and insults, but finding many spirits to whom his words were an inspiration and a solace. His missionary tour in Germany There can be no doubt that this journey had far-reaching results in afterward turning the attention of Germany to-wards Penn's colonizing work in America. Penn afterward published a diary of this missionary tour.[1] A general outline of the route and a few of the interesting scenes must suffice for the present narrative.

[1] It is contained in his *Select Works*, ii. 398–503.

Leaving his wife at the beautiful Sussex home, Penn sailed for Rotterdam on a July day of 1677. Among his companions were George Fox, Robert Barclay, and George Keith, and at Rotterdam they held a great meeting at the house of Benjamin Furly, with such effect, says Penn, that "the dead were raised and the living comforted." With similar success they visited Leyden, Haarlem, and Amsterdam. There the party left Fox behind, but Furly accompanied them into Hanover. After talking with "the man of the inn" at Osnabrug, and leaving with him "several good books of Friends, in the Low and High Dutch tongues, to read and dispose of," the missionaries proceeded next day to Herwerden in Westphalia, where Elizabeth, the Princess

Princess Elizabeth
Palatine, had her court. This Elizabeth, sister of Prince Rupert, cousin to Charles II., and aunt to the German prince who afterwards became George I. of England, was a woman of liberal and cultivated mind. It may have been from her grandfather, James I., that she inherited her bookish proclivities. She had received lessons in philosophy from the immortal Descartes, who was reported to have said that he "found none except her who thoroughly understood his works." She had for a time given protection to Jean de Labadie, and now she cordially welcomed Penn and his companions. After a pleasant day with the Princess Elizabeth and her friend, Anna Maria, Countess of Hornes, the party were invited to return next morning and continue their conference upon sacred themes. So "the next morning we were there between eight and nine; where Robert Barclay falling into some discourse with the princess, the countess took hold of the opportunity, and whispered me to withdraw, to get a meeting for the more inferior servants of the house, who would have been bashful to have presented themselves before the princess. And

Penn preaches to the servants
blessed be the Lord, he was not wanting to us; but the same blessed power that had appeared to visit them of high, appeared also to visit them of low degree; and we were all sweetly tendered and broken

Elizabeth, Princess Palatine

together, for virtue went forth of Jesus that day, and the life of our God was shed abroad amongst us as a sweet savour, for which their souls bowed before the Lord and confessed to our testimony. Which did not a little please that noble young woman, to find her own report of us, and her great care of them, so effectually answered. . . . I must not here

GEORGE KEITH

forget that we found at our inn, the first night at supper, a young merchant, of a sweet and ingenuous tem- A mer-
per, belonging to the city of Bremen, who took chant of
occasion from that night's discourse, the sixth day Bremen
at dinner and supper, and the seventh day also, to seek all opportunities of conference with us ; and, as we have reason to believe, he stayed twenty-four hours in [Herwerden] on

our account. . . . We asked him, in case any of us should visit [Bremen], if he would give us the opportunity of a meeting at his house ; which he readily granted us. So we gave him some books, etc. . . . It being now three in the afternoon, we went to the princess's ; where being come, after some little time, the princess and countess put me in remembrance of a promise I made them in one of my letters out of England, namely, that I would give them an account

Penn tells the ladies of his con- version (at some convenient time) of my first convince- ment, and of those tribulations and consolations which I had met withal in this way of the kingdom which God had brought me to. After some pause I found myself very free, and prepared in the Lord's love and fear to comply with their request ; and so, after some silence, began. But before I had half done it was supper time, and the princess would by no means let us go, we must sup with her ; which importunity not being well able to avoid, we yielded to, and sat down with her to supper.

"Among the rest present at these opportunities, it must not be forgotten that there was a countess, sister to the countess, then come in to visit her, and a Frenchwoman of

A French lady quality ; the first behaving herself very decently and the last often deeply broken ; and from a light and slighting carriage toward the very name of a Quaker, she became very intimately and respectfully kind and re- spectful to us. Supper being ended, we all returned to the princess's chamber ; where making us all to sit down with her, she with both the countesses and the Frenchwoman pressed from me the continuance of my relation ; . . . which, though late, I was not unwilling to oblige them with, because I knew not when the Lord would give me such an opportu- nity."

The ladies listened " with a earnest and tender attention," and afterwards a meeting was appointed for the next day, Sunday, at two o'clock, in Princess Elizabeth's palace ; and so toward midnight the evening came to an end. The next day, at the inn dinner, " there were several strangers that

came by the post-wagon, among whom there was a young
man of Bremen, being a student at the college at Duysburgh,
who informed us of a sober and seeking man of great note in
the city of Duysburgh.   To him we gave some books. . . .
The second hour being at hand we went to the meeting;
where were several as well of the town as of the   A meeting
family. The meeting began with a weighty exercise at the pal-
and travail in prayer, that the Lord would glorify   ace
his own name that day.   And by his own power he made
way to their consciences and sounded his wakening trumpet
in their ears, that they might know that he was God, and
that there is none like unto him.   O, the day of the Lord
livingly dawned upon us, and the searching life of Jesus
was in the midst of us!   O, the Word, that never faileth
them that wait for it and abide in it, opened the way and
unsealed the book of life.   Yea, the quickening power and
life of Jesus wrought and reached to them ; and virtue from
him, in whom dwelleth the Godhead bodily, went forth and
blessedly distilled upon us his own heavenly life, sweeter than
the pure frankincense ; yea, than the sweet-smelling myrrh
that cometh from a far country. . . . As soon as the meeting was done the princess came to me and took me by the
hand (which she usually did to us all, coming and going)
and went to speak to me of the sense she had of   Emotion of
that power and presence of God that was amongst   the princess
us, but was stopped.   And turning herself to the window
brake forth in an extraordinary fashion, crying out, 'I cannot
speak to you ; my heart is full ;' clapping her hands upon
her breast.

      " It melted me into a deep and calm tenderness, in which
I was moved to minister a few words softly to her, and after
some time of silence she recovered herself, and as I was taking leave of her, she interrupted me thus : 'Will ye not
come hither again ? Pray call here as ye return   Penn takes
out of Germany.'   I told her, we were in the hand   leave
of the Lord, and being his, could not dispose of ourselves ;

but the Lord had taken care that we should not forget her and those with her." [1]

From Herwerden our friends proceeded to Paderborn, "a dark popish town, and under the government of a bishop of that religion." Thence in floods of rain, with "only naked carts to ride in," to Hesse-Cassel, and thence to Frankfort. At every place they made converts; at Frankfort "a Lutheran minister was broken to pieces," "a doctor of physic was affected and confessed to the truth." These things happened in the parlour of a young maiden lady, who declared herself ready to go to prison, if need be, for harbouring such preachers. At some places on the route the Quakers were forbidden to preach, but they paid small heed to the injunction. As they made a little circuit through Mannheim, Worms, and Mayence, and back to Frankfort, people thronged from neighbouring towns and villages, in coaches and wagons or afoot, in order to listen to them. Down the beautiful Rhine they went to Cologne, and so on toward Duysburg, near which towered the castle of the gruff old Count von Falkenstein. They carried a letter of introduction to his daughter, "an extraordinary woman," but on the way they met the father, who said that he had no need of Quakers and ordered them to get out of his dominions. The walk to Duysburg was so long that when they arrived there they found the city gates shut and had to sleep under the open sky. As they entered the city in the morning they met with a messenger from the young Countess von Falkenstein, "a pretty young tender man, near to the kingdom, who saluted us in her name with much love; telling us that she was much grieved at the entertainment of her father towards us, advising us not to expose ourselves to such difficulties and hardships, for it would grieve her heart that any that came in the love of God to visit her should be so severely handled; for at some he sets his dogs, upon others he puts his soldiers to beat them." Our pilgrims begged the young man to assure the lady

Frankfort and its neighbourhood

A gruff greeting

[1] Penn's *Select Works*, ii. 414–418.

ANNA MARIA SCHURMANN

"that our concern was not for ourselves, but for her," *i. e.*
since they understood her father's reputation for cruelty.
A walk of eight English miles after dinner brought them to
their next resting-place, and so they kept on, making some
impression wherever they stopped, until they arrived at
Amsterdam.

Thence Penn set out once more, in company with a certain Jan Claus, and visited Leeuwarden, where he met "an
ancient maid, above sixty years of age," Anna Maria Schurmann, the celebrated mystic and friend of Labadie, Anna
and "of great note and fame for learning in lan- Maria
guages and philosophy." This ancient maiden "told Schurmann
us of her former life, of her pleasure in learning, and her

love to the religion she was brought up in ; but confessed she knew not God nor Christ truly all that while . . . she never felt such a powerful stroke as by the ministry of Jean de Labadie. She saw her learning to be vanity, and her religion like a body of death." From Friesland Penn entered Germany again at Emden, and after a stop at Bremen, returned once more to the Princess Elizabeth and her ladies at Herwerden. Thence after affectionate farewells it was a wearisome journey to Wesel : " We rode three nights and days without lying down on a bed or sleeping, otherwise than in the wagon, which was only covered with an old ragged sheet. The company we had with us made twelve in number, which much straitened us. They were often if not always vain ; yea, in their religious songs, which is the fashion of that country, especially by night. They call them Luther's songs, and sometimes psalms. We were forced often to reprove and testify against their hypocrisy, — to be full of all vain and often profane talk one hour, and sing psalms to God the next ; we showed them the deceit and abomination of it. . . . All was very well ; they bore what we said."

Fellow-travellers rebuked

From Wesel through the Netherlands the journey was brief, and at the end of October, after an absence of three months, Penn arrived at Worminghurst, and found wife, child, and family all well. " I had that evening a sweet meeting amongst them, in which God's blessed power made us truly glad together."

At home once more

A charming picture is this of the highly gifted young man, with his noble face, commanding presence, and magnetic demeanour, going about to win souls to a higher life. It was because they felt the divine authority in the nature of his utterances that his hearers were so " broken " and contrite. It was a renewal of Christ's teaching that religion is an affair of the inner soul and not of externals ; and there can be little doubt that the Christian ideal has been, on the whole, more perfectly realized among the Quakers than with any other sect of Christians.

REYS~BOEK.

*Door de Vereenigde Nederlande en Derselver
aen Grensende LandtSchappen en Koninckrijcken*

Amsterdam. Bij Jan ten Hoorn, Boekverkooper.

TITLE OF THE OLDEST BOOK ON TRAVEL THROUGH THE NETHERLANDS

FRIENDS, 3 ohms on pio zo hill London 8

THESE are to Satisfie you, or any other who are Sober, and are any wise
minded to go along with me, and Plant within my COLONY, That
we shall no doubt find, but that New CESAREA or New JER-
SEY, which is the Place which I did Purchase: Together with the Government thereof, is a Healthy Pleasant, and Plentiful Country: According to
the Report of many Honest Men, Friends, and others who has been there,
and the Character given thereof, by John Ogilby in his AMERICA, which
I herewith send. The Method I intend for the Planting of all, or so much thereof, as
I shall reserve to my self, my Heirs and Assigns for ever. Is thus:

1. WHoever is minded to Purchase to them and their Heirs for ever, may for Five
Pound have a Thousand Acres, and so Ten Thousand Acres, and thereby
be made Propriators or Free-Holders.

2. Who is minded to Carry themselves, (and not Purchase) with their Families at
their own Charges, are to have the Freedom of the Country when they Arrive, and one
hundred Acres for every Head they carry above the Age of Fourteen, to them and their
Heirs for ever. At the yearly Rent of a Peny for every Acre, to Me, my Heirs and Assigns for ever.

3. Who are minded to go as Servants, who must be Carried at my Charges, or any
other Propriator, or Purchasors, or Carries themselves with Servants at their own
Charges as aforesaid; they are to Serve 4 years, and then to be made Free of the
Country: Their Masters are to give them a Suit of Cloaths, and other things sutable;
a Cow, a Hog, and so much Wheat as the Law there in that Case allows; with Working Tools to begin with: And then he is to have of me, or his Master out of his Propriety, a hundred Acres, Paying the yearly Rent of a Peny for every Acre: To me and my
Heirs for ever, or to his Master and his Heirs.

And as for the Planting of the Whole, with Ease, Satisfaction and Profit, as well to
the Poor as the Rich: this Method is intended, and approved of by many that are preparing
to go with me, which I intend will be about the middle of the next Month call'd April,
or the end thereof without fail, if the Lord please.

First, 10000. Acres being pitch'd Upon, and divided according to every mans Propriety; then Lots shall be cast, and when every one knows where his Lot lies, there being also a place Chosen and set out for a Town or City to be Built, in which every Purchaser must have a Part, by reason of Delaware River for Trade. Then every one must
joyn their Hands, first in Building the Houses, and next in Improving the Land, casting
Lots whose Houses shall be first built, and whose Land first Improved: And as the Land
is Improved so it shall be for the Use of all the Hands and their Families which are joyned in this Community, until the whole 10000. Acres be Improved; Then every one to
have his own Lot to his own Use: And so this Method to be used till the Country be
Planted.

If any like not this Method, they may be left to Improve their Propriety alone. If
any happen to go who is not Able to get a Livehood here, nor to Pay their Debts out of
their Stocks, the Governor and his Council shall take care, upon notice given thereof by
the Creditors, that such shall make Satisfaction out of their Estates, as the Lord shall
give a Blessing to their Labours, and an Increase of their Substance. Provided the Creditors hinder not their Passage, but give the Governor and his Council a Particular of
their Debts.

The Government is to be, by a Governor and 12 Council to be Chosen every year,
6 of the Council to go out, and 6 to come in; whereby every Proprietor may be made
capable of Government, and know the Affairs of the Country, and Priviledges of the
People.

The Government to stand upon these two Basis, or Leges, viz. 1. The Defence of
the Royal Law of God, his Name and true Worship, which is in Spirit and in Truth.
2. The Good, Peace and Welfare, of every Individual Person.

This 8th. of the 1st. Month,
1675.

I am a Real Friend and Well-
wisher to all Men,
J. Fenwick

TITLE OF "FENWICK'S PROPOSALS"

The importance of this journey in relation to the European peopling of the middle zone of the United States is obvious. It made Penn and his ideas familiarly known to many excellent men and women in Germany, persons of character and influence. At the time when he made the journey his American schemes were rapidly developing. We have now to observe the manner in which his attention was directed to the New World.

Historic significance of the journey

It will be remembered that in 1673 Lord Berkeley sold his half share in the province of New Jersey to a Quaker, John Fenwick, in trust for another Quaker, Edward Byllinge. Fenwick, who is described as a "litigious and troublesome person," soon got into a quarrel with Byllinge, and the affair was referred to William Penn as arbitrator. He adjudged one tenth of the Berkeley purchase to Friend Fenwick, along with a certain sum of money, and directed him to hand over the other nine tenths to Friend Byllinge. At first Fenwick was sorely dissatisfied with the award, and refused to abide by it, whereat he was gravely rebuked by Penn. Meanwhile Byllinge became insolvent. Presently Fenwick yielded, and made over nine tenths of the property to William Penn, Gawaine Laurie, and Nicholas Lucas, as trustees for the benefit of Byllinge's creditors. In 1675 Fenwick sailed for the Delaware River with a party of colonists, and landed at the mouth of a small stream which the Dutch had called by the unromantic name of Varkenskill, or "Hog's Creek," hard by the Swedish settlement of Elsingburgh. There he laid out a town and called it Salem. These proceedings aroused the ire of Andros, who demanded by what authority was Fenwick taking on airs of proprietorship within the Duke of York's dominions. Not getting a satisfactory reply, Andros summoned Fenwick to New York, and when he refused to come the summons was followed by an officer who seized the obstinate Quaker and carried him off to Fort James.

Penn becomes interested in West Jersey

Salem founded by Fenwick

Meanwhile an important question was settled between the proprietors in England. The joint proprietorship of New Jersey between Carteret and Berkeley had passed almost

The lines between East and West Jersey

unconsciously into two proprietorships of East and West Jersey in severalty; and the boundary between the two had been declared to be a straight line running from Barnegat to Rankokus Creek. This was felt to be an inequitable division, and in 1676 the matter was readjusted by what was known as the Quintipartite Deed, between Sir George Carteret on the one hand, and Penn, Laurie, Lucas, and Byllinge on the other. By this instrument it was agreed that the boundary between East and West Jersey should be a straight line running from Little Egg Harbour to the northernmost branch of the Delaware River in latitude 41° 40'.

In the summer of 1677 the good ship Kent, Gregory Marlow, master, dropped down the Thames with 230 passengers bound for West Jersey, including a small

Quakers go to West Jersey

board of commissioners for organizing a government for that province. As they were gliding down-stream, King Charles in his pleasure barge came alongside and asked whither they were bound. Hearing the name West Jersey, he asked if they were all Quakers, and gave them his royal blessing. On arriving at Sandy Hook the Kent dropped anchor while the commissioners went up to New York to pay their respects to Andros. The governor received them politely, but was particular to ask "if they had anything from the duke, his master? They replied, nothing particularly; but that he had conveyed that part of his country to Lord Berkeley, and he to Byllinge, etc., in which the government was as much con-

Peremptory demeanour of Andros

veyed as the soil. The governor replied: 'All that will not clear me. If I should surrender without the duke's order, it is as much as my head is worth; but if you had but a line or two from the duke, I should be as ready to surrender it to you as you would be to ask it.' Upon which the commissioners, instead of excusing their imprudence in not bringing such an order, began to insist upon their right and strenuously to assert their independency.   But Andros, clapping his hand on his sword, told them that he should defend the government [of West Jersey] from them till he received orders from the duke to surrender it.   He, however, softened and told them he would do what was in his power to make them easy till they could send home to get redress ; and in order thereto, would commissionate the same persons mentioned in the commission they produced.   This they accepted, and undertook to act as magistrates under him till further orders came from England, and to proceed in relation to their land affairs according to the methods prescribed by the proprietors." [1]

This incident throws a strong sidelight upon the behaviour of Andros toward Philip Carteret.   Neither personal friendship nor any other consideration could avail against his mastiff-like fidelity to his master.   By their well-timed pliancy Penn's commissioners probably saved themselves from forcible detention in Fort James.   After coming to terms with the governor of New York, the immigrants went on to the Delaware River and proceeded far up-stream, above the Rankokus Creek, as if it were part of their purpose to assert ownership of what had once belonged to East Jersey.   Here they founded a village which they called Burlington, after the town in Yorkshire whence a goodly number of them came.   Andros now, having sufficiently carried his point, released Fenwick.

Founding of Burlington

A letter from one of the settlers, Thomas Hooton, to his wife in England, dated October 29, 1677, is full of interest : " My dear, — I am this present at the town called Burlington, where our land is ; it is ordered to be a town for the ten Yorkshire and ten London proprietors.   I like the place well ; our lot is the second next the water side.   It 's like to be a healthful place and very pleasant to live in.   I came hither yesterday with some friends that

Hooton's letter

[1] Smith's *History of Nova Cæsaria, or New Jersey*, Burlington, 1765, pp. 93, 94.

were going to New York. I am to be at Thomas Olive's
house till I can provide better for myself. I intend to build
a house and get some corn into the ground ; and I know not
how to write concerning thy coming or not coming hither.
The place I like very well, and believe that we may live
here very well. But if it be not made free, I mean as to
the customs and government, then it will not be so well,
and may hinder many that have desires to come. But if
those two things be cleared, thou may take thy opportunity
of coming this [*i. e.* next ?] summer."

The two things that thus needed clearing up were surely
of supreme importance to the colonists. In sending them
to New Jersey, Penn and his colleagues supposed they were
founding a self-governing community. Penn had drawn up
a constitution for it, providing that "no man was to have
power over another man's conscience. A governing assembly was to be chosen by ballot ; every man was eligible to
vote, and to be voted for ; each elected member
was to receive a shilling a day as the servant of
the people. Executive power was to be in the
hands of ten commissioners appointed by the assembly ; and
justices and constables were to be elected by popular vote ;
and it is added, 'All, and every person in the province,
shall by the help of the Lord and these fundamentals be
free from oppression and slavery.'" Here we have democracy in quite modern shape, containing some of the features which are now found to be objectionable (such as an
elective judiciary), as well as those which time and experience
have approved. A friendly message, commenting on the
above provisions, exclaimed, "We lay a foundation for after
ages to understand their liberty as Christians and as men,
that they may not be brought into bondage but by their own
consent, for we put the power in the people." [1] Our worthy
Quakers did not foresee the day when the people,
lured by the bait of high tariffs and the "spoils of
office," would consent to be brought into bondage under

*A demo-
cratic con-
stitution*

*New phases
of tyranny*

[1] Stoughton's *William Penn*, p. 119.

petty tyrants as cheap and vile as ever cumbered the earth. They would have been sorely astonished if told that nowhere could be seen a more flagrant spectacle of such humiliating bondage than in the great commonwealth which bears Penn's name.

Now according to the claim which Andros asserted for the Duke of York, these Quakers were merely landowners in New Jersey under the sovereign jurisdiction of New York; their taxes were to be levied not by their own representative assembly, but by the despotic governor of New York; and at Newcastle on the Delaware there was a custom-house, where goods imported into West Jersey had to pay duties into the New York treasury. Under such circumstances, no wonder that some of the settlers felt dubious about staying and bringing over their wives and children. Nevertheless, people kept on coming and agitating, and as the population grew the question was more and more warmly discussed.

Andros claims West Jersey for the Duke of York

In 1679 there was a strong anti-Catholic excitement in England, due largely to Titus Oates and his alleged detection of a Popish plot in the previous year. The horrors in Scotland and the defeat of Claverhouse by the Covenanters at Drumclog also produced a great effect; and amid it all the friends of the Habeas Corpus Act, led by the Earl of Shaftesbury, wrenched from the king his signature to that famous measure. The Duke of York, as a Romanist, was threatened with exclusion from the throne, and so strong was the feeling against him that he deemed it prudent for a time to leave the country. During his absence the West Jersey question was discussed. Penn argued that Berkeley's conveyance expressly included powers of government along with territorial possession, and that the Duke of York had no authority to levy duties on the colonists in West Jersey, or exclude them of their " English right of common assent to taxes; " and then, skilfully alluding to "the duke's circumstances and the people's jealousies," it was suggested that since he had now an opportunity to

Penn's ingenious argument

free West Jersey with his own hand, "so will Englishmen here [in England] know what to hope for, by the justice and kindness he shows to Englishmen there, and all men to

TITUS OATES

see the just model of his government in New York to be the scheme and draft in little of his administration in Old England at large, if the crown should ever devolve upon his head." [1]

This argument was certainly defective in ignoring the

[1] Broadhead's *History of the State of New York*, ii. 339; an excellent and scholarly work, though occasionally disfigured by a proneness to ascribe unworthy motives to New York's neighbours, whether in Massachusetts, or Connecticut, or Pennsylvania.

legal facts attendant upon the loss and recovery of New
Netherland in 1673–74, which should have made it plain
that Penn and his friends could have no rights of sovereignty
over West Jersey without an explicit release from the Duke
of York.[1] Apparently their minds were not clear on this
point ; or perhaps they acted upon the maxim of worldly
wisdom that it is just as well to begin by "claiming everything." The hope of Penn's subtle and weighty argument
lay not so much in this preamble as in the suggestion of
the duke's true interests. So the duke evidently
understood it, and in August, 1680, he executed a
deed whereby he released all his powers of sovereignty over West Jersey to Byllinge, Penn, and their colleagues. Two months later he released to the Carterets all
his powers over East Jersey, and due notification of these
measures was sent to the peremptory Andros. Thus were
the Jerseys definitively set free from New York.

Final release of the Jerseys

In the course of these discussions Penn had acquired a
wide knowledge of American affairs, and his mind was
turned more and more to thoughts of colonization. The
new settlements at Salem and Burlington were flourishing,
and in England there were thousands of industrious and
thrifty Quakers who would be likely to flock to a new
colony founded expressly in their own behoof by
their trusted leader. Circumstances combined to
favour such a scheme. Penn inherited the claim
to a debt of £16,000 due from the crown to his father, and
there was no way in which such a debt could more easily
be paid than by a grant of wild lands in America. Penn, as
he said of himself, was not destitute of " a moderate and seasonable regard" to worldly interests, and he was shrewd
enough to see that such an American domain might prove
to be better property than the hard cash, even if he were
ever likely to get cash from the needy spendthrift who sat
on the throne or the niggardly brother who was expected to
succeed him. Uppermost in his mind, however, was the

Penn's claim against the crown

[1] See above, p. 37.

hope of planting a free and self-governing community wherein his own ideal of a civil polity might be realized. Irrespective of nationality, from the banks of the Rhine and Weser, or from those of the Thames and the Severn, he might draw people of various kinds and grades of free thinking, and deliver them from the vexations which pursued them in their old homes. The more he dwelt upon this scheme, the more it seemed to him "a holy experiment" which with God's help it was his duty to try. "The Lord is good to me," he wrote to a friend, "and the interest his truth has given me with his people may more than repay [this claim upon the crown]. For many are drawn forth to be concerned with me, and perhaps this way of satisfaction hath more the hand of God in it than a downright payment. . . . For the matters of liberty and privilege I purpose that which is extraordinary, and [to] leave myself and succession no power of doing mischief, that the will of one man may not hinder the good of a whole country." [1]

The "holy experiment"

Penn's petition to the privy council asked for "a tract of land in America, lying north of Maryland, on the east bounded with Delaware River, on the west limited as Maryland, and northward to extend as far as plantable." The determining of these bounds was, as usual, attended with hard feelings and hard words. Lord Baltimore's charter fixed his northern boundary at the 40th parallel of latitude, which runs a little north of the site of Philadelphia. This latitude was marked by a fortress on the Susquehanna River, and when the crown lawyers consulted with Baltimore's attorneys, they were told that all questions of encroachment would be avoided if the line were to be run just north of this fort, so as to leave it on the Maryland side. Penn made no objection to this, but an inspection of maps soon showed that such a boundary would give his province inadequate access to the ocean. Of all the English colonies, his was the only one that had no seaboard, and he was eager to get an outlet at the head of Chesapeake

Boundaries

[1] Clarkson's *Life of Penn*, i. 288.

Bay. His position as a royal favourite enabled him to push the whole line twenty miles to the south of the Susquehanna fort. But this fell short of attaining his object; so he persuaded the Duke of York to give him the land on the west shore of Delaware Bay which the Dutch had once taken from the Swedes. By further enlargement the area of this grant became that of the present state of Delaware, the whole of which was thus, in spite of vehement protest, carved out of the original Maryland.[1] Throughout the colonial period Delaware and Pennsylvania, though distinct provinces with separate legislative assemblies, continued under the same proprietary government, and the history of the little community was to a considerable extent merged in that of the great one.

On the east the Delaware River was a boundary sufficiently definite, and the circumstances of a later day determined at precisely what remote points in the interior the western limit should be fixed. Five degrees of longitude were allowed in the charter, but rather more than this was ultimately obtained. The northern boundary is placed in the charter at the 43d parallel, but in the final compromise between the Penns and Calverts in 1760, when it was decreed that Mason and Dixon should run their division line at 39° 43′ 26.3″ north, the privy council also insisted that the northern boundary of Pennsylvania should be at 42° instead of 43°. This arrangement, like Penn's original charter, ignored the claim of Connecticut, under her Winthrop charter of 1662, to the strip of land between 41° and 42° as far as the Pacific Ocean; an unsettled question which led to the Pennamite-Yankee conflicts, disgraceful alike to both parties. It has been truly said that Penn's charter was the source of more boundary disputes than any other in American history.[2]

It was Penn's intention to call his province New Wales,

Seeds of contention

[1] See *Old Virginia and Her Neighbours*, Illustrated Edition, ii. 130–132.
[2] The subject is ably and succinctly treated in Hinsdale's *Old Northwest*, pp. 98–119.

because he had heard that there were hills west of the Delaware River. But as the king for some reason objected to
this, he changed it to Sylvania, or Woodland. When the
king had in hand the draft of the charter, with this correc-
tion, he added the name Penn before Sylvania. When Penn
saw this he was not at all pleased. It had an egotistical
Name of   look, and he insisted that his own name should
the new   be crossed off; but Charles II. was quick-witted.
common-
wealth   "We will keep it," said he, "but not on your
account, my dear fellow. Don't flatter yourself. We will
keep the name to commemorate the admiral, your noble
father." If there were any answer for this, Penn had it not
forthcoming, and the king's emendation remained. Penn
afterward laughingly argued that, since in the Welsh tongue
pen means "hill," the compound Pennsylvania might well
mean Hilly Woodland or Wooded Hills.[1]

The charter which made Penn lord proprietor of this
goodly domain was drawn up by himself in imitation of the
charter of Maryland, but differed from it in two very important particulars. Laws passed by the assembly of Maryland were valid as soon as confirmed by Lord Baltimore,
and did not need even to be looked at by the king or his
privy council; but the colonial enactments of Pennsylvania
were required to be sent to England for the royal approval.

[1] See his letter to his friend Robert Turner, in Stoughton's *William
Penn*, p. 169. The reader must pardon me for throwing the king's
remark into the *oratio directa*, thus paraphrasing but scarcely amplify-
ing what Penn tells us. The king spake as I have quoted him, or
"words to that effect," as the lawyers say.

It is said that Penn once told the Rev. Hugh David that he was himself of Welsh origin and descended from the Tudors. "My great-
grandfather, John Tudor, lived upon the top of a hill or mountain in
Wales and was generally called John Penmunnith, which in English is
John-on-the-Hilltop. He removed from Wales into Ireland, where he
acquired considerable property," and afterward removed to London.
His Welsh nickname became abbreviated to John Penn, and in the new
surroundings the old name Tudor was forgotten. See Watson's *Annals
of Philadelphia*, i. 119. I relate the tradition for whatever it may be
worth.

FACSIMILE OF THE PENNSYLVANIA CHARTER OF 1682

It was, moreover, expressly provided in the Maryland charter that the crown should never impose any taxes   The char-
within the limits of the province ; and although no-   ters of
                                                        Pennsylva-
thing is said about the authority of parliament in   nia and
such matters, there is no doubt that the proviso was   Maryland
understood to mean that the right of taxing the colony was
entirely disclaimed by the government in England.   For the
views of Charles I. were unquestionably identical with those
of his father, who declared in 1624 that the government of
colonies was the business of the king, and that parliament
had nothing whatever to do with it.[1]   But in the charter of

THE SEAL OF PENNSYLVANIA

Pennsylvania, half a century later than that of Maryland, the
right of parliament to levy taxes in the colony was expressly
maintained. The younger colony was therefore less independent of the mother country than her elder sister, and the position of Penn was distinctly less regal than that of Baltimore.

   This noticeable contrast marks the growth of the imperial
and anti-feudal sentiment in England during those fifty
years, the feeling that privileges like those accorded   Signifi-
to the Calverts were too extensive to be enjoyed by   cance of
                                                        the con-
subjects.   It also marks the great decline in the   trast
royal power and the concomitant increase in the power and

   [1] See *Old Virginia and Her Neighbours*, Illustrated Edition, i. 207.

importance of parliament. We see that august body putting forth claims to a voice in the imposition of American taxes, claims which the American colonies could never be brought to admit, but which were naturally resented and resisted with more alertness and decision by the older colonies than by the younger.

The limitations in Penn's charter show also the influence of the conflict which had been going on for twenty years between Charles II. and the colony of Massachusetts. That stiff-necked Puritan commonwealth had coined money, set the navigation acts at defiance, prohibited the Episcopal form of worship, snubbed the royal commissioners, and passed laws inconsistent with those of England. Hence in the Pennsylvania charter we see imperial claims more carefully guarded. Massachusetts, moreover, had neglected to appoint an agent or attorney to represent her interests at the English court, for, in the rebellious phrase of a later era, all she asked was to be let alone. Accordingly the Pennsylvania charter required that such an agent should be employed. The toleration of Episcopal forms of worship was also expressly provided for.

Influence of the king's experience with Massachusetts

But in spite of these few limitations in the charter,[1] Penn was allowed the widest latitude in shaping the policy of his colony, and nothing could have been less like the principles of the Stuarts than the kind of civil government which he forthwith proclaimed. Absolute freedom of conscience was guaranteed to everybody. It was declared, in language which to the seventeenth century seemed arrant political heresy, that governments exist for the sake of the people, and not the people for the sake of governments ; and side by side with this came the equally novel doctrine that in legislating for the punishment of criminals, the reformation of the criminal is a worthier object than the wreaking of vengeance. The death penalty

Penn's humane and reasonable policy

[1] These were probably added by Lord Chief Justice North, who revised the document.

SOME

ACCOUNT

OF THE

PROVINCE

OF

PENNSILVANIA

IN

AMERICA;

Lately Granted under the Great Seal

OF

ENGLAND

TO

William Penn, &c.

Together with Priviledges and Powers neceſſary to the well-governing thereof.

Made publick for the Information of ſuch as are or may be
diſpoſed to Tranſport themſelves or Servants
into thoſe Parts.

LONDON: Printed, and Sold by *Benjamin Clark*
Bookſeller in *George-Yard Lombard-ſtreet*, 1681.

TITLE OF PENN'S "SOME ACCOUNT OF THE PROVINCE OF PENNSILVANIA" was to be inflicted only in cases of murder or high treason ; a notable departure from the customary legislation of those days. In Massachusetts, for example, there were fifteen capital crimes, including such offences as idolatry, witchcraft, blasphemy, adultery, bearing false witness, and cursing or smiting one's parents.[1] In such wise, with his humane and reasonable policy, did Penn seek to draw men to his new colony. To all who should come he offered land at forty shillings (equivalent to something between $40 and $50) for a hundred acres, subject to a quit-rent of one shilling a year.

In April, 1681, Penn sent his cousin, William Markham, to be deputy-governor of Pennsylvania, and with him a letter to the colonists already settled west of the Delaware River : " My friends : I wish you all happiness, here and hereafter. These are to let you know that it hath pleased God, in his providence, to cast you within my lot and care. It is a business that, though I never undertook before, yet God has given me an understanding of my duty, and an honest mind to do it uprightly.

His letter to the colonists

Wm Markham

I hope you will not be troubled at your change and the king's choice, for you are now fixed at the mercy of no governor that comes to make his fortune great ; you shall be governed by laws of your own making, and live a free, and, if you will, a sober and industrious people. I shall not usurp the right of any, or oppress his person. God has furnished me with a better resolution, and has given me his grace to keep it. In short, whatever sober and free men can reasonably desire for the security and improvement of their own happiness, I shall heartily comply with, and in five months I resolve, if it please God, to see you. In the mean time pray submit to the commands of my deputy, so far as they

[1] *Colonial Laws of Massachusetts*, pp. 14–16.

THE

ARTICLES,
Settlement and Offices

Of the FREE

SOCIETY
OF

TRADERS
IN

PENNSILVANIA:
Agreed upon by divers

MERCHANTS
And OTHERS for the better

Improvement and Government
OF

TRADE
IN THAT

PROVINCE.

LONDON,

Printed for *Benjamin Clark* in *George-Yard* in *Lombard-street*,
Printer to the Society of *Pennsilvania*, MDCLXXXII.

TITLE OF "THE ARTICLES OF SETTLEMENT"

are consistent with the law, and pay him those dues (that formerly you paid to the order of the governor of New York) for my use and benefit, and so I beseech God to direct you in the way of righteousness, and therein prosper you and your children after you.   I am your true friend, — William Penn." [1]

So great was the success of the "holy experiment" that in the course of the first year more than twenty ships sailed A Quaker for the Delaware River,[2] carrying perhaps 3000 exodus passengers.   Penn did not come, as he had hoped, within five months of the date of his letter.   Business connected with the new colony was driving him, and probably for the next year not a man in the three kingdoms worked harder than he.   It is worthy of note that at this time he was chosen a Fellow of the Royal Society.   Devising a frame of government for his colony, making grants of land, sending out detailed instructions to his deputy, and keeping up a huge miscellaneous correspondence, consumed all his time.   In the midst of it all he did not forget to preach. He went with Fox one day to a meeting (once more an "unlawful assemblage" in Gracechurch Street !) ; and Fox informs us that while Penn was speaking "a constable came in with his great staff, and bid him give over and come down ; but William Penn held on, declaring truth in the power of God."   Late in the summer of 1682 he sailed for the New World, leaving his wife and children in England. Penn He sailed from Deal, in the ship Welcome, with a comes to the New hundred passengers, mostly Quakers.   In the two World months' voyage more than thirty of this company died of smallpox.   Toward the end of October Penn landed at Newcastle, amid the welcoming shouts of Dutch and Swedish settlers in woodland garb, the men in leather breeches and jerkins, the women " in skin jackets and linsey petticoats." [3]   Penn showed his deeds of enfeoffment, and

[1] Hazard's *Annals of Pennsylvania*, p. 502.
[2] Proud's *History of Pennsylvania*, i. 216.
[3] Watson's *Annals of Philadelphia*, i. 19.

two of the inhabitants performed livery of seisin by handing over to him water and soil, turf and twig.   Thence he went on to Upland, where there had been for some time a settlement.   Turning to his friend and shipmate, Thomas Pearson, he said, " Providence has brought us here safe.   Thou hast been the companion of my perils.   What wilt thou that I shall call this place ? "   " Call it Chester," re- Chester plied Pearson, who had come from that most quaint and beautiful city of old England.[1]   At this new Chester an

LETITIA COTTAGE, PENN'S HOUSE IN PHILADELPHIA

assembly was held, which passed sixty-one statutes known as the Great Law of Pennsylvania.   After visits to New York and Maryland, Penn sought the spot just above the confluence of the little Schuylkill and the great Delaware rivers, and there laid out the squarest and levelest city, no doubt, that our planet had ever seen.[2]   The plan was like a

[1] Smith's *History of Delaware County*, p. 139.   This Pearson was maternal grandfather of the painter, Benjamin West.   *Id.* p. 170.

[2] But not so level as it has since become.   Many inequalities have been smoothed out.

checkerboard, and the first streets were named after the trees and shrubs, pine and spruce, chestnut and walnut, sassafras and cedar, that grew luxuriantly in the areas now covered with brick and mortar.   The settlers at first came

Founding of Phila-delphia

more rapidly than log huts could be built, so that many were fain to become troglodytes for a while in caves along the river's bank.   Building went on briskly, and settlers kept coming, until by the end of 1683, this new Philadelphia, this City of Brotherly Love, contained 357 dwellings, many of them framed wooden houses, many of them stoutly built of bright red brick, and sometimes so uniform in aspect that a chalk-mark would seem needed to distinguish one from its neighbours, as in the Arabian tale of the Forty Thieves.   The great city on the Delaware, like the great city on the Hudson, had its characteristic features strongly marked from the very outset.

Penn was charmed with his woodland.   In a letter he exclaims, "O how sweet is the quiet of these parts, freed from the anxious and troublesome solicitations, hurries, and perplexities of woeful Europe!"   Again, he says, the land

Penn's opinion of the country

is like "the best vales of England watered by brooks ; the air, sweet ; the heavens, serene like the south of France ; the seasons, mild and temperate ; vegetable productions abundant, chestnut, walnut, plums, muscatel grapes, wheat and other grain ; a variety of animals, elk, deer, squirrel, and turkeys weighing forty or fifty pounds, water-birds and fish of divers kinds, no want of horses ; and flowers lovely for colour, greatness, figure, and variety. . . . The stories of our necessity [have been] either the fear of our friends or the scarecrows of our enemies ; for the greatest hardship we have suffered hath been salt meat, which by fowl in winter and fish in summer, together with some poultry, lamb, mutton, veal, and plenty

A fickle climate

of venison, the best part of the year has been made very passable." [1]   As regards the climate, however, the writer does not find it always mild and temperate ; in

[1] Clarkson's *Life of Penn,* i. 350, 402.

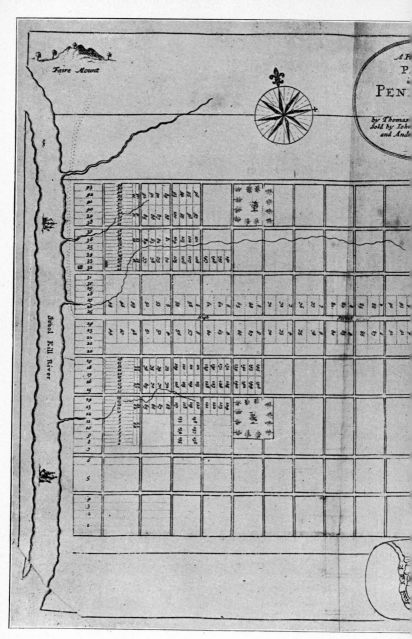

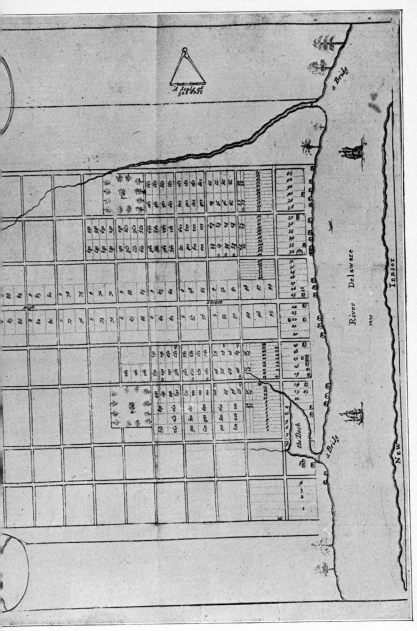

a Bridg

River Delaware

New Jersey

the Dock

a Bridg

a Bridg

A Scale of 528 Feet

A
LETTER
FROM
William Penn
Proprietary and Governour of
PENNSYLVANIA
In America,
TO THE
COMMITTEE
OF THE
Free Society of Traders
of that Province, residing in *London*.

CONTAINING

A General Description of the said *Province*, its *Soil, Air, Water, Seasons* and *Produce*, both Natural and Artificial, and the good Encrease thereof.

Of the *Natives* or *Aborigines*, their *Language, Customs* and *Manners, Diet, Houses* or *Wigwams, Liberality, easie* way of *Living, Physick, Burial, Religion, Sacrifices* and *Cantico, Festivals, Government*, and their order in *Council* upon Treaties for Land, &c. their *Justice* upon *Evil Doers*.

Of the *first Planters*, the *Dutch, &c.* and the *present Condition* and *Settlement* of the said *Province*, and *Courts of Justice, &c.*

As also an Account of the CITY of

PHILADELPHIA
Newly laid out.

Its Scituation between two Navigable Rivers, *Delaware* and *Skulkill*,

WITH A

Portraiture or Plat-form thereof,

Wherein the Purchasers Lots are distinguished by certain Numbers inserted.

And the Prosperous and Advantagious Settlements of the *Society* aforesaid, within the said City and Country, &c.

Printed by Appointment of the said Committee, by Andrew Sowle, *at the Crooked-Billet in* Holloway-Lane *in* Shoreditch, 1 6 8 3:

TITLE OF "A LETTER FROM WILLIAM PENN"

another letter he says, " the weather often changeth without notice, and is constant almost in its inconstancy,"—an excellent description of nearly all weather in the United States, except on the coast of California.

One of the most famous events of Penn's first visit to the New World was his treaty with a tribe of Delawares or Lenapé Indians under the elm-tree at Shackamaxon. Documentary evidence concerning this affair is extremely deficient, but there is little doubt that such a treaty was made,[1] probably in November, 1682, at Shackamaxon, under a great elm which was blown down in 1810. There is no doubt that the Indians from the first were greatly pleased with Penn's looks and manners. None can appreciate better than the red man that union of royal dignity with affable grace which characterized the handsome young cavalier. A lady who was present at a conference between Penn and the Indians, near Philadelphia, gave some detailed accounts of it which were afterward used by the antiquarian John Watson: " She said that the Indians, as well as the whites, had severally prepared the best entertainment the place and circumstances could admit. William Penn made himself endeared to the Indians by his marked condescension and acquiescence in their wishes. He walked with them, sat with them on the ground, and ate with them of their roasted acorns and hominy. At this they expressed their great delight, and soon began to show how they could hop and jump; at which exhibition William Penn, to cap the climax, sprang up and outdanced them all! We are not prepared," continues the worthy Watson, " to credit such light gaiety in a sage Governor and religious Chief; but we have the positive assertion of a woman of truth, who said she saw it. There may have been very wise policy in the measure as an act of conciliation, worth more than a regiment of sharpshooters. He was then sufficiently young for any agility; and we remem-

The Shackamaxon treaty

Penn dances for the Indians

[1] *Memoirs of Pennsylvania Historical Society*, vol. iii. part 2, p. 143.

ber that one of the old journalists among the Friends incidently speaks of him as having naturally an excess of levity of spirit for a grave minister." [1]

The testimony of the "woman of truth" seems to me eminently credible, as the act was highly characteristic. Penn, like Frontenac, knew instinctively what chords in the Indian's nature to touch. The red men always remembered affectionately their *Onas*, for by this Algonquin word, meaning "feather" or "quill," they translated the name of Penn; the name thenceforth always designated the governor of Pennsylvania, and it was an unshakable Lenapé tradition that Onas was a good fellow.

Of the Shackamaxon covenant Voltaire pithily observes that it was "the only treaty between savages and Christians that was never sworn to and that was never broken." [2] The Quaker policy toward the red men was a policy of justice and truth, and deserves all that has been said in its praise. Nevertheless in connection with this subject sundry impressions have obtained currency which are not historically correct. Many people suppose that Penn's conduct, in paying the Indians for the land which he occupied, was without precedent. There could not be a greater mistake. The Dutch settlers of New Netherland were careful to pay for every tract of land which they

Some incorrect impressions

---

[1] Watson's *Annals of Philadelphia*, i. 56.

[2] "Il commença par faire une ligue avec les Américains ses voisins. C'est le seul traité entre ces peuples et les chrétiens qui n'ait point été juré et qui n'ait point été rompu." *Dictionnaire philosophique*, s. v. Quakers, in his *Œuvres*, Paris, 1785, tom. xliii. p. 18. A new sight it was indeed, he goes on to exclaim, that of a sovereign to whom everybody could say Thou and address him with hat on, etc.: "C'était un spectacle bien nouveau qu'un souverain que tout le monde tutoyaient, et à qui on parlait le chapeau sur la tête; un gouvernement sans prêtres, un peuple sans armes, des citoyens tous égaux à la magistrature près, et des voisins sans jalousie. Guillaume Pen pouvait se vanter d'avoir apporté sur la terre l'âge d'or, dont on parle tant, et qui n'a vraisemblablement existé qu'en Pensilvanie." But the good Voltaire, in his enthusiasm, gets his geography mixed up, and places Pennsylvania "au sud de Mariland."

took, and New York writers sometimes allude to this practice in terms which imply that it was highly exceptional.[1]
But similar purchases by the Puritan settlers of New England occurred repeatedly.   In the time of King Philip's
war, Josiah Winslow, governor of Plymouth, said, in a
report to the Federal Commissioners: "I think I can clearly
say that, before these present troubles broke out, the English did not possess one foot of land in this colony but what
was fairly obtained by honest purchase of the Indians."[2]
So the lands of the Providence plantation were bought

Purchases   from Canonicus by Roger Williams; the island of
of land
from   Aquedneck was duly paid for by Hutchinson and
Indians   Coddington; and Samuel Gorton obtained Shawo-
met by fair purchase.[3]   The first settlers of Boston found
in that neighbourhood a solitary survivor of an Algonquin
tribe extirpated by the recent pestilence, and they made a
payment for the land to him.   An Indian village at Beverly
was afterward bought from its tawny occupants for £6 6s.
8d., equivalent to about $158, which was more than Minuit
paid for Manhattan.   In 1638 Davenport's company bought
their New Haven lands for "12 coats of English cloth, 12
metal spoons, 12 hoes, 12 hatchets, 12 porringers, 24 knives,
and 4 cases of French knives and scissors;" and in 1666 the
pilgrims from the New Haven republic paid for the site of
Newark in "50 double hands of powder, 100 bars of lead; of
axes, coats, pistols, and hoes, 20 each; of guns, kettles, and
swords, 10 each; 4 blankets, 4 barrels of beer, 50 knives, 850
fathoms of wampum, 2 anchors of liquor, and 3 trooper's

[1] "Of this purchase [of Manhattan Island by Director Minuit], so
unique and rare an episode in the history of American colonization,
there fortunately exists unassailable proof."   Wilson, *Memorial History of the City of New York*, i. 158.

[2] See Hubbard's *Narrative*, 13.   For the general temper of New
England legislation for Indians, see *General Laws of Massachusetts*,
pp. 74–78; *General Laws of Connecticut*, pp. 32–34; *Plymouth Records*,
ii. 74, 89, 167; iv. 66, 109; Winthrop's *Journal*, i. 120; Trumbull's
History of Connecticut, i. 37.

[3] Arnold's *History of Rhode Island*, i. 70, 125; ii. 112.

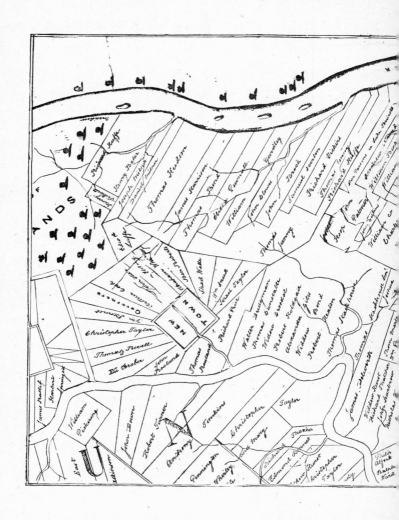

SECTION OF HOLME'S MAP OF PENNSYLVANIA, 1683

coats." So in 1610 Captain West bought the site of Richmond, in Virginia, from The Powhatan; in 1634 Leonard
Calvert bought the Algonquin village on St. Mary's River;
and in 1638 the Swedish settlers paid for their land on the
Delaware.[1]

It appears, therefore, that the custom of paying the
Indians a price for their lands was not peculiar to the
Quakers, or to the Quakers and Dutch. On the contrary,
the European settlers on the Atlantic seaboard of the
United States seem all to have entertained similar ideas on
this matter.

As for the proceedings at Shackamaxon, they seem certainly to have included the welding of a "chain of friendship," with the customary exchange of keepsakes and civil-
ities. Whether any treaty of purchase was then *The price
made is uncertain. At all events, it can hardly paid to
four Dela-
have been completed until a later date, for in 1685, ware chiefs*
after Penn's return to England, the council concluded a
negotiation with four chiefs — Shakkopoh, Sekane, Tangoras,
and Malibore — for a large tract of land extending from the
Delaware to the Susquehanna. The price paid was 44 lbs.
of red lead, 30 pair of hawks' bells, 30 fathoms of duffels,
60 fathoms of "Strandwaters;"[2] of guns, kettles, shirts,
combs, axes, knives, bars of lead, pounds of powder, pair
of scissors, pair of stockings, glasses, awls, tobacco-boxes, 30
each; 12 pair of shoes, 20 tobacco-tongs, 2 papers of beads,
6 draw-knives, 6 caps, 12 hoes, 200 fathoms of wampum.
The worthy chronicler who cites this curious inventory tells
us that he feels "almost ashamed" to name such a shabby
compensation;[3] but who can tell what might have been
an adequate price to the untutored Indian? We have no
standard by which to estimate such things.

Looking back at the situation from the vantage ground of

---

[1] See Ellis, *The Red Man and the White Man*, p. 337; and my
Old Virginia and Her Neighbours, Illustrated Edition, i. 260.

[2] *Duffels* and *Strandwaters* were coarse kinds of cloth.

[3] Watson's *Annals of Philadelphia*, i. 143.

our present knowledge, we must regard it as highly creditable to the early settlers in North America that they felt
bound to give the aborigines some compensation for the
lands of which they deprived them.   When this had been
done they could not understand why the Indians did not
remain satisfied.   But we can understand the case if we
remember that alike in all instances the transaction was not
like a free bargain and sale between members of a civilized
community ; it was much more like an exercise of eminent
domain, in which compensation is allowed.   The white men

A " confu-   came to America uninvited, and having come they
sion of   did not ask the red man's permission to stay.   It
title "   may be doubted if even William Penn would have
consented to abandon his " holy experiment " at the behest
or entreaty of Shakkopoh, Sekane, Tangoras, and Malibore.
It was said by Dr. Increase Mather that " the Lord God of
our fathers hath given to us for a rightful possession " the
lands of " the heathen people amongst whom we live," [1]
whereupon Dr. Ellis has wittily observed that " between
holding lands by fair purchase from the Indians and receiving them as a rightful possession from the Lord God, there
is certainly a confusion of title."   But in spite of the incon-
sistency, Mather gave expression to the principle upon
which all the colonizers implicitly acted.   Everywhere alike
the bottom fact in the situation was that the white man
came here to stay, without saying " By your leave."

It has often been said, and is commonly supposed, that
the kind and just treatment of the Indians by the Quakers
was the principal reason why more than seventy years
elapsed before Pennsylvania suffered from the horrors of

Incorrect   Indian warfare.   This opinion seems closely con-
notions
about red   nected with the notion that the red man is an
men   exceptionally high-minded and peaceably disposed
personage, who would never plunder and slay except under
the stimulus of revenge for grievous wrongs.   Such views

[1] Mather's *Brief History of the War with the Indians,* Boston,
1676, *ad init.*

appear to me inadequately supported. The red man is not, indeed, an unmitigated fiend, but in his wild state he is a man of the Stone Age, whose bloodthirsty policy is swayed by considerations of passion and self-interest, even as the policy of more civilized men is governed. The most successful way of managing him is to keep him impressed with the superior power of the white man, while always treating him with absolute justice and truthfulness. Great credit is due to the Quakers of Pennsylvania for their methods of dealing with the Indians. Their way was the right way, and their success is one of the bright features in American history. Nevertheless it seems to me quite clear that in the long peace enjoyed by Pennsylvania, the controlling factor was not Quaker justice so much as Indian politics. If Penn's colony had been placed in New England, in the days of Pequot supremacy, followed by the days of deadly rivalry between Narragansetts and Mohegans, it is not likely that its utmost efforts could have kept it clear of complications that would have brought on a war with the Indians. On the other hand, if the Puritans of New England had established themselves on the Delaware River about fifty years after the founding of Boston, they would almost certainly have been unmolested by Indians until after 1750. The powerful Iroquois tribe of Susquehannocks, after a long and desperate struggle with their kinsmen of the Long House, finally succumbed in 1675, left their old hunting-grounds, and wandered southward, working mischief in Maryland and Virginia. The red men with whom Penn made his Shackamaxon treaty were Algonquins, remnants of the once formidable confederacy of Lenni Lenapé, called Delawares. They had been so completely broken in spirit by repeated defeats inflicted by the Long House, that they had consented to a treaty in which they were described as "cowards" and "women," and humbly confessed themselves to be vassals and payers of tribute to the terrible Five Nations. Now the Long House, as we have seen, was the irreconcilable foe of Onontio, the power

Indian politics

on the St. Lawrence, and the steadfast friend of Corlear, the power on the Hudson, whether Dutch or English. By the same token it was bound to befriend Onas. For the next seventy years, if any misguided Lenapé had undertaken to ply the tomahawk among Penn's people, Corlear had but to say the word, and the waters of the Susquehanna would soon swarm with canoes of befeathered Senecas and Cayugas, eager for the harvest of Lenapé scalps. Under these circumstances a ruffianly policy, like that of Kieft in New Netherland, might have goaded the Delawares to hostilities; but nothing short of that could have done it. Practically Penn's colony occupied an exceptionally safe position until its westward growth brought it within reach of the Algonquin tribes on the Ohio. These facts in nowise diminish the credit due to the Quaker policy, but they help us to a rational view of the Indian situation.

Penn had much reason to feel contented with the success of his noble experiment. Within three years from its found-

Penn's
return to
England,
1684

ing Philadelphia had 2500 inhabitants, while in the whole province there were more than 8000, — a growth as great as that of New Netherland in its first half century. Having made such an auspicious beginning, Penn heard news from England which made him think it desirable to return thither. He heard of Quaker meetings broken up by soldiers, and the worshippers sent to jail. His presence was needed. He sailed in August, 1684, and arrived at his home in Sussex early in October. He expected soon to return to America, but fifteen years were to elapse and strange vicissitudes to be encountered before he was able to do so.

CHAPTER XIII

DOWNFALL OF THE STUARTS

THE founding of Pennsylvania helped to accelerate the political revolution which had been preparing in New York ever since the first arrival of Andros. During the spring of 1680 many complaints against that energetic governor found their way across the ocean. Not only was fault found with his treatment of New Jersey, but it was said that he showed too much favour to Dutch shipping, and especially that he allowed Boston people to trade in furs with the Mohawks. These rumours led the duke to summon Andros to London in order to justify himself. The governor sailed in January, 1681, expecting to return so soon that he left Lady Andros in New York. He had little difficulty in satisfying the duke as to his official conduct, but during his absence serious troubles broke out in New York, which had been left in charge of Brockholls, the lieutenant-governor. The duke's customs' duties, which had been imposed in 1677 for three years, expired in November, 1680, and by some oversight Sir Edmund neglected to renew them by special ordinance. After he had gone, divers merchants refused to pay duties, and Brockholls did not feel sure that he had sufficient authority to renew them, a squeamishness for which the duke was far from thanking him. As soon as the merchants came to realize the weakness of the situation in which Brockholls was placed, the discontent which had smouldered during long years of autocratic rule burst forth in an explosion that had momentous consequences.

William Dyer, the duke's collector of customs at the port

Andros returns to England

Expiration of the customs law

of New York, detained sundry goods for non-payment of duties. He was promptly indicted for high treason in taking upon himself "regal power and authority over the king's subjects" by demanding the payment of taxes that were not legally due. Brought to trial before a special court, he began by pleading "not guilty," but after a while called in question the competency of the court. The case was a somewhat novel exhibition of legal ingenuity, which puzzled the judges, and it was decided to send Dyer over to England for trial. He was examined in London by the king's legal advisers, who found that he had "done nothing amiss," and presently he returned to New York to be "surveyor-general of his Majesty's customs in the American Plantations."

Indictment of William Dyer

The excitement over Dyer's case found vent in a clamorous demand for a legislative assembly. People wagged their heads as they asked whether the arbitrary rule of a lord proprietor was any better than the arbitrary rule of a mercantile company. The old English and Dutch principle of "taxation only by consent" was loudly reiterated. At this juncture the duke's release of the Jerseys and the founding of Pennsylvania seemed to bring things to a crisis. Here, said the men of New York, in these new colonies, almost at their very door, no laws could be made and no taxes levied except by a colonial assembly of freemen. Why could not James Stuart conduct the business of government upon as liberal principles as his friends, Philip Carteret and William Penn? A petition was accordingly soon sent to the duke, in which the want of a representative assembly was declared an intolerable grievance. The document reached him at a favourable moment. He had been complaining that it was hard to raise a sufficient revenue in his province of New York, that his officers

Demand for a representative assembly

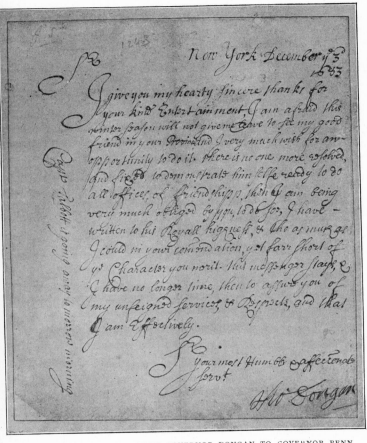

FACSIMILE OF A LETTER FROM GOVERNOR DONGAN TO GOVERNOR PENN

there were in difficulties and the air was full of complaints, so that he had half a mind to sell the country to anybody who would offer a fair price for it.   " What," cried William Penn, " sell New York !   Don't think of such a thing.   Just give it self-government and there will be no more trouble." James concluded to take the advice.   Andros was made a gentleman of the king's chamber and presented with a long lease of the island of Alderney.   In his place James sent a new governor to New York, with instructions to issue the writs for an election of representatives.   With all his faults and in spite of his moroseness, this Stuart prince had many Thomas   excellent men attached to him ; and the new gov-
Dongan   ernor for New York was one of the best of them, Colonel Thomas Dongan, an Irishman of broad statesman-like mind and all the personal magnetism that the Blarney stone is said to impart.   His blithe humour veiled a deep earnestness of purpose, long experience with Frenchmen had fitted him to deal with the dangers that were threatening from Canada, and while he was a most devout Catholic none could surpass him in loyalty to Great Britain and its government.

The arrival of Governor Dongan in New York, with the news of his errand, was hailed with vociferous delight.   The assembly was duly elected and held its first meeting in The first   Fort James on the 17th of October, 1683.   Its com-
assembly,   position forcibly reminds us of what places the
1683   Duke of York's province consisted.   The places represented were Schenectady, Albany, Rensselaerwyck, Esopus, Harlem, New York, Staten Island, Long Island (under the name of Yorkshire in three districts called " ridings "), Martha's Vineyard and Nantucket, and distant Pemaquid.   There were in all eighteen representatives.[1]   Several

[1] This assembly divided New York and its appendages into twelve counties, the names of some of which are curious : New York, Westchester, Dutchess (after the duke's new wife, Mary of Modena), Albany, Ulster (after the duke's Irish earldom), Orange (after William, the duke's Dutch son-in-law, destined to supplant him), Richmond (probably after Louise de Keroualle's bastard), Kings, Queens, Suffolk

wholesome laws were passed, and an admirable charter was drawn up and sent to England for the duke's approval. All this took some time, and before he had signed the charter an event occurred which wrought many changes. In February, 1685, a stroke of apoplexy carried off Charles II., and the duke became king. His proprietary domain of New York thus became a royal province, one among a group of colonies over which he now exercised similar and equal control, and his policy

SEAL OF DONGAN CHARTER

toward it was altered. He did not sign the charter, but let it lie in abeyance while he was turning over in his mind an alternative scheme the outcome of which we shall presently see.

Meanwhile the sagacious Dongan had his hands as full as they could hold of French and Indian diplomacy. Iroquois Happily the determining feature of the situation politics was in his favour. We have seen how the pivotal fact in

(a good name for such a Puritan county), Duke's (including Martha's Vineyard and neighbouring islands), and Cornwall (comprising the Maine districts). See Brodhead's *History of the State of New York*, ii. 385, 386.

early American history was the alliance between the Five Nations and the white men on the Hudson River, first Dutch, afterwards English. We have seen how they dealt with the Dutch, exchanged peltries for muskets, and then entered upon a mighty career of conquest. How they destroyed the French missions in the Huron country in 1649 is one of the most lurid chapters in history. By Governor Dongan's time they had reduced to a tributary condition nearly all the tribes east of the Mississippi and north of the Ohio and Potomac. They had lately wiped out of existence the formidable Susquehannocks, and now guaranteed the safety of Penn's new colony. We have seen how in 1675 they bestowed upon Andros the title of "Corlear," and promised to befriend the English as they had befriended the Dutch. Were they ready to go further, if need be, and attack Onontio himself, the Great White Father, in his strongholds upon the St. Lawrence? It was more than they had yet undertaken, and these dusky warriors of the Stone Age well knew the prowess of the soldiers of France. Dongan with a statesman's foresight knew that a deadly struggle between France and England for supremacy in this wilderness must soon begin, and his military eye saw that the centre of the fight must lie between the Hudson and the St. Lawrence. Either Louis XIV. must be checkmated in Canada or he would drive the English from New York. So Dongan's hands were full of Indian diplomacy as he sought to fan the fires of hatred in the Mohawk valley. His opponent, the Marquis Denonville, viceroy of Canada, was also an astute and keen-witted man, as one had need to be in such a position. No Russian game of finesse on the lower Danube was ever played with more wary hand than the game Some spicy between those two old foxes. While their secret letters emissaries prowled and intrigued, their highnesses exchanged official letters, usually polite in form, but sometimes crusty, and always lively enough, despite the dust of these two hundred years. On one occasion the Frenchman lectures Dongan for allowing West India rum to be sent to

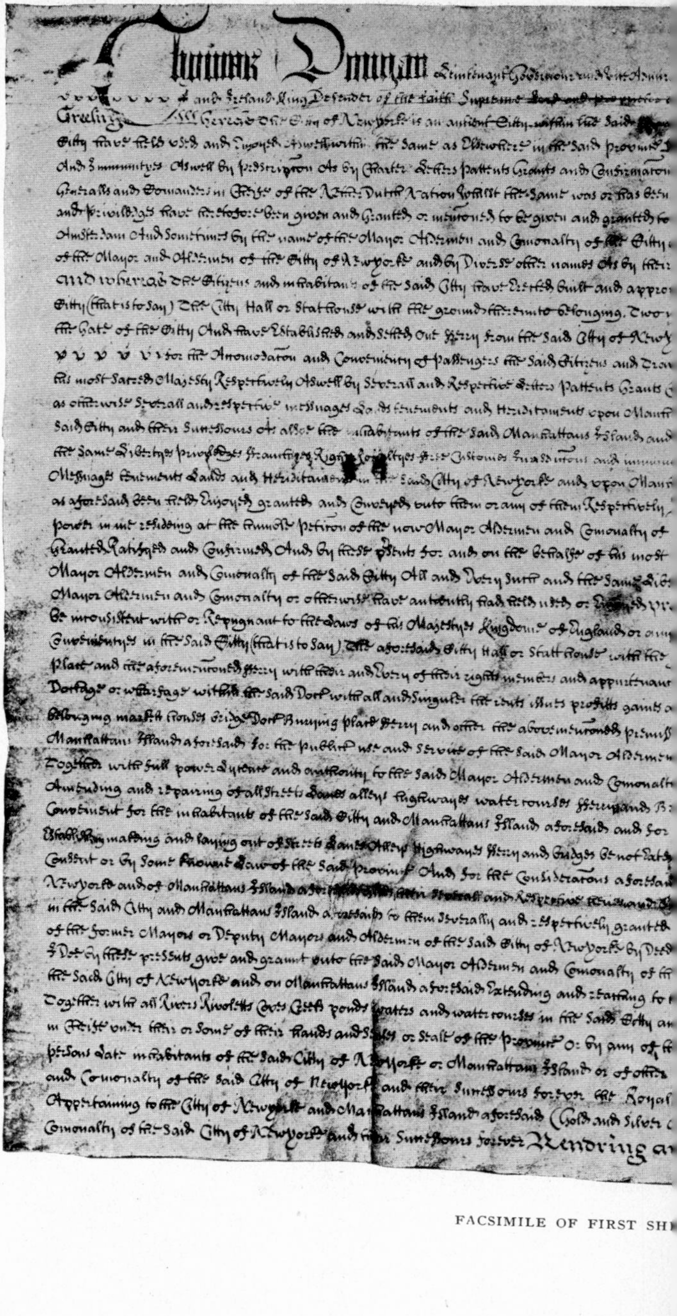

N CHARTER OF 1686

the Long House. "Think you that religion will make any progress, while your traders supply the savages in abundance with the liquor which, as you ought to know, converts them

LOUIS XIV

into demons and their wigwams into counterparts of hell?" One seems to see the Irishman's tongue curl under his cheek as he replies, "Methinks our rum doth as little hurt as your brandy, and in the opinion of Christians is much more wholesome." But presently the marquis gets a chance for a little fling. Dongan writes at the end of a letter, "I desire you would order Monsieur de Lamberville [1] that soe long as he stays among those people of the Five Nations he would meddle only with the affairs belonging to his priestly function. Sir, I send you some oranges, hearing that they are a rarity in your parts." In Denonville's reply the polite attention is thus acknowledged : "Monsieur, I thank you for your oranges. It is a great pity that they were all rotten." [2]

In this diplomatic duel the Blarney stone prevailed, and a black and grewsome war-cloud began gathering over Canada. Meanwhile in a chamber of the palace at Versailles the king was maturing his counterplot with the aid of a greater than Denonville, the wily and indomitable Frontenac. That picturesque veteran, now more than seventy years of age, was coming back to Canada, to undertake what

Plan of Louis XIV. for conquering New York

could be entrusted to no one less fertile in resources. In a word, he was to surprise New York and wrest it from the English, as the English had wrested it from the Dutch. A force of 1000 French regulars with 600 Canadian militia was to pounce upon Albany and there to seize boats, canoes, and small sloops wherein to glide merrily down the river. In New York harbour a French fleet would arrive in season to meet this force, which no defences there were fit to resist. With the capture of New York the supply of firearms to the Long House would cease. The French could then overcome that barbaric confederacy, after which their hands would be free to undertake the conquest of New England. Such was the ambitious scheme of the Most Christian King, but before coming to the latter part of it, New York, the first conquest, must be purged of its damnable heresies. The few Catholic inhabitants must swear allegiance to Louis XIV., and would then be protected from harm. Huguenot refugees were to be sent back to France. All the rest of the people were to be driven to the woods to shift for themselves. Their houses and lands were to be parcelled out

[1] A Jesuit very adroit and busy in political intrigue.
[2] *New York Colonial Documents*, iii. 462–465, 472.

among the French troops ; all their personal property was to be seized and a certain amount of it divided among the troops ; the rest was to be sold at auction and the money paid over into the French treasury.[1]

With these amiable instructions Frontenac was sent to Canada, but when he arrived, in October, 1689, he found things not as he had expected. It was indeed already known in France that the black war-cloud had burst over the colony, but the horrors of that summer had not yet been told. In all directions the ruins of smoking villages bore witness to the frightful ravages of the Iroquois. The environs of Montreal were a scene of mournful desolation, the town itself had barely escaped capture, and the inhabitants, who had looked out upon friends roasted and devoured before the very gates, were sick with terror. It became necessary for Frontenac to send a force at once to Lake Ontario, where the French had abandoned Fort Frontenac after an unsuccessful attempt to destroy it, so that the Iroquois had forthwith occupied it and got hold of more muskets and ammunition than the red man's boldest fancy had ever dreamed of. The fur trade from the upper lakes had been cut off for two years, and so great had been the destruction of property that a military expedition down the Hudson was utterly out of the question.

The Iroquois defeat the plan

Thus it was that the scheme of Louis XIV. against New York collapsed at the outset, and thus it soon sank into oblivion, so that we are liable to forget how much we owe to those dreadful Iroquois. Meanwhile in these six years how had it fared with the knightly Irishman and his fair province ? James, as we have seen, had undertaken to grant constitutional government to New York, and was about ready to sign a charter, when suddenly he became king and changed his mind. This change of purpose had a military reason.

Plan of James II. for uniting all the northern colonies

---

[1] *Mémoire pour servir d'Instruction sur l'Entreprise de la Nouvelle York, 7 juin*, 1689 ; *New York Colonial Documents*, ix. 422.

In order to oppose a more solid front to Canada, James wished to unite all his northern colonies under a single military governor. Circumstances seemed to favour him. Massachusetts, the most populous and powerful of the colonies, had sustained a bitter quarrel with Charles II. during the whole of that king's reign, until just before his death he had succeeded in getting a chancery decree annulling the charter of Massachusetts. In 1686 James II. sent Sir Edmund Andros to Boston to assume the government over all New England. Poor little Plymouth had never had a charter, and those of Connecticut and Rhode Island might be summarily seized. As for New York, the king revoked his half-granted charter and annexed that province to New England. New Jersey soon met the same fate, and legal proceedings were begun

Sir Edmund Andros viceroy of New England

Fr: Nicholson

against the charter of Maryland. Apparently nothing was safe except the sturdy infant colony of William Penn, whose good-will the king could not afford to alienate.

In August, 1688, Andros came in state to New York, and with due ceremonies the seal of that province was broken in his presence, and the seal of united New England was ordered to be used in its stead. Ex-Governor Dongan remained in the neighbourhood for about a year, attending to some private business, and then went home to Ireland, where he afterwards became Earl of Limerick. After a stay of two months in New York and Albany, Sir Edmund Andros returned to Boston in October, 1688, carrying off with him such of the New York public records as he wished to have on hand for reference, and leaving Francis Nicholson behind as his representative and lieutenant. No wonder if the good people on Manhattan Island resented this unceremonious treatment. Thus to

New York annexed to New England

ignore their natural and proper sentiments of local patriotism, and summarily annex them to New England, was
an outrage of the worst sort, and put a severe strain upon
such feelings of loyalty as they may have cherished toward
James II.

But the strain did not endure long.   The rule of Andros
in Boston had already become insupportable.   Arbitrary
taxes were imposed, common lands were encroached upon,
and the writ of *habeas corpus* was suspended.   The rule of
A strict and vexatious censorship was kept over   Andros in
Boston
the press.   All the public records of the late New
England governments were ordered to be brought to Boston,
whither it thus became necessary to make a tedious journey
in order to consult them.   All deeds and wills were required
to be registered in Boston, and excessive fees were charged
for the registry.   It was proclaimed that all private titles to
land were to be ransacked, and that whoever wished to have
his title confirmed must pay a heavy quit-rent, which under
the circumstances amounted to blackmail.   The representative assembly was abolished.   The power of taxation was
taken from the town meetings and lodged with the governor.
And when the town of Ipswich, led by its pastor, John
Wise, one of the most learned and eminent men in his time,
made a protest against this crowning iniquity, the sturdy
pastor was thrown into prison, fined £50 (*i. e.* at least
$1000), and suspended from the ministry.   In view of such
facts the evil repute acquired by Andros in New England
cannot well be said to have been undeserved.   He earned it
by obeying too thoroughly the orders of a master whose
conduct Englishmen could not endure.   Early in 1688 a
commission headed by Increase Mather, president of Har-
vard College, was sent over to England to expostulate with
James II.   They found England aglow with the spirit of
rebellion.   The flames burst forth when on the 5th of
November (Guy Fawkes's day!) the Prince of Orange
landed in Devonshire.   Before Christmas the last Stuart
king had fled beyond sea, leaving a vacant throne.

It was of course a moment of engrossing business for the great Dutch prince, and he took the occasion to prepare a short letter for the American colonies enjoining it upon them to retain all King James's arrangements undisturbed for the present until leisure should be found for revising them.   Dr. Mather did not wish to have any such instructions sent to Boston, for he saw in them the possibility that Andros might hold over until it would be awkward to get rid of him without interfering with some plan of William III.   By skilful pleading with the new king, in which he was aided by Sir William Phips, the wily Mather succeeded in delaying the departure of the letter.   This was in February, 1689, and it was not until late in March that the flight of James II. and the success of the Prince of Orange became known in Massachusetts.   The glowing embers of rebellion were quickly fanned into a blaze.   On the 18th of April armed yeomanry began pouring into Boston in response to the signal on Beacon Hill, and Sir Edmund saw that his hour had come.   He tried to escape to the Rose frigate in the harbour, in the hope of finding a refuge in New York, but his Puritan foes had no mind to let him off so easily. He was seized and securely lodged in jail, and several of his agents and abettors were also imprisoned, among them Chief Justice Dudley, who had lately had the impudence to tell the people of New England that the only liberty left them was that of not being sold for slaves.

Dr. Mather detains King William's letter

Overthrow of Andros

Massachusetts then at once restored her old government as it was before her charter was annulled, and she caused this to be announced in England, explaining that it was done provisionally until the new king's pleasure should be known.   Obviously the improvement in her position through Dr. Mather's astuteness was great. No one could interpret her rebellion as aimed at any other sovereign than the dethroned James. Instantly the other New England colonies followed suit. Plymouth, Rhode Island, and Connecticut quietly resumed

The old governments restored in New England

their old governments. James's consolidated New England thus fell to pieces.

There were people in New York upon whom these events were not for a moment lost. The lieutenant-governor, Francis Nicholson, was in an awkward position. If Andros had come away in the Rose frigate to New York, where he could direct affairs from Fort James, all would have been simple enough. If he had been killed there would have been no difficulty, for Nicholson would have become acting-governor. But as Andros was only locked up, Nicholson did not know just in what light to regard himself or just how much authority to assume. He belonged to that large class of commonplace men who are afraid of assuming responsibility.   So he tried to get messages to Andros in his Boston jail, but found very little counsel or comfort in that way.

Nicholson's government in New York was supported by three members of the council.   They were Dutch citizens of the highest social position : Frederick Philipse, the richest man in the province, Stephanus van Cortlandt, mayor of New York, and Nicholas Bayard, colonel of the city regiment of train-bands.   The other members of the council *Rumours of war* were scattered, some of them as far away as Pemaquid.   These three were the only ones present in the city.   On the 26th of April they heard of the imprisonment of Andros, and the very next day they heard that Louis XIV. had declared war against Great Britain and the Netherlands.   This report was premature, for war was not declared until May 7th, but the very air was full of premonitions of that bloody struggle which was to last for eight years.   Small blame to Nicholson and his three councillors if the grim tidings disturbed them !   Small blame to the mass of worthy citizens if something like a panic was created !   There were many Huguenot refugees in the city ; they had been coming for several years, and especially for the last four years since the king had revoked the Edict of Nantes ; and they had been received with warm welcome.   They knew, as everybody knew, that Louis XIV. had a very long arm.   There was never a time when an attack by France seemed more formidable than in 1689.   The king had not yet been cast down from his pinnacle of military glory, and the spirit of Catholic propagandism had been taking fuller and fuller possession of him. We now know what his truculent purpose was with regard to New York.   Frontenac was just starting to execute it. Of course the burghers of New York did not know of those

secret instructions to Frontenac, but they understood perfectly the danger of the situation.   As for the frightful blow
with which the Iroquois baffled the scheme of Louis XIV.
(which for the sake of clearness we have mentioned by an-
ticipation), it did not come till the summer of 1689, and still
further time was needed to disclose its effects.   In the
spring of that year it was still in the future.

It was not at all strange, then, that the elements of an
anti-Catholic panic were rife in New York.   Other things
contributed to destroy confidence and make men   Causes of
distrustful of one another.   In spite of all pre-   the anti-
                                                    Catholic
tences of liberality, it had always been the design   panic
of James II. to force the Catholic faith upon the American

colonies ; so he afterwards told Pope Innocent XI.[1]   People
were not wrong, then, in suspecting him.   The two regi-
ments of regular troops which Andros had brought to
America were made up of Irish Catholics, and one had been
commanded by Nicholson, who was now in command of
New York.   Nicholson was really an Episcopalian, but it
was rumoured that he had knelt at the Mass once on Houns-
low Heath in the presence of King James, and many people
believed him to be a Papist in disguise.

At the first news of war Nicholson directed the city
train-bands to take turns in guarding Fort James, and a
watch was placed upon Coney Island to look out for French

[1] Brodhead, *History of the State of New York*, ii. 531.

ships. The money collected as revenue was placed within
the fort for safety, and the new receipts after May-
day were to be applied to building new fortifications. At this juncture a cargo of wine arrived
from Europe, consigned to a well-known wine-merchant,
Jacob Leisler. The duty was about a hundred pounds
sterling, and Leisler refused to pay it, on the ground that
Matthew Plowman, collector of the port, was a Roman
Catholic, and that since King James's flight no duly qualified government existed in New York.

Jacob Leisler refuses to pay duties

This Jacob Leisler was a German of humble origin, born
at Frankfort-on-the-Main. In earlier days he had been a soldier in the pay of the West India Company, and had come
to New Amsterdam a few years before its capture by the
English. A residence of thirty years had made
him one of the most prosperous and conspicuous
citizens. Through his marriage with Elsie Tymens, a niece
of Anneke Jans, he had become connected with the aristocracy, but was not cordially welcomed among such people.
One can imagine that Van Cortlandt and Bayard might not
feel proud of such a connection, and that occasions would
be afforded for Leisler to cherish resentment. Indeed,
there had been a bitter quarrel, with one or two lawsuits between Leisler and these two gentlemen, so that their families were not on speaking terms. Leisler was a man of
integrity, noted for fair and honourable dealing in matters
of business. We hear, too, that he was kind-hearted and
generous with money. But he was evidently of coarse fibre,
ignorant, stubborn, and vain, — just the man to be seized
and dominated by a fixed idea. His letters are those of a
man with too little education to shape his sentences correctly. He seems to have had something of the heresy-
hunting temper, for we have already met him once in this
narrative as deacon of Nieuwenhuysen's church, bringing
charges of "false preaching" against Dominie Van Rensselaer, losing his suit, and getting saddled with the costs of
it. But his ruling passion was hatred of Popery, and his

Character of Leisler

dominant idea was rooted in the dread of it. He could see no good in any Romanist; his eyes were blind to the loyal virtues of such a man as Dongan, who was quite above and beyond his ken; he believed Nicholson to be a Papist. These men had been servants of James Stuart, who was now harboured by the French king; what were they staying about New York for if not to deliver it into the hands of the enemy? The Boston men had struck with promptness and decision, New York must do the same, and Jacob Leisler would be God's instrument in bringing this to pass.

Besides this dread of Popery, there was another feeling that Leisler represented. Long-continued arbitrary taxation and the repeated failure to obtain representative government had caused much popular discontent. Though the population of the little city was scarcely more than 4000 souls, a distinction of classes was plainly to be seen. Without regard to race, the small shopkeepers, small farmers, sailors, shipwrights, and artisans were far apart in their sympathies from the rich fur traders, patroons, lawyers, and royal officials. The general disappointment sharpened the distrust felt toward people in high station, especially toward such as had accepted office from the Catholic king, who had not kept his promises. Vague democratic ideas and hopes still hazier were in the air. Along with the indignation at the recent attempt to annex the province to New England, there was exuberant pleasure in the thought that the throne was now to be occupied by a Dutch king; and there was a dim half-shaped notion that a prompt and fervid expression of allegiance to William of Orange would be helpful in winning from him a grant of popular liberties. Coupling all this with the fear that James's officials might betray the city to the French, we find, I think, a certain coherence among the notions that were teeming in Leisler's rugged and fanatical mind. A wealthy and prominent citizen, he was in lack of refinement and education like the mob, and so had its confidence, which was no doubt enhanced by his known integrity and energy.

Vague democratic ideas

He may well have deemed himself marked out for the leader
of a popular movement, and believed that he could establish
a claim upon the good graces of William III. by saving for
him his province of New York despite the diabolical plots
of Catholic officials and the Dutch aristocrats who supported them ; for although such men as Bayard and Van
Cortlandt were thorough Protestants and deacons in the
Dutch Reformed Church, they were none the less to Leisler's distorted fancy a " crew of Papistical renegades."

It is clear that the feelings which found vent in Leisler's
conduct had long been gathering in this little community.
His refusal to pay his tax was followed by other refusals.
Nicholson's act in sheltering the public revenues within the
fort was interpreted as part of a deep-laid plan for using
them against the people.   All through the month of May

Fears of a
French
attack

agitated whispers ran about the town ; a French
fleet was coming, and traitors in power were ready
to welcome it.   Popular imagination filled the woods
on Staten Island with emissaries of Louis XIV., and it was
said that Nicholson had gone over there by night to consult
with them.   Dongan was down at Navesink, getting his
armed brigantine ready to take him back to England ; in
that golden age of pirates it was necessary for ships to go
armed ; that innocent vessel was supposed to be intended
for a part in the plot.

At last on May 30 Nicholson got into an altercation with
an insubordinate lieutenant in Captain De Peyster's train-
band.   " Who commands this fort, you or I ? " shouted the
angry governor.   Probably the lieutenant made some reference to the city being in danger, which caused Nicholson

Nicholson's
rash excla-
mation

to retort, " I would rather see the city on fire than
take the impudence of such fellows as you," or
words to that effect.   What he really said may
have been quite different in purport, but at all events fire
was mentioned, and that was fire enough to kindle insurrection.   The rash remark was overheard, it was said that
the governor had threatened to burn the town, and next

morning the streets were in an uproar. Leisler himself was captain of one of the train-bands. His company, led by Joost Stoll, the sergeant, marched to Fort James, shouting,

WILLIAM III. OF ORANGE

"They have betrayed us, and are going to murder us." The lieutenant whom Nicholson had upbraided let them into the fort, and presently Leisler arrived there and took command. That afternoon while Nicholson and his three councilmen were in the City Hall discussing the situation, Captain Lodwyck, at the head of his company, entered the chamber and demanded the keys of the fort. There was no help for it, so the keys were given him.

Leisler takes command of the fort

Two days of uncertainty followed, while Leisler seems to have been contending with sundry symptoms of timidity and scrupulousness on the part of some of the other captains.   On June 3, an English ship from Barbadoes arrived at Sandy Hook.   Rumour transformed her first into a French ship and then into a French fleet.   Amid wild excitement the militia turned upon their captains and forced them to

Leisler's "Declaration"

sign a "Declaration" prepared by Leisler, in which he announced that since the city was in danger and without any properly authorized government, he proposed in behalf of the people to hold the fort until King William should send some duly accredited person to

Nicholson sails for England

take command.   When this announcement was read aloud to the multitude it was greeted with deafening hurrahs.   One week from that day the discomfited Nicholson sailed for England in Dongan's brigantine.   He thought it best to see the king at once and make his own report.   His departure left the three councilmen as the only regular representatives of royal authority in the province.   But Leisler now assumed more dignity. Some of the insurrectionary party declared that there had been no lawful Christian government in England since the death of Oliver Cromwell.   Leisler likened himself to Cromwell.   He had turned out the traitors and the time had come when the Lord Jehovah must rule New York through the sword in the hands of his saints.   News came that the new sovereigns William and Mary had been officially proclaimed at Hartford, and that post-riders were on their way to New York with a copy of the proclamation. Mayor Van Cortlandt and Colonel Bayard rode many miles out into the country to meet them, but Leisler's emissaries got ahead of those gentlemen and secured the proclamation first, so that next day it was read aloud by Leisler himself in the fort and by one of his captains in the City Hall, and he could claim the credit of having proclaimed the new sovereigns.   At the same time he ordered that Fort James should henceforth be called Fort William.

On the 24th of June a copy of that royal proclamation which Dr. Mather had withheld from the knowledge of Boston reached New York and found its way into the hands of Mayor Van Cortlandt. It continued all King James's appointments provisionally until King William should have time to review the situation. Obviously, then, the government of New York, since The king's proclamation the imprisonment of Andros and the departure of Nicholson, was legally vested in the councilmen Philipse, Van Cortlandt, and Bayard. If this proclamation had arrived a month earlier it would have cut away the ground from under Leisler's feet. Now he had such consolidated popular support as to venture to defy it on grounds of his own. King William was evidently ignorant of the situation. He never would willingly have entrusted responsible command

Jacob Leisler

to these "popishly affected, lying dogs," not he. These rogues must be put down, and the king must be told why. The very next day Leisler turned the city government out of doors, and two or three gentlemen were roughly handled by the soldiers, but Bayard Leisler appointed commander-in-chief escaped and made his way to Albany. Leisler called a convention, and a committee of safety was organized which appointed him commander-in-chief over the whole province.

While these things were going on, Nicholson was in mid-ocean on his way to England. The king, in ignorance of what had occurred, addressed a letter to him with words of advice and counsel; the letter was not The king's letter addressed to Nicholson by name, but to "Our lieutenant-governor and commander-in-chief of our province of New York in America." After sundry vicissitudes this letter reached New York early in December and was received by

Leisler, who understood it to be addressed to himself.[1]   His
vanity was tickled to the bursting point.   He had sent his
friend, Joost Stoll, keeper of a dram-shop, and rather a laugh-
able sort of envoy, to explain matters to the king;
and now, doubtless, this was the response!   So
Leisler at once assumed the title of Lieutenant-
Governor, appointed a council, and took his seat
next Sunday in the gubernatorial pew at church, to the
intense disgust and chagrin of the aristocrats among the
worshippers.

*Leisler as-
sumes the
title of
lieutenant-
governor.*

The summer and autumn had been peaceful, save now and
then for a few arbitrary arrests.   But now troubles began
to thicken about Leisler.   As governor he needed revenue
and began to look at the collection of taxes from a new point

---

[1] The circumstances under which Leisler obtained the letter should
be noted.   The bearer of the king's despatches, John Riggs, expected
to deliver it to the three councilmen, but in passing through Boston he
was told that he ought to deliver it to Leisler, who was actually in command at New York.   To Riggs, coming from England, this was puz-
zling, for he was sure that there was nothing in the packet intended
for any such person as Leisler.   When Riggs arrived in New York
late at night, he met Philipse and Bayard at the latter's house, and they
sent for Van Cortlandt, who was out of town.   On Van Cortlandt's
arrival next morning, Riggs would have delivered the packet to the
three councilmen in presence of each other.   But early in the morning
Leisler sent a party of soldiers who arrested Riggs and took him to
Fort William.   Van Cortlandt and Philipse, hearing of this, followed
him thither, and an altercation ensued, in which Leisler called them
rogues and papistical dogs who had nothing to do with government.   He
showed Riggs his commission from the council of safety, and prevailed
upon him to deliver the packet to himself.   He gave Riggs a written
receipt for the packet.

No doubt Leisler, as a " crank " with his brain dominated by a narrow group of morbid fixed ideas, believed that King William, the Protestant, could not possibly have intended his letters to be received by
three ex-officials of King James, the Catholic.   His subsequent logic, on
opening the letter to Nicholson and understanding it to be addressed to
himself, was crank logic.   Leisler seems to have felt that others might
dispute his conclusion, for he never allowed the contents of the letter
to be made public.

A Modest and Impartial

NARRATIVE

Of several Grievances and

Great Oppressions

That the Peaceable and most Considerable Inhabitants

OF

Their Majesties Province

OF

NEW-YORK

IN

AMERICA

Lie Under,

By the Extravagant and Arbitrary Proceedings of *Jacob Leysler* and his Accomplices.

TITLE OF "A MODEST AND IMPARTIAL NARRATIVE," 1690

of view.   In default of any new statute, he proclaimed that

He revives the Colonial Act of 1683 the Colonial Act of 1683 with regard to customs and excise was still valid and would be rigorously enforced.   That act, albeit passed by New York's first popular assembly,[1] that assembly so long desired and prayed for, had never enjoyed popular favour ; doubtless because it put an end to the two years of free trade which had ensued upon the departure of Andros in 1681.   The history of this piece of legislation was extremely curious. Passed by a popular assembly, it was disallowed by the Duke of York, but was nevertheless continued in operation by Governor Dongan and his council, for want of something better.   But neither under Dongan nor under Nicholson was it very strictly enforced.[2]   Now by adopting this unpalatable act the unhappy Leisler at once sacrificed a large part of his popular support.   People tore down the copies of his proclamation from the walls and trees where they were posted. Merchants declared his title unsound and refused to pay
His authority is defied duties to his collector.   He retorted savagely with fines and confiscations.   Men were dragged to prison till the jails were full.   The fact that he could keep up such a course shows how strong at the outset must have been the popular impulse that brought him into power.

Outside the city his authority was more easily defied. When he appointed new sheriffs and justices, and ordered the old ones to give up their commissions, he was sometimes obeyed but often openly derided.   Albany flatly refused to acknowledge his authority.   Late in the summer the mayor, Peter Schuyler, and his brother-in-law, Robert Livingston, called a convention and took measures for protection against the French, but they would have nothing to say to
Jacob Milborne Leisler.   About that time Leisler's old friend, Jacob Milborne, returned from a visit to Europe and became his most energetic supporter.   Milborne was an

[1] *Colonial Laws of New York*, Albany, 1894, i. 116–121.
[2] Leisler himself had refused to pay duties under it.   See Brodhead, *History of the State of New York*, ii. 599.

Englishman of Anabaptist proclivities. He had some book knowledge and some skill in writing, and was determined to have all the ills in the world mended, say by the year 1700. If he had lived in these days he would have edited some anarchist newspaper. Leisler deemed him a treasure of knowledge and capacity and sent him up the river with three sloops to tame the frowardness of Albany. His persuasive tongue won a number of adherents and succeeded in sowing some seeds of dissension, but Livingston and Schuyler were too much for him, and his mission was unsuccessful.

This was in November, 1689, and Frontenac had arrived in Canada. As we have seen, the Iroquois had been there before him, and his grand scheme for conquering New York dwindled ignominiously into the sending of three scalping parties to destroy the most exposed frontier settlements of the Dutch and English. It was necessary to make some show of strength in order to retrieve in the minds of the Indians the somewhat shaken military reputation of The French the French. The Algonquin allies must be en- war-parties couraged and the Iroquois foes confounded, and there was nothing, of course, that the red men appreciated more highly than a wholesale massacre. The distances to be traversed were long and difficult, and this made it all the easier to surprise the remote villages that sometimes forgot to be watchful against the diabolism that lurked in the forest. The first of the three scalping parties was sent to the Hudson River, the second into New Hampshire, the third into Maine.

The first party consisted of 114 French Canadians skilled in all manner of woodcraft, and 96 Christian Indians ; their leaders were French noblemen, among them the famous LeMoyne d'Iberville, founder of Louisiana. The march of seventeen days was attended with terrible hardships. It was an alternation of thawing and freezing. On one day they were struggling against a blinding snowstorm, on another they were half drowned in the mud and slush of treacherous swamps, on another their ears and toes were frozen in the icy wind.   Their coats and blankets were torn to shreds in the stubborn underbrush, and their stock of food, dragged on sleds, was not enough, so that they had to be put on starving rations.   They could not have encountered more hardship if they had been a party of scientific explorers, and they fought their way through it all with the tenacity and the ferocious zeal of crusaders.   Their original plan was to strike at Albany, but as the limit of human endurance was approaching before they could accomplish the distance, they turned upon Schenectady, some fifteen miles nearer.   This little Dutch village was the extreme frontier outpost of the New York colony.   Its population numbered about 150 souls.   It was surrounded by a palisade and defended by a blockhouse in which there were eight or ten Connecticut militia.   The Leisler affair had bred civil dudgeon in this little community.   Most of the people were Leislerites.   The chief magistrate, John Glen, an adherent of Schuyler, was held in disfavour, and out of sheer spite and insubordination the people disobeyed his orders to mount guard.   They left their two gates open, and placed at each a big snow image as sentinel.   The idea that they could now be in danger from Canada, harrowed and humbled as it had lately been by their friends the Iroquois, they scouted as preposterous.   It was argued that the beaten French were not likely to be in a mood for distant expeditions.

The situation at Schenectady

   And so it happened that toward midnight of the 8th of February, 1690, in the midst of a freezing, lightly whirling and drifting snowstorm their fate overtook them.   The French war-party, haggard and glaring, maddened with suffering, came with crouching stealth and exultant spring, like a band of tigers.   Noiselessly they crept in and leisurely arranged themselves in a cordon around the sleeping village within the palisade, cutting off all escape.   When all was ready, a terrific war-whoop awoke the inhabitants to their doom.   " No pen can write and no tongue express," said brave old Peter Schuyler, "the

Massacre at Schenectady

Le Moyne D'Ieerville.

cruelties that were wrought that night." The work was
sharp and quick. About sixty were killed, and the other
ninety captured. Then the butchers paused to appease
their famine out of the rude cellars and larders of their
victims, and to sleep until morning the sleep of the just.
The Connecticut militia were all among the slain. The

magistrate was strongly fortified in his house on a hill outside the enclosure, but he was not attacked. He had more
than once rescued French prisoners from the firebrands of
the Mohawks, and in requital of this kindness Iberville not
only spared him and his family, but in a spirit of chivalry
gave back to him about sixty out of the ninety prisoners
with polite and edifying speeches. Before noon of the next
day, leaving Schenectady a heap of ashes, mangled corpses,
and charred timbers, the party started on its return march
to Montreal, carrying the other thirty prisoners to be tor-
tured to death in a leisurely and comfortable way. The
news of the disaster spread quickly through the Mohawk
valley, and a sturdy company of warriors of the Long House
pursued the French party with sleuth-hound tenacity until
near Montreal, when at last they overtook them and partially amended the reckoning by killing fifteen or twenty.

As a fresh demonstration of the danger from France, the
affair of Schenectady served to strengthen Leisler's
Albany
yields to   position. He sent Milborne with 160 men to aid
Leisler   in defending Albany. As it was not a time when
one would feel like refusing help from any quarter, Milborne
and his men were admitted into the town, and Leisler's authority was virtually recognized.

When in April, however, he issued writs for the election
of an assembly, his weakness was revealed. Im-
Election of
representa-   perative need of the sinews of war drove him to
tives   this step. Many people refused to pay taxes, and
it was necessary to call an assembly of representatives of
the people. But some towns refused to choose representatives on the ground that Leisler was usurping authority.
This tone was taken especially by the Puritan towns on
Long Island, which wished to be joined to Connecticut and
always welcomed a chance to annoy the government at New
York, whatever it might be.

Leisler's next step was a memorable event in American
history. He called for a Congress of American colonies to
concert measures of attack upon Canada ; and this Congress,

the first of a series which was by and by to end in the great Continental Congress, assembled in New York on the first of May, 1690. None of the southern colonies took part in it. The Carolinas were in their early infancy, Virginia was too remote to feel keenly interested. The task of invading Canada was shared between

The first American Congress, May, 1690

SIR WILLIAM PHIPS

New York, Massachusetts, Plymouth, Connecticut, and Maryland. There were to be 855 men from these colo-nies,[1] and the Iroquois sachems promised to add 1800 war-

[1] The several contingents were, New York 400, Massachusetts 160,

riors.   As finally carried out, a part of the expedition, under Sir William Phips, of Massachusetts, sailed up the St. Lawrence and laid siege to Quebec ; while the rest of the allied forces, under Fitz John Winthrop, of Connecticut, proceeded from Albany toward Montreal.   But these amateur generals were no match for Frontenac, and when they turned their faces southward it was with wiser heads but sadder hearts than when they started. Boston preachers, with bated breath, spoke of " this awful frown of God."   Leisler stormed and raved, and saw disguised Papists everywhere, as usual.   The affair ended in bitter recriminations, and Massachusetts was driven to issue paper money, which plagued her till Thomas Hutchinson got her out of the scrape in 1749.

Unsuccess-ful attempt to invade Canada

What a picturesque creature was Frontenac ! We can seem to see him now, aristocrat and courtier to the ends of his fingers, with his gleaming black eyes, the frost of seventy winters on his brow, and the sardonic smile on his lips, as he presides over a grim council of sachems ; we see him as he suddenly daubs vermilion on his cheeks and seizes a tomahawk, and leads off the war-dance, screaming like a cougar and inflaming to madness those warriors of the Stone Age.   Here it need only be said that after checkmating Leisler he devoted himself to clearing off scores with the Iroquois, and in 1696, in his seventy-eighth year, after one of the most remarkable forest campaigns on record, he dealt the Long House a blow from which it never quite recovered.   Again we may reflect how fortunate it was for New York that the Iroquois were there to serve as a buffer against this redoubtable foe.

Frontenac attacks the Long House

To go back to the May of 1690, the month of the Colonial Congress, — it saw Leisler's doom approaching.   His friend Joost Stoll brought him evil tidings from London. The king had not so much as deigned to look at that gro-

Plymouth 60, Connecticut, 135, Maryland 100 — total, 855 men. The New York contingent was disproportionately large ; on the other hand, Massachusetts furnished most of the naval force.

tesque ambassador. Not a scrap of notice or attention could he get from anybody. But the king had shown favour to Nicholson by making him lieutenant-governor of Virginia. Still worse, he had appointed Colonel Henry Sloughter to be governor of New York, and Major Richard Ingoldsby to be lieutenant-governor. New York was to have a free government with representative assemblies. One of the councilmen was to be Joseph Dudley, the founder of New England Toryism, who had been

Appointment of Henry Sloughter

chief aid and abettor of Andros in Boston. And worst of all, among the old members of the council now reappointed were Philipse and Van Cortlandt and Bayard. As for Jacob Leisler, his existence had not been so much as recognized. There was a terrible sound to this news. Leisler's violence had not spared these members of the council. He had accused them of conspiracy against him. He had seized Bayard and the attorney-general, William Nicolls, and kept them for months in prison and in irons, suffering doleful misery. Now these "Papist rogues," as his distempered fancy called them, were high in the great Protestant king's favour, while Jacob Leisler, most devoted of his Protestant servants, was ominously ignored! I think we may safely suppose that such facts were too much for that poor distorted mind to take in. How could such things be? Stoll must have been deceived; he was a sturdy old toper and must have got things muddled. His news was simply incredible.

Only on the supposition that Leisler's mind was half dazed can we explain his subsequent conduct, which finally reached the heights of madness. Months were yet to pass

before the catastrophe, for various affairs delayed the new
Leisler   governor and his party.   Meanwhile Leisler grew
loses   more and more tyrannical until petitions against
popularity   him were sent to London, the dominies came in and
rebuked him in the name of the Lord, old women taunted
and defied him on the street, and the mob threw stones
at him and called him "Dog driver," "Deacon Jailer,"
"Little Cromwell," "General Hog," and other choice epi-
thets.   The great democrat had fallen from grace.   It was
said that the wedding in January, 1691, when his young
daughter Mary was married to his staunch friend Milborne,
was more like a funeral than a wedding.

It seems proper here to make some mention of a historical novel, "The Begum's Daughter," by the late Edwin
Two his-   Lasseter Bynner, which is based upon the events
torical   of Leisler's time.   Though it does not rise to the
novels   very high level of the same author's "Agnes Sur-
riage," it is an extremely creditable piece of work.   As a
study in history, it reflects a trifle too closely, perhaps, the
bitter feelings of the aristocrats, but after making a slight
allowance for this, "The Begum's Daughter" gives us a
truthful picture of the time, and is worth reading by all who
are interested in American history.[1]

It was sorely against her will that Mary Leisler consented
to become the bride of Jacob Milborne.   It was generally believed that she entertained a very decided preference for Abraham Gouverneur, one of two young Huguenot
brothers, whose family has played an important part in
The mar-   American history.   Against poor Mary's submis-
riages of   siveness to her father's despotic and violent will,
Leisler's
daughters   Mr. Bynner has furnished us with an impressive
contrast in the character which he attributes to her younger
sister, Hester.   The element of domestic conflict needed

[1] Another story, *In Leisler's Times*, written by Mr. Elbridge Brooks
for young readers, but interesting also to older readers, shows a decided
leaning of sympathies in the opposite direction, and undoubtedly takes
more liberties with the records.

in the story is supplied by having Hester betrothed to the handsome and gallant son of Van Cortlandt, while her father is determined that she shall marry Barent Rynders, the sensible but ungainly son of a blacksmith. Hester's will is as strong as her father's, and in spite of his blustering threats, although nearly benumbed with terror, she shows herself as unyielding as adamant. But after the great catastrophe, when her aristocratic lover imprudently identifies himself with the scorn and hatred felt by his family for her unfortunate father's memory, the high-spirited girl instantly and irrevocably dismisses him. The novel skilfully surmounts whatever difficulties there may be in the way of her transferring her affections to the worthy Barent Rynders. Such situations afford fine opportunities for psychological treatment. As a matter of history, Hester Leisler married Rynders, while her widowed sister Mary, set free to consult her own inclinations, became the wife of the brilliant young Huguenot, Abraham Gouverneur. Mary's son, Nicholas Gouverneur, married Hester's daughter, Gertrude Rynders, and a son of this marriage, Isaac Gouverneur, was the grandfather of Gouverneur Morris, one of the ablest members of the immortal convention that framed the Constitution of the United States. This eminent statesman was thus lineally descended from Jacob Leisler through two of his daughters.

To go back to the winter day of 1691, which witnessed Mary's first dreary wedding, that same day saw the little fleet of the new governor, Henry Sloughter, far out on the broad Atlantic, struggling for its life. The ships were separated by the fury of the storm, and the Archangel frigate, with the governor on board, ran aground on one of the Bermuda Islands, and had to wait for repairs. The other three ships, in one of which was Ingoldsby, the lieutenant-governor, arrived in New York harbour on the 29th of January. A small force of regular troops was on board, and Ingoldsby sent word to Leisler to admit these soldiers into Fort William without delay. Leisler

Arrival of Ingoldsby

refused to recognize Ingoldsby's authority or to surrender the fort without a written order from King William or from Governor Sloughter. Unfortunately Ingoldsby had no official documents of any sort with him; they were all in the Archangel. After waiting four days he landed his troops with much circumspection and quartered them in the City

Leisler refuses to surrender the fort

Hall. He demanded the release of Bayard and Nicolls, whom the king had appointed as councilmen. But this simply infuriated Leisler, and confirmed him in a notion which he had begun to entertain, that Ingoldsby and his company were Catholic conspirators who had escaped from England and now wished to seize the fort and hold New York for King James.

In such wise did things remain for six weeks without any event of importance. Ingoldsby, aided by several of the newly named councilmen, began collecting militia to reinforce his regulars, but willingly took the advice of Governor Treat of Connecticut, that he should bear with Leisler as

Ingoldsby waits

patiently as possible until Sloughter's arrival should simplify the situation. Meanwhile Leisler received from Governor Treat and from many friends grave warnings to take heed what he was doing and stop before it should be too late.

All such friendly entreaties were lost upon the infatuated Leisler. On March 17th, quite losing his patience, he sent word to Ingoldsby to disband his forces, and gave him two hours to reply. Not getting a satisfactory answer, he fired upon the king's troops, and a few were killed and wounded.

Leisler fires upon the king's troops

And now occurred an incident of evil omen indeed. Leisler had ordered a militia garrison in the Vly blockhouse at the Water Gate to fire upon a party of Ingoldsby's troops in the Slip; but at this juncture the men threw down their arms, abandoned the blockhouse, and dispersed to their homes!

Nothing was done next day, but the next thereafter at nightfall the Archangel frigate arrived at the Narrows. Word was sent down to Sloughter to make all haste. He

came up the harbour in a boat, went straight into the
City Hall, and read aloud his commission as
royal governor.   After taking the oath of office he
sent Ingoldsby to demand the instant surrender
of Fort William, but with almost incredible fatuity Leisler
insisted upon retaining it until a written order from the
king addressed to him,
Jacob Leisler, by name
should be shown him.
Evidently the poor man's
mind was dazed.   That in view of all that had happened
the king should utterly ignore his faithful Protestant "lieutenant-governor" Leisler was a fact too strange for him to
grasp.   From a soul thus stiffened and benumbed no rational
conduct was to be expected.   Toward midnight a second
demand was made, and then Leisler sent the diplomatic
Milborne to explain that it was against the rules
to surrender the fort in the night.   Sloughter's
only reply was to make a sign to the guards, who forthwith
seized Milborne and dragged him off to jail.

In the morning Leisler sent a conciliatory letter to the
governor, disclaiming any wish to withhold the fort from
him, but asking further explanation on certain points.
Sloughter took no notice of the letter, but sent Ingoldsby
to order the garrison of Fort William to ground arms and
march out, promising full and free pardon to all concerned
in the late proceedings except Leisler and his council.   The
men instantly obeyed, and the forlorn usurper was left alone.
In a few moments Bayard and Nicolls, pale and
haggard with ill usage, were set free from their
dungeon, and Leisler was cast into it, with the same chain
upon his leg that Bayard had worn for more than a year.

On March 30th the prisoners were brought before a
court over which Dudley presided.   They were charged with
treason and murder for refusing to surrender the fort upon
Ingoldsby's arrival, and for firing upon his troops and thereby causing a wanton and wicked destruction of life.   No

notice was taken of Leisler's original usurpation of power,
nor was any allusion made to the complaints brought against
him for tyranny.   After a week's trial Leisler and Milborne
with six others were found guilty and sentenced to death.

Trial and
sentence of
Leislerites

An appeal was taken to the king, but before it was
heard from, the tragedy was ended.   All were pardoned except Leisler and Milborne.   The pressure
brought upon the governor to execute the sentence in their
case was greater than could be resisted.   The hatred they
had aroused was so violent and bitter that their death on
the gallows was hardly enough to appease it.   Sloughter
himself seems to have regarded them as arrant knaves and
unworthy to live, but he hesitated about acting after an
appeal had been made to the crown.   One chief argument
used to overcome his hesitancy was a statement that the
Mohawks were disgusted with Leisler's management of the
war and with his opposition to their esteemed friend and
ally, Peter Schuyler.   So angry were these barbarians, it
was said, that they would refuse to join in the attack upon
Canada until Leisler should be put to death.   Tradition as-
serts that some of Colonel Bayard's friends invited Sloughter
to a wedding feast and plied him with wine and schnapps
until he was induced to sign the death-warrant without
knowing what he was about.   This tradition cannot be cer-
tified, but as it was in existence as early as 1698, it may
very likely have some foundation in fact.

On a dark and rainy morning in May the unfortunate
Leisler and his daughter's bridegroom were led to the gal-

Execution
of Leisler
and Mil-
borne

lows, which stood near the present site of the
World Building in Park Row.   A crowd was assembled in the cold rain to witness the execution,
and in that crowd were two parties.   Some wept and
groaned at the fate of the prisoners, others declared that
hanging was too good for them, — they ought to be burned
with slow fires in the Indian manner.   Milborne spoke in
a tone of vindictive anger, but Leisler behaved with Christian dignity.   He said : " So far from revenge do we depart

this world, that we require and make it our dying request
to all our relations and friends, that they should in time to
come be forgetful of any injury done to us, or either of us,
so that on both sides the discord and dissension (which were
created by the Devil in the beginning) may with our ashes
be buried in oblivion, never more to rise up for the trouble
of posterity. . . . All that for our dying comfort we can say
concerning the point for which we are condemned, is to
declare as our last words, before that God whom we hope
before long to see, that our sole aim and object in the conduct of the government was to maintain the interest of our
sovereign Lord and Lady and the reformed Protestant
churches of these parts."

Concerning Leisler's essential integrity of purpose there
can be little doubt.   His methods were arbitrary and many
of his acts tyrannical, and the bitter hatred felt for him had
doubtless adequate cause.   It has been the fashion with
some writers [1] to treat him as a mere demagogue   *Leisler's*
actuated by no other motive than vulgar ambition.   *honesty*
But this theory does not explain his conduct.   *of purpose*
Insane as was his persistence after Ingoldsby's arrival, it is
not reasonable to suppose that during the two years of his
rule over New York he can ever have deliberately intended
to resist King William and bring about a revolution.   Nor
can it for a moment be allowed, as has sometimes been
insinuated, that the anti-Catholic panic was either got up by
Leisler or used by him as a blind for concealing his real inten-
tions.   There can be no doubt, as we have already seen, that
there was plenty of apparent ground for the panic, or that
Leisler's impulse in assuming the government was thoroughly
honest.   Unquestionably he believed himself, in holding
New York against Papist conspirators, to be doing a great
and needed service to his Protestant king ; and when he
found himself simply ignored and set aside without a word,
his mind was confronted with a fact too deep for him to
fathom.   There is something very pathetic in his utter

[1] Broadhead, for example, can see no good in Leisler.

inability to grasp the fact that there was nowhere a missive from the king addressed to him by name.

Had things gone as Leisler hoped and expected, the aristocratic party and the friends of Andros and Tories like Dudley, and all who had accepted honours or office from James II., would have been snubbed by the new king, while his own prompt action in saving New York would have His motives been cordially recognized by making him governor or at least a member of the council, and thus the cause of democracy would be furthered and helped. Thenceforth the name of Leisler would be inseparably associated with the firm establishment of representative government and the first triumph of democracy in the province of New York. In this dream Leisler was mistaken because he totally misconceived so many essential facts in the case, but the kind of ambition which it discloses is not a vulgar kind or such as to make it proper to stamp him with the name of demagogue. Even as it is, even in spite of his blunders and his failure, in spite of the violence and fanaticism which stain his record, Leisler stands as one of the early representatives of ideas since recognized as wholesome and statesmanlike. Moreover, the name of the man who called together the first Congress of American colonies must always be pronounced with respect.

As for the execution of Leisler and Milborne, it was of course entirely legal. They had caused a wanton loss of life while resisting the king's commissioned officers, and there was no court of that day, as there is no court of the present day, which would not regard such an offence as properly punishable with death. Nevertheless it was afterwards generally admitted that the execution was a mistake. It made martyrs of the two victims. Increase Mather declared that they were "barbarously murdered," and there were many in New York who said the same. Four years afterward Parliament reversed the attainder against Leisler and Milborne, and their estates were restored to their families. But the legacy of hatred remained, and the spirit of dissension so earnestly deprecated in Leisler's dying speech, far from being buried in oblivion with his ashes, renewed its life from year to year, and it was long before it ceased to vex men's minds.

CHAPTER XIV

THE CITADEL OF AMERICA

WHETHER from a commercial or a military point of view, the Dutch and Quaker colonies occupied the most commanding position in North America. It is that part of the continent which sends streams flowing in divergent courses into the Gulf of St. Lawrence, the Atlantic Ocean, and the Gulf of Mexico. Through deep chasms in the Alleghanies, which run irregularly across it, those superb rivers, the Hudson, Delaware, and Susquehanna, flow into the Atlantic; while the Mohawk, coming from the west, serves to join the valley of the Hudson with the Great Lakes; and in like manner the lovely Juniata, rushing down to join the Susquehanna, has its headwaters not far from the spot where the currents of the Alleghany and Monongahela unite to form the Ohio. With such pathways in every direction, whether for peace or for war, the New Netherland (curious misnomer for a region so mountainous) commanded the continent; and could the Dutch settlement at Manhattan have been adequately supported, it might have threatened or prevented the ascendency of England in the New World. It was partly owing to this advantage of position that the League of the Iroquois was enabled to domineer over the greater part of the country between the Atlantic and the Mississippi; and through the divergent river valleys and across the chain of mighty fresh-water seas those ferocious but long-headed barbarians in their bark canoes established those lines of trade which modern civilization, with its steamboat and railway, has simply adopted and improved. For a century after its conquest by the English, New York, with the western mountains of Pennsylvania, served as a military bulwark for New England and for the southern colonies.   The hardest fighting done in the War of Independence was the struggle for the possession of this vantage-ground; and in the second war with England the brilliant victories of Perry and Macdonough maintained on Lakes Erie and Champlain the sanctity of the citadel of America.

It was not, however, until the great immigration of Presbyterians from Ireland and the crossing of Lake Erie by the French that the Pennsylvania frontier acquired its military significance.   At the period with which we are dealing in the present volume, the vital point *The war with France* to be defended in the citadel was the stretch of lakes and woodlands between Albany and Montreal.   The upper Connecticut valley and the Maine frontier also presented opportunities to a watchful enemy.   The danger was sufficiently constant to be an important factor in the policy of all the northern colonies; in New York it was often the dominant factor.   Of the twenty-five years which intervened between the accession of William and Mary and the death of Anne, nineteen were years of deadly warfare between French and English, in the New World as well as the Old.   Then after a lull of thirty years, interrupted by a few local outbreaks like that of Norridgewock in 1724, we come to the final contests in which out of twenty-one years sixteen are years of war.   The burden, at first borne chiefly by New York and New England, comes at last to bear upon all the colonies; but first and last New York takes the brunt of it. The strife which had begun with the diplomacy of Andros and Dongan, and which had broken out in bloodshed in the time of Leisler, was thenceforth forever present to the minds of those who sat in council at Fort William or in the City Hall on the island of Manhattan.   Until the final overthrow of New France, the development of New York was powerfully influenced by the circumstances which made it the citadel of America.

The accession of William and Mary, which precipitated this warfare with the French, marked in other ways an era in New York as it did in other colonies, and notably in Maryland, Plymouth, and Massachusetts. It transformed Maryland into a royal province, and although the proprietary government was by and by to be restored, yet the days of the old semi-independent palatinate were gone never to return.[1]   It abolished the separate existence of Plymouth, and it changed the half-rebellious theocratic republic of Massachusetts into a royal province.   New York also became a royal province after the fashion of Massachusetts, but the change was in the reverse direction.   The days of the autocrats were over.   Self-government gained much in New York, as it lost much in Massachusetts, from the accession of William and Mary. Hereafter New York was to be governed through a representative assembly.

Accession of William and Mary

The first thing which Colonel Sloughter did after the arrest of Leisler was to issue writs for the election of such an assembly ; and the day on which it met in a tavern on Pearl Street, the 9th of April, 1691, marks the beginning of continuous constitutional government in New York.   James Graham, of the famous Grahams of Montrose, was chosen speaker of the assembly,

A representative assembly, 1691

in which the party opposed to Leisler had an overwhelming majority. This assembly declared its enthusiastic loyalty to

William and Mary, while it ascribed its own existence, not to royal generosity, but to the inherent right of freemen to be governed only through their own representatives.   Resolutions were passed, condemning the acts of Leisler.   A grant was made for public expenditures, but only for a period of two years.   The wave of anti-Catholic feeling attendant upon the mighty war between William of Orange and Louis

[1] See *Old Virginia and Her Neighbours*, Illustrated Edition, ii. 154.

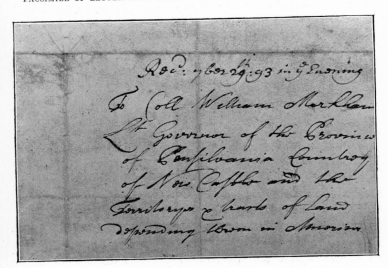

Sr

I have appointed the first wednesday in October next for the meeting of Commissioners from all the neighbouring Colonys and Provinces at Newyorke to consult and agree upon a quota of money for the Defence of the ffrontiers You have seen their Matyes Commands to me as Governor of Pensilvania for that purpose — You are therefore to gett the Councill or a quorum together to consider of a fitt person for Pensilvania & the Country of New Castle as for the abuse in the assessment I leave it to your discretion I did expect they would have been more just to their Own Act

I am yor
loving friend
Benj Fletcher

fort William Henry
the 23th Septr 93

FACSIMILE OF LETTER FROM GOVERNOR FLETCHER TO COLONEL MARKHAM

Recd: 7ber 29th 93 in ye Evening

To Coll William Markham
Lt Governor of the Province
of Pensilvania Country
of New Castle and the
Territoryes & tracts of Land
depending thereon in America

FACSIMILE OF ADDRESS OF ABOVE LETTER

XIV. was revealed in an act prohibiting "Romish forms of worship" in New York.   At the same time the king was requested to annex Connecticut, the Jerseys, and Pennsylvania, with Delaware, to the province of New York, which would thus comprise the whole of the original New Netherland, and somewhat more.

In midsummer of that year the worthless Sloughter died so suddenly that suspicions of poison were aroused, but the particular suspicions were proved to be groundless, and a more probable explanation was to be found in delirium tremens.   Major Ingoldsby then acted as governor until the arrival of Colonel Benjamin Fletcher in August, 1692.   Fletcher was a man of large stature, fair, florid, and choleric, with plenty of energy and a pompous demeanour.   One of the conspicuous sights of the little city was his handsome chariot, drawn by six gaily caparisoned steeds and carrying Mrs. Fletcher and her daughters decked in the latest and most gorgeous European finery. He was devoted to the Church of England and to missionary enterprise ; as a soldier he was so prompt and vigorous that the Mohawks named him "Great Swift Arrow."   Withal it was commonly whispered that he was a consummate adept in the art of feathering his own nest, making both religion and warfare redound to the increase of the credit side of his ledger.

Arrival of Benjamin Fletcher

One of Fletcher's first acts was to go to Albany and take counsel of Peter Schuyler, its mayor.   This gentleman, granduncle of Philip Schuyler, the eminent general of the War of Independence, was a person of extraordinary qualities.   His skill in dealing with red men was equal to that of Frontenac, and the situation called for all such skill that could be had.   The danger lay in the possibility that French diplomacy might succeed in detaching the Iroquois from their English alliance.   Their loyalty to the alliance was of course based much more upon hatred of Onontio than upon love for Corlear, and could they be brought to fear the French as enemies more than they

Peter Schuyler

respected the English as protectors, that loyalty was liable to be weakened. The French realized more clearly than the English the importance of the struggle in which they were engaged, and in comparison with their tireless efforts such energy as the English put forth seemed mere listlessness. In the persuasive tongues of Jesuits reinforcing the mailed hand of Frontenac there was an element of real danger. To the board of Indian commissioners at Albany, and especially to the sagacious mayor, Peter Schuyler, eternal gratitude is due for the skill with which it was averted. The Mohawks entertained boundless respect for "Quidor"[1] (as the name Peter became in their guttural speech), and his influence over them was greater than that of any other man of his time.

Fletcher reinforced Albany with troops under Ingoldsby and returned to Manhattan, but the news soon came that Frontenac, with a large force of French and Algonquins, was on the way from Canada to invade the Iroquois country. The active governor hurried up the river with further reinforcements, to find that in a battle near Schenectady Peter Schuyler had defeated Frontenac. The retreat of the French into Canada was accomplished at the expense of terrible hardships and a heavy loss of life. Such victories for the English were a great help in sustaining the Iroquois alliance. To the Mohawks it seemed

Defeat of the French

---

[1] "Quidor" had a happy knack of adapting himself to the customs and habits of his tawny friends, but once in a while it cost him a few qualms; to judge from an anecdote told me in 1881 by one of the family, the late George Washington Schuyler, of Ithaca, N. Y. After a severe tramp in the wilderness, half starved with hunger and cold, Quidor came one evening upon an encampment of Mohawks, where he was cordially welcomed. In a few moments he was seated before a bright blaze, with a calabash of hot soup, the most delicious he had ever tasted. Presently, when he dipped his rude ladle once more into the kettle and brought up a couple of parboiled human fingers, it gave him a queer turn, but he repressed all show of feeling and quietly asked a feathered chieftain, "What is this soup made of?" The Indian as calmly replied, "Of a Frenchman we killed this morning; is n't it good?"

as if the English were not so much in earnest as the French, and they told Fletcher that if Corlear and all his friends would only join forces they could easily beat the life out of Onontio.

But Fletcher was beginning to find that popular assemblies are crabbed and contentious bodies, and that it was hard enough to get his own people to behave rationally, let alone the difficulty of bringing the other colonies into line. The hatred between "Leislerians" and "Aristocrats" so far pervaded the community as to subordinate other interests. An attempt had been made to appease the friends of Leisler by appointing as mayor of the city Abraham de Peyster, who had been one of his more moderate adherents. The effect was good, but of course insufficient. In the legislature the two parties were far more anxious to trip each other up than to aid the common cause. Besides, many of Fletcher's demands were of very doubtful expediency, and the discussions upon these questions hindered prompt action upon matters of pressing moment. Fletcher was eager to have the Episcopal church established and supported out of the public revenues; and he furthermore wanted the grant of revenue to be made for the lifetime of the reigning king. But the assembly was too "big with the privileges of Englishmen and Magna Charta" to follow in the ways which the governor pointed out. Dudgeon grew high between the two branches of government. The assembly passed a bill to which Fletcher added an amendment. The assembly refused to adopt the amendment, and was forthwith prorogued by the governor with petulant words: "You have shown a great deal of stiffness. You take upon you airs as if you were dictators. I sent down to you an amendment of three or four words in that bill, which, though very immaterial,[1] yet was positively denied. I must tell

Party strife

Fletcher rebukes the assembly

---

[1] O no, good irate governor! very far from immaterial. If it were really of no importance, why this ruffled temper? why so much asperity and gall? The bill provided for the election of rectors by the church

A
JOURNAL
OF THE
Late Actions
OF THE
French at Canada.

WITH

The Manner of their being Repuls'd, by His Excellency, *Benjamin Fletcher*, Their Majesties Governour of *New-York*.

Impartially Related by Coll. Nicholas Reyard, *and Lieutenant* Coll. Charles Lodowick, *who attended His Excellency, during the whole Expedition.*

To which is added,

I. An Account of the present State and Strength of *Canada*, given by Two *Dutch Men*, who have been a long Time Prisoners there, and now made their Escape.
II. The Examination of a *French* Prisoner.
III. His Excellency *Benjamin Fletcher's* Speech to the *Indians*.
IV. An Address from the Corporation of *Albany*, to His Excellency, Returning Thanks for His Excellency's early Assistance for their Relief.

Licensed, Sept. 11th 1693. Edward Cooke.

London, Printed for *Richard Baldwin*, in *Warwick-Lane*, 1693

TITLE OF FLETCHER'S "JOURNAL"

you that it seems very unmannerly. There never was an amendment yet decided by the council but what you rejected ; it is a sign of stubborn ill-temper. . . . . You ought to let the council do their part. They are in the nature of the House of Lords, or upper house. But you seem to take the whole power into your own hands and set up for everything. You have had a very long session to little purpose, and have been a great charge to the country. Ten shillings a day is a large allowance and you punctually exact it. You have been always forward enough to put down the fees of other ministers in the government ; why did you not think it expedient to correct your own to a more moderate allowance ? " [1]

Even when it came to voting supplies for the defence of the colony against actual invasion, Fletcher found his assembly very intractable. But when he tried to exact authority outside of the colony it was still worse. The difficulty of securing that concerted military action which the Mohawk chiefs recommended had led James II. to try to unite the northern colonies under the single rule of Sir Edmund Andros, unhampered by any representative assemblies. To meet the same difficulty, William III. authorized Fletcher to take control of the militia of Connecticut and the Jerseys. In 1693 the king revoked the proprietary grant of Pennsylvania and Delaware to William Penn,[2] and handed over the administration of those two colonies to

Fletcher in Philadelphia

Fletcher as royal governor. Fletcher accordingly spent a few weeks in Philadelphia, where he found the good Quakers so mildly but inexorably intractable that he was fain to write to the king excusing himself from the charge of this additional burden. He left Pennsyl-

wardens and vestrymen, the amendment providing that they must be collated by the governor ! No one but Mr. Totts could say " It 's of no consequence, thank you."

[1] *Journal of the Legislative Council*, i. 47, 48. Compare Governor Spotswood's remarks in dissolving his assembly, in *Old Virginia and Her Neighbours*, Illustrated Edition, ii. 353.

[2] See below, p. 293.

THE
LAWS & ACTS
OF THE
General Assembly
FOR
Their Majesties Province
OF
NEW-YORK,

As they were Enacted in divers Sessions, the first of
which began *April*, the 9th, *Annoq; Domini*,
1691.

At *New-York*,

Printed and Sold by *William Bradford*, Printer to their Majesties, King
William & Queen *Mary*, 1694.

TITLE OF ACTS AND LAWS OF NEW YORK

vania as he found it, and the next year Penn prevailed upon the king to reinstate him in his proprietary rights.

In Connecticut Fletcher had no better success. He visited Hartford in October, 1693, while the assembly was in session, and demanded that the military forces of the colony should be placed at his disposal, at the same time promising to retain Governor Treat in the immediate com-

Fletcher at Hartford

mand over them as his lieutenant. These pro- posals were flatly refused, and the angry Fletcher wrote to the secretary of state in London : " The laws of England have no force in this colony. . . . They set up for a free state." There is a tradition that one bright afternoon the train-bands of Hartford were drawn up before the place where the assembly was in session, and Fletcher ordered his secretary to read aloud his commission and instruc- tions ; whereupon the sturdy Captain Wadsworth, who had once hidden the charter of Connecticut in an oak-tree, or- dered the drums to be beaten. A threatening gesture from Fletcher stopped the drummers, and the reading was begun again. Once more the drums resounded, and once more Fletcher silenced them. Then Wadsworth stepped up to the New York governor and declared that " he would make the sun shine through him " if he dared interfere again. And so the crestfallen Fletcher deemed it wise to retire from the scene.[1] Such is the familiar tradition, but it rests on no good authority, and seems improbable. At all events

[1] Trumbull's *History of Connecticut*, i. 393. I think it not unlikely that this story affords an illustration of one of the normal ways in which legends grow. When Andros came to Saybrook in 1675 and tried to read the duke's patent to Captain Bull and his officers, they foiled him by walking away, but the Hartford magistrates are said afterward to have told them it would have been still better if they had drowned the reading with the noise of drums. (See above, p. 47.) Now for popular tradition to change Andros into Fletcher (one New York governor for another), Bull into Wadsworth (one Connecticut captain for another), and the hypothetical drumbeat into an actual drumbeat, would be the most natural thing in the world, exactly the sort of thing that popular tradition is always doing.

Fletcher was baffled, and when the matter was referred to the privy council it was softened into an order that upon proper notice in war time Connecticut should furnish the governor of New York with 120 men.

No wonder that an officer in Fletcher's position, wielding the forces of a weak colony against a formidable enemy, should fret at being unable to get control of the resources of his stronger neighbour; for in wealth and population Connecticut was at least twice as powerful as New York. Fletcher next appealed to Massachusetts for aid, but without success, for the Quebec affair of 1690 had over-taxed the extensive resources of that colony, and she found it, moreover, necessary to guard her eastern frontier. But in the Jerseys Fletcher fared better, for their men and money were placed at his disposal.

In the double difficulty of obtaining adequate supplies from the legislature and securing concerted action among different colonies, we see the principal causes which led seventy years later to the Stamp Act. Because there was no continental power which could raise troops and levy taxes for continental purposes, the British Parliament, with an entirely friendly purpose, undertook to perform the functions of such a continental power. The experience of those seventy years proved that a single head for the English colonies was an absolute necessity. Either Parliament must be that head, or the colonies must enter into a Federal Union; no third course was practicable. It was the conflict with France that taught this lesson, and therefore the calling of a Continental Congress at New York in 1690 by Jacob Leisler was an event of great interest and significance. Of the same order of importance was the Plan of Union presented by William Penn to the Lords of Trade in 1697. In order to accomplish by rational and constitutional means the ends which William III. was seeking when by a mere order in council he invested the governor of New York with arbitrary control over neighbouring colonies, Penn recommended a Federal

Causes leading toward the Stamp Act

Penn's plan for a Federal Union

Union.   As the earliest suggestion of so great a step in con-
structive statesmanship, his plan must always be interesting.
It provided for a Congress of two deputies from each colony
to meet once a year, and to have for chairman or president
a king's commissioner especially appointed for the purpose.
The place of meeting might be New York, as conveniently
central, and also because the province was a military frontier and under a royal governor.   For further convenience
this governor might be the king's commissioner, "after the
manner of Scotland," and also commander-in-chief of the
forces.   The business of the Congress should be "to hear
and adjust all matters of complaint or difference between
province and province.   As, 1. where persons quit their own
province and go to another, that they may avoid their just
debts though they be able to pay them; 2. where offenders
fly justice . . . ; 3. to prevent or cure injuries in point of
commerce ; 4. to consider of ways and means to support
the union and safety of these provinces against the public
enemies.   In which Congress the quotas of men and charges
will be much easier and more equally set than it is possible
for any establishment made here [*i. e.* in England] to do ;
for the provinces, knowing their own condition and one another's, can debate that matter with more freedom and satisfaction and better adjust and balance their affairs in all
respects for their common safety." [1]

Such was the first simple outline of the scheme which was
further developed in Franklin's Plan, in 1754, and again in
the Articles of Confederation, until maturity was reached
in our present Federal Constitution.   When we fully understand that it was the failure to adopt such wise schemes as
those of Penn and Franklin that ultimately led to the Stamp
Act,[2] we shall be the better prepared to comprehend the

---

[1] Preston, *Documents Illustrative of American History*, p. 147.

[2] This is too large a subject to receive full treatment in the present
volume.   My next work in the present series will be devoted to the
development of the English colonies from 1689 to 1765, under the pressure of the struggle with New France, and it will thus lead naturally to
my volumes on the American Revolution.

American Revolution and to deal with it in a fair and impartial spirit.

The difficulties of Governor Fletcher were increased by the prevalence of piracy on the high seas. I have elsewhere shown how the seventeenth century came to be the golden age of piracy.[1] As a sequel to the long maritime wars in which the Dutch and English put an end to the supremacy of Spain, came the age of buccaneers, when freebooters of all nations joined hands in plundering the Spanish coasts of America. Spaniards had come to be regarded by many people as the enemies of the human race, insomuch that it was hardly deemed criminal to rob and slay them, and thus buccaneering retained a slight flavour of respectability. The buccaneer, however, was not apt to be a person of tender conscience, and frequently developed into the full-fledged pirate, whose hand was against everybody without distinction of race, politics, or creed. Piracy throve greatly in the seventeenth century because maritime commerce expanded far more rapidly than the naval facilities for protecting it. Never before had so many ships been afloat and traversing long distances, loaded with cargoes of such immense value. Moreover the practice of privateering, whereby civilized nations sought to supply the deficiencies in their naval force, was extremely liable to degenerate into piracy. The abominable tariff and navigation acts also, by which commerce was stupidly hampered, aroused in mercantile communities a spirit of lawlessness which tolerated the vile pirate, very much as it aided and abetted the noble army of smugglers. If the pirate could afford to undersell the honest skipper, his customers could easily refrain from asking awkward questions.

The war which brought firebrand and tomahawk upon Schenectady brought many a pirate craft into New York harbour. The principal cruising ground of these rascals was the Indian Ocean, where the richly laden ships of the English and Dutch East India companies were continually

The golden age of piracy

[1] *Old Virginia and Her Neighbours*, Illustrated Edition, ii. chap. xvi.

passing between the coasts of Hindustan or the Spice Islands to the Red Sea or the Cape of Good Hope.   After a
pirate had captured one or more of these vessels and taken
on board all the treasure he could carry, he would make for
The   New York, where he would pull out of his pocket
pirate's lair   some dog's-eared letter-of-marque and swear that he
on Mada-
gascar   had taken all this Oriental stuff from Frenchmen
as a lawful privateer.   It was usually difficult to convict him
of falsehood.   A still more common practice was to sail to
Madagascar with the plunder.[1]   The luxurious tropical for-
ests of that large island furnished an almost inaccessible lair
for the pirates, and thither they repaired from all quarters.
In the intervals between cruises many of them dwelt in
palisadoed castles with moats and drawbridge, approachable
only through labyrinthine paths which for further defence
were studded with sharp thorns to lacerate the ill-shod feet
of the natives.   There they guzzled stolen wines of finest
vintage, kept harems that might have made the Grand Turk
envious, quarrelled and murdered one another, and indulged
in nameless orgies, until they wearied of such pastime and
sallied forth again to the business of ocean robbery.   On
the coast of Madagascar was a strongly defended mart or
emporium where our pirates would meet some merchant
vessel from New York, and exchange their gold pieces and
gems and Eastern shawls for rum or firearms or whatever
else they needed.   Then while the pirate was engaged in
fresh robberies the merchant returned to New York, where
those who bought her merchandise were not bound to know
from whom she got it.   The risks of such a voyage were
considerable, for the merchant ship might itself fall a prey to
Profits of   some pirate, or it might be captured as a receiver
the voy-   of stolen goods by some East India Company's
ages   frigate on patrol.   But while the risks were not
small, the profits were prodigious.   For example, the ship
Nassau, which sailed from New York in 1698, "was laden

[1] There were several haunts of pirates on the African coast, but
Madagascar was the most notorious and important.

with Jamaica rum, Madeira wine, and gunpowder. The rum cost in New York 2s. per gallon, and was sold in Madagascar for £3 per gallon. The wine cost £19 per pipe, and was sold for £300 ; and the gunpowder we may suppose at a similar advance. In return the Nassau purchased East India goods and slaves of the pirates, and, taking 29 of the latter as passengers, sailed for home. The pirates paid £4000 for their passage, and the voyage is said to have netted the owners £30,000." [1]

A trade abounding in such profitable ventures was not easy to suppress. The pirates had convenient lurking-places in the West Indies and the Bahamas, and in the crooked sounds and deep inlets of the Carolina coast. Everywhere they had extensive dealings, underselling the regular merchants and defeating the navigation laws. The citizens of Charleston and of New York, who coveted their wares, knew also that their ships were apt to be formidable, and so treated them usually with politeness. Sometimes the pirate captain was a man of polished address and entertaining speech, who could make himself acceptable at dinner tables and in good society. One of them, we are told, before venturing ashore, was careful to send some silks and cashmeres with a trifle or so in the shape of costly gems, to Mrs. Fletcher and her stylish daughters. For a dozen years or more the streets of New York might have reminded one of Teheran or Bassora, with their shops displaying rugs of Anatolia or Daghestan, tables of carved teakwood, vases of hammered brass and silver, Bagdad portières, fans of ivory or sandalwood, soft shawls of myriad gorgeous hues and white crape daintily embroidered, along with exquisite ornaments of ruby, pearl, and emerald. In the little town which had been wont to eke out its slender currency with wampum, strange pieces of gold and silver now passed freely from hand to hand : Greek byzants, Arabian dinars, and mohurs from Hindustan, along with Spanish doubloons and the louis d'or of France. A familiar sight in

Effects in the city of New York

1 Todd, *The Story of New York*, p. 171.

taverns was the swaggering blade attired in blue coat trimmed with gold lace and pearl buttons, white knee-breeches and embroidered hose, with jewelled dagger in his belt,[1] paying scot for all who would listen to his outlandish yarns, and tipping everybody, from the pot-boy up (as it was whispered) even to the worshipful governor.

The East India companies, English and Dutch, complained of this state of things, and all merchants who felt interested in the navigation laws added their complaints. But the warships of William of Orange were so fully occupied in the waters about France [2] that the Indian Ocean was inadequately guarded. Under these circumstances a scheme was formed which was highly characteristic of the age, and which introduces us to the most famous name, perhaps, in all the annals of piracy.

Whether Captain William Kidd ever really deserved such a grewsome renown is, however, more or less questionable. He was certainly no ruffian, but an educated mariner who for the greater part of his life was esteemed a model of integrity. He was probably the son of a Presbyterian minister at Greenock, in Scotland. In his marriage certificate, in 1691, he is styled "gentleman." At that time he had considerable wealth and lived in a pleasant home on Liberty Street. In earlier days he seems to have been a navigator in various parts of the world. In 1695 King William was discussing with Richard Coote, Earl of Bellomont, and other members of his council, the most feasible means of suppressing piracy, and it was decided to make it a private undertaking. A swift frigate should be sent to the East Indies, under a captain of tried courage and probity, the sea robbers should be vanquished and brought to justice, and their spoil should defray expenses and leave a handsome profit. Robert Livingston and William Kidd happened to be in London, and Livingston recommended

William Kidd

[1] See the description of Thomas Tew, in Todd, _op. cit._ p. 175.

[2] Captain Mahan has treated this war in a masterly manner, in his _Influence of Sea Power upon History_, chap. iv.

Articles of Agreement,

Made the 10th Day of *October*, in the Year of our Lord 1695.
Between the Right Honourable *RICHARD* Earl of
BELLOMONT of the one part, and *Robert Levingston* Esq;

AND

Captain William Kid,

Of the other part.

WHEREAS the said Capt. *William Kid* is desirous of obtaining a Commission as Captain of a Private Man of War in order to take Prizes from the King's Enemies, and otherways to annoy them; and whereas certain Persons did some time since depart from *New-England, Rode-Island, New-York,* and other parts in *America* and elsewhere, with an intention to become Pirates, and to commit Spoils and Depredations, against the Laws of Nations, in the *Red-Sea* or elsewhere, and to return with such Goods and Riches as they should get, to certain places by them agreed upon; of which said Persons and Places, the said Capt. *Kid* hath notice, and is desirous to fight with and subdue the said Pirates, as also other Pirates with whom the said Capt. *Kid* shall meet at Sea, in case he be impowered so to do; and whereas it is agreed between the said Parties, That for the purpose aforesaid a good and sufficient Ship, to the liking of the said Capt. *Kid*, shall be forthwith bought, whereof the said Capt. *Kid* is to have the Command. Now these Presents do witness, and it is agreed between the said Parties,

I. That the Earl of *Bellomont* doth covenant and agree, at his proper Charge, to procure from the King's Majesty, or from the Lords Commissioners of the Admiralty (as the Case shall require) one or more Commissions, impowering him the said Capt. *Kid* to act against the King's Enemies, and to take Prizes from them, as a private Man of War in the usual manner; and also to fight with, conquer and subdue Pirates, and to take them and their Goods; with other large and beneficial Powers and Clauses in such Commissions as may be most proper and effectual in such Cases.

II. The said Earl of *Bellomont* doth covenant and agree, That within three Months after the said Capt. *Kid*'s departure from *England*, for the purposes in these Presents mentioned, he will procure, at his proper charge, a Grant from the King, to be made to some indifferent and trusty Person, of all such Mechandizes, Goods, Treasure and other things as shall be taken from the said Pirates, or any other Pirate whatsoever, by the said Capt. *Kid*, or by the said Ship, or any other Ship or Ships under his Command.

III. The said Earl doth agree to pay four Fifth parts, the whole in Five parts to be divided, of all Moneys which shall be laid out for the buying such good and sufficient Ship for the purposes aforesaid, together with Rigging and other Apparel and Furniture thereof, and providing the same with competent victualling the said Ship, to be approved of by the said Parties; and the said other one Fifth part of the said Charges of the said Ship to be paid for by the said *Robert Levingston* and *William Kid*.

IV. The said Earl doth agree, That in order to the speedy buying the said Ship, in part of the said four parts of Five of the said Charges, he will pay down the sum of sixteen hundred Pounds, by way of Advance, on or before the sixth day of *November* next ensuing.

V. The said *Robert Levingston* and *William Kid* do jointly and severally covenant and agree, That on and before the sixth day of *November*, when the said Earl of *Bellomont* is to pay the said Sum of sixteen hundred pounds as aforesaid, they will advance and pay down four hundred pounds in part of the Share and Proportion which they are to have in the said Ship.

VI. The said Earl doth agree, to pay such further Sums of Money as shall compleat and make up the said four parts of Five of the Charges of the said Ship's Arrival, Furniture and Victualling, unto the said *Robert Levingston* and *William Kid* within seven Weeks after the date of these Presents; and in like manner the said *Robert Levingston* and *William Kid* do agree to pay such further Sums as shall amount to a fifth part of the whole Charge of the said Ship within seven Weeks after the date of these Presents.

A   VII. The

CAPTAIN WILLIAM KIDD'S COMMISSION (FIRST PAGE)

VII. The said Capt. *Kid* doth covenant and agree to procure and take with him on board of the said Snip. one hundred Mariners or Seamen, or thereabouts, to make what reasonable and convenient sp ed he can, to set out to Sea with the said Ship, and to sail to such parts or places where he may meet with the said Pirates, and to use his utmost Endeavours to meet with, subdue and conquer the said Pirates, or any other Pirates, and to take from them their Goods, Merchandizes and Treasure, also to take what Prizes he can from the King's Enemies, and forthwith to make the best of his way to *Boston* in *New-England*, and that without touching at any other port or harbour whatsoever, or without breaking Bulk, or diminishing any part of what he shall so take or obtain, on any pretence whatsoever, of which he shall make Oath, in case the same be desired by the said Earl of *Bellomont*, and thereto deliver the same into the hands and possession of the said Earl.

VIII. The said Capt. *Kid* doth agree, That the Contract and Bargain which he will make with his said Ships-Crew shall be *No Purchase no Pay*, and not otherwise; and that the share and proportion which his said Ships-Crew shall by such Contract have of such Prizes, Goods, Merchandizes and Treasures as he shall take as prize, or from any Pirates, shall not at the most exceed a fourth part of the same, and shall be less than a fourth, in case the same may reasonably and conveniently be agreed upon.

IX. The said *Robert Levingstone* and Capt. *William Kid*, do jointly and severally agree with the said Earl of *Bellomont*, That in case the said Capt. *Kid* do not meet with the said Pirates which went from *New-England*, *Rode-Island*, *New-York*, and elsewhere as aforesaid, or do not take from any other Pirates, or from any of the King's Enemies, such Goods, Merchandize, or other things of Value, as being divided, as herein after is mentioned, shall fully recompence the said Earl for the Moneys by him expended, in buying the said four fifth parts of the said Ship and Premises, that then they shall refund and pay to the said Earl of *Bellomont* the whole Money by him to be advanced in Sterling Money or Moneys equivalent thereunto, on or before the five and twentieth day of *March*, which shall be in the Year of our Lord 1697. (the Danger of the Seas, and of the Enemies, and Mortality of the said Capt. *Kid* always excepted) upon payment whereof the said *Robert Levingstone* and *William Kid* are to have the sole property in the said Ship and Furniture, and this Indenture to be delivered up to them, with all other Covenants and Obligations thereunto belonging.

X. It is agreed between the said parties, That as well the Goods, Merchandizes, Treasure and other things which shall be taken from the said Pirates, or any Pirates, by the said *William Kid*, as also all such Prizes as shall be by him taken from any of the King's Enemies, shall be divided in manner following, that is to say, Such part as shall be for that purpose, agreed upon by the said Capt. *Kid* (so as the same do not in the whole exceed a fourth part) shall be paid or delivered to the Ships-Crew for their use, and the other three parts to be divided into five equal parts, whereof thesaid Earl is to have his own use four full parts, and the other Fift his to be equally divided between the said *Robert Levingstone* and *William Kid*, and is to be delivered them by the said Earl of *Bellomont*, without Deduction or Abatement on any pretence whatsoever; but it is always to be understood, that such Prizes as shall be taken from the King's Enemies, are to be lawfully adjudged Prize in the usual manner, before any Division or otherwise intermedling therewith, than according to the true Intent of the said Commission to be granted in that behalf.

XI. Lastly, it is covenanted and agreed between the said parties to these presents, That in case the said Capt. *William Kid* do bring to *Boston* aforesaid, and there deliver to the Earl of *Bellomont* Goods, Merchandizes, Treasure or Prizes to the value of one hundred thousand Pounds or upwards, which he shall have taken from the said Pirates, or from other Pirates, or from the King's Enemies; that then the Ship, which is now speedily to be brought by the said Pirates, shall be and remain to the sole use and behalf of him, the said Capt. *William Kid*, as a Reward and Gratification for his good Service therein.

Memorandum, Before the Sealing and Delivery of these Presents it was covenanted and agreed by the said Earl of *Bellomont*, with the said *Robert Levingstone* Esq; and Captain *William Kid*, that the person to whom the Grant above-mentioned in these Articles, shall be made by His Majesty, shall within eight Days at the most after such Grant has passed the Great Seal of *England*, assign and transfer to each of them, the said *Robert Levingstone* Esq; and Captain *William Kid*, their Heirs and Assigns one full tenth part (the Ship-Crew's share and proportion being first deducted) of all such Goods, Treasure, or other thing as shall be taken by the said Captain *Kid* by virtue of such Commissions as aforesaid; and the said Grantee shall make such Assignment as aforesaid, in such manner as by the said *Robert Levingstone* Esq; and Capt. *William Kid*, or their Council Learned in the Law shall be reasonably advised and required. And then these Presents were sealed and delivered (the Six-penny Stamp being first afixed) in the presence of us

Martha Breken
John Maddock
John Moulder.

BELLOMONT.

Licensed according to Order.

LONDON, Printed for *J. Richardson*, near *Ludgate*, 1701.

CAPTAIN WILLIAM KIDD'S COMMISSION (LAST PAGE)

Kidd to Lord Bellomont as the very man for the enterprise.
These three, with several members of the council, entered
into partnership, and subscribed £6000.   Kidd re- His com-
ceived letters-of-marque authorizing him to capture mission for
arresting
French vessels, and a special commission instruct- pirates
ing him to arrest all pirates wheresoever found, and bring
them to trial.   After reserving a royalty of 10 per cent. for
the king, the proceeds of the cruise were to be divided
among the partners.   Kidd was to render a strict account
of all prizes to Lord Bellomont, and Livingston became his
surety.[1] A 36-gun frigate, the Adventure, was duly equipped,
and in May, 1696, Kidd sailed from Plymouth, with a crew
of 80 men.   In New York he picked up about 90 more, and
in February, 1697, set sail for Madagascar.   The civilized
world saw nothing more of him for more than two years.

In the mean time the Leislerites brought about the recall
of Governor Fletcher.   Two of them — Leisler's son Jacob,
and Abraham Gouverneur, who was presently to marry
the widowed Mary Milborne — were very busy in London.
They secured the restoration of Leisler's estates and the
rehabilitation of his memory so far as that could be done by
an act of Parliament.   Lord Bellomont, who was Charges
one of the king's most trusted advisers, declared against
Fletcher
that the execution of Leisler and Milborne was a
judicial murder.   He was a nobleman of generous and lofty
character and entertained sundry democratic notions, so that
he soon became a favourite with the Leislerians.   They accused Fletcher of complicity with the pirates, or, at the
very least, of accepting from them bribes or hush-money.
It is difficult to tell how far these charges were He is su-
founded on fact.   Fletcher always resented them, perseded
by Lord
and they were not irrefragably proved; but such Bellomont
charges are apt to be hard to prove, even when true.   At all

---

[1] Kidd's name often appears in tradition as Robert Kidd, and is
sometimes so given in books that should know better.   I have sometimes wondered if this might have been a confusion arising from some
vague memory of his connection with Robert Livingston.

events, they led to the recall of Fletcher and the appointment of Bellomont to be governor of New York, with explicit
instructions to move heaven and earth for the suppression of
piracy.   This appointment was made before Kidd sailed, but
various causes delayed Bellomont so that he did not arrive
in New York until April, 1698.

In order to effect as much concentration as possible without creating disturbance, Bellomont was appointed royal
governor of Massachusetts and New Hampshire, as well as
New York.   His graceful and courteous manners made him
generally popular, but his administration was not a tranquil
one.   As Fletcher quarrelled with the Leislerians, Bellomont kept himself in hot water with the aristocrats.   He
began by issuing a writ of restitution to put the families of
More party   Leisler and Milborne in possession of their estates,
strife   and turmoil at once ensued, for many pieces of this
property had passed into the hands of innocent purchasers
who were now despoiled.   He tried to enforce the navigation laws and to confiscate ships and cargoes for non-payment of custom-house dues.   This brought on a quarrel
with the merchants and with the collector of the port, whom
he cashiered for remissness in enforcing the laws.   As the
Leislerites had accused Governor Fletcher of receiving
stolen goods from the pirates, so Bellomont in turn charged
some of the members of his aristocratic council with similar
practices.   Mrs. Bayard one evening wore an extraordinary
diamond, which rumour said had been given to her husband
as hush-money by some scoundrel who had robbed and murdered an Eastern princess.   It was also reported that Gabriel Minvielle had under his bed a big chest full of gold
dinars, which, could they have spoken, would have told just
as foul a tale.   And as for Philipse, why did his son go
down to the Narrows in a pinnace, to meet some merchant-
men just come from Madagascar ?

Bellomont was the more inclined to believe such rumours
because of his engrained prejudices against rich men.   He
was inclined to regard great wealth as incompatible with

Bellomont

perfect honesty. The immense landed estates of the patroons and their feudal privileges disgusted him. Bello-
He lost no opportunity of attacking land grants levelling
in which any flaw could be suspected, and he even tendencies
proposed a bill which should make it illegal for any person
in the province to hold more than one thousand acres.

With these levelling tendencies, which accorded well with
his Leislerian sympathies, Bellomont was only too ready to
believe ill of Bayard and his friends. He accused them of
complicity with pirates and removed Bayard, with four other
gentlemen, from his council. In their place he appointed
able and well-known Leislerians. Much commotion was
thus excited throughout the province, and the next election
of representatives was fiercely contested. Never before in
America had an election day consumed so much Election
grog or broken so many pates. The aristocracy of 1699
suffered a crushing defeat at the polls, and the government
thus became Leislerian in all its branches.

This result created something like a panic among the
merchants and great landowners, and a report was circulated
that the Leislerians were intending to obtain compensation
for all the damages which they had suffered since the beginning of the troubles. The king felt it necessary to warn
Bellomont against such a policy, which would tend to drive
some of the best citizens away from New York. Bellomont
replied that he was not so foolish as to countenance such
measures. But the complaints against him multiplied, and
were presently complicated by a quarrel with the dominies.
In the midst of these dissensions came the rumour that
William Kidd, the pirate-catcher, from whom nothing had
been heard for two years, had himself turned pi- Strange
rate! This was a dire mortification for the gov- rumours
ernor. The friends of the displaced councilmen about Kidd
could now wag their heads and cry, "Aha! just see what
sort of agents and tools this Earl of Bellomont, so prudish
in all such matters, employs!" We can fancy that the
need for attending to the affairs of Massachusetts and New

Hampshire afforded the governor some relief from this sti-

fling atmosphere of contention and distrust. We can also see that it will be likely to go hard with Captain Kidd if ever he falls into the hands of honest Richard of Bellomont.

Nevertheless it happened, curiously enough, that scarcely had the governor been a month in Boston when a message addressed to him by that mariner disclosed his presence in

Narragansett Bay. The message informed Bellomont that he was in a sloop with £10,000 worth of goods on board, and was entirely innocent of the acts of piracy which lying rumour had laid to his charge. Let us briefly note some of the events in this career of innocence.

After a tedious voyage of nine months from New York, during which the stores were nearly exhausted and the crew threatened with famine, Kidd arrived off Madagascar in the autumn of 1697. He had encountered neither pirates nor French vessels on the way, and now at the island he found no prey; all the pirates were off on business. So Kidd filled his water-casks, bought food, and sailed over to the Malabar coast without meeting a ship of any sort. Provisions and money were nearly all gone, and the crew insisted upon

attacking the first ship they should meet, whether lawful prey or not, in order to get the means of sustenance. Kidd afterward stoutly maintained that he did not follow this advice until he was compelled by his starving and mutinous crew. However that may have been, he did follow it, and began by capturing a few ships of the Great Mogul. Probably his noble patrons in England, on payment of a goodly dividend, would not inquire too closely into damage inflicted upon mere heathen. It seems probable that Kidd did not at first take willingly to this course. He had some disputes with his crew, in one of which he seized a bucket and struck a gunner, William Moore, over the head, inflicting fatal injuries. The work of piracy went on, and presently it was not only heathen but Christian ships that suffered. So things went until December, 1698, when Kidd captured a large East Indiaman, named the Quedah Merchant, owned by Armenian traders and commanded by an English skipper. His own ship, the Adventure, was badly out of repair; so he set ashore the crew of the Quedah Merchant, transferred to her his own armament and crew, burned the Adventure, and made for the pirate mart at Madagascar, where his cargo fetched £64,000, equivalent to more than a million dollars of the present day. Of this sum his own portion amounted to $320,000. After losing two thirds of his men by desertion, and enlisting a new crew, our amateur pirate sailed for the West Indies. There he was met by appalling news. Not only had his acts of piracy been reported in England, but a parliamentary committee had been appointed to inquire into the nature of his commission and the character of the partnership from which he had received it. A royal proclamation had been issued, The king's moreover, offering free pardon to all pirates who proclamation would surrender themselves for acts committed before May-day of 1699. Only two pirates were excepted by name; one was a fellow named Avery, one of the worst scoundrels of his time, the other was William Kidd.

The reason for this was that Kidd's conduct reflected upon the whole group of powerful noblemen who had sent him to the East Indies. He was the agent not only of Bellomont, but of the Lord Chancellor Somers, of Orford the First Lord of the Admiralty, of the Earl of Shrewsbury, even in a sense of King William. The Tories exultingly threw his misdeeds in the face of these Whig statesmen; it was their purpose to impeach the Lord Chancellor, and it pleased them to be able to say that he had a pirate in his Kidd's employ. Under these circumstances the Tories desperate magnified the rumours of Kidd's villainies, while situation the Whigs could not incur the responsibility of contradicting them; they must wash their hands of him as quickly as possible. Hence he was excepted from the offer of pardon.

Had Kidd fully grasped the hopelessness of the situation, or had he been an unmitigated ruffian, like Blackbeard or

Olonnois, he would most likely have accepted an outlaw's career. With his powerful ship and vast treasure he might roam the seas and play the corsair, or seek refuge in some inaccessible spot. But one may fancy that a castle in Madagascar was not the sort of home that he wanted. The pleasant fireside in Liberty Street, where wife and children awaited him, may well have been in his thoughts ; and if he could make Lord Bellomont believe his story, there might be a good chance for him. So he bought at the island of Curaçoa a small sloop, in which he put his gold coins, gold-dust, and jewels, and with a crew of forty men started for New York. At San Domingo he stopped and left the Quedah Merchant, with her armament of 50 guns and cargo of immense value. What became of her is not known. As Kidd stealthily approached New York he learned that the governor had gone to Boston. He contrived to get a letter ashore to his wife and children, who joined him at Block Island. Arriving in Narragansett Bay, he sent to Boston the message already mentioned. Bellomont replied that if Kidd could satisfy him of his innocence he might count upon his pro-

Kidd lands in Boston, and is arrested

tection. Accordingly on the first day of July Kidd landed in Boston, and paid his respects to the governor, handing him a present of rare jewels for Lady Bellomont. With the approval of the council Bellomont accepted the present, lest a refusal should put Kidd too keenly on his guard. As his story did not satisfy the governor, he was arrested on July 6, and the jewels were handed to a trustee as part of the documents in the case.

He is sent to London

After a while Kidd was sent to London and kept in prison more than a year while evidence was sought in the East Indies. In the spring of 1701 he was brought to trial for sundry acts of piracy and for the murder of William Moore. Kidd's defence as to the first charge was that he had only captured vessels sailing under French colours, except in one or two cases when his crew overpowered him and took the command out of his hands. As to the second charge, he averred that Moore was engaged in

To his Excellency the Earle of Bellomont, Cap:t:n Gen:ll
Gov:r in Chief of his Maj:ties provinces of the Massachusetts
Bay New yorke &c:a in America, and of the Territory
thereon depending & vice Admiral of the same:

The petition of Sarah Kidd the wife of
Cap:n W:m Kidd

Humbly Sheweth.

That on the Sixth day of July Inst: Some of the
Magistrates and officers of this place, came into your
Pet:rs lodgings at the house of Duncan Campbell,
& did there Seize and take out of ar Trunck a Silver
Tankard, a Silver Mugg, Silver Porringer, Spoons
forcks & other pieces of Plate, and two hundred and
Sixty pieces of Eight, yo:r Pet:rs Sole and proper
Plate & mony; brought with her from New yorke
whereof She has had the possession for Several years
last past, as She can truely make oath; out of w:ch
S:d Trunck was also took Twenty five English Crowns
w:ch belonged to yo:r Pet:rs Maid

These premisses and most deplorable
Condition of yo:r Pet:r considered
She humbly intreats yo:r hon:rs
Justice, That Returne be made of
the Said Plate & mony.

Sarah SK Kidd

18:th July (99)

In Council July 18: 1699.

Advised That m:rs Kidd makeing Oath That
She brought the Plate and money abovem:sntioned
from New yorke with her. It be restored unto
her. As also That Cap:t: Kidd and Company:s wearing
Apparel under Seizure be return:d to them.

PETITION OF MRS. WILLIAM KIDD

mutiny and rightfully slain; nevertheless the homicide was unintentional; he had not used pistol nor dagger, but only struck the offender with a bucket, and on the worst construction was guilty only of manslaughter. The prosecution did not break down this defence, and one cannot read the report of the trial without feeling that the verdict of guilty was predetermined. Kidd was hanged in May, 1701. In spite of the unfairness of the trial, he had probably done enough to deserve his sentence; but his preeminent notoriety is clearly due to other causes than preëminence in crime.

His trial and execution

Lord Bellomont's stay in Boston was little more than a year, and his acquaintance with New Hampshire was limited to a fortnight. He was much liked in Boston for his personal qualities and his opposition to the Toryism represented by the friends of Joseph Dudley. For his own part he liked the people of Boston, but as a liberal-minded Episcopalian he confessed he could not see how so much learning could coexist with so much fanaticism as in some of the Puritan clergymen and professors. In the summer of 1700 he returned to New York. He had long been troubled with gout, and in the following winter died very suddenly.[1]

Death of Bellomont

His death was the signal for an explosion which had long been preparing. It soon appeared that some of the reports which had been circulated as to the designs of the Leislerians were well founded. That party had a majority both in the assembly and in the council, and now that Bellomont's restraining hand was removed, they brought in a bill to enable the Leisler family to institute lawsuits for damages which they alleged they had sustained at the hands of the aristocracy during the change from the House of Stuart to the House of Orange. They also brought outrageous charges against prominent members of the aristocratic party. They accused Robert Livingston

Violent proceedings of the Leislerites

[1] His mortal remains now rest in St. Paul's churchyard. See Mrs. Lamb's *History of the City of New York*, ii. 446.

THE
Arraignment, Tryal, and Condemnation
OF
Captain William Kidd,
FOR
MURTHER
AND
PIRACY,

Upon Six several Indictments,

At the Admiralty-Sessions, held by His Majesty's Commission at the *Old-Baily*, on *Thursday* the 8th. and *Friday* the 9th.
of *May*, 1701. who, upon full Evidence, was found Guilty,
receiv'd Sentence, and was accordingly Executed at *Execution-
Dock*, *May* the 23d.

AS ALSO,

The TRYALS of *Nicholas Churchill*, *James Howe*, *Robert
Lamley*, *William Jenkins*, *Gabriel Loff*, *Hugh Parrot*, *Richard Barlicorn*,
Abel Owens, and *Darby Mullins*, at the same Time and Place
for PIRACY.

Perused by the Judges and Council.

To which are added,

Captain *KIDD*'s Two Commissions:
One under the Great Seal of *ENGLAND*, and the Other under
the Great Seal of the Court of *Admiralty*.

LONDON:
Printed for *J. Nutt*, near *Stationers-Hall*. 1701.

TITLE OF KIDD'S TRIAL

of defalcation in his accounts, and petitioned the king to remove him from his office of secretary of Indian affairs; they made a similar charge against the late Stephanus van Cortlandt, and brought suits against his widow.   In view of the anticipated passage of their Leisler Act for damages, they invited all the injured persons to bring in an inventory of their losses, and some astounding estimates followed, as when a rusty sword and dilapidated gun, which Governor Sloughter had seized, were valued at £40 (say, nearly $800).

This last step was unwise, for it seemed to herald a carnival of spoliation and created intense alarm.   There was a rumour that Viscount Cornbury had been appointed governor, to succeed the Earl of Bellomont.   A petition to the crown was prepared, urging that he might be sent with all possible haste.   It had more than 600 signatures, including most of the aristocratic leaders.   The chief justice and solicitor-general, who were fierce Leislerians, saw fit to call this paper " seditious," and indictments for high treason were brought against Nicholas Bayard and an alderman named Hutchings, at whose house the petition had been signed.

Petition to the crown

What followed would have been a ludicrous farce had it not been so execrably wicked.   The intention was to avenge the death of Leisler upon the person of his old enemy, Bayard; and in the proceedings all law and decency were trampled under foot.   In a scurrilous speech the solicitor-general accused Bayard of complicity with the pirates and of plotting to introduce Popery into New York.   Such invective did duty for evidence, a jury, half packed and half browbeaten, quickly found a verdict of " guilty," and the chief justice forthwith sentenced Bayard and Hutchings to be disembowelled and quartered.   The poor alderman, it may be supposed, was to atone for Milborne.   At about the same time the Leisler Act was passed by the assembly, and Livingston was turned out of his offices, while all his property was confiscated.

Shameful trial of Bayard and Hutchings

A new governor, however, was even then on his way from

AN

ACCOUNT

OF THE

Illegal Profecution

AND

TRYAL

OF

Coll. Nicholas Bayard

In the Province of New-York,

For Suppofed

High - Treafon,

In the Year 170½.

Collected from feveral Memorials taken by
divers Perfons privately, the Commiffioners having
ftrictly prohibited the taking of the Tryal in open
COURT.

Printed and Sold by *William Bradford*, at the Sign of
the Bible in *New-York*, MDCCII.

TITLE OF BAYARD'S TRIAL

England.   On March 7, 1702, the king breathed his last, and Anne ascended the throne.   Edward Hyde, Viscount Cornbury, was grandson of the great Earl of Clarendon, the

Lord Corn-bury statesman and historian, and own cousin to Queen Anne.   The late king had appointed him governor, and Anne at once confirmed the appointment.   Cornbury was a trained soldier, and not wholly wanting in ability, but his character was far from estimable.   He had gross vices, and some contemptible follies. His strong likeness to his cousin Anne attracted much notice and led him often to make a guy of himself by dressing in elaborate and sumptuous female attire, like a lady of the court.   His name is now chiefly remembered for this tomfoolery.   Yet much

good was effected by his coming to New York.   One of his first acts was to dissolve the assembly.   The recent scanda-lous trials were investigated, and those legal luminaries, the solicitor-general and the chief justice, absconded and hid themselves in Virginia under assumed names.   Bayard and Hutchings were set free and reinstated in their property ; Livingston was replaced in his offices and estates ; the Leis-ler Act was quashed by the Lords of Trade ; and the public alarm was allayed.

Having performed this much needed service, Cornbury went on unwittingly to perform another and soften the ani-mosities between the Leislerites and the aristocracy by unit-ing them to some extent in opposition to himself.   He thus introduced fresh grievances, but some of these were of a kind conducive to growth in constitutional liberty.   He ob-tained from the assembly a grant of £1500 for fortifying

A treasurer for the as-sembly the Narrows against French fleets, and was very wroth at the suggestion that the assembly should appoint a treasurer to handle the money.   What ! did they distrust his integrity ?   So the business was left to

his integrity and three years slipped by, until one fine afternoon a French warship sailed in through the Narrows, and
great was the commotion.   The batteries had not been built ;
what had been done with the £1500 ?   Cornbury protested
that he had never seen the money, but the assembly knew
better.   There was a sound, wholesome discussion, in the
course of which the doctrine was plainly stated that the
rights of a colonial assembly were precisely the same as
those of the House of Commons.   The matter was referred
to the queen in council, and it is an interesting fact that the
assembly was sustained against the governor.   Henceforth
it appointed a treasurer and saw that his accounts were
properly audited.

It was not only with the New York assembly that Cornbury had contentions, for he was also governor of New Jersey.   Since the overthrow of Andros, the history   The gov-
of the two provinces of East and West Jersey had   ernorship
                                                        of New Jer-
been a plexus of difficulties which need not here   sey united
concern us, until in 1702 all the proprietors agreed   with that of
                                                        New York
in surrendering their proprietary rights of sovereignty to Queen Anne.   Their ownership of their landed
estates was not disturbed by this surrender.   The two provinces were united into one, and thenceforward until 1738
New Jersey was an appendage to New York, in much the
same way that Delaware was an appendage to Pennsylvania.
There was the same governor, but the assemblies were distinct and independent.   This preserved the local life, and
prevented New Jersey from being merged in New York, and
Delaware from being merged in Pennsylvania.   Any such
absorption would have been a calamity, for what the civilized
world most needs is variety and individual colour in social
development, and the more that local independencies can be
preserved, in so far as such preservation is compatible with
general tranquillity, the better.

Governor Cornbury's first demand upon the New Jersey
assembly was for a yearly salary of £2000, to be granted for
twenty years.   When we bear in mind that this sum repre-

sented nearly $40,000 in our present currency, we shall ap-
Disputes
over sal-
aries
preciate the comment of the Quaker member who
turned upon Cornbury with the remark, "Thee
must be very needy!" The assembly voted only
£1300 for three years, and thus began its bickerings with
the spendthrift governor. Such contentions over salaries
were flagrant during the eighteenth century, and must be
taken into the account if we would understand how the
Townshend Act of 1767 led directly to the War of Independence.

It was Cornbury's fate to antagonize not only the legislatures but the dominies. There were but few Episcopalians
Cornbury's
debts
in New York, though the civil government was
always trying to help that church, and people already noticed that it flourished better in Pennsylvania, under
Penn's grand policy of a fair field for all, and no favour.
But Cornbury tried to help Episcopacy in his feeble way,
by making warfare upon other sects, which in New York
were in the majority. In such ways, but perhaps still more
through his private affairs, he came to grief. He was steeped
in debauchery and never paid his debts; and when, in 1708,
Queen Anne yielded to the general clamour and sent out
Lord Lovelace to supersede him, no sooner had he ceased
to be governor than his creditors sprang upon him. Besieged with bills innumerable from butcher and baker and
candlestick-maker, the unhappy Cornbury was thrown into
jail and stayed there till next year, when the death of his
father made him Earl of Clarendon. Then he paid up his
debts and went home, leaving unsavoury memories behind
him.

Lord Lovelace, nephew of the governor who succeeded
Nicolls, lived but a few months after his arrival. His place
was taken by our old acquaintance, Ingoldsby, once more
lieutenant-governor. Danger was again threatening from
Canada. The strife of Leislerian and anti-Leislerian had
absorbed the attention of the province, weakened its resources, and loosened its grasp upon the Long House,

SA GA YEATH QUA PIETH TOW
King of the Maquas

TEE YEE NEEN HO GA ROW
Emperor of the Six Nations

HO NEE YEATH TAW NO ROW
King of the Generethgarich

ETOW OH KOAM
King of the River Nation

insomuch that Onontio had actually achieved a treaty which
secured its neutrality. Peter Schuyler now persuaded those barbarians to put on their war paint,
and took command of them in person. A force of
1500 men from New York, New Jersey, and Connecticut,
commanded by another of our old acquaintances, Francis
Nicholson, marched to Lake Champlain, while 1200 men
raised by Massachusetts awaited the arrival of a promised
British fleet which was to take them up the St. Lawrence.
This force was to attack Quebec while Nicholson advanced
upon Montreal. But the loss of the battle of Almanza made
it necessary for England to send to Portugal the force designed for America; and so the expedition against Canada
came to nothing.

As a partial compensation for this disappointment, Nicholson, in the course of the next year, conquered Nova Scotia.
Schuyler was more than ever impressed with the necessity
of driving the French from the valley of the St. Lawrence,
and in order to urge the matter upon Queen Anne's ministry he went over to England in 1710, taking with him
four Iroquois chiefs.[1] These barbarians made as
great a sensation in London as Pocahontas had
done in the days of Queen Anne's great grandfather. They were received with much ceremony by
the queen, on which occasion they made a solemn
speech on the necessity for conquering Onontio, and presented her with a belt of wampum. It was agreed that
Canada should once more be invaded, and Colonel
Robert Hunter was sent out to be governor of
New York. This Scottish gentleman was the ablest
and best of the English governors since Richard Nicolls;
broad-minded and sagacious, cultivated and refined, upright
and genial, a thoroughly admirable man. He was an intimate friend of Addison and Swift, and could himself write
witty poems and essays. He had served with credit in King

[1] One of them was a Mohawk of the Wolf clan, grandfather of the
great Thayendanegea, better known as Joseph Brant.

William's army, and now came to oppose the French arms in the New World. His arrival on such an errand was enthusiastically welcomed. The assembly was less niggardly than usual, partly, perhaps, because it was voting away not real money but promissory notes. It issued £10,000 of this pernicious currency, hoping to redeem it within five years. There was a conference of governors at New London, and a plan was made essentially similar to the former one. Nicholson, with the troops from Connecticut, New

York, and New Jersey, and Schuyler's Indians, was to advance upon Montreal by way of Lake Champlain ; while the Massachusetts, New Hampshire, and Rhode Island troops, aided by a powerful English fleet, should ascend the St. Lawrence and take Quebec. But the enterprise failed ignominiously. On the last *Another abortive attempt against Canada* day of July, 1711, the fleet, commanded by Sir Hovenden Walker, sailed from Boston Harbour, carrying about 2000 provincial troops, with 5000 regulars under General Hill, commonly known about London as " Jack Hill," brother of the queen's favourite lady, Mrs. Masham. The admiral, who had too much of the proud spirit that goeth before a fall, would not take the advice of his Yankee pilots ; wherefore during their second day upon the St. Lawrence several ships were wrecked upon ledges of rock, with the loss of more than 1000 lives. Then with preposterous logic a council of war decided that the mighty river was impracticable for such vessels as theirs, and so the fleet returned to England. The disaster was reported to Nicholson in time

to prevent his imperilling his army.   The affair ended in
recriminations, and presently the treaty of Utrecht allowed
New France another half century of life.

Amid these incidents of war the business of legislation
was encumbered with the usual difficulties.   The council,
though by no means a tool in the governor's hands, was very

Difficulty
of raising
money for
military
purposes

apt to agree with his views of constitutional questions.   The assembly, on the other hand, was almost
certain to differ from the governor on questions
relating to revenue, if on no others.   In most of the
colonies military exigencies made a greater demand upon the
exchequer than people could comfortably meet.   Hence the
governor's requests did not usually meet with prompt or adequate response, and operations were apt to languish.   There
is no doubt that despotic Onontio could mobilize his forces
much more speedily than constitution-hemmed Corlear.   It
was half a century of this sort of experience that led to the
Stamp Act.

Under these circumstances the constitutional position and
functions of the council gave rise to important discussions.

Constitu-
tional dis-
cussions

The council maintained that it was properly an
upper house, like the House of Lords, and this was
generally the governor's opinion ; but the assembly insisted that the council was merely an advisory board.
Especially jealous was the assembly of any pretension on
the part of the council to initiate or amend money bills.
Then there was the burning question of the governor's salary, which the assembly usually insisted upon granting only
for a year at a time, in order to keep a check-rein upon the
governor.   Sometimes an earnest patriot, like Hunter, bent
upon getting things done, would furnish the money from his
own pocket.   From some of Hunter's letters to Dean Swift
we catch glimpses of his feeling about the people's representatives : " This is the fine stair to live upon in the universe ;
and if our trees and birds could speak, and our assembly-
men be silent, the finest conversation also.   The soil bears
all things, but not for me.   According to the custom of the

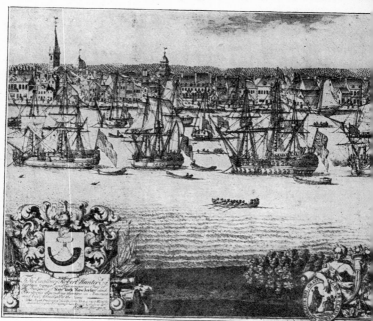

country, the sachems are the poorest of the people. . . . I thought in coming to this government I should have hot meals and cool drinks, and recreate my body in Holland sheets upon beds of down; whereas I am doing penance as if I were a hermit. . . . I am used like a dog, after having done all that is in the power of man to deserve better treatment."

Notwithstanding such expressions of feeling, and in spite of many altercations with the assembly, Governor Hunter was greatly liked and admired, and there was much sorrow when private business called him back to England in 1719. His friend and successor, William Burnet, who came next year, was another upright and able governor. He was a son of Gilbert Burnet, Bishop of Salisbury, the famous historian, and was himself a man of learning and accomplishments, with much practical sagacity and rare personal charm. One of his first measures, however, was for a time extremely unpopular. There was far too much intercourse between the French and the warriors of the Long House. It was an excellent instance of the shrewdness with which Onontio made trade and religion support each other. Jesuit priests had made converts to Christianity even among their arch-enemies, the Mohawks, and with these converts they formed a colony at Caughnawaga, a place on the right bank of the St. Lawrence, a short distance above Montreal. These Caughnawaga Indians soon became a source of danger to New York. The most prolific source of the furs which made so large a part of the wealth of the province was the country about the Great Lakes, inhabited by Ottawas, Sacs and Foxes, Pottawatomies and other Algonquin tribes, besides Dakotahs. These were commonly called the " Far Indians." Now since the English commercial policy, however narrow, was far more liberal than that of Louis XV., the best supply of goods for the Indians was in New York and Albany, not in Montreal. Knives and guns, powder and blankets, were apt to be plenty and cheap among the

Hunter is succeeded by William Burnet

The Caughnawagas and their trade

English, while scarce and dear among the French.   Accordingly the Caughnawagas soon became the middlemen in a brisk and lucrative trade.   By way of the St. Lawrence and Lake Champlain they brought furs from the Great Lakes to Albany and exchanged them there for tools and weapons, blankets and beads, which they forthwith carried to Montreal and sold to the French traders.   It was often in this way only that the Frenchmen obtained the wares which they needed for getting furs from the " Far Indians." [1]

Now this trade through the Caughnawagas was profitable to merchants in New York and Albany, as well as in Montreal.   But every Caughnawaga was a Jesuit spy whose presence upon English soil was a possible source of danger.   Moreover, the use of the St. Lawrence route played into the hands of the enemy by diverting trade from the safer avenue of the Mohawk valley.   With a statesman's glance Governor Burnet comprehended the situation, and his action was prompt and decisive.   He procured an act of the assembly prohibiting trade with Montreal under the penalty of £100 fine with forfeiture of goods ; while at the same time he bought the land at Oswego from the Six Nations [2] and built a small fort there, and as the assembly was slow in providing the money, he paid the expenses out of his own pocket.   Much to the delight of the Long House, some forty young men, headed by Quidor's son, Philip Schuyler, came among them to carry on trade.   It was decidedly for the interest of the Six Nations to become the middlemen in a flourishing trade between the " Far Indians " and Albany. Accordingly the measures of Governor Burnet had lasting

Its dangers

Founding of Oswego, and closer relations with the Mohawk valley

[1] See Parkman, *A Half-Century of Conflict*, i. 15.

[2] After the crushing defeats of the Tuscarora tribe of Iroquois in North Carolina, by Barnwell in 1712 and by Moore in 1713, the remnant of the tribe migrated into New York and were admitted into the confederacy of the Long House, as a sixth nation.   The territory there assigned to the Tuscaroras lay south of the Oneidas and southeast of the Onondagas.   For their career in North Carolina, see *Old Virginia and Her Neighbours*, Illustrated Edition, ii. 277–286.

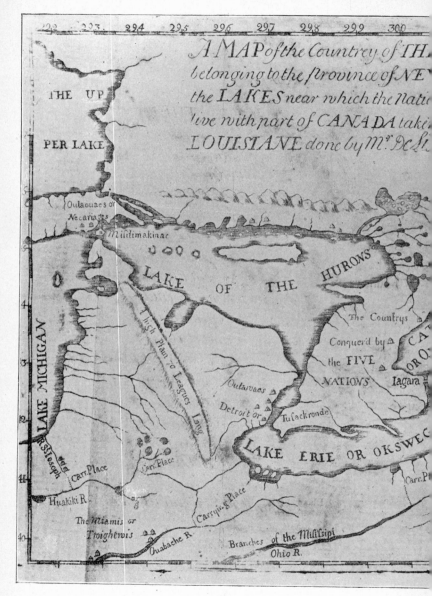

A MAP of the Countrey of TH.
belonging to the Province of NE
the LAKES near which the Natic
live with part of CANADA taken
LOUISIANE done by M.. De St.

THE UP

PER LAKE

Oulaoüaes or
Necariages

Mifsilimakinac

LAKE   OF   THE   HURONS

The Countrys

Conquer'd by

the FIVE

NATIONS

CA

OR

Iagara

Oulaoüaes

Detroit or a

Tufackronde

LAKE MICHIGAN

High Plain 70 Leagues long

St. Joseph R.

LAKE ERIE OR OKSWEC

Carr. Place

Carr. Place

Carr. P

Huakiki R.

The Miamis or
Twightwis

Carrying Place

Ouabache R.

Branches of the Mifsisipi

Ohio R.

MAP

results, although his prohibitory act was after a few years
quashed by the Lords of Trade. The main course of the
fur trade was in great measure diverted from Fort Frontenac
and Lake Champlain to Oswego and the Mohawk valley.
Intercourse between the
English and the Six Na-
tions thus grew closer
and the danger from
Canada was lessened.
Probably the action of Burnet was the most important event
in the history of the Anglo-Iroquois alliance between the
death of Frontenac in 1698 and the arrival of William Johnson in 1738.

Upon the accession of George II., Burnet was transferred
from the governorship of New York to that of Massachusetts and New Hampshire. His successor, John Montgomery, died in 1731, and the next year came Colonel William
Cosby, who had been governor of Minorca and acquired
there a reputation for gross avarice. The prin- Cosby's
cipal event of his administration in New York dispute
with Rip
was a money dispute with Rip van Dam, who as van Dam
president of the council had conducted affairs during the
interregnum after Montgomery's death. Out of this dis-

pute grew a trial which excited intense interest throughout
the English colonies, and deserves mention in every account
of the development of political liberty.

Since 1725 New York had had a newspaper,[1] edited by

---

[1] The first newspaper printed in English America was " Public
Occurrences, both Foreign and Domestic," Boston, September 25,
1690. Only this first number was printed. The first permanent news-
papers were as follows : —

The Boston News-Letter, Boston, April 17, 1704.

William Bradford, a gentleman who had come from Pennsylvania in 1693 and brought with him the art of printing. He

LARGE SEAL OF THE MONTGOMERIE CHARTER

was printer for the government, and his paper, the " New York Gazette," of which the first number appeared November 1, 1725, was to some extent a government organ. Bradford and Zenger One of Bradford's apprentices was John Peter Zenger, a German who had come over from the Palatinate in 1710, being then a lad of thirteen. In 1733 Zenger started ed an opposition paper, called the "Weekly Journal." He had no money, but received help

The Boston Gazette, Boston, December 21, 1719.
The American, Philadelphia, December 22, 1719.
The New York Gazette, New York, November 1, 1725.
The Maryland Gazette, Annapolis, June, 1728.
The South Carolina Gazette, Charleston, January 8, 1732.
The Rhode Island Gazette, Newport, September 27, 1732.
The Weekly Journal, New York, November 15, 1733.
The Virginia Gazette, Williamsburg, 1736.
The Connecticut Gazette, New Haven, January 1, 1755.
The North Carolina Gazette, New Berne, December, 1755.
The New Hampshire Gazette, Portsmouth, August, 1756.
See Isaiah Thomas's *History of Printing*, Worcester, 1810, 2 vols.; Frothingham's *Rise of the Republic*, p. 129.

Numb. 113.

THE

New-York Gazette,

From *December* 25. to Monday *January* 1. 1727.

CADIZ, September 12. N.S.

IT having been customary to Print Weekly Accounts of the Ships arriving, sailing from, and remaining in the Bay, the *French Admiral* taking Notice that the *English* Ships were placed before the *French* in the said List, has complained of it as an undue Preference; upon which the Governor of this Place sent to the Printer, and ordered him to place the *French* first; but the *British Factory* looking on this as a publick Affront, found means to prevent it: However, the Governor has wrote about it to Court, and in the mean time the printing the said List is forbid. Orders are arrived for breaking up the Blockade of *Gibraltar*, but the said Garrison is not suffered to have Communication with the Country.

Malaga, Sept. 16. N.S. By a Ship arrived here we learn that Sir *Charles Wager* was on the 31st past in the Bay of *Tangier* with 11 Men of War; and that the *Orford, Preston* and *Weymouth* Men of War, from *England*, joyned him in the said Bay; where he then remained with the said 14 Men of War.

Marseilles, Sept. 19. N.S. The French Court is very busy in endeavouring to promote the Navigation of this Kingdom; and Orders are frequently brought to our Magistrates, by which the Ships belonging to Foreign Nations are very much affected. These Orders are judged here to to interfere with Privileges formerly granted to this Place, and as such will be represented to the Court. Two French Ships are arrived here with 10,000 Quintals of Baccalas from Cape Briton, where they have had a very good Fishery.

Extract of a Letter from Paris, Sept 27.

WE learn that Count *Rothembourg*, who is gone to *Madrid* in Quality of Ambassador Extraordinary of his Majesty, is not only charged with the Order of the Holy Ghost for the Infant Don Louis, but also to declare that his Majesty still resolves to maintain his Engagements with his Allies, and expects the Preliminaries to be ratified in the Sense which the King of *Great Britain* takes them; that he cannot dispense with desiring his Catholick Majesty to terminate immediately his Differences with *Great Britain* in raising the Siege of Gibraltar, in restoring the Ship Prince Frederick, and in distributing the Effects of the Flotilla, that afterwards the Galleons may return home, &c.

LONDON, September 30.

Yesterday the Commissioners of the Customs in Town, viz. Sir *Walter Tonge*, Sir *John Stanley*, *Thomas Walker*, Esq; Sir *Charles Peers*, Sir *John Evelyn*, *Bryan Fairfax*, Esq; *Humphry Brent*, Esq; and *Alan Broderier*, Esq; and *Charles Carkesse*, Esq; their Secretary, were introduced to his Majesty at St. James's, by the Right Honourable Sir *Robert Walpole* Chancellour of the Exchequer, and had the Honour to kiss his Majesty's Hand: At the same Time Sir *Robert Baylis*, who was lately in that Commission, and since made Receiver General of the Taxes for the City of *London* and *Westminster*, and the County of *Middlesex*, had also the Honour to kiss his Majesty's Hand.

They had afterwards the Honour to kiss her Majesty's Hand.

They write from Sheerness, That two Ships of War lately put in Commission, are sheathing with all Expedition, for foreign Service, and several of the Workmen being sick, they are supplyed with Men from other Yards.

At a Council held at Fort George, in New-York *November* 25. 1727.

Present, His Excellency *William Burnet*, Esq; &c. Capt. *Walter*, Mr *Van Dam*, Mr. *Harrison*, Dr. *Colden*, Mr. *Alexander*, Mr. *Lewis Morris*, jun. Mr. *Abraham Van Horn*, Mr. *Kennedy*.

HIS Excellency was pleased to declare the General Assembly of this Province Dissolved, with the unanimous Consent and Approbation of this Board, on Account of the following Resolves made by them, viz.

Die Sabbat. 25 *November*, 1727.

Coll. *Hicks*, from the Committee of Grievances, reported, That as well by the Complaints of several People, as by the general Cry of his Majesty's Subjects inhabiting this Colony, they find That the *Court of Chancery* as lately assumed to be set up here, renders the Liberties and Properties of the said Subjects extreamly precarious: And that by the violent Measures taken in and allowed by it, some have been ruined, others oblig'd to abandon the Colony, and many restrained in it, either by Imprisonment, or by excessive Bail exacted from them not to depart, even when no Manner of Suits are depending

against

Numb. I.

THE
New-York Weekly JOURNAL.

Containing the freſheſt Advices, Foreign, and Domeſtick.

MUNDAY November 5, 1733.

Mr. *Zenger*,

UNDERSTANDING you intend ſhortly to publiſh a Weekly Paper, I recommend to your diſpoſal the incloſed Verſes upon Wiſdom; which is ſo noble a Theme, that whoever takes the Pains ſeriouſly to reflect thereon, will find himſelf happily loſt in the boundleſs Ocean of Benefits and Satisfaction attending it. It is without Diſpute the chief Wood of Mankind; the firm Bank that conſtantly ſecures us again the impetuous Raging of that turbulent Sea of Paſſions, which inceſſantly daſh againſt the Frame of human Nature. It is a Fort impregnable by all Aſſaults of Vice, Folly, and Misfortunes, and a ſecure Rock againſt all the Caſualties of Miſery. It is a Guide and Security to Youth, Health, and Vigour to Old Age; and a Remedy and Eaſe in Sickneſs and Infirmity. It is Comfort in Adverſity, it is Plenty in Poverty, and a conſtant Source of true Joy and Delight. It is infinitely beyond all that the feigned *Fortunatus* ever could wiſh, or *Gyges's* Treaſures purchaſe; *For her Ways are Ways of Pleaſantneſs, and all her Paths are Peace.* She is of eaſy acceſs to all that diligently ſeek her; and refuſes none that with Sincerity apply to her, and is always a ready Help in Time of Need: Therefore pray continue to recommend the earneſt Purſuit of Her to all Mankind; and you will particularly oblige.

PHILO-SOPHIA.

On WISDOM.

Victorious Wiſdom whoſe ſupreme Command
Extends beyond the Bounds of Sea and Land;
'Tis thou alone that doſt reward our Pains,
With Pleaſures that endure, and ſolid Gains.

But Oh! What art thou, and where doſt thou dwell?
Not with the Hermit in his lonely Cell;
The ſullen Fumes of whoſe diſtemper'd Brain,
Make the dull Wretch torment himſelf in vain:
Whilſt of the World affectedly afraid,
He ſhuns the End for which Mankind was made.

Not with the Epicure in all his Pleaſures,
Nor with the Miſer in his Bank of Treaſures,
The one's a Slave bound faſt in golden Chains,
The other buys ſhort Joys with laſting Pains.

Not in the vain Purſuit of partial Fame,
The gaudy Outſide of an empty Name;
When moved by Chance, not Merit common Breath
Gives the falſe Shadow ſudden Life or Death.

Honour, when meritoriouſly aſſigned,
The noble Actions of a God like Mind,
Is then indeed a Bleſſing ſent from Heaven,
A bright Reward for human Labour given.

But when 'tis Fame's miſtaken Flattery,
A popular Applauſe of Vanity,
The worthleſs Idol ought to be abhor'd;
And is by none but Knaves and Fools ador'd.

Thus as I'm ſearching with the feeble Light
Of human Reaſon, in dark error's Night,
For what has oft eſcap'd the curious Eye,
Of lofty Wit, and deep Philoſophy,
From the bright Regions of eternal Day,
Methinks I ſee a ſmall but glorious Ray,
Dart ſwift as Lightning throug the yielding Air,
To an unſpotted Breaſt, and enter there.

This is the Wiſdom I ſo much adore;
Grant me but this, kind Heaven, I aſk no more,
This once obtain'd, how happy ſhall I be?
Kings will be little Men, compar'd to me:
They in their own Dominions only great,
I Conquer of the World, my ſelf and Fate.

Thus arm'd, let Fortune uſe me as ſhe will,
I ſtand prepar'd to meet with Good or Ill.
If I am born for Happineſs and Eaſe,
And proſp'rous Gales ſalute the ſmiling Seas;
This Path I'll tread, (the Bleſſings to repay)
Where Virtue calls and Honour leads the Way,

But if the Weather of my Life prove foul,
Though Storms ariſe that makes whole Kingdoms rowle.

Yet

and encouragement
from some of the
ablest and best men
of the province, in-
cluding Lewis Morris,
Rip van Dam, James
Alexander,[1] and oth-
ers. In point of tell-
ing argument and bold
sarcasm Bradford was
no match for Zenger,
and when sundry deeds
of Cosby were held up
to scorn the governor
writhed under the in-
fliction. At last, in
November, 1734, the
council could endure
it no longer. They
pronounced four num-

LEWIS MORRIS'S BOOK-PLATE

bers of the "Weekly Journal" "seditious" and ordered the
common hangman to make a public bonfire of them in front
of the pillory. The mayor and aldermen, however, pronounced
this order of the council illegal, and would not allow the hangman to obey it. The papers were accordingly burned by one
of the sheriff's negro slaves. Then Zenger was im-   Persecu-
prisoned on a warrant from the governor and coun-   tion of
cil, who requested the assembly to concur with them   Zenger
in prosecuting him ; but the assembly simply laid the request
upon the table. He was brought before Chief Justice De
Lancey, and his counsel, James Alexander and William Smith,
two of the foremost lawyers in the province, wished to have
him admitted to bail, but as he was unable to find the exces-

1 This eminent lawyer was a Scotch Jacobite who had found the old
country too hot for him after the rebellion of 1715. His son, William
Alexander, was the Revolutionary general commonly known as " Lord
Stirling."

sive sum of £800 which was required, he was remanded to
jail, where he continued to edit his paper by dictating to his
clerks through a chink in the door.   A grand jury was im-
panelled, but refused to indict him.   Therefore the attorney-
general filed an "information"[1] against him for "false, scandalous, malicious, and seditious libels."   Six months elapsed
before the trial came on, and meanwhile the plain speaking
Zenger was kept in durance.   His counsel, Smith and Alexander, attacked the commissions of the chief justice and
another judge as unconstitutional, because it had appointed
them "during pleasure" instead of " during good behaviour."
This was for many years a very sore point with the people,
and the move of Smith and Alexander was hailed with ap-
plause. De Lancey had but one way of meeting it. He said,

" You have brought it to that point, gentlemen, that either
we must go from the bench, or you from the bar ; " and he
summarily disbarred the two eminent lawyers for contempt
of court.

Zenger was thus left without counsel, but the popular sympathy for him was increased, and his friends succeeded in engaging the services of Andrew Hamilton, of Philadelphia, the greatest lawyer in the English
colonies, the first, indeed, who attained a truly continental
reputation.   The thoughts of all English America were then
turned upon the poor German printer in a New York jail,
and Hamilton undertook the case without fee or reward.   If
a government could use the law of libel to suppress freedom

Andrew Hamilton

---

[1] An information " differs in no respect from an indictment in its form
and substance, except that it is filed at the mere discretion of the proper
law officer of the government *ex officio*, without the intervention of a
grand jury."   Bouvier, *Law Dictionary*, s. v. ; Blackstone's *Commentaries*, iv. 308.

A. Hamilton

A Song made upon the Election of new Magistrates for this City.

To the tune of, To you fair Ladies now on land

To you good lads that dare oppose
    all lawless power and might,
You are the theme that we have chose,
    and to your praise we write:
You dar'd to shew your faces brave
In spight of every abject slave ;
             with a fa la la.

Your votes you gave for those brave men
    who feasting did dispise ;
And never prostituted pen
    to certify the lies
That were drawn up to put in chains,
As well our nymphs as happy swains ;
             with a fa la la.

And tho the great ones frown at this,
    what need have you to care ?
Still let them fret and talk amiss,
    you'll shew you boldly dare
Stand up to save your Country dear,
In spight of usquebaugh and beer ;
             with a fa la la.

They beg'd and pray'd for one year more,
    but it was all in vain :
No wolawants you'd have, you swore ;
    By jove you made it plain :
So sent them home to take their rest.
And here's a health unto the best ;
             with a fa la la.

A Song made upon the foregoing Occasion.

To the Time of, Now, now, you Tories all shall stoop.

Come on brave boys, let us be brave
    for liberty and law,

Boldly despise the haughty Knave,
    that would keep us in aw.
Let's scorn the tools bought by a sop,
    and every cringing fool.
The man who basely bend's a sop,
    a vile insipid tool.

Our Country's Rights we will defend,
    like brave and honest men ;
We voted right and there's an end,
    and so we'll do again.
We vote all signers out of place
    as men who did amiss,
Who sold us by a false adress,
    I'm sure we're right in this.

Exchequer courts, as void by law,
    great grievances we call ;
Tho' great men do assert no flaw
    is in them ; they shall fall,
And be contemn'd by every man
    that's fond of liberty.
Let them withstand it all they can,
    our Laws we will stand by.

Tho' pettyfogging knaves deny
    us Rights of Englishmen ;
We'll make the scoundrel raskals fly,
    and ne'er return again.
Our Judges they would chop and change
    for those that serve their turn,
And will not surely think it strange
    if they for this should mourn.

Come fill a bumber, fill it up,
    unto our Aldermen ;
For common-council fill the cup,
    and take it o'er again.
While they with us resolve to stand
    for liberty and law,
We'll drink their healths with hat in hand,
    whoraa ! whoraa ! whoraa !

ZENGER'S SEDITIOUS SONGS

By his Excellency

William Cosby, Captain General and Governour in Chief
of the Provinces of *New-York*, *New-Jersey*, and Territories thereon
depending in America, Vice-Admiral of the same, and Colonel in His Majesty's
Army.

A PROCLAMATION.

Hereas Ill-minded and Disaffected Persons have lately dispersed
in the City of *New-York*, and divers other Places, several
Scandalous and Seditious Libels, but more particularly two Printed
Scandalous Songs or Ballads, highly defaming the Administration of
His Majesty's Government in this Province, tending greatly to
inflame the Minds of His Majesty's good Subjects, and to disturb
the Publick Peace. And *Whereas* the Grand Jury for the City and
County of New-York did lately, by their Address to me, complain
of these Pernicious Practices, and request me to issue a Proclamation
for the Discovery of the Offenders, that they might, by Law, receive
a Punishment adequate to their Guilt and Crime. *I Have* therefore
thought fit, by and with the Advice of his Majesty's Council, to
issue this Proclamation, hereby Promising *Twenty Pounds* as a Reward,
to such Person or Persons who shall discover the Author or Authors
of the two Scandalous Songs or Ballads aforesaid, to be paid to the
Person or Persons discovering the same, as soon as such Author or
Authors shall be Convicted of having been the Author or Authors
thereof.

*GIVEN under My Hand and Seal at Fort-George in New-York this Sixth Day
of November, in the Eighth year of the Reign of Our Sovereign Lord G* ORGE
*the Second, by the Grace of G O D of Great-*ritain, France *and* Ireland, KING,
Defender of the Faith, &c. and in the year of Our LORD, 1734.

By his Excellency's Command,
Fred. Morris, D. Cl. Conc.   **W. COSBY.**

GOD Save the KING.

PROCLAMATION AGAINST ZENGER

of speech and of the press, it would be the end of liberty in these colonies. All that Zenger had said, in the paragraph chiefly relied on by the prosecution, was the plain truth. He

Rip Van Dam

said that judges were arbitrarily displaced and new courts erected without consent of the legislature, by which means jury trial was taken away whenever a governor felt so disposed; and furthermore he declared that the tendency of such tyrannical acts was to drive residents of New York away to other colonies. But let us see his very words : —

"One of our neighbours of New Jersey being in company, observing [certain persons] of New York full of complaints, endeavoured to persuade them to remove into Jersey; to which it was replied, that would be leaping out of the frying-pan into the fire; for, says he, we both are under the same governor, and your assembly have shown with a witness what is to be expected from them. One that was then moving from New York to Pennsylvania (to which place it is reported several considerable men are removing) expressed much concern for the circumstances of New York, and seemed to think them very much owing to the influence that some men had in the administration; said he was now going from them, and was not to be hurt by any measures they should take, but could not help having some concern for the welfare of his countrymen, and should be glad to hear that the assembly would exert themselves as became them; by showing that they have the interest of the country more at heart than the gratification of any private view of any of their members, or being at all affected by the smiles or frowns of a governor; both which ought equally to be despised when the interest of their country is at stake. 'You,' says he, 'complain of the lawyers, but I think the law itself is at an end.' We see men's deeds destroyed, judges arbitrarily displaced, new courts erected without consent of the legislature, by which it seems to me trials by juries are taken away when a governor pleases; men of known estates denied their votes, contrary to the received practice of the best expositor of any law. Who is there in that province that can call anything his own, or enjoy any liberty longer than those in the administration will condescend to let them, for which reason I left it, as I believe more will." [1]

The words of the alleged libel

If such plain speaking were to be in our days condemned as libellous, which of our newspapers could survive for four-

[1] *Report of Zenger Trial*, Boston, 1738.

and-twenty hours ? Hamilton admitted that this paragraph
had been printed, whereupon the attorney-general Hamilton's
at once claimed a verdict for the crown. But the argument.
"information" had described the paragraph as "false, scandalous, malicious, and seditious," and Hamilton fastened

LORD MANSFIELD

upon the allegation of falsehood. He declared that the paragraph simply stated plain and well-known facts. Lord Man-
The chief justice and the attorney-general reminded field's
opinion,
him that the truth of a libel could not be admitted 1770
in evidence. This was the English law at that time, and
a few years later Lord Mansfield, in commenting upon it,
declared that "the greater truth, the greater libel." It was

then held that the only question for the jury was the fact of publication. But the contrary view was pressing for recognition, and in the famous cases of Woodfall and Miller, in 1770, before the same eminent judge, the jury fairly took the matter into their own hands, deciding among themselves that certain expressions were not libellous, and returning a peremptory verdict of not guilty.[1] The question was put to rest in 1792 by Fox's Libel Act, which declared it to be the law of England that the truth of a so-called libel is admissible in evidence, and that the jury have a right to examine into the innocence or criminality of the writing and to give their verdict peremptorily without stating their reasons.

Fox's Act, 1792

We can thus see the vast importance of the step taken by the Philadelphia lawyer, Hamilton, in 1735, when he insisted not only that the jury should listen to proof of the truthfulness of Zenger's paragraph, but should also decide whether it could properly be condemned as libellous, or not. Hamilton may be said to have conducted the case according to the law of the future, and thus to have helped to make that law. In the history of the freedom of the press his place is beside the great names of Erskine and Fox. A few extracts from his speech must be quoted : —

The "law of the future" in 1735

"Years ago it was a crime to speak the truth, and in that terrible court of Star Chamber many brave men suffered for so doing ; and yet, even in that court a great and good man durst say what I hope will not be taken amiss of me to say in this place, to wit : ' The practice of *informations* for libels is a sword in the hands of a wicked king, and an arrant coward, to cut down and destroy the innocent ; the one cannot because of his high station, and the other dares not because of his want of courage, revenge himself in any other manner.' . . . Our Constitution gives us an opportunity to prevent wrong by appealing to the people. . . . But of what use is this mighty privi-

Part of Hamilton's speech

[1] Sir Erskine May, *Constitutional History of England*, ii. 115.

By his Excellency

William Cosby, Captain General and Governour in Chief of the Provinces of *New-York*, *New-Jersey*, and Territories thereon depending, in America, Vice-Admiral of the same, and Colonel in His Majesty's Army.

A PROCLAMATION.

Whereas by the Contrivance of some evil Disposed and Disaffected Persons, divers Journals or Printed News Papers, (entitled, *The New-York Weekly Journal, containing the freshest Advices, Foreign and Domestick*) have been caused to be Printed and Published by *John Peter Zenger*, in many of which Journals or Printed News-Papers (but more particularly those Numbred 7, 47, 48, 49) are contained divers Scandalous, Virulent, False and Seditious Reflections, not only upon the whole Legislature, in general, and upon the most considerable Persons in the most distinguish'd Stations in this Province, but also upon His Majesty's lawful and rightful Government, and just Prerogative. Which said Reflections seem contrived by the wicked Authors of them, not only to create Jealousies, Discontents and Animosities in the Minds of his Majesty's Leige People of this Province, to the Subversion of the Peace & Tranquility thereof, but to alienate their Affections from the best of Kings, and raise *Factions, Tumults* and *Sedition* among them. *Wherefore* I have thought fit, by and with the Advice of His Majesty's Council, to issue this Proclamation, hereby Promising a Reward of *Fifty Pounds* to such Person or Persons who shall discover the Author or Authors of the said *Scandalous, Virulent* and *Seditious Reflections* contained in the said *Journals* or *Printed News-Papers*, to be paid to the Person or Persons discovering the same, as soon as such Author or Authors shall be Convicted of having been the Author or Authors thereof.

GIVEN under My Hand and Seal at Fort-George *in* New-York *this Sixth Day of* November, *in the Eighth year of the Reign of Our Sovereign Lord* GEORGE *the Second, by the Grace of* GOD, *of* Great-Britain, France *and* Ireland, KING *Defender of the Faith, &c. and in the Year of Our LORD* 1734.

By his Excellency's Command,   W. COSBY.
   Fred. Morris, D. Cl. Conc.

GOD Save the KING.

PROCLAMATION AGAINST ZENGER'S "JOURNAL"

A brief Narrative of the Case and Tryal of *John Peter Zenger*, Printer of the New-York weekly *Journal*.

AS There was but one Printer in the Province of *New-York*, that printed a publick News Paper, I was in Hopes, if I undertook to publish another, I might make it worth my while ; and I soon found my Hopes were not groundless: My first Paper was printed, *Nov. 5th, 1733.* and I continued printing and publishing of them, I thought to the Satisfaction of every Body, till the *January* following; when the Chief Justice was pleased to animadvert upon the Doctrine of Libels, in a long Charge given in that Term to the Grand Jury, and afterwards on the third *Tuesday of October, 1734.* was again pleased to charge the Grand Jury in the following Words.

‘ *Gentlemen* ; I shall conclude with reading a Paragraph or two out of the ‘ same Book, concerning Libels ; they are arrived to that Height, that they ‘ call loudly for your Animadversion ; it is high Time to put a Stop to them ; ‘ for at the rate Things are now carried on, when all Order and Government ‘ is endeavoured to be trampled on ; Reflections are cast upon Persons of all ‘ Degrees, must not these Things end in Sedition, if not timely prevented? Lenity, ‘ you have seen will not avail, it becomes you then to enquire after the Of‘fenders, that we may in a due Course of Law be enabled to punish them. ‘ If you, *Gentlemen*, do not interpose, consider whether the ill Consequences ‘ that may arise from any Disturbances of the publick Peace, may not in part, ‘ lye at your Door?

‘ *Hawkins*, in his Chapter of Libels, considers three Points, 1*st*. *What shall* ‘ *be said to be a Libel.* 2*dly*. *Who are lyable to be punished for it.* 3*dly*. *In what* ‘ *Manner they are to be punished.* Under the 1*st*. he says, §. 7. *Nor can there be* ‘ *any Doubt, but that a Writing which defames a private Person only, is as much* ‘ *a Libel as that which defames Persons intrusted in a publick Capacity, in as much* ‘ *as it manifestly tends to create ill Blood, and to cause a Disturbance of the publick Peace;* ‘ *however, it is certain, that it is a very high Aggravation of a Libel, that it tends to* ‘ *scandalize the Government, by reflecting on those who are entrusted with the Admini-* ‘ *stration of publick Affairs, which does not only endanger the publick Peace, as all other* ‘ *Libels do, by stirring up the Parties immediately concerned in it, to Acts of Revenge,* ‘ *but also has a direct Tendency to breed in the People a Dislike of their Governours,* ‘ *and incline them to Faction and Sedition.* As to the 2*d*. Point he says §. 10. ‘ *It is certain, not only he who composes or procures another to compose it but* ‘ *also that he who publishes, or procures another to publish it, are in Danger of being* ‘ *punished for it* ; *and it is said not to be material whether he who disperses a Libel,* ‘ *knew any Thing of the Contents or Effects of it or not* ; *for nothing could be more*

A *easy*

lege if every man that suffers must be silent; and if a man
must be taken up as a libeller for telling his sufferings to his
neighbour? . . . Prosecutions for libels since the time of the
Star Chamber have generally been set on foot at the instance
of the crown or his ministers, and countenanced by judges
who hold their places at pleasure . . . If a libel is understood in the large and unlimited sense urged by Mr. Attorney, there is scarce a writing I know that may not be called
a libel, or scarcely any person safe from being called to
account as a libeller. Moses, meek as he was, libelled Cain;
and who has not libelled the Devil? for, according to Mr.
Attorney, it is no justification to say that one has a bad
name. . . . How must a man speak or write, or what must
he hear, read, or sing, or when must he laugh, so as to be
secure from being taken up as a libeller? I sincerely believe
that if some persons were to go through the streets of New
York nowadays, and read a part of the Bible, if it were not
known to be such, Mr. Attorney, with the help of his innuen-
does, would easily turn it to be a libel; as for instance, the
sixteenth verse of the ninth chapter of Isaiah: 'The leaders
of the people (*innuendo*, the governor and council of New
York) cause them (*innuendo*, the people of this province)
to err, and they (meaning the people of this province) are
destroyed (*innuendo*, are deceived into the loss of their liberty, which is the worst kind of destruction).'"

After concluding his argument, the learned counsel, pale
and haggard from an illness, turned to the jury with the following impressive peroration: —

"You see I labour under the weight of years, and am borne
down with great infirmities of body; yet, old and weak as I
am, I should think it my duty, if required, to go to His pero-
the utmost part of the land, where my service ration
could be of use in assisting to quench the flame of prosecutions upon *informations* set on foot by the government, to
deprive a people of the right of remonstrating and complaining of the arbitary attempts of men in power. Men who
injure and oppress the people under their administration

provoke them to cry out and complain, and then make that very complaint the foundation for new oppressions. . . . I wish I could say there were no instances of this kind. But to conclude: the question before the court, and you, gentlemen of the jury, is not of small or private concern; it is not the cause of a poor printer, nor of New York alone, which you are now trying. No! it may in its consequences affect every freeman that lives under a British government on the main of America! It is the best cause, it is the cause of liberty, and I make no doubt but your upright conduct this day will not only entitle you to the love and esteem of your fellow-citizens, but every man who prefers freedom to a life of slavery will bless and honour you, as men who have baffled the attempt of tyranny, and by an impartial and uncorrupt verdict have laid a noble foundation for securing to ourselves, our posterity, and our neighbours, that to which nature and the laws of our country have given us a right, — the liberty both of exposing and opposing arbitary power . . . by speaking and writing *truth !* "

After this eloquent appeal De Lancey's charge to the jury fell upon deaf ears. They had scarcely left the court-room when they returned with the verdict, "Not guilty." The scene of the trial was the new City Hall on Wall Street, which had been built in Bellomont's time; and never perhaps, not even on the day that witnessed the inauguration of George Washington as president of the United States, did it hear such a shout as that which greeted the acquittal of John Peter Zenger. The judges tried by threats to quell the tumult; they might as well have tried to stop the flow of the North River. An English naval officer, Captain Norris, of the frigate Tartar, called out that hurrahs were as lawful there as in Westminster Hall, where they were somewhat loud when the seven bishops were acquitted. At this popular allusion, renewed cheers upon cheers made the welkin ring. A public dinner was given to the venerable Hamilton by the mayor and aldermen, and when it was time for him to start for Philadelphia he was

Trium-
phant ac-
quittal of
Zenger

escorted to his sloop with drums and trumpets, like a conquering hero.

Here we may leave, for the present, the story of the
political vicissitudes of the Citadel of America. We may
hope to resume the narrative in a later volume, in its connection with the mighty drama of the rise and fall of New
France. At present some features of social life among the
Knickerbockers demand our attention.

CHAPTER XV

KNICKERBOCKER SOCIETY

AT the time of the Zenger trial the population of the province of New York had reached 50,000, about one fifth of which was in the city on Manhattan Island. On the east side of the city the growth in half a century was noticeable, though very slow if rated by modern standards. Houses had arisen pretty closely as far up as John Street, and more sparsely as far as Beekman Street. Especially noteworthy was the increase in wharves and docks, quays and shipyards, which came close upon one another all the way from Whitehall to near the site of the Catharine Street ferry. Pearl Street was no longer the river bank, for Water Street had been raised above the waves. Looking across to the Brooklyn shore, you would have seen there a dozen or more wooden farmhouses.

New York in 1735

On the west side of the island the aspect of things was still more rural. There was no northerly and southerly thoroughfare west of Broadway, but cross streets were opened as far up as Cortlandt Street, and on the North River were two docks. Up near the present foot of Chambers Street was a garden for popular resort, with a new bowling green or skittles ground. Most of the open country between Cortlandt Street and the village of Sappokanican or Greenwich, an area of more than sixty acres, was then known as the King's Farm. It was the land which the blooming widow Anneke Jans had brought to Dominie Bogardus, and it was long known as the Dominie's Bowery. In 1664 it was confirmed by Governor Nicolls to Anneke Jans and her heirs. In 1671 five of the

The farm of Anneke Jans

JAMES LYNE'S PLAN OF NEW

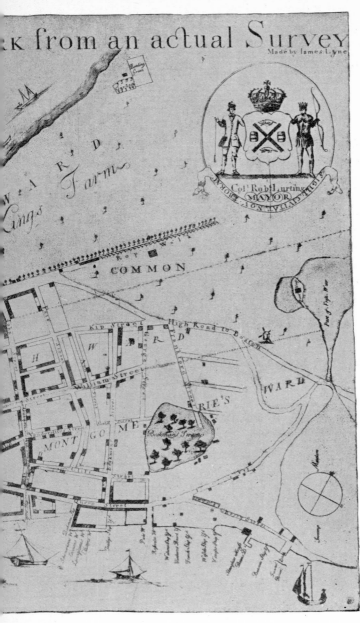

k from an actual Survey

Made by James Lyne

Col.ª Rob.ª Lurting
MAYOR

W A R D

Kings Farm

COMMON

Rope Walk

Kid Street

High Road to Boston

William Street

W A R D

H

Bower Street

WARD

Place of Pipe Maker

RIE'S

MONTGOME

Richard Twenty

W. BRADFORD, CIRCA 1731

heirs sold the farm to Governor Lovelace, and in 1674 the Duke of York confiscated it, so that it was the Duke's Farm until 1685, when with James's accession to the throne it became the King's Farm. In Governor Fletcher's time Trinity Church was founded, and in 1705 Queen Anne granted this farm to the church. It happened that one of the sons of Anneke Jans had not joined in the sale to Lovelace, and the heirs of this son claimed that his failure to join invalidated the sale. At first the property was not of great value, but with the growth of the city its value increased enormously, and suits in ejectment were brought against

ANNEKE JANS'S MARK

Trinity Church by the heirs who coveted the property. Between 1750 and 1847 not less than sixteen or seventeen such suits were brought, with a persistency which seemed to learn no lessons from defeat. In 1847 Vice-chancellor Sanford decided that, after waiving all other points, the church had acquired a valid title by prescription, and all the adverse claims were vitiated by lapse of time.

Above the Freshwater Pond in 1740 there had been little change since 1680, except that there were a few more country houses along the Bowery Lane. While we note the slow rate of growth in the city, we must also bear in mind the limited extent of the province. Its 50,000 inhabitants lived on Long Island and the banks of the Hudson, all save some 2000 Germans who had come in Governor Hunter's time, and had pushed up the Mohawk valley beyond Schenectady, making settlements at German Flats, Palatine Bridge, and Stone Arabia. Far beyond these

Narrow limits of the province

and quite alone in the wilderness stood the fortified trading-post of Oswego. The territory of the Six Nations, stretching northerly toward the Adirondacks, southerly into the Susquehanna valley, and westward to Lake Erie, was of course claimed by Corlear as protector and overlord; but for the present he had as little control over it as the Grand Turk has over Tripoli. It is important to remember, if we would do justice to the pivotal part played by New York in early American history, that so late as 1776, with a population of 170,000, she ranked only seventh among the thirteen states, while her geographical limits had scarcely changed since 1720. The supreme greatness of New York dates from a period subsequent to the Revolution, and in its origin was closely connected with the westward migration from New England, the settlement of the northwestern states, and the opening of the Erie Canal. In the colonial period the agriculture of New York was considerable, and a great deal of wheat was exported; but the fur trade was always the controlling interest, and was often the source of immense wealth. Nevertheless, inasmuch as New York was preëminently the frontier colony against the French, and as it was made the scene of military operations to a much greater extent than any other colony, it was always necessary to keep up an army. Besides the British regular forces, which were stationed on Manhattan Island, there was a colonial regular army of 2500, and there were more than 15,000 trained militia. These circumstances, as well as the actual frequency of wars between 1690 and 1760, entailed ruinous expense and oppressive taxation, and interfered seriously with the normal growth of

Some causes of slowness in growth the colony. Such a state of things had been to some extent foreseen and dreaded by Andros and Dongan, as it was deplored by the later governors who had to contend with it. One of the worst ills was the chronic affliction of a depreciated paper currency. By the end of the French wars New York had a public debt of £300,000, and the taxation, including direct levies upon real and personal property as well as duties on imports, was an acute annoyance.

It was probably due to the prevalence of warfare that the power of the assembly was somewhat less and the arbitrariness of the governor somewhat greater than in the other colonies. After seventy years of arbitrary rule, representative assemblies and incessant warfare began at just the same time in the citadel of America, with Governor Fletcher. The most important part of the constitutional progress achieved by the assemblies came within the interval of peace between the Treaty of Utrecht and the War of the Austrian Succession. Usually the headquarters of the commanding general were in the city of New York, and various courtly visitors were attracted by the army. More than elsewhere the royal governor had somewhat the air of a sovereign holding court, and the political atmosphere about him was thick and heavy with Toryism. The officials generally were demonstrative in their loyalty, keeping the king's birthday with festivities and speeches. Under such auspices a powerful Tory party was developed in New York, and in the War of Independence it was made to seem all the more powerful in that the Tory Johnsons controlled the military policy of the Long House. Nevertheless the Whig party in New York was also very strong and vigorous, nor was it by any means confined to the lower grades of society. Among the leaders of the Revolutionary party were the Schuylers and Livingstons, Van Rensselaers, Van Cortlandts, Morrises, Alexanders, Clintons, and Jays. It is a common mistake to overrate the strength of New York Toryism. The truth is that both parties were very powerful in their leaders, while beneath there was a surging mass of people with uncertain proclivities, some strongly Whig, some strongly Tory, some independent, some stolidly indifferent to everything outside of private business. The result was seen in excitement and disorder at elections, and occasional violent vicissitudes in party supremacy. In Massachusetts or Virginia you could usually foretell the action of the assembly upon an important question, there was so much homogeneity of thought among the members

Comparative weakness of the assembly

Whigs and Tories

of those purely English communities. But in New York the effects of the few independent thinkers and of the stolid mass were things with which it was difficult to reckon quanti-

Great value of New York as a "doubtful state" tatively. Similar characteristics have distinguished the state of New York down to the present day. The politics of some communities are so swayed by the inert mass of engrained prejudice that independent thinking finds it nearly impossible to reverse the customary verdict. You know beforehand that in these days the vote of Vermont will be Republican and that of Alabama will be Democratic, no matter what are the principles and issues at stake ; but in New York an immense majority on one side may be followed the next year by an equally overwhelming majority on the other side. This uncertainty, combined with the great magnitude of its vote, almost enough of itself to determine a national election, has made New York a factor of inestimable value in American history. It has made that state one of the chief safeguards of the republic, and for it we have largely to thank the spirit of cosmopolitanism which has characterized it ever since the days of Peter Minuit. That cosmopolitan spirit, weakening the grasp of local prejudices, leaves the public mind responsive to the needs and exigencies of the time. One of the worst calamities that could happen in our time would be the conversion of New York into a "sure" state ; one of the greatest benefits would be the change of Pennsylvania into a perennially "doubtful" state.

Returning to our old Knickerbocker community, we may note that the old antagonism between the Leislerians and the Aristocrats was not parallel to the opposition between Whigs and Tories. Some features of Leislerism were reproduced in the democratic views of Jefferson's extremest followers in the days of the French Revolution. Among our

The old aristocracy Revolutionary leaders there was aristocracy enough in temper and views, as exemplified in Washington, Schuyler, Jay, Trumbull, and Hancock. Especially in New York we may note the conspicuousness of well-born and accomplished leaders as hardly less notable than in Virginia. This fact was an outcome of the social conditions established early in the colonial period.

The tone of colonial New York was always aristocratic. Neither Maryland nor Virginia furnished a much stronger contrast to that peculiar type of New England democracy which was exemplified perhaps most completely in Connecticut. In the latter colony, with its lowest stratum of society far above the peasant type, there were few if any great landed estates or accumulations of wealth in any form. Yet nowhere else in America were so large a proportion of the people in easy circumstances; nowhere was there more comfort and refinement "to the square mile." The relation of landlord and tenant was seldom met with in Connecticut. Education was universal, and the country squire was a much more cultivated person than his contemporary in England, as the country minister was more learned. Self-government by town meeting was ubiquitous, public debts were very unusual, taxation was light, governors as well as assemblies were chosen by the people, and the commonwealth was for all practical purposes as independent of Great Britain as it is to-day. Connecticut in the eighteenth century was preëminently the home of unpretentious and refined democracy, a "land of steady habits," but with perhaps a little more monotony and provinciality than its neighbours on either side.

The Connecticut type of democracy.

In New York, on the other hand, there was a considerable stratum of peasantry, among the Germans and Dutch at least, and in the city there was something of a "populace" of rough water-side characters, discontented artisans, and idlers in tap-rooms. In New York, as in Boston, it was this sort of populace that now and then relieved the tedium of existence by mobs and riots. Yet neither New York nor Boston could be called an unruly town. Between the peasantry and the patroons, as between the populace and the merchant princes, the social interval was very wide. Of the lowest and poorest classes it must

Peasantry and populace of New York

be said that there were extremely few paupers or beggars. But at the other extreme of society immense fortunes were accumulated ; and there was a distinct consciousness of a gulf between high and low which gave to Leislerism certain features that in Connecticut would have been impossible. The relation of landlord and tenant was extremely common. The great manors of the Cortlandts and Van Rensselaers and Livingstons extended over many square miles and were cultivated by a vast number of tenants. Each of these manors had a representative in the assembly ; their lords held court-baron and court-leet, very much as in Maryland,[1] and could even in some instances inflict capital punishment. On rent-days, twice a year, the tenants came flocking to the manor-house and, after paying their rent in coin or produce, were entertained by the landlord with a barbecue and plentiful draughts of 'Sopus ale.[2] These vast estates were held together by primogeniture, usually somewhat qualified by small legacies to the younger sons and the daughters. The prevalence of this manorial system was often cited, and no doubt correctly, as one reason for the slow increase of population in New York ; a small farmer would prefer to be a landowner in New Jersey or Pennsylvania, rather than the tenant of a manor on the Hudson. Most of the manorial privileges were swept away during the War of Independence, and the patroons lost their position of political superiority.

The manors and their tenantry

As an example of a rural mansion may be cited that of the Schuylers at the Flats, near Albany, as described by Mrs. Grant of Laggan, in her charming "Memoirs of an American Lady." The estate ran along two miles of the western bank of the Hudson, bordered with drooping elm-trees of enormous girth. "On the right you saw the river in all its beauty, there above a mile broad. On the opposite side the view was bounded by steep hills, covered with lofty pines,

---

[1] See *Old Virginia and Her Neighbours*, Illustrated Edition, 131–134.
[2] At Esopus and elsewhere the water of the Hudson has always made a light ale of fine body and extremely delicate flavour.

Lady Anne Grant

from which a waterfall descended. . . . Opposite to the grounds lay an island, above a mile in length, and about a quarter in breadth, which also belonged to the colonel; exquisitely beautiful it was, and though the haunt I most delighted in, it is not in my power to describe it. . . . Southward, on the confines of an interminable wild, rose two gently sloping eminences, about half a mile from the shore. From each of these a large brook descended, bending through the plain, and having their course marked by the shades of primeval trees and shrubs left there to shelter the cattle when the ground was cleared. On these eminences, in the near neighbourhood and full view of the mansion at the Flats, were two large and well-built dwellings, inhabited by Colonel Schuyler's two younger sons, Peter and Jeremiah. To the eldest was allotted the

Description of the Schuyler manor

SCHUYLER MANSION AT THE FLATS, ERECTED IN 1666

place inhabited by his father, which, from its lower situation and level surface was called the Flats. . . . They had also a large house in Albany, which they occupied occasionally."

The mansion at the Flats "was a large brick house of two or rather three stories (for there were excellent attics), besides a sunk story, finished with the exactest neatness.

The lower floor had two spacious rooms, with large light closets ; on the first there were three rooms, and in the upper one four.   Through the middle of the house was a The Schuy- very wide passage, with opposite front and back ler mansion doors, which in summer admitted a stream of air peculiarly grateful to the languid senses.   It was furnished with chairs and pictures like a summer parlour.   Here the family usually sat in hot weather, when there were no cere- monious strangers. . . . The mirrors, the paintings, the china, but above all the state bed, were considered as the family Teraphim, secretly worshipped and only exhibited on very rare occasions. . . . The rooms were shut up to keep the flies, which in that country are an absolute nuisance, from spoiling the furniture.   Another motive was that they might be pleasantly cool when opened for company.   This house had also two appendages common to all those belong- ing to persons in easy circumstances there.   One was a large portico at the door, with a few steps leading up to it, and floored like a room ; it was open at the sides, and had seats all around.   Above was either a slight wooden roof, painted like an awning, or a covering of lattice-work, over which a transplanted wild vine spread its luxuriant leaves and numer- ous clusters.   These, though small and rather too acid till sweetened by the frost, had a beautiful appearance.   What gave an air of liberty and safety to these rustic porticoes, which always produced in my mind a sensation of pleasure that I know not how to define, was the number of little birds domesticated there.   For their accommodation there was a small shelf built round, where they nestled, safe from the touch of slaves and children, who were taught to regard them as the good genii of the place, not to be disturbed with impunity."

The protection which these little birds bestowed " was of more importance than any inhabitant of Britain can imagine. American . . . The insect population is numerous beyond insects belief. . . . These minute aerial foes are more harassing than the terrible inhabitants of the forest, and more difficult to expel.[1]   It is only by protecting these little winged allies, who attack them in their own element, that the conqueror of the lion and tamer of the elephant can hope to sleep in peace, or eat his meals unpolluted. . . .

" At the back of the large house was a smaller and lower one, so joined to it as to make the form of a cross.   There one or two lower and smaller rooms below, and the same number above, afforded a refuge to the family during the rigours of winter, when the spacious summer rooms would have been intolerably cold, and the smoke of prodigious wood fires would have sullied the elegantly clean furniture.   Here too was a sunk story, where the kitchen was immediately below the eating parlour, and increased the general warmth of the house.   In summer the negroes resided in slight outer kitchens, where food was drest for the family. Servants' quarters Those who wrought in the fields often had their simple dinner cooked without, and ate it under the shade of a great tree.

" One room in the greater house was open for the reception of company ; the rest were bed-chambers for their accommodation, while the domestic friends of the family occupied neat little bedrooms in the attics, or in The bed-rooms the winter house.   This house contained no drawing-room ; that was an unheard-of luxury.   The winter rooms had carpets : the lobby had oil-cloth painted in lozenges, to imitate blue and white marble.   The best bedroom was hung with family portraits, some of which were admirably executed ; and in the eating-room were some fine scripture paintings. . . .

"The house fronted the river, on the brink of which,

[1] A London newspaper of 1710 thus speaks of the mosquito: " The New York people are greatly troubled with a little insect which follows the hay that is made in the salt meadows, or comes home with the cows in the evening.   This little animalcule can disfigure most terribly a person's face in a single night.   The skin is sometimes so covered over with small blisters from their stings, that people are ashamed to appear in public."   Mrs. Lamb's *History of the City of New York*, ii. 490. Among the agreeable features of life in England are the absence of mosquitoes and scarcity of flies.

OLD DUTCH CHURCH, ERECTED IN 1715

under shades of elm and sycamore, ran the great road towards Saratoga, Stillwater, and the northern lakes. A little
simple avenue of morella cherry trees, enclosed with a white
rail, led to the road and river, not three hundred yards distant. Adjoining to this, on the south side, was an enclosure
The   subdivided into three parts, of which the first was
approaches a small hayfield, opposite the south end of the
house; the next, not so long, a garden; and the third, by
far the largest, an orchard. These were surrounded by simple
deal fences.

"Adjoining to the orchard was the most spacious barn I
The barn   ever beheld, . . . at least a hundred feet long and
             sixty wide. The roof rose to a great height in the
midst, and sloped down till it came within ten feet of the
ground, when the walls commenced; which, like the whole of
this vast fabric, were formed of wood. It was raised three
feet from the ground by beams resting on stone; and on

these beams was laid a massive oak floor. Before the door was a large sill, sloping downwards, of the same materials. About twelve feet in breadth, on each side of this capacious building were divided off for cattle ; on one side ran a manger, at the above-mentioned distance from the wall, the whole length of the building, with a rack above it ; on the others were stalls for the other cattle. . . . The cattle and horses stood with their hinder parts to the wall, and their heads projecting towards the threshing floor. There was a prodigious large box or open chest in one side built up, for holding the corn after it was thrashed ; and the roof, which was very lofty and spacious, was supported by large cross-beams ; from one to the other of these was stretched a great number of long poles, so as to form a sort of open loft, on which the whole rich crop was laid up. The floor of those parts of the barn, which answered the purposes of a stable and cow-house, was made of thick slab deals, laid loosely over the supporting beams. And the mode of cleaning those places was by turning the boards and permitting the dung and litter to fall into the receptacles left open below for the purpose. . . . In the front of this vast edifice there were prodigious folding doors, and two others that opened behind."[1]

Mrs. Grant's description of Albany is too much to our present purpose to be omitted : " One very wide and long street lay parallel to the river, the intermediate space between it and the shore being occupied by gardens. A small, steep hill rose above the centre of the town, on The town which stood a fort, intended (but very ill-adapted) of Albany for the defence of the place and of the neighbouring country. From the foot of this hill another street was built, sloping pretty rapidly down till it joined the one before mentioned. . . . This street was still wider than the other ; it was only paved on each side, the middle being occupied by public edifices. These consisted of a market-place, a guard-house, a town hall, and the English and Dutch churches. The Eng-

1 *Memoirs of an American Lady*, i. 142, 143, 147, 164–168, 171–173, 176–178.

lish church, belonging to the Episcopal persuasion and in the diocese of the Bishop of London, stood at the foot of the hill, at the upper end of the street. The Dutch church was situated at the bottom of the descent where the street terminated. Two irregular streets, not so broad but equally long, ran parallel to those, and a few even ones opened between them. . . . This city was a kind of semi-rural establishment ; every house had its garden, well, and a little green behind ; before every door a tree was planted, rendered interesting by being coeval with some beloved member of the family ; many of their trees were of a prodigious size and extraordinary beauty, but without regularity, every one planting the kind that best pleased him, or which he thought would afford the most agreeable shade to the open portico at his door, which was surrounded by seats, and ascended by a few steps. It was in these that each domestic group was seated in summer evenings to enjoy the balmy twilight or serenely clear moonlight. Each family had a cow, fed in a common pasture at the end of the town. In the evening they returned all together, of their own accord, with their tinkling bells hung at their necks, along the wide and grassy street, to their wonted sheltering trees, to be milked. . . . At one door were young matrons, at another the elders of the people, at a third the youths and maidens, gaily chatting or singing together, while the children played around the trees, or waited by the cows for the chief ingredient of their frugal supper, which they generally ate sitting on the steps in the open air. . . .

"At the further end of the town was a fertile plain along the river, three miles in length and near a mile broad. This was all divided into lots, where every inhabitant raised Indian corn sufficient for the food of two or three slaves (the greatest number that each family ever possessed), and for his horses, pigs, and poultry ; their flour and other grain they purchased from farmers in the vicinity. Above the town, a long stretch to the westward was occupied first by sandy hills, on which grew bilberries of uncommon size and flavour in prodigious quantities ; beyond rise heights of a poor

ST. PETER'S CHURCH, ERECTED IN 1714

hungry soil, thinly covered with stunted pines, or dwarf oak.
Yet in this comparatively barren tract there were Pictur-
several wild and picturesque spots, where small esque surroundings
brooks, running in deep and rich bottoms, nour-
ished on their banks every vegetable beauty. There some
of the . . . settlers had cleared the luxuriant wood from
these charming little glens, and built neat cottages for their
slaves, surrounded with little gardens and orchards, sheltered
from every blast, wildly picturesque and richly productive.
. . . One of their sequestered vales was in my time inhabited by a hermit. He was a Frenchman, and did not seem
to inspire much veneration among the Albanians. They
imagined, or had heard, that he retired to that solitude in
remorse for some fatal duel in which he had been engaged ;
and considered him an idolator because he had an image
of the Virgin in his hut. I think he retired to Canada at
last ; but I remember being ready to worship him for the

sanctity with which my imagination invested him, and being cruelly disappointed because I was not permitted to visit him." [1]

In the middle of the eighteenth century Albany was much more distinctively Dutch than the city of New York, which was so cosmopolitan. In general Dutch habits held their own with much more conservatism in towns like Esopus, or Sche-

A Flatbush country house

nectady, or Flatbush, than in the centre of travel and traffic. With some Flatbush details we may complete our sketch of the Dutch country house. Ordinarily it had not three stories, like the Schuyler mansion, but was a low and rambling affair, covering much territory but needing few stairs. It was usually built of brick. In the earlier times the front roof swept down without break from ridgepole to eaves and beyond, so as to cover a veranda, while the much longer back roof sometimes came within eight feet of the ground. Sometimes in the front were dormer windows. About the middle of the eighteenth century the hipped roof with dormer windows came into vogue. From tin spouts at the end of the gutters the clear rain water fell into tubs or casks. It was not unusual to have a projecting beam from the gable end of the spacious garret, so that heavy articles might be hoisted into it with tackle, as is often seen in Holland to this day.[2] The shutters were usually of solid wood, with a crescent-shaped aperture near the top, and held back when open by a piece of iron shaped like a letter S. Instead of the huge central chimney of New England houses, there were usually two broad and stately chimneys, one on each gable end. The Dutch front door was almost always divided into an upper and a lower half, so that when the lower half was shut the upper half served the purposes of an open window. The upper half when shut was usually lighted with a large pair of glass bulls'-eyes. Quaint

---

[1] *Memoirs of an American Lady*, i. 44–49.

[2] I am indebted for many details to Mrs. Vanderbilt's *Social History of Flatbush*, New York, 1881, an excellent and scholarly work; but the absence of an index to such a book is an unpardonable sin.

knockers and spoon-shaped latches of iron or polished brass were the outfit of the door. The spacious "stoop" outside, with its long seats cosily facing each other, was a very important adjunct to the house. In summer time it fulfilled the functions of family sitting-room and reception- The stoop

THE SCHUYLER MANSION, ERECTED IN 1761

room ; neighbours gathered there and talked politics and gossip amid the fragrance of tobacco smoke.

In the interiors of these Dutch houses the heavy oak beams which supported the upper floor often projected below the ceiling of the room underneath, a pleasing architectural feature. In the humbler houses a plain protecting board, known as a "chair rail," ran round the plaster walls about three feet above the floor ; but panelled wainscots were not very uncommon, and sometimes a wainscoting of tiles might be seen. The jamb of the enormous fireplace was usually faced with blue or pink tiles, upon which were often represented scenes from the Bible. In winter time the fireside played a part similar to that of the stoop in warm weather. The one in the dining-room was likely to be the place of chief resort. Its dancing flames lighted up the china and silver in the cupboard opposite, and the moon's The dining-room face on the tall clock in the corner, and afforded enough illumination for a game of backgammon or dominoes on the cherry dining-table, though many worthy Dutch families esteemed such diversions, even to the noble chess, as fit only for alehouse parlours. The same flickering light, eked out perhaps by a couple of dip candles, sufficed for grandma with her knitting, beside the chintz-curtained window in her low rush-seated chair with bright red cushion. Other chairs in the room were of mahogany, high-backed, with claw feet, their broad seats covered with brocade. Often, however, the chairs were of painted wood and rush-work, and the table of deal, and the family living-room the ample kitchen. In the latter case there was usually a separate back kitchen for the servants, who were likely to be negro slaves.

The deep dark cellar, with its coolish and even temperature, was for much more than half the year a storage-place for provisions. The farmers of New York raised upon their own farms the greater part of the food which they consumed, and The cellar even in the city, where orchards, kitchen-gardens, and hen-coops were not yet uncommon, there was no such complete dependence upon markets as in our time. A large part of the autumn work was the preparation of the stores that were to be put away in the spacious cellar. The packing of butter in firkins and pickled pork in barrels, the smoking of hams and bacon, the corning of beef rounds and briskets, the chopping of sausage-meat and head-cheese, the trying of lard, the careful and dainty salting of mackerel and other fish, — made it a busy time for all the household. In the cellar might be found all these good things, with kegs of soused pigs' feet, stone jars of pickles, barrels of red and green apples, bins heaped high with potatoes, parsnips, and turnips ; along with barrels of vinegar, cider, and ale, and Here's canty brown jugs of rum. In the houses of the your good health, and wealthier sort there was also plenty of wine, either your fam- of the claret family or some kind of sack, which ily's! was a generic name covering sherries, Canaries, and Madeiras. For your new-fangled hothouse notions of "teetotalism" would have been quite unintelligible to the farmer or burgher of those healthy days of abundant and breezy activity out-of-doors. In the Dutch cupboard or on the sideboard always stood the gleaming decanter of cut glass or the square high-shouldered magnum with its aromatic schnapps.[1]

In the bedrooms, or sometimes in an entry way, you would come here and there upon a long deep chest of cherry or oak, filled with rolls of homespun linen, or with blankets and coverlets. A different kind of fore- *Chests and secretaries* sight was then needed from that of the present day, when all manner of shops are so accessible. Large quantities of linen were spun and woven into pieces, from which table-cloths, sheets, and garments could be cut when wanted. A bride's trousseau was not ordered all at once from fashionable modistes and milliners, but was taken from family stores of silks and cambrics and laces that years had accumulated.

---

[1] In connection with the subject of eating and drinking it may be interesting to cite the caterer's bill for the banquet given by the corporation of New York to Lord Cornbury, upon his arrival as governor, in 1704.

1704.   THE MAYOR, ALDERMEN, ETC., *Dr.*

		£	s.	d.
Dec. 19	To a piece of beef and cabbage	0	7	6
	To a dish of tripe and cowheel	0	6	0
	To a leg of pork and turnips	0	8	3
	To 2 puddings	0	14	6
	To a surloyn of beef	0	13	6
	To a turkey and onions	0	9	0
	To a leg mutton and pickles	0	6	0
	To a dish chickens	0	10	6
	To minced pyes	1	4	0
	To fruit, cheese, bread, etc.	0	7	6
	To butter for sauce	0	7	9
	To hire of 2 negroes to assist	0	6	0
	To dressing dinner, etc.	1	4	0
	To 31 bottles wine	3	2	0
	To beer and syder	0	12	0
		10	18	6

This is cited from Todd's *City of New York*, p. 224.

Chests were therefore indispensable, and tall cases of drawers were very common. A very beautiful piece of furniture was the secretary or covered writing-desk, with drawers below ; it was usually made of mahogany adorned with polished brass, and it was apt to contain secret drawers or pigeon-holes, where gold, coins, or jewels, or valuable papers could be hidden.

The bedstead was almost always the kingly " four-poster," with its feather-beds resting upon a straw mattress supported by tight cords. It was draped with white dimity curtains and coverlet, or, perhaps, instead of dimity a kind of chintz was used, with vines and birds and flowers in bright colours.

Beds   The legs of the bedstead were so long that there was plenty of room beneath for the low children's bed which was kept there during the day and trundled out at bedtime.   In the days before Satan had invented hot air furnaces and steam radiators, it was apt to be cold in the

NORTH PEARL STREET, FROM STEUBEN STREET SOUTH

bedroom on winter nights. Sometimes water froze in the ewer ; and at such times, in spite of Sergeant Buzfuz, there were those who did trouble themselves about the brass warming-pan, filled with glowing embers, which was thrust here and there between the linen sheets to take off the chill.[1]

[1] For further information concerning the contents of the house, I cite from an appraisement in 1792 the following list, in which the pound sterling has approximately its present value : —

	£	s.	d.
25 pewter plates, 1s. each	1	5	0
37 earthen plates	0	10	0
9 pewter dishes, 4s. each	1	16	0
8 earthen dishes, 2s. 6d. each	1	0	0
2 waffle-irons, 6s. each	0	12	0
1 musket	0	16	0
1 saddle and bridle	3	0	0
10 keelers (wooden milk-tubs)	1	0	0
6 spinning wheels, 12s. each	3	12	0
1 pair kitchen andirons	0	8	0
2 bookcases, 1s. 6d. each	0	3	0
1 bed, bedstead, and curtains	10	0	0
1 dining-table	16	0	0
1 looking-glass	1	10	0
15 Windsor chairs, 6s. each	4	10	0
12 rush-bottom chairs, 2s. each	1	4	0
4 mahogany chairs, 8s. each	1	12	0
8 old chairs, 6d. each	0	4	4
1 mahogany dining-table	4	0	0
1 writing-desk	0	10	0
1 cupboard	0	16	0
1 large chest	0	16	0
1 looking-glass	1	0	0
1 large Dutch cupboard	4	0	0
1 bed, bedstead, and curtains	15	0	0
1 wild-cherry dining-table	1	0	0
1 looking-glass	1	5	0
1 eight-day clock	14	0	0
1 looking-glass	5	0	0
1 desk and bookcase	20	0	0
1 mahogany tea-table	2	0	0
1 bed, bedstead, and curtains	10	0	0
1 Dutch Bible	2	0	0
1 English dictionary	1	0	0
1 parcel of books	7	0	0
6 sets of china cups and saucers	3	0	0
27 Delft plates	0	13	6

In general, so far as concerned the homestead with its equipments, the style of living in colonial New York was one of much comfort with little display. But when we come to the subject of dress, the case was somewhat different. In all parts of the world, and in all ages down to the present, display has been the primary motive in dress, and considerations of comfort have been distinctly secondary. Of late years marked improvement has been shown, and possibly in the endeavour to subordinate display, too little heed has been given to æsthetic requirements. Early in the eighteenth century the streets of New York were gorgeous with costumes. One eminent citizen is described as clad in a long-skirted coat and knee-breeches of cinnamon cloth trimmed with silver lace ; the coat is lined with sky-blue silk, the hose are of dove-coloured silk, and the shoes have large silver buckles. Over his enormous wig, elaborately curled and scented with ambergris, he wears a wide-brimmed hat of black felt with a band of gold lace ; through the opening of his red satin waistcoat finely bestrewn with threads of gold peep the dainty ruffles of the white Holland shirt ; and at his left side, fastened with a bright scarlet swordknot, hangs a diamond-hilted sword. And as for the ladies, with blue-and-gold atlas gowns "laced over very tight stays," showing glimpses of black velvet petticoat trimmed with silver, and not falling so low as to hide the crimson stockings and fine Morocco shoes,[1] we should soon lose ourselves if we were to try to describe more closely the dress-stuffs of the time, with their weird names, — "chilloes, betelees, deribands, tapsiels, surbettees, sannoes, gilongs, mulmuls, and cushlashes " that were familiar enough over the shop coun-

1 silver tankard	.	.	.	.	.	.	. 15	0 0
1 silver sugar-cup	.	.	.	.	.	.	. 14	0 0
1 silver milk-pot .	.	.	.	.	.	.	. 4	0 0
13 silver table-spoons	.	.	.	.	.	.	13	0 0

This is cited from Mrs. Vanderbilt's *Social History of Flatbush*, pp. 81, 82.

[1] Todd, *The City of New York*, pp. 207, 208, 230.

ters in the days when New York was so near to the Indian Ocean.

One fancies that something of the same undefinable but potent charm for which New York is to-day so eminent among the world's great bustling cities must already have characterized it when its roof-trees sheltered but ten thousand souls. Whether it be in the jour- Cheerful-ness of New York nals of visitors, or in private correspondence, we always get the impression of a lively and cheerful town, where people like to come, and from which they are sorry to go away. In the old days, indeed, there was a restful sense of leisure which the rapid pace of modern life has ruthlessly destroyed. For architecture, for other fine arts in their various forms, for learning, for intellectual stimulus of whatever sort, the New York of Burnet's time could not be compared with its mother-city, Amsterdam, to say nothing of such centres of civilization as Venice, or Florence, or Paris; but there was about the little city an air of dignity and refinement which scholars and men of the world found attractive. In 1668 Governor Lovelace wrote, in a letter to Charles II., " I find some of these people have the breeding of courts, and I cannot conceive how such is acquired." The explanation was simple enough; the manners of an old and refined civil-ization had been brought from Europe and retained under the new conditions. Among the settlers who came from the Netherlands there were so many of excellent character, with advantages of education and social position, as to set the standard for the community. The English and French immigrations brought many persons of similar character. Nearly all, outside of the official class and the learned pro-fessions, were merchants or tradesmen, among whom there was an abounding appreciation of the amenities of life; while the continual meeting of different nationalities and different mental habits preserved the cosmopolitan spirit and pre-vented the growth of such self-centred provincialism as has always been a besetting weakness of Boston.

In the olden times society in New York, as elsewhere, got

up with the dawn, took its dinner at noon, and devoted its
evenings to recreation.   Sleighing parties in winter
and fishing picnics in summer were common amuse-
ments ; and there were private theatricals, as well
as balls and concerts.   The first theatre in America was
established in Beekman Street, about the middle of the
eighteenth century, without serious opposition.   There were
more holidays than in other parts of America, and for
this we have doubtless to thank the Dutch.   While in New
England we had little beside the annual Thanksgiving and
Fast days, and frowned upon Maypoles and Christmas pud-
dings, the Dutch kept the church festivals of Christmas,
Easter, and Whitsuntide, as well as the heathen St. Valen-
tine's and May-day, and the specially Dutch St. Nicholas's
day, and New Year's, and Pinkster, which was a day of
June picnics.   As for the urchins, they made life hideous
with gunpowder and fish-horns on Guy Fawkes's day until
the events of 1776 provided them with the Fourth of July
instead.

*Amuse-
ments and
holidays*

New York has always been preëminent for the excellence
of its clubs, and this feature in its social life had become
marked as early as Bellomont's time.   Pleasant
decorum and cordiality ruled in these clubs then as
now.   At first they were usually domiciled in some tavern
or coffee-house, and of these there were many and good ones.
At the time of the Zenger trial the most fashionable inn was
the Black Horse, kept by Robert Todd, vintner, in William
Street, and thither society was wont to repair, not only for
a good dinner and a convivial glass, but for concerts, balls,
and public receptions.   Several of the taverns and coffee-
houses took in the newspapers from the different colonies
and from London.

*Clubs and
inns*

Of reading more profitable and solid than the newspaper
there was not a great deal in colonial New York.
The first public library, with about 1600 volumes,
was established in 1729, in a room in the City
Hall on Wall Street.   It was known as the Corporation

*Reading
and litera-
ture*

Library until 1754, when it was merged in the New York Society Library, founded in that year. In the Dutch period there were some good schools, but these declined under English rule. In 1757 the historian William Smith ex- William claimed : "What a contrast in everything respect- Smith ing the cultivation of science between this and the colonies first settled by the English. . . . Our schools are of the lowest order ; the instructors want instruction ; . . . and the evidences of bad taste, both as to thought and language, are visible in all our proceedings, public and private." [1] This William Smith, son of the accomplished lawyer in the Zenger case, was himself one of the few literary men of the province, the author of a " History of New York to the Year 1732," which is sturdy and racy, but so full of partisan bitterness that Smith himself admits it " deserves not the name of a history." As literature, however, it has decided merits. The only other literary name which needs to be mentioned before the Stamp Act period is that of Cadwalla- Cadwalla-der Colden, son of a Scottish parson in Berwick- der Colden shire. He was born in 1687 and educated at the University of Edinburgh, after which he studied medicine and began the practice of it in Philadelphia. In 1718 Governor Hunter made him surveyor-general of the province of New York. The next year Colden bought a fine estate in Orange County, some 3000 acres, and built a house on it. There he lived for many years in rural quiet, devoting himself to the physical sciences and to history, and keeping up a correspondence with the most eminent scholars and philosophers of Europe. At the time of the Stamp Act he was lieutenant-governor of New York, acting as governor. The work by which he is best known is his " History of the Five Nations."

No outline of the Knickerbocker social life can pass without mention the lower strata of society, the servile classes. These were the same in kind as in Virginia, indented white servants and negro slaves. I have discussed them so elabo-

[1] Smith's *History of New York*, i. 328, ii. 379.

rately in that connection that I need not here repeat myself.[1]

White ser-
vants
In New York, as in Virginia, the indented white servants were either, 1, convicts shipped from Great Britain, to get rid of them ; 2, poor men and women kidnapped and sold into servitude; or, 3, redemptioners, who paid their passage by servile labour after arriving in this country. As the great landed estates of New York were mostly worked by free tenant farmers, the demand for servile labour was very much smaller than in any of the southern colonies, and the indented white servants were much less numerous.

As for negro slavery in New York, it never seemed to be an economic necessity, as in the southern colonies. The

Negro
slaves
interests of no great staple industry seemed inseparably bound up with it, as was the case in Virginia with tobacco, in South Carolina with rice and indigo. The abolition of slavery was therefore easily accomplished by the act of 1785, which declared that from that time forth all children born of slave parents should be born free.[2]

Negro slaves were brought to New Amsterdam as early as 1625 ; they were bought and sold during the entire colonial period at an average price, whether for men or for women, of from $150 to $250. They were employed in all kinds of service, agricultural and domestic, as ploughmen and gardeners, or as cooks and porters and valets, but children were seldom consigned to their care, as with southern "mammies." Ladies might be seen carried about town in sedan chairs borne by coloured men, or in coaches with negro drivers and footmen. They served in almost every menial capacity. In the city they never, perhaps, formed so large a portion of the population as in 1746, when a census showed 2444 slaves in a total of 11,723. It appears that the slaves were generally not overworked or ill-treated. Mrs. Grant

[1] See *Old Virginia and Her Neighbours*, Illustrated Edition, ii. 159–185.

[2] See my *Critical Period of American History*, Illustrated Edition, p. 76. The census of 1820 showed 10,088 slaves in a total population of 1,372,111 ; that of 1830 showed only 75 slaves ; that of 1840 only 4.

THE
HISTORY

Of the PROVINCE of

NEW-YORK,

FROM THE

First Difcovery to the Year M.DCC.XXXII.

To which is annexed,

A Defcription of the Country, with a fhort Account of the Inhabitants, their Trade, Religious and Political State, and the Conftitution of the Courts of Juftice in that Colony.

Lo ! fwarming o'er the new difcover'd World,
Gay Colonies extend; the calm Retreat
Of undeferv'd Diftrefs. ———
——— Bound by focial Freedom, firm they rife;
Of Britain's Empire the Support and Strength. THOMSON.

Nec minor eft Virtus, quàm quærere, parta tueri.

By WILLIAM SMITH, A.M.

LONDON:

Printed for THOMAS WILCOX, Bookfeller at *Virgil's Head*, oppofite the New Church in the *Strand*.

M.DCC.LVII.

TITLE OF SMITH'S HISTORY

tells us that among the people of Albany "even the dark aspect of slavery was softened into a smile." [1]   Manumission was not infrequent ; the slave was often allowed to choose his home among the heirs of his deceased master ; and it is said that " if a slave was dissatisfied with his master, it was very common for the master to give him a paper on which his age, his price, etc., were written, and allow him to go and look for some one with whom he would prefer to live, and who would be willing to pay the price stated." [2]   When the purchaser was found, the master would hand over the slave and take the money, and we may hope that Cuffee found no reason to regret the change.

Even in these kindly circumstances, however, slaves now and then ran away.   The statute-book, moreover, shows
Dread of   that they were regarded with some fear by their
the slaves   masters.   They were prohibited from gathering in
groups of more than four, and they were forbidden to carry guns, swords, or clubs, under penalty of ten lashes at the whipping-post.   One curious act provided that no slave could go about the streets after nightfall anywhere south of the Collect without a lighted lantern, "so as the light thereof may be plainly seen." [3]

In 1712, during Governor Hunter's administration, there was an attempt at a slave insurrection.   A party of negroes, armed with guns, knives, and hatchets, assembled one even-
The negro   ing, in an orchard near Maiden Lane, and set fire to
plot of 1712   an outhouse.   At sight of the flames people came
running to the spot, and as fast as they came were shot or slashed.   Nine had been killed and six wounded when a squad of soldiers came upon the scene and captured the murderers.   Many negroes were arrested, and twenty-one were executed in ways intended to strike terror.   One was broken on the wheel, and several were burned alive at the stake, while the rest were hanged.[4]

[1] *Memoirs of an American Lady*, i. 51.
[2] *Social History of Flatbush*, p. 249.
[3] Morgan, *Slavery in New York*, p. 13.
[4] *Colonial Documents*, v. 341, 346, 356, 367, 371, 525.

The recollection of this affair may have had something to do with the virulence of the panic that was brought on in 1741 by what has been called the " Great Negro Plot." This was a melancholy instance of panic and delusion, not wholly unmingled with fraud, and has often been likened to the witchcraft delusion at Salem Village in 1692. It might also be compared with Titus Oates's miserable " Popish Plot," inasmuch as it was a symptom of a wave of fierce anti-Catholic excitement. To the generally mild and tolerant policy of New York we have now and then had occasion to note some exceptions. At the close of the seventeenth century, when the Counter-reformation was still showing such formidable strength in the giant war between Louis XIV. and William III., the dread of Catholics showed itself again and again in the legislative acts of Protestant countries. For example, in 1700 it was enacted in New York that any Popish priest discovered within the province after the first day of November of that year should be seized and imprisoned for life ; and for every such person who should escape and be found at large, the penalty should be the gallows. Any person convicted of aiding or concealing such priest should be set in the pillory for three days and give bonds at the discretion of the court.[1] This act was really and avowedly called forth by the persistent intrigues of Jesuit missionaries with the Long House. Under such circumstances it was not strange that a Catholic priest should be deemed an " incendiary and disturber of the public peace." Considerations of a religious nature had very little to do with the matter.

The "Great Negro Plot" of 1741

Dread of Catholic priests

In the year 1741 this act had not yet been repealed, and the feelings that prompted it were once more stimulated into activity by the war with Spain that had been going on for

[1] *Colonial Laws of New York*, i. 428. About the same time the law was passed in Rhode Island, debarring Catholics from the franchise ; see Arnold's *History of Rhode Island*, ii. 490–494. In Massachusetts a Romish priest was liable to imprisonment for life.

two years. In 1740 the fleet of Admiral Vernon had returned from Cartagena, discomfited by yellow fever rather
than the prowess of the enemy. Preparations were now going on in the colonies for an attack upon Havana.
A letter from Governor Oglethorpe in Georgia
mentioned a rumour that Catholic priests were to be fur-
tively introduced into all the English colonies in the guise
of dancing-masters, and at some concerted signal were to
set fire to the principal towns, by way of forestalling and
crippling the proposed expedition against Cuba.

The Span-
ish war

Shortly before this time a large number of negroes, including many savages lately kidnapped from Africa, had
been brought to New York from Spanish America; and
they seem to have aroused a feeling of dread, both for their
own uncouthness and on account of the region from which
they came. On the last day of February, 1741, a house in
Broad Street was robbed of some silverware, coins,
and pieces of linen. Suspicion fell upon a negro in
the owner's employ; the negro was proved to be in the habit
of meeting other negroes at Hughson's Tavern on the North
River; a search was made, and some of the stolen articles
were found in a pig-pen behind the house.

Hughson's
Tavern

This Hughson's was a low place; among its inmates was
an indentured white servant, Mary Burton, an abandoned
girl, only sixteen years of age, who had been brought over
from some English bridewell. Arrested on suspicion of complicity with the thieves, this creature
sought to screen herself by charges and insinuations impli-
cating her master and his family as well as sundry negroes.
She found herself suddenly invested with an importance
which she was cunning enough to seek to increase by ap-
pearing to know much more than she had yet told.

Mary
Burton

On the 18th of March, owing it is thought to the careless-
ness of a plumber, a fire broke out in Fort George [1] and the
governor's house was consumed, with some other buildings.

[1] So the old Fort Amsterdam was called after the accession of
George I.

A
JOURNAL

OF THE

PROCEEDINGS

IN

The Detection of the Conspiracy

FORMED BY

Some *White* People, in Conjunction with *Negro* and other *Slaves*,

FOR

Burning the City of *NEW-YORK* in AMERICA,
And Murdering the Inhabitants.

Which Conspiracy was partly put in Execution, by Burning His Majesty's House in Fort GEORGE, within the said City, on Wednesday the Eighteenth of *March*, 1741. and setting Fire to several Dwelling and other Houses there, within a few Days succeeding. And by another Attempt made in Prosecution of the same infernal Scheme, by putting Fire between two other Dwelling-Houses within the said City, on the Fifteenth Day of *February*, 1742; which was accidentally and timely discovered and extinguished.

CONTAINING,

I. A NARRATIVE of the Trials, Condemnations, Executions, and Behaviour of the several Criminals, at the Gallows and Stake, with their *Speeches* and *Confessions*; with Notes, Observations and Reflections occasionally interspersed throughout the Whole.

II. AN APPENDIX, wherein is set forth some additional Evidence concerning the said Conspiracy and Conspirators, which has come to Light since their Trials and Executions.

III. LISTS of the several Persons (Whites and Blacks) committed on Account of the Conspiracy; and of the several Criminals executed; and of those transported, with the Places whereto.

By the Recorder of the City of NEW-YORK.

Quid faciènt Domini, audent cum talia Fures? Virg. Ecl.

NEW-YORK:

Printed by *James Parker*, at the New Printing-Office, 1744.

TITLE OF BOOK ON THE GREAT NEGRO PLOT

Within another week Sir Peter Warren's chimney took fire, but no harm was done. Then a fire broke out in a store-house, which was traced to the careless dropping of ashes from a tobacco pipe. Three days afterward the hay in a cow-stable was found burning; there was an alarm and the fire was put out, but people had scarcely left the scene, when flames were descried shooting up in a loft over a kitchen where negroes were known to lodge. "The next morning coals were found under a haystack near a coach-house on Broadway. The following day a fire burst forth from the house of Sergeant Burns opposite the fort; and a few hours later, the roof of Mr. Hilton's house near the Fly Market was discovered on fire, and, on the same afternoon, Colonel Frederick Philipse's storehouse was all ablaze." [1]

Alarms of fire

From such alarming incidents there was nothing at all strange in the rapid genesis of a fierce and bloodthirsty panic. On April 11 the common council offered £100 reward, with a full pardon, to any conspirator who should tell what he knew about a plot for burning the city. This offer elicited a "confession" from Mary Burton, who swore that, in meetings at Hughson's Tavern, certain negroes had matured such an incendiary plot, as the first step in a revo-lution which was to make Hughson *king* and a darky named Cæsar *governor*. She further averred that Colonel Philipse's Cuffy used to say that "some people had too much and others too little, but the time was coming when master Philipse would have less and Cuff more." The only white people present at these meetings besides herself were Hughson and his wife and a loose woman named Carey. After a while, however, she "confessed" that a poor school-teacher, John Ury, who was known to be a Catholic, had taken part in the affair. The result of these disclosures was a reign of terror which lasted until September. In the course of it, Hughson and his wife, the teacher Ury, and the woman Carey were hanged, and twenty other

The alleged conspiracy

Wholesale executions

[1] Mrs. Lamb's *History of the City of New York*, ii. 582.

white persons were imprisoned. One hundred and fifty-four negroes were arrested, of whom fourteen were burned alive at the stake, and eighteen were hanged. Throughout the affair Mary Burton seems to have played the part which at Salem was shared among the " afflicted children," and just as at Salem, when the panic was clearly waning, the end was hastened by her aiming the accusations too high and striking at persons of consequence. The wretched girl received £100, the wages of her perjury. But after the terror was over, it began to be doubted, and has ever since been doubted, whether the " Great Negro Plot " was anything more than a figment of the imagination.[1]

It is only a shallow criticism, however, and utterly devoid of historic appreciation, that would cite this melancholy affair in disparagement of the good people of colonial New York. The panic, as we have seen, arose very naturally from the circumstances, and it was not strange that some of the strongest and clearest heads in the community were turned by it. He would be a rash man who should venture to predict that even in the most enlightened communities in the world a recurrence of such horrors has for- *Revulsion of feeling* ever ceased to be possible. It is pleasant to add that by a wholesome revulsion of popular feeling, soon after the panic of 1741, a sentiment was aroused in favour of the negroes ; within ten years they were admitted to the franchise, and New York soon became honourably distinguished among the states that actively endeavoured to loosen their chains and insure their welfare.

[1] Dunlap's *History of New York*, chapter xxi.; Smith's *History of New York*, ii. 70, 71 ; *Colonial Documents*, vi. 186, 196, 199, 201–203; Horsmanden's *Negro Plot*, New York, 1744.

CHAPTER XVI

THE QUAKER COMMONWEALTH

When William Penn sailed from Philadelphia to England, in the summer of 1684, it was in the hope of soon returning to take personal supervision of the affairs of his rapidly growing colony. But he soon discovered that England was full of troubles for him. The accession of James II. brought Penn into a prominence that had its unfortunate side.

We have seen how it was the dying request of Admiral Penn that the Duke of York should have a care for the welfare of his son. The trust thus confided to James was amply redeemed. There can be little doubt that he was really fond of the young Quaker, and felt in his presence something of the fascination that the brilliant mind will often exert upon minds too narrow and dull to understand it. Moreover, in this case James's policy happened to coincide with his personal inclination. It would be impossible for any two sects within the limits of the Christian Church to differ more profoundly than the Roman Catholics and the Quakers. Yet circumstances were such in Penn's time that this radical hostility did not prevent the existence, for a moment, of something like a tacit alliance between the two ; and the same cruel king, who broke the legs and crushed the thumbs of his Scottish Presbyterian subjects with all the zest of an inquisitor, was glad to seize an occasion for setting free the Quakers who crowded the jails of England. This was because Quakers and Catholics differed so far, though in opposite directions, from the opinions generally held by the English people that they were alike condemned by everybody. Even the warmest advocates

Friendship between Penn and James II.

Good Order Established

IN

Pennsilvania & New-Jersey

IN

AMERICA,

Being a true Account of the Country ;
With its Produce and Commodities there made.

And the great Improvements that may be made by
means of 𝔓𝔲𝔟𝔩𝔦𝔠𝔨 𝔖𝔱𝔬𝔯𝔢-𝔥𝔬𝔲𝔰𝔢𝔰 for 𝔥𝔢𝔪𝔭, 𝔉𝔩𝔞𝔵 and
𝔏𝔦𝔫𝔫𝔢𝔫-𝔠𝔩𝔬𝔱𝔥 ; also, the Advantages of a 𝔓𝔲𝔟𝔩𝔦𝔠𝔨-
𝔖𝔠𝔥𝔬𝔬𝔩, the Profits of a 𝔓𝔲𝔟𝔩𝔦𝔠𝔨-𝔅𝔞𝔫𝔨, and the Probability of its arising, if those directions here laid down are
followed. With the advantages of publick 𝔊𝔯𝔞𝔫𝔞𝔯𝔦𝔢𝔰.

Likewise, several other things needful to be understood by
those that are or do intend to be concerned in planting in
the said Countries.

All which is laid down very plain, in this small Treatise ; it
being easie to be understood by any ordinary Capacity. To
which the *Reader* is referred for his further satisfaction.

By Thomas Budd.

Printed in the Year 1685.

A Further Account of the Province of PENSYLVANIA, and its Improvements.

For the Satisfaction of those that are Adventurers*, and Inclined to be so.*

IT has I know, been much expected from me that I should give some farther Narrative of those parts of *America*, where I am chiefly interested, and have lately been; having continued there above a Year after my former *Relation*, and receiving since my return, the freshest and fullest Advices of its *Progress* and *Improvement*. But as the reason of my coming back, was a *difference* between the Lord *Baltamore* and my self, about the *Lands of Delaware*, in consequence, reputed of mighty moment to us, so I wav'd publishing any thing that might look in favour of the Country or inviting to it, whilst it lay under the Discouragement and Disreputation of that Lord's claim and pretences.

But since they are, after many fair and full hearings before the *Lords* of the *Committee* for *Plantations* justly and happily *Dismist*, and the things agreed; and that the *Letters* which daily press me from all parts, on the subject of *America*, are so many and voluminous, that to answer them severally, were a Task too heavy, and repeated to perform, I have thought it most easie to the Enquirer, as well as my self, to make this Account *Publick*, lest my silence, or a more private intimation of things, should disoblige the just inclinations of any to *America*, and at a time too, when an extraordinary Providence seems to favour its plantation, and open a Door to *Europeans* to pass thither. That then which is my part to do in this Advertisement is,

First, *To Relate our Progress, especially since my last of the Month called* August, 83.

Secondly, *The Capacity of the place for farther Improvement, in order to Trade and Commerce.*

A 2

Lastly,

TITLE OF PENN'S "A FURTHER ACCOUNT," 1685

of toleration were wont to make an exception in the case of Catholics and Quakers, who for different reasons were regarded as hardly within the pale of Christianity. Hence Quakers and Catholics had, for the moment, an interest in common, as opposed to the intermediate Christian sects, and hence, both as duke and afterward as king, the Catholic James found it worth his while to befriend the chief of the Quakers. It was a singular alliance, that between the man for whom such words as pity and clemency were meaningless terms, and the man whose faith in the ethical teachings of Jesus was so genuine that he was eager to see them embodied in civil legislation and made the cornerstone of a new Christian state. It is strange to think of the champion of truthfulness and toleration as a Jacobite, leagued in political bonds of sympathy with a family whose very name has come to be almost a synonym for bigotry and falsehood. It is this singular alliance which once kindled the wrath of the prejudiced and impetuous Macaulay, and led him to bring some foul charges against Penn's integrity. *Macaulay's hasty charges*

Of Macaulay's charges, the only one that needs mention [1] is that which relates to the affair of the Maids of Taunton. When the handsome Duke of Monmouth was making his silly attempt to dethrone James II., and on a bright June day of the year 1685 rode into Taunton with much bustle and parade, he was met in the market-place by a procession of school-girls, from ten or twelve to sixteen years, all in their prettiest summer gowns. They gave him a royal standard richly embroidered, and the good schoolmistress gave him a Bible, and all felt, no doubt, that they *The Maids of Taunton*

---

[1] They were conclusively refuted by W. E. Forster, in his preface to a new edition of Clarkson's *Life of Penn*, London, 1850; and by Hepworth Dixon, in his *Life of Penn*, London, 1851; and others. After Macaulay had replied to his critics, the matter was again taken up and treated with consummate ability, by John Paget, in his *New Examen*, London, 1861. Mr. Paget's evidence and arguments are absolutely conclusive, and leave Macaulay in a very sorry plight.

had done what was right. A few weeks later, when Monmouth had begged for life in vain, and the ghastly skulls of his adherents were bleaching over many a city gate, and the execrable Jeffreys was holding his Bloody Assizes, some of the queen's maids of honour asked the king for permission to threaten these poor children, of whose frolic they had heard, in order to extort blackmail from their parents. James granted the infamous permission. The story of the consequent distress and misery at Taunton almost makes one ashamed of belonging to the human race. One young girl was snatched from home and thrown into a dungeon, where she died of fever. Another mustered courage to go into court and declare her innocence of evil intent and beg the hyena Jeffreys for mercy. His only answer was to put on one of his hideous frowns and shout, " Take her away, jailer ! " She was led away shivering and sobbing, and died within a few hours, literally frightened to death. Out of such sufferings the queen's ladies tried to make £7000, but were obliged to desist long before their greed was satisfied.

Now, when Macaulay found that the name of the solicitor who represented the maids of honour in this devil's work was " Mr. Penne," it seemed to him to furnish welcome proof that anybody who stood high in favour with James II. must be more or less of a knave. So he seized the occasion for inculcating a moral lesson for the benefit of all admirers of the founder of Pennsylvania. " The maids of honour," says Macaulay, " requested William Penn to act for them, and Penn accepted the commission. Yet it should seem that a little of the pertinacious scrupulosity which he had often shown about taking off his hat would not have been altogether out of place on this occasion." [1] Macaulay went on to speculate ingeniously as to the arguments by which Penn might have succeeded in silencing the voice of conscience. Many of us can still remember how Macaulay's readers, more than forty years ago, were astounded by this grave accusation. But when, after more

Macaulay's discreditable blunder

[1] Macaulay's *History of England*, cabinet edition, ii. 235.

careful inquiry, it turned out that the " Mr. Penne " in question was not the great Quaker at all, but a certain George
Penne, a notorious pettifogger and pardon-broker at the vile
Stuart court, the historian's moral lesson lost much of its
point, and one could not help feeling that once more in this
dull world there had been some very vigorous barking up the
wrong tree !

None of the charges brought against William Penn have
been adequately supported ; and so far was his character from
deteriorating through his intimacy with James II., that at no
time in his life does he seem more honest, brave, and lov-
able than during the years, so full of trouble for him, that
intervened between the accession of James and the accession
of Anne.   As for the king, Penn always maintained that,
with all his faults, he was not so black as people painted
him ; and this we may readily admit.   A man who had and
retained such friends as Nicolls and Dongan could   Penn was
not have been entirely devoid of redeeming traits.   not awake
                                                      to James's
But there was one side of James's character to   treacherous
which Penn was not sufficiently awake.   Unlike   qualities
other Stuarts in many respects, James was as false as any of
the race, but his treacherousness was more or less concealed
under an appearance of honest and awkward dulness.   One
would not look for Machiavelism in such a dense atmosphere.
Nevertheless, James was able to impress Penn with the belief
that in extending royal favour to Quakers he had the interests of religious liberty at heart, and, so long as Penn was
thus hoodwinked, his demeanour towards the king was liable
to be such as to excite the suspicion of patriots, who realized
how dangerous that personage really was.   When the great
Quaker came to be known as a royal favourite, and scores
of people crowded his doorsteps, in order to obtain through
him royal aid for their schemes, he was at once placed in a
position that could hardly fail to be misunderstood.

The difficulty of his position was well illustrated in the
famous case of the Seven Bishops.   It should be distinctly
understood that in 1687 England was in serious danger, and

that the interests of civil and religious liberty were gravely

imperilled. All over Europe the Counter-Reformation had made alarming progress; and the ground gained by the peace of Westphalia, in 1648, seemed for the moment lost again. The most recent great event was the revocation of the Edict of Nantes, and Louis XIV. seemed as formidable as in later days Napoleon at Tilsit. Under these circumstances the intense anti-Catholic excitement in England was natural; it was one of the forms assumed by the instinct of self-preservation. The new king of England intended to destroy Protestantism, and civil liberty with it, wherever he could. To achieve his ends he relied ultimately upon military force to be summoned from Ireland, and aid to be extended by the king of France, as well as upon the development of a strong party loyal to himself in England. For this latter purpose he offered favours to Dissenters, hoping to secure their support until the time when he should feel strong enough to desert and betray them. Hence his attempt, under the hypocritical pretence of liberality in matters of religion, to annul the various test acts which, in the course of his brother's reign, had been passed against Presbyterians, Independents, Baptists, and Quakers, as well as Roman Catholics. Parliament would not repeal these acts, and so James tried to override them by a royal Declaration of Indulgence, thus setting himself up above the law. Such favours law-abiding Englishmen were slow to avail themselves of; there were many, like Richard Baxter, who suspected the trick and warned their fellow-dissenters. The king, by an order in council, commanded the ministers of all persuasions, in all churches and chapels throughout the kingdom, to read his Declaration aloud to their congregations on two successive Sundays. Before the first Sunday arrived, a petition signed by Sancroft, Archbishop of Canterbury, and six suffragan bishops, protesting against the order in council, was served upon the king. When Sunday came, not more than two hundred clergymen in all England read the Declaration. In West-

minster Abbey it was read amid such murmurs that not a
word could be heard.   In another church the minister sar-
castically observed that, though he was commanded to read
it, the people were not commanded to hear it ; so he waited
till all had gone out, and then read it to the walls.[1]   Forthwith the seven recalcitrant bishops were brought to trial on
a criminal information for seditious libel ; and in the shouts
with which London greeted the verdict of " Not guilty "
there resounded the death-knell of Stuart kingcraft.

Now, while this intense popular excitement was thoroughly sound, it cannot be denied that the refusal of the
seven bishops was, on the face of it, a protest against a policy
of religious toleration, and doubtless, among the motives by
which they were actuated, there was something of narrow
bigotry as well as of patriotism and reverence for law.[2]   It
was therefore impossible for William Penn to sym-   *Penn's lack
pathize with these prelates, or with the popular en-   *of sympa-
thusiasm by which they were supported.   He did   *the popular
not suspect the king's double-dealing ; his zeal for   *feeling
perfect liberty of conscience was much greater than his dread
of the Counter-Reformation ; and from Episcopacy he and
his friends had met with little save contumely and oppression.   Politically, while he was as far as possible from sym-
pathizing with the Tories, Penn was clearly not a Whig.
His ideals were strongly republican.   With regard to the
much-desired boon of religious liberty, the object of his life-
long yearning, it seemed too great a boon to refuse, no matter
how objectionable the shape in which it might be offered.
He would have preferred to see all test acts abolished by
Parliament, but when a king undertook to override such vile
laws, he could not find it in his heart to oppose him.   Thus
did Penn find himself, in this national crisis, quite out of
sympathy with the national feeling.   The natural results

---

[1] Burnet's *My Own Times*, iii. 218.
[2] This view of the case is urged, with plausible eloquence but somewhat superficial argument, by Buckle, in his *History of Civilization*,
i. 361–373.

followed.   He was called " William the Jesuit," an emissary
in the pay of Rome ; he was accused of saying mass at
Absurd   Whitehall ; he was supposed to have prompted the
notions   king to his Declaration of Indulgence ; and even
about Penn   the high-handed arrest of the seven bishops was
laid at his door, although he earnestly disapproved of it.   No
aspersion was too black to be cast upon him.[1]   He suffered
all the more injustice because of the noble courage with
which he declared his opinions, then as always.   When William III. arrived, and it became fashionable to vilify or de-
ride the exiled James, Penn's beautiful fidelity to his old
guardian was unimpaired, and he had always his good word
to say for the fallen prince.

It followed from all this that many persons believed our
Penn sus-   good Quaker to be implicated in Jacobite plots, and
pected of   in the year 1691 he felt that prudence required him
complicity
with the   to live very quietly in obscure lodgings in the city
Jacobites   of London.   For an innocent man it seemed better
thus than to seek safety abroad,[2] and Penn was sure that he
could satisfy William III. of his innocence of any complicity
with Jacobite intrigues.   For more than two years he continued to live thus in retirement, writing a number of admirable books and pamphlets, one of which, entitled " Fruits
of Solitude," is in some respects the most charming of his

[1]   Clarkson's *Life of Penn*, ii. 11.

[2]   Macaulay, indeed, makes him escape to France in the autumn of
1691, but his only authority is the Diary of the book-collector Narcis-
sus Luttrell, as worthless a mess of rubbish as was ever printed.   On
the other hand, Paget has proved that Penn was in London during the
whole of his " retirement."

Macaulay goes on : " Scarcely had he again begun to harangue in
public about the unlawfulness of war, when he sent a message earnestly
exhorting James to make an immediate descent on England with 30,000
men." (*History of England*, vi. 32.)   The memorandum on which this
charge is based is, as Macaulay tells us, " among the Nairne MSS. and
was translated by Macpherson," whereat the reader is no doubt duly
overawed.   Macaulay ought to have added that the writer of the memorandum was one Captain Williamson, a hired spy of low character,
whose unsupported statements are of no value.

works. During this period an incident occurred which deserves mention for its intrinsic interest in coupling Penn's name with that of John Locke. In 1685, during Monmouth's insurrection, the great philosopher was in Holland. His patron, Lord Shaftesbury, had once supported Monmouth's claim to the succession, and there were dastardly creatures who whispered in King James's ear suspicions of Locke. At that time Penn wrote to Locke, offering him from the king full pardon and amnesty for whatever he might have done, and bidding him feel quite free to return to England; for, quoth Penn most naïvely, " I am sure none can mistrust the king's word! "

Penn and Locke

But the sagacious Locke did mistrust it. He replied sententiously that "he had no occasion for a pardon, having committed no crime," and he stayed in the Netherlands. Now in 1691, while Penn was under a cloud, Locke stood very high in the favour of William III., and the spirit moved him to do something for his old Oxford friend. He made his way to Penn's lodgings in the city, and offered to secure for him from the king full pardon and grace for whatsoever complications he might have been drawn into. One fancies it must have been with a merry laugh that Penn, in declining the friendly offer, quoted against Locke his own sentiment, "the innocent need no pardon."[1]

King William was doubtless quite satisfied of Penn's innocence of complicity with Jacobite schemes, but other circumstances came in to influence his conduct toward the proprietor of Pennsylvania. In the mighty and irrepressible conflict with the powers of darkness as embodied in Louis XIV., who could tell what would become of the Dutch and Quaker colonies that occupied the citadel of North America? It would not do to leave Pennsylvania in the hands of men who had conscientious scruples about drawing a sword or firing a gun. Military policy forbade such a thing. Accordingly, in March,

William III. deprives Penn of his proprietary government

[1] Stoughton's *William Penn*, p. 262; Fox-Bourne's *Life of John Locke*, ii. 24.

1693, an order in council deprived Penn of his proprietary government. Pennsylvania was made into a royal province and consigned to the rule of Benjamin Fletcher, the soldier who then governed New York.

This blow was made all the more shocking for Penn by the news of the defection of his old friend, George Keith, who
George Keith's defection
had been one of his companions in the memorable Low German tour of 1677. Keith enjoyed a high reputation for linguistic and scientific attainments. In 1689 he was headmaster of the first Quaker school in Philadelphia, now known as the William Penn Charter School, and there he began to find fault with his brethren for making too much of the Inward Light and too little of Christ and the Scriptures. His dissent grew more and more emphatic, and extended to such matters of detail as the condemnation of capital punishment. The Yearly Meeting at Philadelphia rejected his views, but he had many sympathizers, who were known for some time as "Keithian Quakers." It was not long, however, before Keith passed over to Episcopacy. After a visit to England he came back to America in 1700 as the first missionary of the Society for Promoting Christian Knowledge, and travelled about the country making converts and organizing new Episcopal churches. Most of the Keithian Quakers likewise went back into the Church of England.

The loss of his province, the defection of his old friend, and the knowledge that some of his fellow-Quakers suspected him of sympathy with Jesuits were blows which it taxed all of Penn's buoyant strength to bear. Added to those calamities came the loss of his wife, in February, 1694. But soon after, in the midst of the valley of the shadow of
The king restores Penn's government
death, there came voices of comfort. Renewed expressions of love and trust on the part of his brethren were followed, in August, 1694, by an order in council restoring to Penn the proprietary government of his woodland in the New World. Again we find

HANNAH CALLOWHILL

him travelling and preaching in England and Ireland: in 1696 he is married to Hannah Callowhill, a "devout and comely maiden" of Bristol ; and in 1699, with this new wife and his grown-up children, William and Letitia, he comes once more across the wave to visit his woodland.

When Penn arrived in Philadelphia, the city had scarcely recovered from the panic into which it had been thrown by a deadly visitation of yellow fever. But, in spite of the pale, scared faces, the evidences of prosperity abounded on every side. There were more than

His return to Philadelphia

700 houses in the city, indicating a population of not less than 4000 souls.   There were some spacious and well-built brick warehouses, and two Friends' meeting-houses, as well as an Episcopal church.   Here and there were gardens brilliant with roses, lilies, and carnations.   Penn now dwelt for a while in the famous "Slate-roof House," at the corner of Second Street and Norris Alley, which was pulled down in 1867.   But he much preferred a country home, called Pennsbury, in Bucks county, northeast of the little city.   There in 1682 he had begun building a fine house, which cost him £7000.   An inventory of the furniture mentions plush couches, embroidered chairs, curtains of camlet and satin, and in the drawing-room such a carpet as was seldom seen outside of a palace.   The silver and china were of the finest, and Penn's orders to his steward show that asceticism formed no part of his theory of life. Not vain display, but refined and bountiful comfort, was his ideal.   He could appreciate a toothsome haunch of venison, and tells how "the old priest at Philadelphia had rare shads." With such a companion he would sit till a late hour discussing learned questions over a stoup of good ale or wine.[1] He was much interested, like Washington, in the details of domestic affairs ; and the devout maiden of Bristol, whose executive ability was marked and manifold, proved a most competent housewife.

His home and habits

Between his rural mansion and Philadelphia, the Lord Proprietor used either to ride his horse by the river's bank, or to go on the river in a six-oared barge, of which he was very fond.   "Above all dead things," he wrote to his steward, "take care of my barge."   Once, on a stormy day, as he was fighting the waves with it, the governor of New Jersey overhauled him, and expressed surprise that he should thus venture out against such a wind and tide.   Quick and pithy was the reply : "I have been sailing against wind and tide all my life."

His ready wit

[1] See Swift's letter to Stella, September 30, 1710, in his *Works*, ed. Scott, ii. 37.

In the government of his New World province he encountered other adverse winds and tides than those of the
Delaware River.   From the outset, there was a human
element of strife in the City of Brotherly Love.   There was,
first, the question as to how much or how little democracy
might best comport with the proprietary rule.   Penn was,
for his age, an advanced democrat ; yet he never ceased to
regard himself as a kind of patriarch who knew much better
what was good for his little sylvan community than   Democratic
the people themselves.   In this assumption he was   questions
very likely correct ; but it is one of the essential features of
thorough-going democracy that those who do not know what
is best should have a much greater part in governing than
those who do know, since they are much the more numerous.

THE "SLATE-ROOF HOUSE"

In the minds of many people, democracy rests upon the
colossal untruth that "one man is as good as another," [1] so
that a large number are more likely to be right than a small
number.   In reality democracy rests upon the ubiquitous

[1] The only sense in which this can at all be said to be true is the
Irishman's : "Why, Patrick," exclaims the landlord, whose mind is
dallying with Bentonian ideas, "is n't one man as good as another ?"
"Faith, he is, your honour, and a d—d sight better !"

fact that all men are directly interested in securing good government, while its successes have often been due to its practical recognition of the truth that some men are born to lead and others to follow.   The fact that William Penn was a born leader was too obvious to be questioned, and between him and his people there was not much contention.   But with his deputies, when he was absent in England, the case was different.   Constitutional questions at once came to the foreground, and one of the first was that which concerned the shares to be taken by the assembly and the council in the work of legislation.   It was Penn's original intention to give the sole power of originating laws to the council, while all laws required confirmation by the assembly.   But this scheme was never realized.   By 1693 all power of law-making was absorbed by the assembly, while the council became a mere board of advisers to the governor ; and thenceforth for a hundred years the government of Pennsylvania was practically unicameral.

Along with such questions there were disagreements between the "province" and the "territories," or between Pennsylvania and Delaware, which resulted permanently in separate legislatures for the two.   There were also troubles between Quakers and non-Quakers, especially the members of the Church of England. Some increment of confusion and bitterness came from Keith's apostasy.   Meanwhile the quit-rents failed to be collected, and each dissatisfied party was inclined to accuse its antagonists of surreptitious dealings with the ubiquitous pirates.

Penn approached the situation in a most amiable spirit. "Friends," said he, "if in the constitution by charter there be anything that jars, alter it."   The revised charter of 1701 comprised but nine articles.   The first grants liberty of conscience to all who "confess and acknowledge Almighty God," which, on a strict interpretation, would have admitted Mussulmans and Jews, and would have excluded such persons as Denis Diderot or the late Mr.

Pennsylvania and Delaware

The revised charter

Bradlaugh.   At the same time, the right to hold executive or legislative offices was restricted to persons " who profess to believe in Jesus Christ," a provision which ought hardly to have barred out Unitarians, but was sometimes used for that purpose.

The second article "requires an assembly to be chosen yearly by the freemen, to consist of four persons or more from each county.   This assembly has full powers to choose its officers, to judge of the qualifications of its own members, to adjourn itself, to prepare bills and make laws, impeach criminals and redress grievances, ' with all other powers and privileges of an assembly, according to the rights of free-born subjects of England.'

" The third requires the freemen to elect two or three people for each position of sheriff or coroner or other court officers, and the governor to choose among them ; or, if the governor fails to select, the first named shall serve.

" The fourth declares that all laws shall be issued in the form, ' By the Governor, with consent and approbation of the freemen in General Assembly met.'

" The fifth allows all criminals to have the same privileges of witnesses and counsel as their prosecutors.

" The sixth requires that all cases concerning property shall be decided by courts of justice, and not by governor and council.

" The seventh prevents any one receiving a tavern license who is not recommended by the justices and allows the justices to suppress a disorderly public house.

" The eighth prevents the forfeiture of the estates of suicides or intestates ; prohibits any law contrary to this charter without the consent of the governor and six sevenths of the assembly ; and pledges the Proprietor to observe inviolably the first article concerning liberty of conscience.

" Lastly, the Proprietor binds himself and heirs not to destroy the liberties of the charter, and declares such actions, if attempted, to be of no force or effect." [1]

[1] Sharpless, *A Quaker Experiment in Government*, pp. 64–66.

Scarcely had this charter begun to go into operation when Penn felt it necessary to return once more to England. There was always a more or less powerful opposition to his lord-proprietorship, and he felt that he must be near the throne in order to protect his interests and ensure the success of the holy experiment. The accession of Queen Anne,

Divergence in policy between Penn and William III.

in 1701, was in many ways favourable to Penn. The late king, who could admire him for his fearlessness and his breadth of view, was never fully in sympathy with him. Something like a gulf divided the preacher of universal peace and brotherly love from the warlike king to whose lot it had fallen to defeat a most formidable conspiracy for depriving human civilization of all that it had gained since the days of Wyclif. Louis XIV. was the great champion of ideas and methods which would have made Europe no better than Cathay, of the spirit of civil and religious despotism, — the accursed thing which Voltaire afterward stigmatized as "The Infamous." The policy of *L'Infame* was one of blood and iron, and with blood and iron the mighty Dutchman must oppose it. Thus William of Orange was beset by a chronic temptation to interfere with the holy experiment. In 1701 he asked Pennsylvania to contribute £350 toward erecting fortifications upon the northern frontier of New York, and thus a serious question was raised. Could a Quaker legislature properly

Could Quakers fight in self-de-. fence?

vote money for military purposes? Different opinions were expressed. Some worthy Friends, who abhorred warfare as much as any, nevertheless did not feel bound to sit still and let the enemy cut their throats. Others deemed it right to adhere to their principles and trust in Providence for the result. So for four days "there was an unpleasant parley" which ended in a postponement of the vote, while sundry resolutions were adopted, vague and ambiguous enough for any modern political platform. Warned by such symptoms, Penn was careful to leave in the province deputy-governors who were not averse to fighting in self-defence.

In the Christmas time of 1701, Penn arrived once more in England; before Easter the great king had passed away, and by Whitsuntide the gigantic war of the Spanish Succession had begun. Queen Anne was inclined to befriend Penn for her father's sake, and there was no further serious risk of his losing his province. Of his military deputies, however, one contrived, through excess of zeal, to make much trouble. The appointment of this man, John Evans, was one of a number of instances which seem to show that Penn was liable to err in his judgments of character. He was apt to be too generous in his estimates of men. Evans was a youth of five-and-twenty or so, with some scholar-like traits which attracted Penn's admiration, but he soon showed himself unworthy of trust. There was not much danger of an attack upon the little Quaker commonwealth on the Delaware River; that community did not extend westward enough, nor did the French - Algonquin conflagration, against which New York and New England were fighting, as yet extend westward enough; the Five Nations, an insuperable barrier, stood between. But Evans, who was not a Quaker, believed in going forth to smite the hosts of Amalek, and to help the cause of England wherever it was imperilled. His call for troops met with no response, whereupon he resorted to an almost incredibly shameful and puerile trick. On a bright spring day in 1706, while the good people of Philadelphia were holding their annual fair, a courier came spurring into the town with consternation depicted upon his face, and announced that a dozen French warships were coming up the river. The governor straightway sprang upon his horse and cantered about the streets, waving a drawn sword and calling people to arms. At this sudden alarm, which was simply a brazen falsehood, some people threw their silver spoons and goblets into their wells for

Penn's return to England

The deputy-governor, John Evans

His folly

hiding, some ran out to the woods, some crowded into boats and hurried up the river, a few poor women were frightened into miscarriage ; but the scare was soon over, and the silly Evans became an object of scorn.[1]   The failure of this arti- ficial attempt to create a panic, in the absence of the natural conditions, is instructive.   Of the Quakers it is said that very few took part in the momentary excitement.   Most of them were gathered at a religious meeting, and during the hubbub they went on quietly with their devotions.   Only four Quakers were found under arms at the governor's place of rendezvous.

Still bent upon contributing something to the war against Antichrist, the clumsy Evans persuaded the people of the Delaware settlements to build a fort at Newcastle, and to clap a duty on cargoes passing either to or from Philadelphia.   This tax, which was known as "powder money" was a violation of Penn's charter ; whereupon three stout Quakers — Richard Hill, Isaac Norris, and Samuel Preston, gentlemen of high consideration — ran a sloop down past the fortress, at the cost of a bullet-hole in their main-sail, and when the commander gave chase they captured him and carried him to Salem, on the Jersey shore, where, after some coarse rebuke from Lord Cornbury, who happened

Powder money

---

[1] It is of course this false alarm to which one of the old settlers, Thomas Makin, alludes in his *Descriptio Pennsylvaniæ*, 1729, dedicated to James Logan : —

> Sed semel hæc rumor mendax clamavit ad arma,
> Incola cui nimium credulus omnis erat.
> Hæc malesana die fuit acta tragœdia quadam,
> Cum convenerunt undique turba frequens;
> Scilicet ut major fieret commotus in urbe,
> Notior et mutis rumor ubique foret.
> Usque adeo fuit hac confusus in urbe tumultus,
> Ut neque tunc leges, ordo nec ullus erat.
> Hic removere sua instanti properabat ab hoste,
> Ille nihil contra jussit ab urbe vehi :
> Sed quodcunque sibi voluit dementia talis,
> Hæc damno multis est memoranda dies :
> Vespere sed tandem fuit hoc stratagema detectum,
> Fabula tunc istam finiit acta diem.

See Proud's *History of Pennsylvania*, Philadelphia, 1797, i. 469.

to be there, he was sent about his business. This was the end of "powder money."

Evans, moreover, disgusted people by his loose living. Rumour attributed to him scandalous adventures with Indian squaws and white women,[1] and he seems to have been something of a tippler and a brawler withal; for once the watchman, "Solomon Cresson, going his rounds at night, entered a tavern to suppress a riotous assembly, and found there John Evans, Esq., the governor, who fell to beating Cresson."[2] On such occasions one of the governor's boon companions was young William Penn, the unworthy son of the Proprietor. The antics of this graceless boy nearly broke his father's heart.

Penn's wretched son

These troubles were presently followed by a dire calamity. For steward of his province Penn had appointed one Philip Ford, who turned out to be a scoundrel. It was a fresh illustration of Penn's weakest point, an occasional slowness in recognizing the bad side of human nature. With all the worldly wisdom of which he had so much, Penn now and then showed a streak of guilelessness that reminds one of Tom Pinch. This trait helps us to understand his belief in the honesty of James II. The wretched Ford died in 1706, leaving a very murky set of accounts, and a widow and son as unscrupulous as himself. In these days Penn, in spite of his wealth, often found himself in need of ready money. Large sums were sunk in his holy experiment; his dissolute son had debts amounting to £10,000; and his daughter's husband, William Aubrey, a mean-spirited creature, extorted money from him. At one time Penn borrowed money of Ford, and mortgaged his province of Pennsylvania as security; when he repaid the loan, he neglected to get back from Ford the bond and mortgage. So after Ford's death his widow and son brought against Penn a trumped-up claim for £14,000, and petitioned Queen Anne to hand over to them the proprietorship of Pennsylvania. The base at-

Philip Ford

[1] Watson's *Annals of Philadelphia*, ii. 273.
[2] *Id.* ii. 481.

tempt failed, but not until it had led to Penn's incarceration for nine months in the Fleet prison.

By 1712 Penn was on the point of selling for £12,000 his proprietary government to the crown, while retaining the landed estates which he owned in Pennsylvania. But in the course of that year a paralytic stroke nearly put an end to his power of doing business. He lingered for six years, with memory failing until he could scarcely recognize his nearest friends. The contemplated surrender of the proprietary government was never made; but after divers questions had been decided by the courts, it passed to the founder's three surviving sons by his second wife. Of these the eldest, John Penn, called "the American" because he was born in Philadelphia in 1700, died in England in 1746 without issue. The second brother, Thomas Penn, died in England in 1775, leaving two sons, John and Granville, both of whom attained distinction. The third brother, Richard Penn, died in England in 1771, leaving two sons, John and Richard, who were successively lieutenant-governors of Pennsylvania. When the proprietary government came to an end in 1776, it was in the possession of these heirs of Thomas and Richard. For seven years after the founder's death, while his three sons were still young, the interests of the proprietorship were managed with great ability by his widow.

Penn's illness and death

One of the most important personages in the Quaker commonwealth was James Logan, the friend of the founder and representative of his ideas. This remarkable man, a native of Ulster, was descended from the Scotch Logans of Restabrig who lost their estates for connection with the mysterious Gowrie conspiracy. James was an infant prodigy; at the age of twelve his attainments in Greek, Latin, and Hebrew had attracted much notice, and he afterward attained distinction in modern languages, mathematics, physics, and natural history. Penn brought him to Philadelphia on his second coming, in 1699, and for the next forty years he was always in some high position, — secretary of the

James Logan

James Logan

province, member of the council, judge of common pleas, chief justice, mayor of Philadelphia, and, in 1736–38, acting governor of Pennsylvania. Like his friend Penn, he knew how to win and keep the confidence of the red men, and it was in honour of him that the chieftain Tagahjutè received the name of Logan, long to be remembered for the tale of woe which cast such unjust aspersions upon the fame of Captain Michael Cresap.[1] The singular variety of his genius is shown by the fact that his friend Linnæus, in compliment to his botanical attainments, named after him a natural order of herbs and shrubs, the Loganiaceæ, containing some 30 genera in 350 species, of which *strychnos nux vomica* is one of the best known. He published Latin essays on reproduction in plants, and on the aberration of light; translated Cato's "Disticha" and Cicero's "De Senectute ; " and bequeathed to the city his library of 2000 volumes, comprising all the Latin classics, and more than a hundred folios in Greek, with the original edition of Ptolemy's "Almagest " and Timon's commentary, "from my learned friend Fabricius, who published fourteen volumes of his 'Bibliotheca Græca' in quarto, in which, after he had finished his account of Ptolemy, on my inquiring from him at Hamburg how I should find it, having long sought for it in vain in England, he sent it to me out of his own library, telling me it was so scarce that neither price nor prayers could purchase it."

A very different figure was that of the stout Welshman, David Lloyd, whom Penn sent over in 1686 to be attorney-general of the province. At various times Lloyd David was member of the assembly and of the council, Lloyd judge of admiralty, and chief justice of the commonwealth. Without any pretence to such profound and varied attainments as Logan's, he was a learned jurist and had an extensive knowledge of Welsh history and philology. In politics Lloyd represented the popular party, while Logan stood for the proprietary interests and prerogatives of the Penns, and the strife between them was often intense and bitter. The

[1] See my *American Revolution*, Illustrated Edition, ii. 102.

general character of Pennsylvania politics early in the eighteenth century we have already indicated; the details are so closely implicated with the struggle against France that they will be best treated in my future volumes which are to deal with that mighty conflict. Lloyd was contentious, and his methods were sometimes objectionable, but they surely

helped to carry out Penn's democratic ideas to their logical conclusions.[1]

The associations connected with such men as Logan and Penn served at once to give something of a literary atmosphere to Philadelphia, which was greatly heightened after the return of Benjamin Franklin from London in 1726. The founding of the Philadelphia Library in 1731, of the American Philosophical Society in 1743, and of the University of Pennsylvania in 1749–55, were evidences of the rapid development of the Quaker commonwealth in scholarship and in literary tastes. In these respects Philadelphia was in contrast with New York, and by the middle of the eighteenth century her reputation for culture was second only to that of Boston and Cambridge. The immense contributions made by Franklin to the higher life of Philadelphia are a striking commentary upon the excellence of Penn's unflinching insistence upon "soul liberty." Franklin, though born in Boston, was hardly a product of the Puritan theocracy. His parents, who did not quit their ancient home in Northamptonshire until a few years before his birth, were Puritans of a liberal type who had but lately left the Church of England. The atmosphere of Boston was too stifling for the youthful Benjamin, who was born with the

[1] Cf. Sharpless, *A Quaker Experiment in Government*, p. 97.

Numb. XL.

THE
Pennſylvania GAZETTE.

Containing the freſheſt Advices Foreign and Domeſtick.

From Thurſday, September 25. to Thurſday, October 2. 1729.

THE Pennſylvania Gazette *being now to be carry'd on by other Hands, the Reader may expect ſome Account of the Method we deſign to proceed in.*

Upon a View of Chambers's *great Dictionaries, from whence were taken the Materials of the* Univerſal Inſtructor *in all Arts and Sciences, which uſually made the Firſt Part of this Paper, we find that beſides their containing many Things abſtruſe or inſignificant to us, it will probably be fifty Years before the Whole can be gone thro' in this Manner of Publication. There are like-wiſe in thoſe Books continual References from Things under one Letter of the Alphabet to thoſe under another, which relate to the ſame Subject, and are neceſſary to explain and compleat it; theſe taken in their Turn may perhaps be Ten Years diſtant, ſince thoſe who* deſire to acquaint themſelves with any particular Art or Science, *would gladly have the whole before them in a much leſs Time, we believe our Readers will not think ſuch a Method of communicating Knowledge to be a proper One.*

However, tho' we do not intend to continue the Publication of thoſe Dictionaries in a regular Alphabetical Method, as has hitherto been done; yet as ſeveral Things exhibited from them in the Courſe of theſe Papers, have been entertaining to ſuch of the Curious, who never had and cannot have the Advantage of good Libraries; and as there are many Things ſtill behind, which being in this Manner made generally known, may perhaps become of conſiderable Uſe, by giving ſuch Hints to the excellent natural Genius's of our Country, as may contribute either to the Improvement of our preſent Manufactures, or towards the Invention of new Ones; we propoſe from Time to Time to communicate ſuch particular Parts as appear to be of the moſt general Conſequence.

As to the Religious Courtſhip, *Part of which has been retail'd to the Publick in theſe Papers, the Reader may be inform'd, that the whole Book will probably in a little Time be printed and bound up by it-ſelf; and thoſe who approve of it, will doubtleſs be better pleas'd to have it intire, than in this broken interrupted Manner.*

There are many who have long deſired to ſee a good News-Paper *in* Pennſylvania; *and we hope thoſe Gentlemen who are able, will contribute towards the making This ſuch. We ask Aſſiſtance, becauſe we are fully ſenſible, that to publiſh a good* News-Paper *is not ſo eaſy an Undertaking as many People imagine it to be. The Author of a Gazette (in the Opinion of the Learned) ought to be qualified with an extenſive Acquaintance with Languages, a great Eaſineſs and Command of Writing and Relating Things cleanly and intelligibly, and in few Words; he ſhould be able to ſpeak of War both by Land and Sea; be well acquainted with Geography, with the Hiſtory of the Time, with the ſeveral Intereſts of Princes and States, the Secrets of Courts, and the Manners and Cuſtoms of all Nations. Men thus accompliſh'd are very rare in this remote Part of the World; and it would be well if the Writer of theſe Papers could make up among his Friends what is wanting in himſelf.*

Upon the Whole, we may aſſure the Publick, that as far as the Encouragement we meet with will enable us, no Care and Pains ſhall be omitted, that may make the Pennſylvania Gazette *as agreeable and uſeful an Entertainment as the Nature of the Thing will allow.*

The Following is the laſt Meſſage ſent by his Excellency Governour *Burnet*, to the Houſe of Repreſentatives in *Boſton*.

Gentlemen of the Houſe of Repreſentatives,

IT is not with ſo vain a Hope as to convince you, that I take the Trouble to anſwer your Meſſages, but, if poſſible, to open the Eyes of the deluded People whom you repreſent, and whom you are at ſo much Pains to keep in Ignorance of the true State of their Affairs. I need not go further for an undeniable Proof of this Endeavour to blind them, than your ordering the Letter of Meſſieurs *Wilks* and *Belcher* of the 7th of *June* laſt to your Speaker to be publiſhed. This Letter is ſaid (in Page 1. of your Votes) *to incloſe a Copy of the Report of the Lords of the Committee of His Majeſty's Privy Council, with his Majeſty's Approbation and Order thereon in Council*: Yet theſe Gentlemen had at the ſame time the unparallell'd Preſumption to write to the Speaker in this Manner; *You'll obſerve by the Concluſion, what is propoſed to be the Conſequence if your not complying with His Majeſty's Inſtruction (the whole Matter to be laid*

FIRST PAGE OF FIRST NUMBER OF THE "PENNSYLVANIA GAZETTE"

temperament of a free-thinker, and soon began to hear himself called an "infidel." There can be no doubt that this circumstance was potent in turning the young man's attention to the more liberal Dutch and Quaker commonwealths,[1] and thus his footsteps were led to Pennsylvania, which could furnish more work for printers than New York. Thus Boston's loss was Philadelphia's gain.

In spite of their liberalism, the Quakers attached far less importance to education than the Puritans of New England. Attitude of Quakers toward learning The majority of their preachers and instructors were men of high moral tone and spiritual insight with scant learning, like George Fox himself. Fox used to say that " God stood in no need of human learning," and that " Oxford and Cambridge could not make a minister." Quakers, in studying the Bible, depended upon their Inner Light rather than that critical interpretation of texts to which the orthodox Puritans attached so much importance. A knowledge of Hebrew, therefore, was not highly valued ; and as for Greek and Latin literature, it was the unsanctified work of pagans, while the poets of France and Italy dealt with worldly and frivolous themes. In these respects we must remember that Penn was as far from being a typical Quaker as Milton, with his pervading artistic sense, his love of music and the theatre, and his long curling hair, was from being a typical Puritan. George Fox and John Cotton are respectively the typical men. The latter, who spent twelve hours a day in study and said, "I love to sweeten my mouth with a piece of Calvin before I go to sleep," could write and speak fluently in Greek, Latin, and Hebrew, besides carrying a ponderous burden of philological, metaphysical, and theological erudition. Among the Puritan divines of New England, real scholarship was commonly

[1] " I was rather inclined to leave Boston when I reflected that I had already made myself a little obnoxious to the governing party, . . . and farther, that my indiscreet disputations about religion began to make me pointed at with horror by good people as an infidel or atheist." Franklin's *Autobiography*, ed. Bigelow, 1868, p. 106.

found, and it was sometimes of a high order ; and this was
because sound scholarship was supposed to be conducive to

BENJAMIN FRANKLIN

soundness in doctrines.   This explains the founding of Har-
vard College in the wilderness in 1636.

To the Quaker, whose mind was directly illuminated by
light from above, this elaborate equipment was mere rubbish.   It was therefore not strange that in colonial times the
higher education in Pennsylvania owed little to Quakers.
They were nevertheless careful, as people of practi-   The first
cal sense, to teach their children "the three R's,"   schools
and it was unusual to find a member of the community who
could not write and cipher.   The first school in Philadelphia
was opened in 1683, when the town was scarcely a year old.

In that humble establishment the master, Enoch Flower, taught reading for four shillings per quarter ; for six shillings the pupil could add writing, and for eight shillings arithmetic likewise, to his initial accomplishment. In 1689 the Society of Friends set up their public school, which was chartered by Penn in 1711.

The impulse toward literary culture, given from the outset by Penn and his friends, was visible in the early estab-

The Bradfords lishment of a printing-press, the first one south of New England, by William Bradford, in 1685. In 1690 the same Bradford set up a paper-mill on the bank of the Schuylkill. After his removal to New York in 1693,[1] his son Andrew kept up the press, with a considerable bookstore, and in 1719 issued the first newspaper in the middle colonies. In 1735 he was finely established as a bookseller the sign of the Bible in Second Street, whence he afterward moved to South Front Street, and in 1741 began to publish " The American Magazine." In the following year Andrew's nephew, William Bradford, started the " Pennsylvania Journal," which was continued under that name until 1801, when it became " The True American." It was in Andrew Bradford's office that Franklin in 1723 found work as a compositor. The standard English books of the period could be found on the shelves of Philadelphia booksellers, and the demand for such works as Robertson's "Charles V." and Blackstone's " Commentaries " was so great that they were reprinted. Among Pennsylvanians who attained distinction for scientific or literary achievement were the astronomer David Rittenhouse, the botanists John Bartram and his son William, the self-taught mathematician Thomas Godfrey, one of the inventors of Hadley's so-called quadrant,[2] and his son Thomas, author of the first American dramatic

---

[1] See above, p. 235.

[2] This useful instrument, which is more properly called a sextant, was invented by Thomas Godfrey and also by John Hadley. The Royal Society decided that both were entitled to the credit of the invention, and awarded to each a prize of £200.

The AMERICAN
Weekly Mercury,

December 22, 1 7 1 9.

From the NORTH.

HAMBURGH *August,* 29. All Our Letters from *Sweden,* are full of the Dismall Ravages committed by the Muscovites there, Those *Semi Christians* have burnt the fine Towns of *Nykopping, Nordkopping, North Telle, South Telle, Ortoll, Oshammers, Oregrund, Forslenar, Ortela,* &c. with all the Castles and Gentlemens Seats near them & ruined all the fines, utterly Destroy'd the Copper and Salt Works, burnt the Woods and carried Thousands of the People on Board their Gally's in Ord r to Transport them into *Russia.* the Rainage is computed at severall Millions, and a Hundred Years wont Retrieve the Loss the Country has Sustained in their Woods and Mines.

Whatever the End proposed by the Muscovite in the present Ravage of Sweden, may be, we think they have neither pursued the Maxims of Christianity or Human Policy.

It was the Maxim of *Augustus* the greatest and mightiest Czar that ever reigned on the Earth, that Princes who would he truly great, should conquer for the Good of Mankind, and triumph only over themselves. The present Czar triumphs not over himself but lets his rage triumph over his Reason in his Passion triumph over his Christianity, and his Revenge over his Humanity, he is for far from Conquering for the good of Mankind, that he seems to make the Destruction of Mankind the Design of his Conquests.

And we cannot but think that the Czar has Acted a most Impolitick as well as Unchristian part, in making a brave Warlike Nation the Hereditary Enemies of his Country by his Barbarous Usage's. In short he has made a powerfull Nation Desperate, and a Severe Revenge is become the popular Vow in *Sweden,* Princes often vow Revenge in their own or other people's Names and are restrained even by their own people, but when whole Nations Vow Revenge, they seldom give it over;

If it be not reckoned prudence to make a private Enemy or Army desperate, much less is it to make a Nation desperate. The *Swedes,* left in Possession of their Estates and Land, Houses and Towns, though reduced and brought low, may, though even conquered, had been a Nation of Christians still ; and being brought low by their Misfortunes, would, as it is most natural, to all People, have been the more humble and apt to submit to the Conqueror ; but the *Swedes* ruined, starved, beggar'd, Irretrievably impoverish'd, stript of all, their Houses, Towns, land Ships burnt and destroyed, the whole Country laid waste, and themselves exposed to Hunger, Want, Nakedness, and all the Horrors of an approaching Lapland Winter ; what will this make them, but an enraged Nation of meer desperate distracted Men ? and that is, in plain English, a Nation of wild Beasts ; for without any Reproach upon the Swedes, who are a brave and gallant as well as generous and Christian Nation, a Man made desperate is more raging, more furious, more fierce than a *Lyon* ; a Man Stript naked, injured, starved, oppressed, as a Bear robbed of her Whelps, and the braver and more daring he is, the more furious raging he grows, made mad by Oppression.

Letters from *Paris* are still surprizingly filled with the Progress of Monsieur Lawes and his new Company ; the Subscription of fifty Millions in New Actions, which the King gave them Liberty to add to their Stocks, was filled up, in a few Hours ; the Price it was filled up at being a thousand Livres for every Share of one hundred Livres of Original Stock, has brought the Company in such an immense sum in Specie, that it is no Wonder they should be able to pay off the King's Debts of twelve hundred Millions, seeing they are Gainers by that particular Subscription, no less than four hundred and fifty Millions at one Blow in ready Money, and 'tis now said they will still have Leave to advance and enlarge their Subscription for fifty Millions more, and so on to fifty more, if they please, in which Case they may easily pay twelve hundred Millions ; and it is said already from *Paris,* that they have eighteen hundred Millions in Cash now by them, in order to pay the publick Debts, if the People demand their Money, which it is thought no Body would do. They are now, it is talked there, to buy all the Plate with the old Species, and bring it into the Mint, and to oblige the People to part with it. Mr. *Lawes,* they say, has found out a miraculous Expedient for this, so advantageous that no Body will be able to resist it.

They write us further from *Paris,* that the Joy of the People there is not to be expressed, it is impossible to describe it : The poor find themselves all discharged at once from their Taxes and Provisions, which pinched them severely ; and when the Turn-Pikes and Watch Houses which were set up at all the Out-Parts of the City were taken down, as they were begun to be the 23d, the People went dancing and jumping about Streets as if they were distracted for Joy. They now pay not one Farthing Tax for Wood, Coal Iron, Oats, Oil, wine, Beer, Bread, Cards, Soap, Cattle, Fish, or, in a Word, for any thing ; and a middling Family can now live cheaper in *Paris,* than they could a Week ago by a fifth Part, at least, of their Expence. The 23d the Marescbal D' *Estree* coming to see the Regent at the Opera, told him in publick, that he came to acquaint him with the good News which he had just received Advice of, that the Company's Ships had actually seized upon the Spanish Port of *Pensacola,* at the most Navigable mouth of the Mississippi, River in the Gulph of *Mexico,* which News the Regent received with great Satisfaction.

Among all their good News at Paris they have one affliction, which is very heavy upon them, that the Small-Pox makes terrible Havock amongst their great People ; the Marquis de Lovois, Grandson to the famous Minister of State of that Name, Counsellour and Secretary of State to the late King, is dead of it ; his Regiment of Horse is given to *Monsieur de Biron,* and his Office of Captain of the Band of a Hundred Swifs, is given to his Son, tho' at present he is not above six Months old.

It Causes some Speculations at Paris, that the Marquis de *Scotti* who, it was said, had Proposals of peace to make from Spain, and to whom the Regent Refused to give Passports to go to the *Hague,* because he would not make known those Propositions, has at length, obtained the Passports without communicating his Proposals ; and not-withstanding the *Emperor* opposed the receiving that Minister, as a person not acceptable to his Imperial Majesty.

They continue to say at Paris, that the Duke of Berwick pursues his March with the French Army towards Catalonia ; but they talk now, that he will not attempt the Siege of Roses, but will march directly into Catalonia, where the Miquelets are, as they say, in a Readiness to revolt, and take up Arms in favour of the French ; these having promised to procure them the Restoration of all their Privileges whenever a Peace shall be made, and that no Peace shall be made with the King of Spain, but upon the express Condition of satisfying those Malecontents.

From the Camp before Meſſina, Auguſt 6 N. S.

On the 23. paſt Sir George Byng left Naples and came off the Phare of Meſſina; and having had an Account that the Spaniſh Squadron in that Harbour were making ready, as if they intended to puſh to Sea, he ſent another Ship to Strengthen Captain Walton, who lay within the Phare to watch the Motions of the Spaniſh Ships, and kept four with himſelf without the Phare, ſhould they attempt coming out that Way. Hitherto the Spaniſh Ships continue in Meſſina, and it will be very difficult for them to get away. General Zuminguen having remov'd from his Camp at Francavilla, where he left the Spaniſh Army in their Intrenchments, march'd by ſome Paſſes which were in the Enemy's Poſſeſſion, but gave him little Oppoſition in his Way by them to Meſſina, before which Town the Imperialiſts are now encamped on the South and South Weſt Part of it, and have form'd the Siege. The Paſs of St. Aleſſio, which was taken in their March hither, is maintain'd ſtill by the Imperialiſts, but they have quitted Tarremina as lying too far off. General Mercy, arriv'd there from Reggio ſome Days ago; he has cauſed two Batteries of ſix Pieces of Cannon each, to be raiſed againſt the Caſtle Gonzaga, and has without much Loſs carry'd on his Approaches ſo as to ſet Miners to work at the Foot of the Wall, by which or by Breach, he hopes to be Maſter of it in four or five Days. He has alſo a Battery of 12 Pieces of Cannon againſt the Baſtion of the Town call'd Secretto, which has already done good Execution; and laſt Night a Battery of eight Mortars began to play upon the Town. The Enemy is ſaid to have 3000 Regular Troops in the Citadel and Town, of which the Marquis Spinola is Governor, who obliged the Burghers to take Arms in Defence of the Place. However, it is judg'd that within a Fortnight after the taking of the Caſtle of Gonzaga, we may be Maſters of the Town; tho' the Siege of the Citadel will be a Work of more Time. It is rumoured amongſt the Country People that the Marquis de Lede will come to the Relief of the Place. The Hills and Eminences about the Town are Poſſeſs'd by the Troops, and it will be difficult for the Spaniards to diſlodge them. We are yet in no Apprehenſion they can give us much Diſturbance, but promiſe our ſelves Succeſs in taking the Town. At General Mercy's deſire Sir George Byng came hither in his Boat Yeſterday from his Ships which lie without the Phare to confer with him. This Evening Sir George will go over to the Squadron at Pentemelia, to confer with Captain Walton who commands the Ships there, after which he will return to thoſe without the Phare.

By ſubſequent Advices we are inform'd, That on the 7th of Auguſt, N. S. the Imperialiſts took the Caſtle of Gonzaga, and the Tower of the Phare; and that on the 9th the Town of Meſſina ſurrendred to them, without making any Conditions, ſubmitting entirely to the Emperor's Mercy and Generoſity.

LONDON.

One Mr. Harring, an Engine-Maker joyning to the Wind-mill near Cupid's Bridge on the Thames ſide, has made a Clock which is kept going by the Natural Motions of the Elements, without any other Supply or winding up ſo long as the Materials can laſt. The ſaid Clock will be placed in the Front of his Work-houſe for publick View of ſuch as paſs that-way by Water: This Clock has already been ſeen by ſome Gentlemen of the Royal Society, who have named it the Lunar Cronometer, by Reaſon its Motion is continued by the Influence of the Moon's Attraction, and the Projector propoſes to make St. Paul's Clock go by the ſame Motions.

PHILADELPHIA, December 22d By the Sloop Samuel and Sarah, Matthew Phillips Commander from Providence, we have received Advice that the Spaniards, having fitted Out Seven Ships, at the Havana with Soldiers and Ammunition to retake Penſacola, near the Mouth of the Miſſiſippi Rivers and after-wards to goe and Deſtroy the Engliſh Settlement at Providence were met at Sea by a French Squadron, who let but one Brigantten, Eſcape to carry news of their Wonderfull Succeſs.

Boſton, Entred Inwards, Ralph Ellinwood, John Wharffe and John Prince, from Piſcataqua, Jonah Gitts from New London, Timothy Yeals, from North Carolina, Lemuel Drew, Sterling, Joſiah Carver, Unity, Joſeph Farrington, Mary and Joſeph Newel, Return from Barbados.

Cleared Outwards, Dan. Wait Joſ. Jackſon. and Tho. Miller for Piſcataqua, Jonath. Chaſe for Rhode Iſland. Edward Wilkinſon for Connecticut, Wm. Gold for Annapolis. Royal, John Jackſon for New York, Joſ. Prince, James Wall and Job Chamberlin for North Carolina, Edward Cooper, Lemuel Drew, Joſeph Douglaſs and Eben. Norwood for Barbadoes, Dan. Beekman for South Carolina, Wm Roby, for Antigua, Joſiah Carver for Weſt Indies and Archibald Blackader for London.

Outward Bound, Joſ. Johnſton. Jer. Simmons and John Royal for North Carolina, Joſ. Gorham for Rhode Iſland and Connecticut, Charles Hogg, Venice, and James Wiſton Argile, for South Carolina, John Buikley, John Feſter Suſan and John Whittemore, Robert for Weſt Indies, Wm. Hodes Speedwell for Leeward Iſland, Geo. Burchan, Mary and Abigail for Jamaica. John Ellery, Sarah and Peter Klagg, Mary for Barbadoes, Eben Allen, Joſeph and Mary for St Thomas, John Bolderſon, May-flower. for Liſbon, and Alex Beckley, Benſon, for Briſtol.

New York, December 9th. On the 6th. Inſtant arrived Nathaniel Owen in a Sloop from Jamaica.

Entred Out Tickel. Fred and Beardſit Junior for Curacoa, and Nicholas and Web for Barbados, cleared out Ford for Jamaica Welman and Rhein, Moor for St Chriſtophers.

PHILADELPHIA.

Entred Inwards, Sloop Unity Henry Stevens from Jamaica, Mary Galley Stephen Simmonds from London, Matthew Phillips from Providence and Sherlock Rivers from Antigua.

Cleared Out, Brigantine Montroſe David Lindſay and the Dolphin Sloop Robert Palmer, for Jamaica Peel for Berbadoes, King and Naſh for Madera, Ratford for Surinam Curtis for Barbadoes and Hadden for Carolina.

Advertiſement.

This Paper will be Publiſh'd Weekly, and ſhall contain an Impartial account of Tranſactions, in the Several States of Europe, America, &c. All Perſons that are willing to Encourage ſo Uſeful an Undertaking at the Moderate rate of Ten Shillings, a Year for the City of PHILADELPHIA Fifteen Shillings, for New Jerſey, New-York and Maryland Twenty Shillings, for Virginia, Rhode Iſland, and Boſton Proclamation Money, (to be paid Quarterly) are Deſired to ſend their Names, and places of abode, to any of the following Perſons. Viz.

Mr. William Bradford in New York, Mr. Evan Jones at the City of Annapolis Mr. Robinſon, Poſt-Maſter at Williams-Burgh, Mr. Jacob Walter, at Hamton in Virginia Docter Ryley at New-Caſtle, Mr. Thomas Hill, at Salem Mr. Campbell Poſt-maſter at Rhode-Iſland, Mr. John Barclay at Amboy. Mr. John Coſtard at Burlington and Mr. ANDREW BRADFORD, at Philadelphia.

PHILADELPHIA Printed, and Sold by ANDREW BRADFORD, at the Bible in the Second Street and John Copſon in Market Street 1719.

SECOND PAGE OF THE "AMERICAN WEEKLY MERCURY"

DAVID RITTENHOUSE

work, "The Prince of Parthia." This tragedy, rapid and strong in action, and dignified, if somewhat mono- tonous and conventional in its language,[1] suggests that, had not the author been cut off at the early age of seven-and-twenty, he might have won honourable mention among English poets.

The first American drama

[1] On a stormy night two arch conspirators thus parley together : —

VARDANES. —Why rage the elements? They are not cursed
    Like me! Evanthe frowns not angry on them ;
    The wind may play upon her beauteous bosom,
    Nor fear her chiding ; light can bless her sense,
    And in the floating mirror she beholds
    Those beauties which can fetter all mankind.

At the time when the first American drama was written, the stage was generally viewed with strong disapproval, except in New York, where the first theatre was opened in 1761, in spite of some feeble remonstrances. In Philadelphia a little company of players undertook in 1749 to give the public a taste of Shakespeare under improvised conditions, but the performance was suppressed by the magistrates. After two or three further abortive attempts, the Old Southwark Theatre went into operation in 1766, and the most vehement efforts to close it were unsuccessful. It is worthy of note that, among the strait-laced persons who deemed it scandalous to look on at "Hamlet" or "Othello," there were not a few who took delight in cock-fighting and bull-baiting.[1]

Beginnings of the theatre

LYSIAS. — My lord, forget her ; tear her from your breast.
Who, like the Phœnix, gazes on the sun,
And strives to soar up to the glorious blaze,
Should never leave ambition's brightest object,
To turn and view the beauties of a flower.
VARDANES. — O Lysias, chide no more, for I have done.
Yes, I 'll forget the proud disdainful beauty.
Hence with vain love ! ambition now alone
Shall guide my actions. Since mankind delights
To give me pain, I 'll study mischief too,
And shake the earth, e'en like this raging tempest.
LYSIAS. — A night like this, so dreadful to behold,
Since my remembrance' birth I never saw.
VARDANES. — E'en such a night, dreadful as this, they say,
My teeming mother gave me to the world.
Whence by those sages who, in knowledge rich,
Can pry into futurity and tell
What distant ages will produce of wonder,
My days were deemed to be a hurricane.
LYSIAS. — Then, haste to raise the tempest.
My soul disdains this one eternal round,
Where each succeeding day is like the former.
Trust me, my noble prince, here is a heart
Steady and firm to all your purposes ;
And here 's a hand that knows to execute.
Whate'er designs thy daring breast can form,
Nor ever shake with fear.

See Godfrey's *Juvenile Poems*, ed. Evans, Philadelphia, 1767. The volume contains also, among other things, a poem in pentameter couplets, entitled "The Court of Fancy," a sort of study after Chaucer.
[1] Cf. Miss Repplier's *Philadelphia*, p. 69.

The chief occupation of Pennsylvanians was agriculture, but there was also a brisk commerce, and towns grew up rapidly. Soon after the middle of the century, Philadelphia, with a population of 30,000, was the largest city of the English colonies; Lancaster, with 10,000, was the largest inland town; York was nearly as large; while Wilmington and Newcastle, in Delaware, were thriving places. Wheat, timber, and furs were exported in such quantities as to employ more than 500 ships and 7000 sailors. Sugar, wines and liquors, and most kinds of manufactured articles, were imported; but some manufactures flourished almost from the start. The ale brewed in Philadelphia soon became deservedly famous. Bradford's printing-press and paper-mill have already been mentioned, and good German glass was made at Germantown and Manheim.

Agriculture and commerce

OLD SOUTHWARK THEATRE

By the middle of the eighteenth century, the export of pig iron to England reached 3000 tons.

In such a community negro slavery could not come to be regarded as an economic necessity. As a rule, every farmer owned the house in which he dwelt, and the land

which he cultivated with the aid of the members of his family and hired servants. But there were a good
many indented white servants,[1] partly convicts and
kidnapped waifs, but in greater part Irish and German "redemptioners" who sold themselves into temporary servitude
to defray the cost of their ocean voyage. In the eighteenth
century, probably more such redemptioners came to Pennsylvania than to any of the other colonies. They were in
general kindly treated. The regular term of service was four
years, with five days additional for every day of truancy.
They could not be sold out of the province without their consent freely given in open court, or before a justice of the
peace ; and good behaviour entitled them at the end of their
service to a suit of clothes and a set of farm tools. These
white freedmen often became useful and respectable members of society.

Slaves and servants

From the first there were negro slaves in Pennsylvania,
used mostly for household service, but seldom as field-hands
except in Delaware. But the Quaker conscience was aroused
on the subject of slavery at a time when other Christians
could see nothing wrong in it. The Memorial of
1688, in which the German Friends of Germantown protested against "the buying and keeping of
negroes," is still in existence. During the next half-century
the assembly laboured assiduously to check the importation
of slaves by imposing prohibitory duties on such traffic.
Some years before 1776 slaves had ceased to be brought
into Pennsylvania. In 1758 the Yearly Meeting enjoined
all Friends to set free their slaves, "making a Christian
provision for them." Many complied, but a few held out
until "in 1776 a declaration of independence for all slaves
held by Friends was decreed, and monthly meetings were directed, after proper effort, to exclude from membership all
Quakers who refused to comply."[2] Long before the Revo-

Quaker opposition to slavery

[1] I have discussed the subject of indented servants at some length in
Old Virginia and her Neighbours, Illustrated Edition, ii. 159–171.
[2] Sharpless, *A Quaker Experiment*, pp. 31–33.

END OF PROTEST WITH SIGNATURES

FACSIMILE OF PROTEST (1688) AGAINST "THE BUYING AND KEEPING OF NEGROES"

lution the practice of manumission had been sufficiently frequent to create a much larger class of free blacks than could be found in any of the other colonies.

The Quaker spirit in dealing with pauperism and crime was equally admirable, although with regard to capital punishment it proved impossible to realize the ideal of Penn and confine the death penalty to cases of murder and treason. The list of capital offences grew to fourteen, including highway robbery, horse-stealing, and counterfeiting. In 1731 Catherine Bevan was burned alive at Newcastle for the murder of her husband. It was intended to strangle her before the fire could reach her, but a sudden outburst of flame severed the rope, and drove away the executioner, so that she died in torment. For larceny, fornication, and assault, the usual penalties were pillory and whipping-post. It was said that the indented white servants furnished the great majority of offenders. In 1703 we find the grand jury presenting all persons known to play at cards in public; nine persons at one time for selling strong drink without a license; "John Walker for using Sassafras Street as a ropewalk;" three barbers for "trimming people on First day," etc.[1] *Crimes and punishments*

The practice in such matters was therefore not very different from that of the other colonies. But Pennsylvania was honourably distinguished for the good care of prisons and the humanity of prison discipline. Visitors from Europe remarked upon Philadelphia prisons as the best in the world. Philadelphia had also the only lunatic asylum in America that was managed upon something like modern methods. It had, moreover, an excellent hospital, a reform school, and no city in the world devoted a larger share of time and thought to philanthropic purposes. In all this we see the direct influence of Quakerism, and of the ideals of William Penn. *Philanthropy*

Indeed, to cite the words of the illustrious lawyer, Andrew Hamilton, on retiring from his place as speaker of the as-

[1] Watson's *Annals of Philadelphia*, i. 308, 309.

sembly, in 1739: "It is not to the fertility of our soil or the commodiousness of our rivers that we ought chiefly to attribute the great progress this province has made within so small a compass of years in improvements, wealth, trade, and navigation, and the extraordinary increase of people who have been drawn from every country in Europe; it is all due to the excellency of our Constitution. Our foreign trade and shipping are free from all imposts except those small duties payable to His Majesty by the statute laws of Great Britain. The taxes are inconsiderable, for the sole power of raising and disposing of public money is lodged in the assembly. . . . By many years' experience we find that an equality among religious societies, without distinguishing one sect with greater privileges than another, is the most effective method to discourage hypocrisy, promote the practice of moral virtues, and prevent the plagues and mischiefs which always attend religious squabbling. This is our Constitution, and this Constitution was framed by the wisdom of Mr. Penn."

Hamilton's tribute to Penn

Hamilton was right in attributing the extraordinary increase of people drawn from all parts of Europe to the excellency of Penn's ideas. Although Pennsylvania began her existence seventy-five years later than Virginia and fifty-two years later than the colony of Massachusetts Bay, although she was the youngest of all the colonies save Georgia, yet before the Revolution she had come to rank next after Virginia and Massachusetts in populousness. The chief elements in this rapid increase were two great streams of immigration — the Palatinate German and Scotch-Irish streams — which were drawn thither in consequence of Penn's ideas. One of the most interesting aspects in which to consider Pennsylvania is as the chief centre of diffusion of the people who became afterward the pioneers of the democratic West. In our next and concluding chapter, something must be said concerning this matter.

Significance of Pennsylvania's rapid growth

CHAPTER XVII

THE MIGRATIONS OF SECTS

THE colonies of New York and Pennsylvania were not only more heterogeneous in population than any of the others, but they were the principal centres of distribution of the non-English population from the seaboard to the Alleghany mountains. In the New England colonies, during the seventeenth century, the non-English element might most succinctly be described by saying that there was no such element; in the eighteenth century it was extremely small, though not without importance. Virginia and Maryland also were at first purely English, but the tidewater region, in the eighteenth century, received some foreign accessions and the Appalachian region far more. Among the oldest colonies, therefore, New York was the only one which had any considerable foreign population, and there it formed a large majority of the whole. Of the younger colonies the two Carolinas had a large foreign element among the dwellers on the seaboard, and still larger in the back country. But all this mountain population, in the Carolinas as well as in Virginia and Maryland, entered the country by way of Pennsylvania; and this migration was so great, both in its physical dimensions and in the political and social effects which it has wrought, that Pennsylvania acquires especial interest as the temporary tarrying-place and distributing centre for so much that we now call characteristically American.

Of the different classes of non-English immigrants during the colonial times, while all were represented in the city of New York, the Jews and the French Protestants settled chiefly on the seaboard, and on the other hand the Germans and the so-called Scotch-Irish found their way in great numbers to what was then the western frontier. We must devote a few words to each of these classes.

The city of New York has always been the principal home of the Jews in the United States, and it was in connection with the Dutch enterprise in founding New Netherland that they were first brought here. It was from various quarters, but mainly from the Spanish peninsula that they The Jews had come to Holland. In all the history of this in Spain wonderful people there is no more brilliant chapter than that of their career in Spain under the Mohammedan dynasties between the tenth and fourteenth centuries. In point of civilization, in the days when Philip Augustus and lion-hearted Richard went together on their crusade, such cities as Toledo and Cordova were as far in advance of London and Paris as London and Paris are now in advance of Toledo and Cordova, and in this Spanish preëminence the Jews played a foremost part. Such men as Ibn Gebirol and Maimonides were the great teachers of their time, and influences wafted across the Pyrenees had much to do with the Albigensian culture in southern France. As the Christians in Spain slowly conquered and drove back the Mussulmans, the persecution of Jews began and steadily increased in virulence, until the year 1492, which witnessed the surrender of Granada and downfall of the last Moorish kingdom, saw also the abominable edict which drove from their homes and their native land 200,000 honest and industrious Spanish citizens of Hebrew race and faith. In that eventful year, when an inscrutable Providence put into the hands of Spain the rich prize of America, did she enter upon that course of wholesale persecution which proved her to be unworthy of such opportunities and incapable of using them. The cost of Columbus's second voyage was partly defrayed with stolen money, the property of Jews who had been dragged on shipboard and carried over to Morocco. Meanwhile several industries received a death-blow, and in particular many cities were left without a single physician or any person qualified to act as notary public.[1] But the edict of 1492, savagely as it was executed, did not suffice to remove all Jews, and for

SPINOZA

the next century a large part of the work of the Inquisition consisted in burning them and seizing their goods.

The revolt of the Netherlands gave them an opportunity for emigration of which they were not slow even to avail themselves, and by the end of the sixteenth century they were to be found in all the cities of Holland, especially in Amsterdam, whereby Andrew Marvel was provoked to write a poem in which that city is said to

Their migration to the Netherlands

[1] Graetz, *Les Juifs d'Espagne*, 121.

have its "bank of conscience," where "all opinions find credit and exchange;" yea, continues the poet, with what is meant for withering sarcasm : —

"The Universal church is only there." [1]

Among these settlers in Holland were some from Poland and Germany, but the great majority were from the Spanish peninsula, and some of the most highly cultivated of these were Portuguese. Of such parents was born at Amsterdam, in 1732, Benedict Spinoza, one of the most exalted names in all the history of human thought and human character.

In Holland, as usual, many of the Jews were bankers. They were liberal subscribers to the stock of the West India Company, and there were several Hebrew names on the list of directors. When the Dutch took possession of Brazil in 1624, a party of Jews went over and settled there ; but

Arrivals of Jews in New Netherland and Rhode Island in 1645 the Portuguese rose against the Dutch and after nine years of desultory fighting compelled them to sign a treaty in which they gave up all claim to the country. As for the resident Jews, the Portuguese agreed to give them "an amnesty, in all wherein they could promise it," — too vague an assurance to be very assuring. In the autumn of that year, 1654, the barque Santa Caterina arrived at New Amsterdam from Brazil, with 27 Portuguese Jews on board, men, women, and children. They had apparently embarked in haste, taking such effects as they could, for upon their arrival at Manhattan the skipper sold all their goods at public auction to pay for their passage. Another party presently came from the Dutch island of Curaçoa. These arrivals did not please Director Stuyvesant, who wrote home to the Company, begging that "none of the Jewish nation be permitted to infest New Netherland." Before getting an answer he contrived to annoy the newcomers, so that some went to Newport, feeling sure of toleration there, while others stayed at Manhat-

[1] Daly, *Jews in North America*, 3.

tan in the hope of being set right by the Company's orders. In that hope they were not disappointed. The Company replied to Stuyvesant that his request "was inconsistent with reason and justice," and the States General followed this up with the act of July 15, 1655, "expressly permitting the Jews to trade to New Netherland, and to reside there, only on the simple condition that they should support their own poor." [1] This condition has been well fulfilled, for such a kind of person as a Jewish pauper has seldom been seen.

The incidents here recounted were the beginnings of thrifty and valuable Jewish settlements in New York and Rhode Island. After the English conquest of New Netherland, the Duke of York was led, as we have seen, by considerations of expediency, to continue the liberal policy of the Dutch. The instructions to Governor Andros, on his first coming, were to give full toleration to persons "of what religion soever," but perhaps the failure to exclude Jews may have been due to oversight ; for this clause was omitted from the instructions to Governor Dongan, and when in 1685 the Jewish residents in New Amsterdam petitioned for leave to build a synagogue, he referred the petition to the mayor and common council, who refused to grant it, on the ground that toleration of public worship extended only to sects professing faith in Christ. But Dongan, himself an Irish Catholic, was a man of extremely liberal views. Next year, whether at his own instance or not, a fresh set of instructions was sent him, in which the omitted clause was restored. Probably Dongan took advantage of this to grant the Jews' petition, for neither Andros, who came back as his successor, nor Leisler, was at all likely to take such a step ; and we know that in 1691 the Jews had a place for public worship. In 1695 there were *The synagogue in New York* 20 families, or probably about 100 souls, in the city, and their little synagogue stood on the south side of the present Beaver Street, midway between Broadway and Broad Street. In 1712 an English clergyman informs us that one can learn

[1] Daly, *op. cit.* 10.

Hebrew in New York as easily as in Europe, because of divers ingenious and learned men of that nation that dwell there. In 1748 the Swedish traveller, Peter Kalm, tells of the fine shops, the large country estates, and the richly freighted ships belonging to the Jews whom he visited in New York. At that time they possessed all civil rights and privileges in common with the other inhabitants, except that of voting for members of the legislature. In 1737 this point was decided by the New York assembly itself in a contested election case. The decision was that, since Jews did not possess the parliamentary franchise in England, they did not possess it in New York, in the absence of any special enactment for that purpose.

It may have been because New York absorbed so large a part of the Jewish immigration that comparatively little was left for Pennsylvania. There were nevertheless a good many Jews in Philadelphia, and some were citizens of great influence. The name of Haym Salomon, a very wealthy Polish Jew, deserves to be coupled with that of Robert Morris for the financial aid which he extended to Congress during the War of Independence. Mr. Salomon advanced to the United States nearly $700,-000, not a cent of which was ever repaid.

The difference in point of liberality between William Penn's idea of toleration and Cecilius Calvert's idea was shown in the fact that Maryland's deservedly famous Toleration Act extended only to Trinitarians. By that very act disbelief in the doctrine of the Trinity was made a crime punishable with death. We need not be surprised, therefore, that Jews did not flock to Maryland. But in Georgia and South Carolina, where a more liberal policy was pursued toward them, a good many found homes and proved valuable citizens. At the time of the Revolution the principal Jewish population of North America was in Newport, New York, Philadelphia, Charleston, and Savannah.

The French Protestants next claim our attention. During the seventeenth century, while the colonization of North America was going on, they met with their final defeats in France, and thereafter continued to exist merely on sufferance until even that privilege was withdrawn. There was something extraordinary in this tragic end of a mighty struggle, and to us who look back upon it after this interval it is one of the most impressive spectacles in history. In 1558, when Elizabeth ascended the English throne, The while Martin Luther's Reformation was not yet Huguenots half a century old, its prospects of success seemed at least as bright in France as in England. Within four years at least 2000 Protestant churches had sprung up in France, and with their local consistories and provincial synods, sustaining a national synod, a powerful and aggressive Calvinistic organization was rapidly coming to the front. Half the aristocracy, including a large majority of the noblemen below forty years of age, were in favour of the Reform, and of the clergy a strong party comprising one cardinal, one archbishop, six bishops, and hundreds of priests, were numbered among its friends. But, on the other hand, not more than one tenth of the people had become Protestants. An educated rural middle class, such as played so great a part in England and planted Virginia and New England, did not exist in France. The peasantry through sheer conservatism kept on in the old ways. The popular strength of the reformers was chiefly among the urban middle class, educated craftsmen, merchants, and professional men ; this class was hampered in national action for want of rural support. Below it the populace, whether conservative or anarchist, looked upon the respectable middle class chiefly as fit subjects for plunder and murder. The mob of Paris, which in the midst of civilization for age after age remains an untamed primeval tiger, was the deadly enemy of the reformers. There was another circumstance ; the submission of the great nobles to the overshadowing power of the crown was not yet completed, so that the Protestant cause, when upheld by these nobles against the crown, ran counter to the popular instinct of national unity.

In spite of all these drawbacks the Protestants made a noble fight, and had it not been for the untoward issue of another great struggle, more than three centuries earlier, even they might very probably have triumphed. One of the blackest chapters in European history is that which records

Effect of the extermination of the Albigenses

the ruin of a brilliant civilization and wholesale slaughter of a noble people in the thirteenth century in what we are used to call the south of France. It is a commonplace remark that religions thrive upon persecution, and that truth is sure in the long run to prevail. It is nevertheless true that a sufficiently thorough persecution may inflict such damage upon mankind as many long ages may fail to repair. Nothing can be clearer than that France has not yet recovered from the horrors wrought nearly seven hundred years ago in Languedoc. The Albigenses of France were exterminated. When the last 200 of them were shut up within palisades in a high gorge of the Pyrenees and burnt to death in a holocaust, it was the end of all that their preachings and their modes of life could do for France. Could these influences have survived, in all probability the aspirations afterward represented by the Huguenots would have so far prevailed that the moral tone of the whole nation in the seventeenth century would have been far higher than it was, the absolutism reached under Louis XIV. might have been avoided and the awful retribution of 1793 might have been escaped.

Every one will remember how in 1555 the great Coligny entertained the idea, which afterward passed from him to

Defeat of Coligny's schemes for a Huguenot colony in America

Sir Walter Raleigh, of founding a Protestant state in America. His two attempts, in Brazil and in Florida, both ended in grim disaster. In 1603 a scheme not wholly dissimilar was put into operation by Henry IV., when he made a grant of Acadia to Pierre du Gua, the Sieur du Monts, a sagacious and valiant Huguenot knight of Saintonge. To him was entrusted the enterprise of founding a colony where liberty of conscience was to be respected. Under his auspices the first attempts

were made in Acadia and Samuel de Champlain founded a
trading-post at Quebec ; but the enterprise did not flourish.
In 1610 the murder of the great king deprived the Huguenots of their best friend ; and in the course of the next year
the Sieur du Monts sold out his rights in New France to Ma-
dame de Guercheville, by whom the work of colonization in
the New World was handed over to the Jesuits. Thus all
hopes of a colony where Huguenots might live peaceably
were at an end.

After Henry's death the Protestants in France saw more
and more reason for anxiety lest the privileges which he had
extended to them in the Edict of Nantes should be curtailed. The brief war which ended with the loss of Rochelle
in 1628 was a heavy blow to them. The same reign   First arri-
witnessed the cessation of the meetings of the na-   vals of
                                                      Huguenots
tional legislature, and presently with the failure   in New
                                                      Netherland
of the Fronde rebellion the absolute despotism of
Louis XIV. was riveted upon unhappy France. At this
time many Huguenots fled to Holland, whence some of them
made their way to New Netherland. The Bayards, one of
whom was the wife of Peter Stuyvesant, were a prominent
Huguenot family, and from this time more or less migration
from France to the Hudson River was kept up.

In April, 1655, occurred the awful massacre of Waldenses
in Piedmont which called forth from John Milton that solemn
denunciation, like the message of a Hebrew prophet : —

> " Avenge, O Lord, thy slaughtered saints, whose bones
>   Lie scattered on the Alpine mountains cold," etc.

The Elector Palatine, who was one of the leading Protestant
powers of Germany, offered a refuge to the persecuted Waldenses, and many made their way through Switzer-   Arrivals of
                                                   Waldenses
land to the Palatinate, where some stayed while   and Wal-
others kept on to Holland and so to America. A   loons
colony of these interesting primitive Protestants was formed
upon Staten Island in 1662. Many Huguenots also found a
refuge in the Palatinate, as well as Walloons, who were be-

ginning to suffer fresh molestation in the Flemish Netherlands. A party of such Walloons, led by Louis du Bois,
made up their minds in 1660 to remove from the banks of
the Rhine to those of the Hudson. They settled in Esopus,
in what is now Ulster county, and there made the beginnings
of the towns of Kingston and New Paltz, the name of which
commemorates their brief sojourn on the Rhine.

In 1661, in his twenty-third year, Louis XIV. took the
government of France into his own hands, and in the same
year entered upon a series of measures designed to
undermine and neutralize the Edict of Nantes. It
was decreed that Protestant boys might lawfully
abjure the faith of their parents at fourteen years and girls
at twelve years. This rule was soon made to justify the
most shameless kidnapping. Any child who could be coaxed
or bribed with trinkets to enter a church while mass was
going on, or even to repeat a verse of Ave Maria in the
street, was liable to be forthwith claimed as a Catholic and
dragged off to some convent, and the courts paid no heed to
the protests and entreaties of the outraged parents. Protestant schools were shut up by sovereign decree. Sometimes the buildings which they had erected for the purpose
were confiscated and handed over to Jesuits. The dull ego-
tist at Versailles had but to say what should be done, and it
was done. Thus the five great Protestant colleges, including
that one at Saumur where William Penn had studied, were
broken up. Protestant churches were shut up either on slight
pretexts or without a word, or were now and then burned by
a mob with the connivance of the magistrates. Huguenots,
moreover, were excluded from many public offices, and were
forbidden to practice law or medicine, or to print or sell
books. Huguenot women were not allowed be milliners or
laundresses.

Finally in 1681 began the infamous *dragonnades*. All over
the kingdom troops were quartered upon Huguenot households, as if in an enemy's country, with
liberty to commit any outrage short of murder. Upon this

Decrees of Louis XIV. against Huguenots

The dra-gonnades

device the king especially plumed himself. At the same time he issued a decree lowering the age at which children might abjure Protestantism to seven years. The revocation of the Edict of Nantes followed in 1685, but the great Huguenot exodus began in 1681. Immediately England, Holland, Denmark, Sweden, and the Protestant states of Germany offered especial inducements to these people. They were at once to be naturalized, with all the rights and privileges of born subjects; in England sums of money were subscribed toward the expenses of their journey thither, and all their goods were admitted free of custom-house charges; in Holland they were exempted from all taxes for twelve years. Thus there came about such a migration as the civilized world has rarely seen; within twenty years something like a million Huguenots fled from

The Huguenot exodus

their country, or at least seven per cent. of the entire population. As soon as the king discovered that such an exodus was beginning, he issued decrees forbidding Protestants to leave the kingdom under heavy penalties, and guards were stationed on the frontiers to intercept them, while cruisers patrolled the coasts. But these measures were ineffective, for popular sentiment was very far from keeping pace with the tyrant's besotted zeal, and many fugitives were helped on their way by compassionate Catholics. Drink-money, too, played exactly the same part as now and always. Guards for a small tip, instead of detaining refugees, would pass them on or even furnish them with guides; and captains of ships were equally obliging. Where such methods were unavailable, people travelled on foot by night or disguised as peasants, driving a cow, or carrying a hod, or trundling a wheelbarrow; wealthy men and women, clothed in rags, begged from door to door; and so in one way or another the exodus was accomplished.

Concerning the damage which this wholesale emigration inflicted upon France, little need be said, for the tale has often been told. It cannot be expressed in statistics. This seven per cent. of the total French population included a far higher proportion of skilled craftsmen, prosperous merchants,

Terrible
loss to
France professional men and scholars.   So largely was the marine represented that the French navy has never recovered from the loss.   And then there was the weeding out of a certain earnest Puritan type of character which no nation can afford to weaken.   Altogether this emigration was in many respects a skimming of cream.

The Huguenots were largely represented in the maritime provinces of Normandy, Brittany, Saintonge, and Languedoc, and sometimes they made the voyage directly to America. But more often the first flight was to England or Holland, where parties were formed for crossing the ocean.   There was no part of English or Dutch America where they were not welcome.   They maintained friendly relations with the Church of England as well as with the Independents in Boston.   Numbers came to Massachusetts and Virginia, but much greater numbers to New York and South Carolina. In Boston the marks of them are plentiful.   Opposite the hotel named for Paul Revere, in the square named for James Bowdoin, comes the street named for Pierre Chardon, of Touraine, whence it is but a short walk to the public hall

The Hu-
guenots in
Boston built by the grandson of Pierre Faneuil, of Rochelle. The family of Governor Bowdoin, or Baudouin, was a cultured and respectable one in southwestern France.   The French look of the name is not always so well preserved as in those cases; sometimes it is quite anglicized. Thus the name of the Salem family of Brownes, eminent in the eighteenth century, is simply the translation of Le Brun, from the island of Jersey ; and the name of Philip English, which is remembered in connection with the witchcraft panic, was L'Anglois, from the same island.   So Olney represents Aulnoy, and Dabney, of Massachusetts and Virginia, is curtailed from D'Aubigné ; and not only such names as Gillet and Lambert, but now and then a Collins, or a Lewis, or a Basset, or a Lawrence, may indicate French origin.   Louis XIV., who had a capacity for details, liked to gather information concerning these refugees.   Reports from Canada assure him that there are many of the "vile miscreants" on the Hudson River, and on a map of Boston, drawn for the king in 1693, the situation of the Huguenot meeting-house, on the south side of School Street, is shown by the words "renegats françois," French renegades. But not all settled in Boston. There were the Le Barons at Plymouth, and the Sigourneys, Bernons, Bondets, Germaines, and Martins at the village of Oxford, up in the Nipmuck country, until an Indian massacre dispersed them in 1696.

Nowhere, however, did Huguenots fill a larger place than in New York. There came Jacques Desbrosses from Poitou, whose grandson was President of the Chamber of Commerce, the first organized mercantile society in America, and whose family name is left upon a well-known street and ferry. There came Étienne de Lancey, from Caen, whose son James was chief justice and lieutenant-governor of New York, and from the neighbouring city of Rouen came Guillaume Le Conte, among whose descend- Huguenots in New York ants in these latter days are numbered two of the most eminent men of science that our country has produced. In 1689 a party of these Frenchmen obtained from acting-governor Jacob Leisler a grant of land on Long Island Sound, where they founded the pretty town of New New Rochelle Rochelle. In 1693 they built a church there, but before this was accomplished the settlers used to walk every Sunday morning to New York, a distance of 20 miles, to attend the regular service at the Église du Saint Esprit, in Pine Street, and then they would walk back in the evening. Four times a year — at Christmas, Easter, Whitsuntide, and Michaelmas — the sacrament of the Lord's Supper was administered at New Rochelle, but at all other times it was necessary to go to the city. First the young children were carefully gathered together and left in charge of faithful friends. Then the procession started, with measured tread keeping time to music as men's and women's voices joined with fervour in some grand old psalm of Clement Marot. At a half-way place where a huge rock was shaded by cedars and fragrant pines they rested and took lunch, and then went on their way. We are assured that it was no unusual thing for men and women to do the 40 miles.[1] For more than half a century they retained their native speech.

In the ancient city of Rochelle, whence most of these devoted worshippers came, one of the most important families was that of the Jays, apparently a branch of the Jays who were lords of Montonneau in Poitou. From that province, as early as 1565, the first Jean Jay whom we know, already converted to Protestantism, had come to live in Rochelle. His descendant, Pierre Jay, who was living there in 1685, was a wealthy merchant. One day in October a corps of 7000 fusileers from Béarn marched into Rochelle and began plundering as if in an enemy's country. The house of Pierre Jay was one of those that had been especially marked out for pillage. He succeeded in getting his wife and children out of the house, and, although the shore was closely patrolled on land by troops of cavalry and watched from the sea by warships, he contrived to elude this guard and put them safely on board a vessel that was just starting for Plymouth in England. After they had sailed out of harm's way they were missed, and Jay was forthwith thrown into prison for assisting them to escape. Some Catholic friends procured his release, but there was manifestly no hope of saving his property. He was expecting, however, one of his own ships from Spain, with a rich cargo of which he was sole owner. Taking into his confidence a bold and faithful pilot, he bade him watch out at sea for the ship and not let her come ashore but bring her to anchor off the island of Rhé. This was punctually done, and Jay, after lying hidden for some hours in the bottom of the pilot-boat, so near to a royal cruiser that he could hear the sailors talk, at length boarded his own ship and sailed away to Plymouth. Shortly afterward his eldest son, Auguste, returning from a

The Jay family

---

[1] Bolton's *Hist. of the County of Westchester*, 1848, i. 400. A slight pinch of salt seems to be needed, which I will leave it for the reader to supply at discretion.

voyage to Africa, found the homestead deserted and dismantled, and all the property of the family confiscated. He contrived to slip on board a ship bound for the West Indies, and after a while the family were all united in the hospitable city of New York.

One of Pierre Jay's friends and neighbours in Rochelle was the ancestor of Henry Laurens, of South Carolina, and in the next town, only eleven miles away, dwelt the ancestor of Elias Boudinot, of New Jersey ; — three presidents of our Continental Congress from one little corner of the coast of France ! In Benjamin West's well-known picture of the American Commissioners at Paris, in 1783, John Jay and Henry Laurens are standing while the others sit, and Laurens's face is turned with a satisfied expression toward Jay, who had detected and defeated the insidious scheme of France which would fain have made the independent United States stop short at the Alleghany Mountains. When all the past circumstances crowd in upon our memory, there is something deeply impressive in the picture.

Three presidents of Congress

The Huguenots, as we have observed, were free to come to any of the American colonies, but showed a marked preference for New York and South Carolina. The choice of the Quakers, and of various German sects akin to them, was much more limited, and after the founding of Pennsylvania offered them such strong inducements, they were sure to go there. For the Quakers the state which Penn founded ensured them a much greater and more useful future than they could have had in England, where they have dwindled in numbers to less than 15,000. In America there are probably not less than 150,000. From Pennsylvania they have been to some extent distributed in the west and southwest, and the civilizing work which they have done, especially perhaps in the eighteenth century in North Carolina, has been of inestimable value. It was the coming of the Quakers to Pennsylvania in 1681

Dimensions of the Quaker exodus from England

that brought also the first Germans. They came and made their first home in Germantown, hard by Philadelphia, and the reasons for their coming were closely connected with the sympathy between their views and those of the Quakers. We have seen how William Penn, who was himself half a Dutchman, made visits occasionally to Holland, and extended them into preaching tours through portions of Germany. He thus discovered many kindred spirits and held out inducements for them to come to his new colony. The

The Mennonites and Dunkers

first to come were the Mennonites, who were spiritual descendants of the mediæval Quietists, and may probably have contained in their ranks a few Waldenses and Anabaptists. Their differences from the Quakers were so slight that they often held meetings together, and it was not uncommon to hear the Mennonites called German Quakers. In Germany and Switzerland they were savagely persecuted by Protestant and Catholic alike; so they gladly followed Penn to the New World. Their leader, Francis Daniel Pastorius, was an enthusiastic scholar, studying science, philosophy, jurisprudence, or whatever came to hand, and reading eight or ten languages. The Mennonites were followed by the Dunkers, a sect of German Baptists who came to Pennsylvania between 1719 and 1729, leaving none of their number behind. There are said to be more than 200,000 in the United States to-day. About 1732, under the preaching of a singular mystic, Conrad Beissel, a portion of this sect broke off as Seventh Day Baptists, and founded a community at Ephrata, in some respects analogous to those of the Shakers. An interesting feature of these German sects is their learning and their devotion to literature. The Ephrata Community printed religious books in handsome type upon very fine paper; and they also knew good music. Besides these sects were the Labadists and Moravians, whom I must for the present dismiss with this mere mention.[1]

[1] See in this connection the admirable work of Sachse, *The German Pietists of Provincial Pennsylvania*, Philadelphia, 1895.

Another migration from Germany, of a different kind and far more numerous, was that which came from the Rhenish Palatinate. The nearness of that province to Alsace, Lorraine, and Franche-Comté, upon which Louis XIV. waged a war of conquest, often brought serious trouble upon it. The first devastation of the Palatinate in 1674 is the The one dark spot upon the honourable career of Tu- Palatines renne, but it had a strategic excuse. The second devastation, in 1688, partly intended as a chastisement for harbouring Huguenots, was far more barbarously performed. Sad havoc was wrought at Heidelberg and Mannheim, and that beautiful country did not recover itself for more than two generations. Thousands of peasantry were reduced to a state of abject misery. This attracted the attention of British statesmen in the reign of Queen Anne, and a systematic effort was made to induce them to come to England in order to be shipped to America.[1] Thus in the years 1708 and 1709 more than 30,000 Germans crossed the Channel, and were soon afterward brought in English ships to New York and the Carolinas, but above all to Pennsylvania. This was but the beginning of a vast stream of migration in which Palatine peasants were taken down the Rhine to Rotterdam and there shipped to Philadelphia. Some, indeed, came to New York and settled in the Mohawk valley, where they gave us Nicholas Herkimer in the Revolutionary War; but most went into the valley of the Susquehanna in such large numbers, and remained so long without much in- Pennsyl-termixture, that their language still survives in the vania dialect which we call Pennsylvania Dutch, but which German is really High German with a quaint admixture of English.[2]

[1] A competent scholar assigns the travels of Penn in Germany in 1671 and 1677 as the chief cause of the direction of this wave of migration to Pennsylvania. See Diffenderffer, *The German Exodus to England in* 1709, Lancaster, 1897, p. 30. See, also, Sachse, *The Fatherland*, Philadelphia, 1897, pp. 142–144.

[2] For example, Emerson's verses :

> 'T was one of the charmed days
> When the genius of God doth flow,

Not all the Palatine immigrants tarried here, however ; there were some, and those, I dare say, the most enterprising, who pressed onward and spread along the Appalachian frontier.[1] Here they have played an important part, usually in association with a race of men of still more vigorous initiative, the so-called Scotch-Irish.

The name Scotch-Irish is an awkward compound, and is in many quarters condemned. Curiously enough, there is

The Scotch-Irish

no one who seems to object to it so strongly as the Irish Catholic. While his feelings toward the "Far-Downer" are certainly not affectionate, he is nevertheless anxious to claim him with his deeds and trophies, as simply Irish, and grudges to Scotland the claim to any share in producing him.[2] It must be admitted, however, that there is a point of view from which the Scotch-Irish may be regarded as more Scotch than Irish. The difficulty might be compromised by calling them Ulstermen, or Ulster Presbyterians.

It is said to have been the poet Edmund Spenser who first suggested to Queen Elizabeth — perhaps when he came to

> The wind may alter twenty ways,
>   A tempest cannot blow;
> It may blow north, it still is warm;
>   Or south, it still is clear;
> Or east, it smells like a clover farm ;
>   Or west, no thunder fear

have thus been rendered into Pennsylvania German : —

> 'S waar eens vun de harrliche Daage
>   Wann dar Himmel scheint uf ze sei ;
> Dar Wind maag zwanzig Wege jaage
>   'Es Wetter bleibt doch fei.
> Bloost's vun de Nard, 's is waarm un schee ;
>   Odder vun de South, 's bleibt hell :
> Vun Marrige haer, mar riecht dar Klee ;
>   Vun Owet, clear wie 'n Bell.

Zeigler, *Drauss un Deheem: Gedichte in Pennsylvanisch Deitsch*, Leipzig, 1891, — a charming little book.

[1] A good account of this migration is given in Cobb, *The Story of the Palatines*, New York, 1897.

[2] Amusing illustrations may be found in the correspondence appended to S. S. Green's excellent pamphlet, *The Scotch-Irish in America*, Worcester, 1895, pp. 42–59.

London in 1594 to look after the publication of his "Faery Queene" — the plan of putting into Ireland a Protestant population that might come to outnumber and control the Catholics. It was in 1611 that James I. began to put this scheme into operation, sending from Scotland and the northern counties of England a Presbyterian company of picked men and women of the best sort, yeomanry and craftsmen like those who settled Massachusetts and Connecticut, with many generations of ancestry behind them on a far higher level of intelligence and training than the native peasantry of Ireland. At the beginning of the eighteenth century the percentage of illiteracy in Ulster was probably smaller than anywhere else in the world. There were then more than a million of these Presbyterians in Ulster. About 1720, when they began coming in great numbers to America, those families that had been longest in Ireland had dwelt there but three generations, so that there is surely some laxity of speech in calling them Irish without some qualifying adjective.

Scotch planting of Ulster

The English experiment of thus scotticizing Ireland was defeated by a crass policy of protectionism combined with petty religious persecution. Flourishing linen and woollen industries had sprung up in Ulster, and sundry legislative handicaps were laid upon them for the "protection" of native industries in England. Thus did government treat its own pioneers as "foreigners" whom it was meritorious to plunder. At the same time divers civil disabilities were enacted for Presbyterians. The result of this twofold tyranny was the largest exodus from Europe to America that ever took place before the nineteenth century. Between 1730 and 1770 more than half of the Presbyterian population of Ulster came over to America, where it formed more than one sixth part of our entire population at the time of the Declaration of Independence.[1]

Exodus from Ulster to America

[1] Much detailed information may be found in the *Proceedings of the Scotch-Irish Congress*, published annually since 1889, first at Cincinnati, afterwards at Nashville.

A few of these Presbyterians came to New England, where they have left their mark. But the great majority came to Pennsylvania and occupied the mountain country west of the Susquehanna. Thence a steady migration was kept up southwesterly along the Appalachian axis into the southern colonies. Now there was one very important re-spect in which these Presbyterians of Ulster had come to differ from their Presbyterian brethren in Scotland. In the "land of cakes" the kirk ruled things pretty much at its own sweet will, and was therefore in favour of keeping civil and spiritual affairs united. But in Ulster, whether in relation to their Catholic neighbours or more especially to the English parliament, Presbyterians were in a harassed minority, and therefore became convinced of the desirableness of divorcing church from state. Accordingly, in spite of a very rigid theology, they stood for a liberal principle, and other Protestant sects, such as Lutherans, Mennonites, and Dunk-ers, found it possible to harmonize with them, especially in the free atmosphere of Pennsylvania. The result was the partial union of two great streams of immigration, the Ulster stream and the Palatinate stream. It influenced South Carolina and Maryland most powerfully, completely renovated society in North Carolina, and broke down the sway of the Cavalier aristocracy in Virginia. While it sent southward men and women enough to accomplish all this, enough more remained in Pennsylvania to form more than half its population, raising it by 1770 to the third place among the thirteen colonies, next after Virginia and Massa-chusetts. From the same prolific hive came the pioneers of Kentucky and Tennessee, with their descendants throughout the vast Mississippi valley and beyond. In all these directions, as I have elsewhere shown,[1] this sturdy population, distilled through the Pennsylvania alembic, has formed the main strength of American demo-cracy, and its influence upon American life has been manifold.

[1] *Old Virginia and Her Neighbours*, chap. xvii.

In thus taking our leave of the Dutch and Quaker Colonies in America, we must not forget that the close association between them was due to no mere accident of contiguity.
William Penn was Dutch on his mother's side, and one sees
in all his political ideas the broad and liberal tem- Fruitful-
per that characterized the Netherlands before and ness of
Dutch
beyond any other country in Europe. The two ideas
great middle colonies present a most interesting subject of
comparative study because both have been profoundly influenced by Holland, but in the one case the Dutch ideas have
been worked through the crucible of an individual genius,
while in the other case they have flowered with random
luxuriance. In the cosmopolitanism which showed itself so
early in New Amsterdam and has ever since been fully maintained, there was added to American national life the variety, the flexibility, the generous breadth of view, the spirit
of compromise and conciliation needful to save the nation
from rigid provincialism. Among the circumstances which
prepared the way for a rich and varied American nation, the
preliminary settlement of the geographical centre by Dutchmen was certainly one of the most fortunate.

APPENDIX I

SOME LEISLER DOCUMENTS

A

AFFIDAVITS AGAINST NICHOLSON

THE deposition of Nicholas Brown Aged Twenty three Years, the said Deponent declares that he being in the Service of ye late King Anno One thousand six hundred Eighty Six some time in July & August, did see Frances Nicholson Ye late lieu^t Governor of Ye fort at New York Several times in Ye Masse, but especially two times in Ye Kings tent at Hunsloheath in old ingland, being there to Exercise his devotions, & did Ye the same upon his Knees before the Alter in the papist Chappel, where the Mass was said, that himself, this deponent is ready to Confirm and declare upon Oath in testimony of the truth & have hereunto Set my hand, In New York this 12th day of Septem^r Anno 1689.

   Signed   NICHOLAS BROWN.
1689 the 13th 7^{ber} in New York.

Then appeared before me Nich^{ls} Brown & Sworn before me the aforesaid to be the truth.

   Signed   G. BEEKMAN Justice.

B

COMMISSION FROM THE COMMITTEE OF SAFETY

APPOINTING JACOB LEISLER TO BE CAPTAIN OF THE FORT

There being a Present necessity that a Capt. of Ye fort at New Yorke should be appointed to be constantly there attending and to Command & order ye Soldiers appointed by this Committee of Safety to Serve ye fort in behalfe of their Majesties till orders Shall come and to order all matters of ye fortifications of said fort necessary at present this Committee therefore doe think fitt that Cap^{tn} Jacob Leisler shall be Captain of said fort as abovesaid Till orders shall come from their Majesties, & that the said Captn Jacob Leisler, shall have all aid and assistance, if need be & demanded by him from City and Country to suppress any foren Enemy & prevent all disorders which Evidently may appear

dated this 8th of June 1689, Signed Sealed

RICHARD DANTON	(L. S.)	SAM^L EDSALL	(L. S.)
THEUNIS ROELOFSE	(L. S.)	P DELA NOY	(L. S.)
JEAN DE MAREST	(L. S.)	MATHIAS HARVEY	(L. S.)
DANIEL DE KLERCKE	(L. S.)	THO^s WILLIAMS	(L. S.)
JOHANNES VERMILLYE	(L. S.)	WM LAURENCE	(L. S.)

C

COMMISSION TO CAPT. LEISLER TO BE COMMANDER IN CHIEF

Forasmuch the Committee of Safety do apprehend the difficulty & inconveniency by reason of their remote habitants and ye insuing season of ye year to commence & abide in ye City of New York to advise recommend order, & appoint ye present affairs in hand for the Interest of their most Excelent Majesties King William & Queen Mary and due preservation of ye inhabitants in ye province of New York & some others near adjacent towns, it is thought convenient and concluded by ye Committee for ye most Safety of ye province by reason of Sundry intervals & accidental motions which may arise & for the orderly way to direct all necessary matters touching ye ruling & ordering of ye inhabitants in the Province, it being uncertain whether ye orders shall Come from their Majesties, that Captain Jacob Leisler is hereby appointed to Exercise & use the Power & Authority of a Commander in Chief of the said Province to administer such Oaths to the people, to issue out such Warrants, and to order such Matters as shall be necessary & requisite to be done for the preservation and protection of the peace, of the inhabitants tak-

ing all ways, seasonable advice with Militia and Civil Authority as Occasion require   Dated ye 16th day Augt 1689 —
Copy was Signed Sealed as followeth,

WILLIAM LAURENCE	(L. S.)	SAM^L EDSALL	(L. S.)
D^L DE KLERCKE	(L. S.)	JEAN DEMAREST	(L. S.)
JOHANNES VERMILLYE	(L. S.)	P. DE LA NOY	(L. S.)
RICHARD DANTON	(L. S.)	MATHIAS HARVEY	(L. S.)
THEUNIS ROELOFSE	(L. S.)	THO^s WILLIAMS	(L. S.)

D

SCHUYLER'S PROTEST AGAINST MILBORNE

FORT ALBANY ye 15th day of novemb^r 1689

Whereas one Jacob Milborne hath with a Comp^e of armed men, come up to there Maj^{e}s fort in a hostile manner with full arms and Demanded Possession thereof from ye May^r of ye Citty who has ye Command of ye same, who Declared to keep said fort for there Maj^{es} William & Mary untill there orders comes but ye said Jacob Milborne as a Tumultuous & Mutinous Person doth Proceed to occasion great Disturbance to there Maj^{es} Liege People, by again faceing to ye fort with Loaden arms, Especially so many heathens to witt Maquase being ye Spectators thereof who seems to be upon ye Point to undertake some Dangerous Design, The Convention of ye Civil & Military officers of ye Citty & County of albany now p'sent in ye fort doe therefore Protest hereby in their Maj^{es} King William & Queen Maryes name before god and ye world against ye s^d Milborne and his Seditious Troops, for all Dammages, Murthers Bloodsheds Plunderings and oy^r mischieffs which may Ensue by his Rebellious actions and charge him & them forthwith to withdraw themselves from there s^d May^{es} fort.

P^R SCHUYLER May^r
and Commander of there Maj^{es} fort

The Protest being Read hille akus Sister told y^t ye Indians were ^{very} much Dissatisfyed & if Milborne did not withdraw with his Comp^e they would fyre upon him, whereupon ye May^r Desyred Doctor Dellius & ye Recorder to goe to ye Indians to Pacify and quiet them for ye Bussinesse was y^t a Person without Power or authority would be Master over ye gent^n here which they would nott admitt; the Indians answered goe and tell him that if he come out of ye gates we will fyre upon him, which Doctor Dellius forthwith Communicated to ye s^d Milborne at ye head of his Comp^e in ye Presence of a great many Burghers who made no further attempt to goe to ye fort, but Marched doune ye towne and Dismissed his men.

E

LEISLER TO THE OFFICERS OF WESTCHESTER

FORT WILLIAM February 15, 1689 [90]

GENTLEMEN, — Whereas ye ffrench have surprized Schanegtade, & killed & taken Prisoners the most of their Maties Subjects burning & destroying ye s^d Place: and fearing too great a Correspondency hath bean maintained between ye s^d ffrensch & disaffected P'sons amongst us.

These are in his Maties Name to will & require you to secure all Such Persons who are resputed Papists or Do any wise despise or reflect against this Governm^t or hold or maintaine any Commissions from the Late Govern^rs Col^o Thomas Dongan or Sr Edmund Andros by virtue of their Authority derived from King James the second & ye same Safely to Convey to mee forthw^th Given under My hand & seale this 15th ffeb^y 1689 and in ye first yeare of their Maties Reigne.

JACOB LEISLER

To the Officers Military & Civill &
ye Sheriffe of the County of Westchester
Ye same to Richmond County
Ye same to ye County of Suffolk
Ye same to Kings County
Ye same to ye Country of East Jersey
Ye same to Queens County

F

LEISLER TO HIS COMMISSIONERS AT ALBANY

A 1690 1st July In Fort William

GENTLEMEN — Yesterday was my last to which I Referr you, You have Referred us to ye Messengers who brought our letter but

we cane understand nothing of them, my opinion Is they came here
to consult with there parties. If they may safely Receive a Commission of mee what alteration in your place, there Coming here
may cause us, the time will learne, beshure they are not well Tu-
tered & keept from us I have writt you our meaning which we hoop
you may be able to observe touching the major, Inclosed is a copy
of a Letter Received of Governour Treat which I perceive was
lifft upon the table wherein the major is absolutely Refused If
Boston & Connecticut sends not their Compliment Ingaged In
ye Result & approved by ye government they Brook ye Covenant &
we are not obliged to any article therein the Barers are made sensible y^t what we propose about ye Council of Warr y^t the Cap^n by
Turnes Every week should bee president In said Councel and so
in gods name go one without a major — Except Cap^n Browne ac-
cepts of ye place but no other whatsoever — Except Mausachu-
setts, Plymouth & Connecticutt Colonyes Comply fully with there
promise y^e ffrench Knight begins to be moved of (our) march and
desires to prevent y^e cruelties of our Indians against y^e ffrench
wimens and children which Indied would bee generous if possible
It could be prevented we have sent $Mest^r$ Stole who has a speciall
maxim to gaine the people & is able to assist you much in forward-
ing y^e Business and if he should go he most be commissionated
he is true, full mettall able and politique the news of Colonell
Slayter is quitt vanised It would not hould — [1]we have gott yesterday the Inclosed nues from neu England En send It for the
Everi direcktet als the copie, to day the 25 I gott the Inclosed
from Southampton I wish Ensign Stole was heer En Iff possible
also Major Milborn we expeckt the franch ships heer the messenger raports the ar all ships, pray God to grand & give vs courage
to resist them after min respects I remain

Sr^s

Your reall frind to serve your

JACOB LEISLER

Addressed, To the $Hono^{ble}$ The $Commission^{rs}$ Cap^n
John De Bruyn, Mr Johannes Provoost
and Major Jacob Milborne Esq^{rs} In
Albany

G

LEISLER TO GOV. SLOUGHTER

FORT WILLIAM March the 20. 1609-1

May it Please Your Excellency — This his Majesty's fort being besieged by Major Ingoldsby so farre that not a boat could depart, nor Persons conveyed out of the same without to be in danger of their Lives which hath occasioned that I could not be so happy as to send a messinger to give me the certainty of Your excellency's Safe arrival & an account of what was published, of which I am ignorant still but the Joy I had by a full assurance from Ensign Stoll of your Excellency's arrival has been something troubled by the detencon of Ye two my Messengers, I see very well the stroke of my enemies who are wishing to cause me some mistakes at the End of the Loyalty I owe to my gracious King & Queen & by such ways to Blatt out all my faithfull service till now but I hope have care to commit such an error, having by my duty & faithfulnesse being vigerous to them, Please only to Signify & order the Major in releasing me from his Majesties fort delivering him only his Majesties Armes with all the Stores & that he may act as he ought with a person who shall give Your excellency an exact account of all his actions & conduct, who is with all the request, Your Excellency's Most Humble Servt

JACOB LEISLER

H

DYING SPEECHES OF LEISLER AND MILBORNE

Colleccons made on the Dying Speeches of Captain Jacob Leisler & Jacob Milborne, his son in Law, who both Suffered in New York City on the 16th of May being Saturday in the Year of our Lord 1691.

— The great wise & omnipotent creator of all things visible & invisible who from the time of our first coming a Shore in the Vale of tears, misery & affliction, hath to this present moment protected us be magnified. Praysed & Glorified for ever, Amen,

Gentlemen And Fellow Brethren all I hope in the grace & fear of the Lord Jesus, we are not at present unsensible of our dying State & Condition, as to this world a State which all the Sons &

Daughters of Adam in this globe must now one after another run through ere they can be satisfied with that eternity of which so often by Divines is treated of — In consideration of which for death we may be better prepared, like penitent Mortals here on earth, we Submit our lives. & all that unto us appertaineth into the hands of divine protection prostrating ourselves before the foot Stoole that immaculate Lamb of God who taketh away the Sinns of the world hoping that through his meritorous death & passing our iniquities shall be done away & our pardons Sealed on earth before we go hence & are seen no more, humbly imploring that not through our own meritts of Justification but rather through the merit of him that is willing to save our souls, might become precious in the Eyes of God & live forever in the Kingdome of Eternall Glory when time shall be no more — as to our State in this world among the rest of our hard fortunes in this seat of tears it is true we have lately on the important request of a Committee choose by the Major Part of the Inhabitants of this province & taken (to the present griefe & vexation of our poore afflicted relations left behind) great & weighty matters of State affairs requiring at Such an helme more wise & Cunning powerful Pilotts. then either of us ever was. but considering that in the time of this distracted Countrey's greatness, necessity amongst us — no such Persons could be found but that those that were any wayes, in Capasity of Uniting us against a Common enemy would not undertake, we conceive for the Glory of the protestant interest the Establishment of the present Government under our Sovereign Lord & Lady King W^m & Queen Mary &c — & the Strengthening against all foreign attempts, of this confused City & Province, thought it a very serviceable Act that our poore endeavours should not be wanting in anything that was needful for the Support of ourselves & posterity hereafter whereby we must confess & often times against our will several enormities have been committed from the day of our first undertakings until the arrival of his excellency the Honorable Col^l Henry Sloughter. who now for his Majesties Sake, we love & Honour & often times, during our unhappy abode in power longed to see that a periode thereby might be put to such distracted orders, as then were raging all of which some we must Confess on our side hath been committed through Ignorance some through a Jealous fear that disaffected persons would not be true to the present interest of the Crowne of England some peradventure through misinformation & misconstruction of People's intent & meaning, some through rashness by want of Consideration, & then through passion haste & anger, which According to orders for to declare would take up more time than present can be afforded, however for every such offence. seeing there is no recalling of the same, or possibility of given further Satisfaction, first of the great god of heaven & then afterwards of the several offended persons, we humbly begg pardon & forgiveness, desiring them every one with a Christian Charity in our graves with us to bury all malice, hatred & Envy that therein might be incurred & further before God & the World here we do declare & protest as Dying Sinners that we do not only forgive the greatest & most inveterate of our enemies, but According to that most Excellent patron of our dying Saviour. we say to the God of Justice, father forgive them for they know not what they do & so farre from revenge we do depart this world, that we require and make it our dying supplication to every of our relations & friends & acquaintances, that they should in time to come forever be forgetfull of any injury done to us or either of us, so that on both Side, that discord & dessention (which by the devil in the beginning was created) might with our dying sides be buried in oblivion, never more to raise up to the inflamation of future posterity, the Lord grant that the offering up of our blood might be a full satisfaction for all disorders to this present day committed, & that forever after the Spiritt of unity might remaine among our felow brethren continuing upon earth, knowing that in a Strange land it is the divine providence of heaven not our desarts that have so well protected our unhappy province this day all that for our dying comfort we can say, as concerning the point for which we were condemn'd, is to declare as our last words. before that God whom we hope before long to see that our maine end, totall Intent & endeavors to the fullness of that understanding with which we were endowed — who had no other than to maintaine against popery or any Schism or heresy whatever the interest of our Sovereign Lord & Lady that now is & the reformed protestant Churches in those parts, who ever things otherwise Since have hapined or being misconstructed & Scandalous reports (we at present must confess by divers are thrown upon us) as tho we intended to Support the dying, intrest of the late King James & the Contradiction of which we need not trouble many arguments, being persuaded that every

good protestant of this Country who have been for any time acquainted with our transactions can from his conscience averre the
falsehoods & maliciousness of such aspersions, as concerning
Major Ingoldesby's coming to demand the Garrison after his
arrival, he but in the least produced any Satisfaction of his power
to receive the same and discharge us, we would as readily have
delivered the fort, as he could demand the same, all of which seeing past & gone is Scarce worthy nothing —

The Lord of his infinite Mercy preserve the King & Queen from
all their traytors and deceitfull Enemies, God be merciful unto &
bless with peace & unity these their Kingdoms unto which we belong, God preserve this province from greedy outrageous Enemies
abroad and Spite full inveterate wretches at home God bless the
Governor of this place, God bless the council Assembly & Government now Established that they all may be united to propagate
their Majesties interest, the Country's good & the Establishment
of Piety, the Lord of Heaven of his infinite mercy bless all that
wish well to Zion & Convert those that are out of the way, let his
mercies likewise administer true Comfort to all that are desolate,
grieved & oppressed in misery & necessity or any other affliction,
Especially the deplored Souls of that poor family unto which we
did formerly belong, our only comfort, in this case, is that God
has promised to take care for the Widows and fatherless, recom-
mending them all this dying moment into the hands of one that
is able and willing. to save these that seek him desiring them to
put their perpetuall confidence in the mercies of one that never
faileth, & not to weep for us that are departing to our God but
rather to weep for themselves that are here behind us to remain
in a State of Misery and Vexation.

Gentlemen you will, I hope all Christian like be Charitable to
our poor distressed family that are to remain among you (as long
as God please) that you will Join with us in prayer for the preservation of our immortal Soules in a kingdom of never Dying Glory,
unto which God of his infinite mercy bring us all   Amen Amen.

The Sheriff asking him if he was ready to die, he replied Yes,
& lifting up his Eyes he prayed & then said that he had made his
peace with God & that death did not scare him, & desired that
his Corpse might be delivered to his wife, and declared that he
Educated his family as a good Christian & hoping they should

continue, accordinly & he said that you have brought my body to shame, I hope you will not despise my family therefore, I have not much more to say on this world, for we read in the Lords prayer, forgive us our trespasses as we forgive them that trespass Against us, but hereafter we shall appear before God's Tribunal & there shall we be judged, our Lord Jesus Christ suffered so much in this world, why Should I not suffer a little —

Then to his Son Milborne he said. I must now die, why must you die? You have been but a Servant to us & further he declared I am a dying man & do declare before god & the world that what I have done was for king William & Queen Mary, for the defence of the protestant religion & the Good of the Country & therefore I must die upon which I will receive Gods Judgment, and then he said, when this my skin shall be eaten through, with this my flesh shall I see God, my Eyes shall see him & no stranger, when the Handkerchief was put about his head, he said, I hope these my Eyes shall see our Lord Jesus Christ in Heaven I am ready. I am ready.

Of Jacob Milborne —

He prayed for the King & Queen the Governor & Council he pardoned the Judge that had condemned him Saying that the Lord would forgive him, he was ready to lay down his terrestral coat, being assured that his heavenly father would cloath him with a new one in the Kingdom of Heaven, then to Mr Levingston he said you have caused the King (that) I must now die, but before gods tribunal I will implead you for the same. then to his father he said we are thoroughly wet with rain, but in a little while we shall be rained through with the Holy Spirit The sheriff asked him whether he would not Bless the King and Queen, he answered it is for the King and Queen I die & the protestant Religion to which I was Borne & Bred, I am ready I am ready. father into thy hands I recommend my soule —

APPENDIX II

CHARTER FOR THE PROVINCE OF PENNSYLVANIA —
1681

CHARLES the Second, by the Grace of God, King of *England, Scotland, France*, and *Ireland*, Defender of the Faith, etc. To all whom these presents shall come, *Greeting*. WHEREAS Our Trustie and well-beloved Subject William Penn, Esquire, Sonne and heire of Sir William Penn deceased, out of a commendable Desire to enlarge our *English* Empire, and promote such usefull comodities as may bee of Benefit to us and Our Dominions, as also to reduce the Savage Natives by gentle and just manners to the Love of Civil Societie and Christian Religion, hath humbley besought Leave of Us to transport an ample Colonie unto a certaine Countrey hereinafter described, in the Partes of *America* not yet cultivated and planted ; And hath likewise humbley besought Our Royall Majestie to Give, Grant, and Confirme all the said Countrey, with certaine Privileges and Jurisdictions, requisite for the good Government and Safetie of the said Countrey and Colonie, to him and his Heires forever: KNOW YE THEREFORE, That Wee, favouring the Petition and good Purpose of the said *William Penn*, and haveing Regard to the Memorie and Meritts of his late Father in divers Services, and perticulerly to his Conduct, Courage, and Discretion under our Dearest Brother JAMES Duke of *York*, in that Signall Battell and Victorie fought and obteyned against the *Dutch* Fleete, command by the Heer *Van Opdam*, in the yeare One thousand six hundred and sixty-five: In consideration thereof, of Our Speciall grace, certaine Knowledge, and meere Motion have Given and Granted, and by this Our present Charter, for Us, Our Heires and Successors, Doe give and Grant unto the said *William Penn*, his Heires and Assignes, all that Tract or Parte of Land in *America*, with all the Islands therein conteyned, as the same is bounded on the East by *Delaware* River, from twelve miles distance Northwards of *New Castle* Towne unto the three and fortieth degree of Northerne Latitude, if the said River doeth extende so farre Northwards; But if the said River shall not extend soe farre Northward, then by the said River soe farr as it doth extend; and from the head of the said River, the Easterne Bounds are to bee determined by a Meridian Line, to bee drawne from the head of the said River, unto the said three and fortieth Degree. The said Lands to extend westwards five degrees in longitude, to bee computed from the said Easterne Bounds; and the said Lands to bee bounded on the North by the beginning of the three and fortieth degree of Northern Latitude, and on the South by a Circle drawne at twelve miles distance from *New Castle* Northward and Westward unto the beginning of the fortieth degree of Northern Latitude, and then by a streight Line Westward to the Limitt of Longitude above-mentioned. WEE do also give and grant unto the said *William Penn*, his heires and assignes, the free and undisturbed use and continuance in, and passage into and out of all and singular Ports, Harbours, Bays, Waters, Rivers, Isles, and Inletts, belonging unto, or leading to and from the Countrey or Islands aforesaid, And all the Soyle, lands, fields, woods, underwoods, mountaines, hills, fenns, Isles, Lakes, Rivers, waters, Rivuletts, Bays, and Inletts, scituate or being within, or belonging unto the Limitts and Bounds aforesaid, togeather with the fishing of all sortes of fish, whales, Sturgeons, and all Royall and other Fishes, in the Sea, Bayes, Inletts, waters, or Rivers within the premisses, and the Fish therein taken; And also all Veines, Mines, and Quarries, as well discovered as not discovered, of Gold, Silver, Gemms, and Pretious Stones, and all other whatsoever, be it Stones, Mettals, or of any other thing or matter whatsoever, found or to bee found within the Countrey, Isles, or Limitts aforesaid; AND him, the said *William Penn*, his heirs and assignes, Wee doe by this Our Royall Charter, for Us, Our heires and Successors, make, create, and constitute the true and absolute Proprietarie of the Countrey aforesaid, and of all other the premisses, Saving always to Us, Our heires and Successors, the Faith and Allegiance of the said *William Penn*, his heires and assignes, and of all other Proprietaries, Tenants, and Inhabitants that are or shall be within the Territories and Precincts aforesaid; and Saving also, unto Us, Our heires and Successors, the Sovereignty of the aforesaid Countrey; TO HAVE, hold, possess, and enjoy the said Tract of Land, Countrey, Isles, Inletts, and other the premisses unto the said *William Penn*, his heires and assignes, to the only proper use and behoofe of the said *William Penn*, his heires and assignes for ever, to bee holden of Us, Our heires and Successors, Kings of *England*, as of Our Castle of *Windsor* in our County of *Berks*, in free and comon Socage, by fealty only for all Services, and not in *Capite* or by Knights Service: Yielding and paying therefore to Us, Our heires and Successors, Two Beaver Skins, to bee delivered at Our said Castle of *Windsor* on the First Day of *January* in every Year; and also the Fifth Part of all Gold and Silver Oare, which shall from Time to Time happen to bee found within the Limitts aforesaid, cleare of all Charges. And of Our further Grace, certaine Knowledge, and meer motion, We have thought fitt to erect, and We doe hereby erect the aforesaid Countrey and Islands into a Province and Seigniorie, and do call itt PENSILVANIA, and soe from henceforth we will have itt called.

AND forasmuch as wee have hereby made and ordained the aforesaid *William Penn*, his heires and assignes, the true and absolute Proprietaries of all the Lands and Dominions aforesaid, KNOW YE THEREFORE, That We reposing speciall trust and Confidence in the fidelitie, wisedom, Justice, and provident circumspection of the said *William Penn* for us, our heires and Successors, Doe grant free, full, and absolute power by vertue of these presents to him and his heires, and to his and their Deputies, and Lieutenants, for the good and happy government of the said countrey, to ordeyne, make, and enact, and under his and their Seales to publish any Lawes whatsoever, for the raising of money for the publick use of the said Province, or for any other End, apperteyning either unto the publick state, peace, or safety of the said Countrey, or unto the private utility of perticular persons, according unto their best discretions, by and with the advice, assent, and approbation of the Freemen of the said Countrey, or the greater parte of them, or of their Delegates or Deputies, whom for the enacting of the said Lawes, when, and as often as need shall require, Wee will that the said *William Penn* and his heires, shall assemble in such sort and forme, as to him and them shall seeme best, and the same Lawes duly to execute, unto and upon all People within the said Countrey and the Limitts thereof.

AND wee doe likewise give and grant unto the said *William Penn*, and his heires, and to his and their Deputies and Lieutenants, such power and authoritie to appoint and establish any Judges and Justices, Magistrates and Officers whatsoever, for what causes soever, for the probates of wills, and for the granting of Administrations within the precincts aforesaid and with what Power soever, and in such forme as to the said *William Penn* or his heires shall seeme most convenient: Also to remitt, release, pardon, and abolish whether before Judgement or after all Crimes and Offences whatsoever comitted within the said Countrey against the said Lawes, Treason and wilful and malitious Murder onely excepted, and in those Cases to grant Reprieves, until Our pleasure may bee known therein and to doe all and every other thing and things, which unto the compleate Establishment of Justice, unto Courts and Tribunalls, formes of Judicature, and manner of Proceedings doe belong, altho in these presents expresse mention bee not made thereof ; And by Judges by them delegated, to award Processe, hold Pleas, and determine in all the said Courts and Tribunalls all Actions, Suits, and Causes whatsoever, as well Criminall as Civill, Personall, reall and mixt ; which Lawes, soe as aforesaid to bee published, Our Pleasure is, and soe Wee enjoyne, require, and command, shall bee most absolute and avaylable in law ; and that all the Liege People and subjects of Us, Our heires and Successors, doe observe and keepe the same inviolabl in those partes, soe farr as they concerne them, under the paine therein expressed, or to bee expressed. PROVIDED nevertheless, that the said Lawes be consonant to reason, and bee not repugnant or contrarie, but as neare as conveniently may bee agreeable to the Lawes and Statutes, and rights of this Our Kingdome of *England;* And Saving and reserving to Us, Our heires and Successors, the receiving, heareing, and determining of the appeale and appeales of all or any Person or Persons, of, in, or belonging to the Territories aforesaid, or touching any Judgement to bee there made or given.

AND forasmuch as in the Government of soe great a Countrey, sudden Accidents doe often happen, whereunto it will bee necessarie to apply remedie before the Freeholders of the said Province, or their Delegates or Deputies, can bee assembled to the making of Lawes ; neither will itt bee convenient that instantly upon every such emergent occasion, soe greate a multitude should be called

together : Therefore for the better Government of the said Countrey Wee will, and ordaine, and by these presents, for us, our Heires
and successors, Doe Grant unto the said *William Penn* and his
heires, by themselves or by their Magistrates and Officers, in that
behalfe duely to bee ordeyned as aforesaid, to make and constitute fitt and wholesome Ordinances, from time to time, within the
said Countrey to bee kept and observed, as well for the preservation of the peace, as for the better government of the People
there inhabiting ; and publickly to notifie the same to all persons,
whome the same doeth or anyway may concerne. Which ordinances, our Will and Pleasure is, shall bee observed inviolably
within the said Province, under Paines therein to be expressed,
soe as the said Ordinances bee consonant to reason, and bee not
repugnant nor contrary, but soe farre as conveniently may be
agreeable with the Lawes of our Kingdome of *England*, and soe
as the said Ordinances be not extended in any Sort to bind, charge,
or take away the right or Interest of any person or persons, for
or in their Life, members, Freehold, goods, or Chattles. And our
further will and pleasure is, that the Lawes for regulateing and
governing of Propertie within the said Province, as well for the
descent and enjoyment of lands, as likewise for the enjoyment and
succession of goods and Chattles, and likewise as to Felonies,
shall bee and continue the same, as they shall bee for the time
being by the generall course of the Law in our Kingdome of *England*, until the said Lawes shall bee altered by the said *William
Penn*, his heires or assignes, and by the Freemen of the said Province, their Delegates or Deputies, or the greater Part of them.

AND to the End the said *William Penn*, or heires, or other the
Planters, Owners, or Inhabitants of the said Province, may not att
any time hereafter by misconstruction of the powers aforesaid
through inadvertencie or designe depart from that Faith and due
allegiance, which by the lawes of this our Realme of *England*,
they and all our subjects, in our Dominions and Territories, alwayes owe unto us, Our heires and Successors, by colour of any
Extent or largenesse of powers hereby given, or pretended to bee
given, or by force or colour of any lawes hereafter to bee made in
the said Province, by vertue of any such Powers ; OUR further
will and Pleasure is, that a transcript or Duplicate of all Lawes,
which shall bee soe as aforesaid made and published within the
said Province, shall within five years after the makeing thereof, be

transmitted and delivered to the Privy Councell, for the time being, of us, our heires and successors : And if any of the said Lawes, within the space of six moneths after that they shall be soe transmitted and delivered, bee declared by us, Our heires and Successors, in Our or their Privy Councell, inconsistent with the Sovereignty or lawful Perogative of us, our heires or Successors, or contrary to the Faith and Allegiance due by the legall government of this Realme, from the said *William Penn*, or his heires, or of the Planters and Inhabitants of the said Province, and that thereupon any of the said Lawes shall bee adjudged and declared to bee void by us, our heires or Successors, under our or their Privy Seale, that then and from thenceforth, such Lawes, concerning which such Judgement and declaration shall bee made, shall become voyd : Otherwise the said Lawes soe transmitted, shall remaine, and stand in full force, according to the true intent and meaneing thereof.

FURTHERMORE, that this new Colony may the more happily increase, by the multitude of People resorting thither ; Therefore wee for us, our heires and Successors, doe give and grant by these presents, power, Licence, and Libertie unto all the Liege People and Subjects, both present and future, of us, our heires, and Successors, excepting those who shall bee Specially forbidden to transport themselves and Families unto the said Countrey, with such convenient Shipping as by the lawes of this our Kingdome of *England* they ought to use, with fitting provisions, paying only the customes therefore due, and there to settle themselves, dwell and inhabitt, and plant, for the publick and their owne private advantage.

AND FURTHERMORE, that our Subjects may bee the rather encouraged to undertake this expedicion with ready and cheerful mindes, KNOW YE, That wee, of Our especiall grace, certaine knowledge, and meere motion, Doe Give and Grant by vertue of these presents, as well unto the said *William Penn*, and his heires, as to all others, who shall from time to time repaire unto the said Countrey, with a purpose to inhabit there, or trade with the natives of the said Countrey, full Licence to lade and freight in any ports whatsoever, of us, our heires and Successors, according to the lawes made or to be made within our Kingdome of *England*, and unto the said Countrey, by them, theire Servants or assignes, to transport all and singular theire wares, goods, and

Merchandizes, as likewise all sorts of graine whatsoever, and all other things whatsoever, necessary for food or cloathing, not prohibited by the Lawes and Statutes of our Kingdomes, without any Lett or molestation of us, our heires and Successors, or of any of the Officers of us, our heires and Successors ; saveing alwayes to us, our heires and Successors, the legall impositions, customes, and other Duties and payments, for the said Wares and Merchandize, by any Law or Statute due or to be due to us, our heires and Successors.

AND Wee doe further, for us, our heires and Successors, Give and grant unto the said *William Penn*, his heires and assignes, free and absolute power, to Divide the said Countrey and Islands into Townes, Hundreds and Counties, and to erect and incorporate Townes into Borroughs, and Borroughs into Citties, and to make and constitute ffaires and Marketts therein, with all other convenient privileges and munities, according to the meritt of the inhabitants, and the ffitness of the places, and to doe all and every other thing and things touching the premisses, which to him or them shall seeme requisite and meet ; albeit they be such as of their owne nature might otherwise require a more especiall commandment and Warrant then in these presents is expressed.

WE WILL alsoe, and by these presents, for us, our heires and Successors, Wee doe Give and grant Licence by this our Charter, unto the said *William Penn*, his heires and assignes, and to all the inhabitants and dwellers in the Province aforesaid, both present and to come, to import or unlade, by themselves or theire Servants, ffactors or assignes, all merchandizes and goods whatsoever, that shall arise of the fruites and comodities of the said Province, either by Land or Sea, into any of the ports of us, our heires and successors, in our Kingdome of *England*, and not into any other Countrey whatsoever : And wee give him full power to dispose of the said goods in the said ports ; and if need bee, within one yeare next after the unladeing of the same, to lade the said Merchandizes and Goods again into the same or other shipps, and to export the same into any other Countreys, either of our Dominions or fforeigne, according to Lawe : Provided alwayes, that they pay such customes and impositions, subsidies and duties for the same, to us, our heires and Successors, as the rest of our Subjects of our Kingdome of *England*, for the time being, shall be bound to pay, and doe observe the Acts of Navigation, and other Lawes in that behalfe made.

AND FURTHERMORE, of our most ample and esspeciall grace, certaine knowledge, and meere motion, Wee doe, for us, our heires and Successors, Grant unto the said *William Penn*, his heires and assignes, full and absolute power and authoritie to make, erect, and constitute within the said Province and the Isles and Islets aforesaid, such and soe many Sea-ports, harbours, Creeks, Havens, Keyes, and other places, for discharge and unladeing of goods and Merchandizes, out of the shipps, Boates, and other Vessells, and ladeing them in such and soe many Places, and with such rights, Jurisdictions, liberties and privileges unto the said ports belonging, as to him or them shall seeme most expedient; and that all and singuler the shipps, boates, and other Vessells, which shall come for merchandize and trade unto the said Province, or out of the same shall depart, shall be laden or unladen onely at such Ports as shall be erected and constituted by the said *William Penn*, his heires and assignes, any use, custome, or other thing to the contrary notwithstanding. Provided, that the said *William Penn*, and his heires, and the Lieutenants and Governors for the time being, shall admit and receive in and about all such Ports, Havens, Creeks, and Keyes, all Officers and their Deputies, who shall from time to time be appointed for that Purpose by the ffarmers or Commissioners of our Customs for the time being.

AND Wee doe further appoint and ordaine, and by these presents for us, our heires and Successors, Wee doe grant unto the said *William Penn*, his heires and assignes, That he, the said *William Penn*, his heires and assignes, may from time to time for ever, have and enjoy the Customes and Subsidies, in the Portes, Harbours, and other Creeks and Places aforesaid, within the Province aforesaid, payable or due for merchandizes and wares there to be laded and unladed, the said Customes and Subsidies to be reasonably assessed upon any occasion, by themselves and the People there as aforesaid to be assembled, to whom wee give power by these presents, for us, our heires and Successors, upon just cause and in dudue p'portion, to assesse and impose the same; Saveing unto us, our heires and Successors, such impositions and Customes, as by Act of Parliament are and shall be appointed.

AND it is our further will and pleasure, that the said *William Penn*, his heires and assignes, shall from time to time constitute and appoint an Attorney or Agent, to reside in or neare our City of *London*, who shall make knowne the place where he shall dwell or may be found, unto the Clerke of our Privy Counsell for the time being, or one of them, and shall be ready to appeare in any of our Courts att *Westminster*, to Answer for any Misdemeanors that shall be comitted, or by any wilfull default or neglect permitted by the said *William Penn*, his heires or assignes, against our Lawes of Trade or Navigation ; and after it shall be ascertained in any of our said Courts, what damages Wee or our heires or Successors shall have sustained by such default or neglect, the said *William Penn*, his heires and assignes shall pay the same within one yeare after such taxation, and demand thereof from such Attorney : or in case there shall be noe such Attorney by the space of one yeare, or such Attorney shall not make payment of such damages within the space of one yeare, and answer such other forfeitures and penalties within the said time, as by the Acts of Parliament in *England* are or shall be provided according to the true intent and meaneing of these presents ; then it shall be lawfull for us, our heires and Successors, to seize and Resume the government of the said Province or Countrey, and the same to retaine untill payment shall be made thereof : But notwithstanding any such Seizure or resumption of the government, nothing concerneing the propriety or ownership of any Lands, tenements, or other hereditaments, or goods or chattels of any of the Adventurers, Planters, or owners, other then the respective Offenders there, shall anyway be affected or molested thereby.

PROVIDED alwayes, and our will and pleasure is, that neither the said *William Penn*, nor his heires, or any other the inhabitants of the said Province, shall at any time hereafter have or maintain any Correspondence with any other king, prince, or State, or with any of theire subjects, who shall then be in Warr against us, our heires or Successors ; Nor shall the said *William Penn*, or his heires, or any other the Inhabitants of the said Province, make Warre or doe any act of Hostility against any other king, prince, or State, or any of theire Subjects, who shall then be in league or amity with us, our heires or successors.

AND, because in soe remote a Countrey, and scituate neare many Barbarous Nations, the incursions as well of the Savages themselves, as of other enemies, pirates and robbers, may probably be feared ; Therefore Wee have given, and for us, our heires and Successors, Doe give power by these presents unto the said *William Penn*, his heires and assignes, by themselves or theire Captaines or other their Officers, to levy, muster and traine all sorts of men, of what condition soever or wheresoever borne, in the said Province of *Pensilvania*, for the time being, and to make Warre, and to pursue the enemies and Robbers aforesaid, as well by Sea as by Land, even without the Limitts of the said Province, and by God's assistance to vanquish and take them, and being taken to put them to death by the Lawe of Warre, or to save them, att theire pleasure, and to doe all and every other Art and Thing which to the Charge and Office of a Captaine-Generall of an Army belongeth or hath accustomed to belong, as fully and ffreely as any Captaine-Generall of an Army hath ever had the same.

AND FURTHERMORE, of Our especiall grace and of our certaine knowledge and meere motion, wee have given and granted, and by these presents, for us, our heires and Successors, do Give and Grant unto the said *William Penn*, his Heires and Assignes, full and absolute power, licence and authoritie, that he, the said *William Penn*, his Heires and Assignes, from time to time hereafter forever, att his or theire own Will and pleasure may assigne, alien, Grant, demise, or enfeoffe of the Premises soe many and such partes and parcells to him or them that shall be willing to purchase the same, as they shall thinke fitt, To have and to hold to them the said person and persons willing to take or purchase theire heires and assignes, in ffee-simple or ffee-taile, or for the terme of life, or lives or yeares, to be held of the said *William Penn*, his heires and assignes, as of the said Seigniory of Windsor, by such services, customes and rents, as shall seeme ffitt to the said *William Penn*, his heires and assignes, and not imediately of us, our heires and successors. AND to the same person or persons, and to all and every of them, wee doe give and grant by these presents, for us, our heires and successors, licence, authoritie and power, that such person or persons may take the premisses, or any parcell thereof, of the aforesaid *William Penn*, his heires or assignes, and the same hold to themselves, their heires and assignes, in what estate of inheritance soever, in ffee-simple or in ffee-taile, or otherwise, as to him, the said *William Penn*, his heires and assignes, shall seem expedient : The Statute made in the parliament of *EDWARD*, sonne of King *HENRY*, late King of

England, our predecessor, commonly called *The Statute QUIA EMPTORES TERRARUM,* lately published in our Kingdome of *England* in any wise notwithstanding.

AND by these presents wee give and Grant Licence unto the said *William Penn,* and his heires, likewise to all and every such person and persons to whom the said *William Penn* or his heires shall att any time hereafter grant any estate or inheritance as aforesaid, to erect any parcells of Land within the Province aforesaid into Mannors, by and with the Licence to be first had and obteyned for that purpose, under the hand and Seale of the said *William Penn* or his heires ; and in every of the said Mannors to have and to hold a Court-Baron, with all things whatsoever which to a Court-Baron do belong, and to have and to hold View of ffrank-pledge for the conservation of the peace and the better government of those partes, by themselves or their Stewards, or by the Lords for the time being of the Mannors to be deputed when they shall be erected, and in the same to use all things belonging to the View of ffrank-pledge. AND Wee doe further grant licence and authoritie, that every such person or persons who shall erect any such Mannor or Mannors, as aforesaid, shall or may grant all or any parte of his said Lands to any person or persons, in ffee-simple, or any other estate of inheritance to be held of the said Mannors respectively, soe as noe further tenures shall be created, but that upon all further and other alienations thereafter to be made, the said lands soe aliened shall be held of the same Lord and his heires, of whom the alienor did then before hold, and by the like rents and Services which were before due and accustomed.

AND FURTHER our pleasure is, and by these presents, for us, our heires and Successors, Wee doe covenant and grant to and with the said *William Penn,* and his heires and assignes, That Wee, our heires and Successors, shall at no time hereafter sett or make, or cause to be sett, any impossition, custome or other taxation, rate or contribution whatsoever, in and upon the dwellers and inhabitants of the aforesaid Province, for their Lands, tenements, goods or chattells within the said Province, or in and upon any goods or merchandize within the said Province, or to be laden or unladen within the ports or harbours of the said Province, unless the same be with the consent of the Proprietary, or chiefe governor, and assembly, or by act of Parliament in *England.*

AND Our Pleasure is, and for us, our heires and Successors, Wee charge and comand, that this our Declaration shall from henceforth be received and allowed from time to time in all our courts, and before all the Judges of us, our heires and Successors, for a sufficient and lawfull discharge, payment and acquittance ; commanding all and singular the officers and ministers of us, our heires and Successors, and enjoyneing them upon pain of our high displeasure, that they doe not presume att any time to attempt anything to the contrary of the premisses, or that doe in any sort withstand the same, but that they be att all times aiding and assisting, as is fitting unto the said *William Penn* and his heires, and to the inhabitants and merchants of the Province aforesaid, their Servants, Ministers, ffactors and Assignes, in the full use and fruition of the benefitt of this our Charter.

AND Our further pleasure is, and wee doe hereby, for us, our heires and Successors, charge and require, that if any of the inhabitants of the said Province, to the number of Twenty, shall at any time hereafter be desirous, and shall by any writeing, or by any person deputed for them, signify such their desire to the Bishop of *London* that any preacher or preachers, to be approved of by the said Bishop, may be sent unto them for their instruction, that then such preacher or preachers shall and may be and reside within the said Province, without any deniall or molestation whatsoever.

AND if perchance it should happen hereafter any doubts or questions should arise, concerneing the true Sense and meaning of any word, clause, or Sentence conteyned in this our present Charter, Wee will ordaine, and comand, that att all times and in all things, such interpretation be made thereof, and allowed in any of our Courts whatsoever, as shall be adjudged most advantageous and favourable unto the said *William Penn*, his heires and assignes : Provided always that no interpretation be admitted thereof by which the allegiance due unto us, our heires and Successors, may suffer any prejudice or diminution ; Although express mention be not made in these presents of the true yearly value, or certainty of the premisses, or of any parte thereof, or of other gifts and grants made by us and our progenitors or predecessors unto the said *William Penn:* Any Statute, Act, ordinance, provision, proclamation, or restraint heretofore had, made, published, ordained or provided, or any other thing, cause, or matter whatsoever, to the contrary thereof in any wise notwithstanding.

IN WITNESS whereof wee have caused these our Letters to be made patents: Witness OUR SELFE, at *Westminster*, the *Fourth* day of *March*, in the *Three and Thirtieth* Yeare of Our Reign.

By Writt of Privy Seale,

PIGOTT.

INDEX

62, 66; French fur-traders' village on, 67;
Dutch traders at, 88; Argall warns them,
89; meaning of the name, 105; purchased,
106. *See also* New Amsterdam, New York
city.

Manors (patroonships), establishment in New
Netherland, i. 116–121; inducement, 121;
failure of first, 116–123; success of Rensselaerwyck, 123, 178; attempt to introduce
indented servants, 149; disputes between
Rensselaerwyck and the government, 179–
184; system in New York, ii. 256; Schuyler's manor, 256–262.

Mansfield, Lord, opinion on libel, ii. 243.

Manufacturers, in the Netherlands, i. 13, 14,
30; influence of Dutch, on English, 30–33,
40; forbidden to the patroons, 120; prohibition removed, 150.

Marathon, Greece, importance of battle, i.
190.

Markham, William, deputy-governor of
Pennsylvania, ii. 142.

Martha's Vineyard, Mass., Duke of York's
claim, ii. 7.

Mary, Lady, of Burgundy, marriage, i. 24;
and the Great Privilege, 24.

Maryland charter, ii. 138–140.

Mason, Arthur, Boston constable, and the
royal commissioners, ii. 8–10.

Massachusetts, and the royal commissioners,
i. 248, 249, ii. 8–10; and the Duke of York's
claim, 7; persecution of Quakers, 102;
tyranny of Andros, 165; overthrow of Andros, 166; refuses to aid Fletcher, 205;
Bellomont governor, 214. *See also* Colonies, New England.

Mather, Increase, on King Philip and the
Mohawks, ii. 55 n.; in England, 165, 166.

Maurice of Orange, Prince, leads war party
in the Netherlands, i. 84; and Olden-
Barneveld, 94.

Maverick, Samuel, intrigue against New Netherland, i. 245; royal commissioner, 248; in
Boston, ii. 8.

May, Cornelius, in Delaware Bay, i. 91; first
director-general of New Netherland, 102.

Mazarin, Cardinal, dissatisfied with treaty of
Münster, i. 214.

Megapolensis, John, Dutch clergyman in New
Netherland, intolerance, i. 202.

Melyn, Cornelius, arrival in New Netherland, i. 150; settlement on Staten Island,
156; member of Board of Eight Men, 164;
petition against Kieft, 174; accusations
against, 175; banished and fined, 175; ship-
wrecked, 176; justified, 177; return with
mandamus, to Stuyvesant, 188.

Mennonites, persecution and migration to
Pennsylvania, ii. 332.

Mercator, Norumbega on his 1569 map, i. 66.

Merchant Adventurers in England, i. 34.

Merchants' Exchange, first New York, ii. 26.

Meteren, Emanuel van, Dutch consul at London, and Hudson, i. 71, 72.

Middle Kingdom. *See* Lotharingia.

Milborne, Jacob, Leisler's lieutenant, ii. 178;
marries Leisler's daughter, 186; arrest, 189;
trial and execution, 189–191, 348.

Milt, Anthony de, and the oath of allegiance,
ii. 41.

Minuit, Peter, director-general of New Netherland, i. 105; discussion with Bradford,
108; recalled, 124; leads colony to New
Sweden, 206.

Mohegan Indians, and the Mohawks, i. 107,
249; in the Connecticut valley, 130, 132.

Money, wampum as, i. 152; chaotic condition in early New York, ii. 45; Massachusetts issues paper, 184; New York issues
paper, 229.

Monopoly in New Netherland, i. 90, 91, 98,
120; abolished, 148; New York city flour,
ii. 85.

Montgomery, John, governor of New York,
ii. 233.

Monts, Sieur du, attempted colony, ii. 325.

Moravians, migration to Pennsylvania, ii. 332.

Morris, Gouverneur, ancestry, ii. 187.

Mosquitoes in New York, ii. 258 n.

Motley, J. L., *Rise of the Dutch Republic*, i.
39.

Muscovy Company, organized, i. 49, 69.

Music in the Netherlands, i. 14.

Names, changes in Huguenot, in America, ii.
328.

Nantucket, Mass., Duke of York's claim, ii.
7.

Narragansett Bay, R. I., Verrazano in, i. 58.

Navigation laws, origin, i. 218; and trade
with New Netherlands, 244, 245.

Naylor, James, religious enthusiast, ii. 101.

Netherlands, and the Roman Empire, i. 4;
and the Frankish Empire, 6–9; in Lotharingia, 9–11; growth of little states, 11;
resulting political advantages, 12, 35; agricultural and industrial growth, 12–14; topo-
graphy, 13; fine arts, 14, 20; culture, 14–
17; urban and rural population, 17; burgher type, 18; discordant political factors,
20–22; conditions of civil liberty, 22, 195;
absorption by the House of Burgundy, 22;
under Charles the Bold, 23; Great Privilege
24; under the Hapsburgs, 24–26; commercial influence on England, 30–33, 40, 41; influence on American progress, 28, ii. 336;
importance of the woollen industry, i. 31;
religious influence on England, 32–36; Protestantism, 36; persecution and revolt, 37–
39; division, 39; further history of the
Flemish, 39, 42; growth of the Dutch at
expense of the Flemish, 42; sea power, 43;
East Indian empire, 43–47; Australasian
explorations, 47; control of Brazil, 48;
Arctic explorations, 50; Antarctic explorations, 51; independence acknowledged, 83;
parties in 1609, 85–87; divergent views on
colonization, 86–88; triumph of the war
party, 94; inauguration of a colonial policy,
96; charter of the Dutch West India Company, 98; alliance with England, 104; renewed war with Spain, 110; English friendship, 211; effect of treaty of Münster,
211; government, 211–213; parties after
treaty of Münster, 213–216; attempted union
with the Commonwealth, 216; commercial
rivalry with England, 216; wars with England, 216–220, 227–235, 246–255, ii. 19, 27,
28, 35–37; personal union with England, i.
220; immigration of Jews, ii. 319; inducement to Huguenots, 327. *See also* New
Netherland.

New Amstel, Del., resists the English, ii. 4;
called Newcastle, 4.

New Amsterdam, beginnings, i. 106, conditions, 121, 143–144, 148, 200, 229; subscription for a church, 159; municipal government
desired, 189; incorporated, 199; defences,

END OF VOLUME II

The Riverside Press

Electrotyped and printed by H. O. Houghton & Co.
Cambridge, Mass., U. S. A.